Journal publishing

Journal publishing

Gillian Page
Pageant Publishing

Robert Campbell
Blackwell Science Ltd

Jack Meadows
Loughborough University

CAMBRIDGE
UNIVERSITY PRESS

CAMBRIDGE UNIVERSITY PRESS
Cambridge, New York, Melbourne, Madrid, Cape Town, Singapore, São Paulo

Cambridge University Press
The Edinburgh Building, Cambridge CB2 2RU, UK

Published in the United States of America by Cambridge University Press, New York

www.cambridge.org
Information on this title: www.cambridge.org/9780521441377

First published 1997
This digitally printed first paperback version 2006

An original edition, on which this revised, updated and extended
edition is based, was published as *Journal Publishing: Principles
and Practice,* by Gillian Page, Robert Campbell and Jack Meadows
(Butterworths, 1987)

A catalogue record for this publication is available from the British Library

Library of Congress Cataloguing in Publication data
Page, Gillian.
Journal publishing / Gillian Page, Robert Campbell, Jack Meadows.
– Rev., updated and expanded ed.
    p.   cm.
Revised, updated, and expanded edition of: Journal publishing, 1987.
Includes bibliographical references and index.
ISBN 0 521 44137 4
1. Scholarly periodicals – Publishing. 2. Learned institutions and
societies – Publishing. 3. Periodicals, Publishing of. 4. Scholarly publishing.
I. Campbell, Robert. II. Meadows, A. J. (Arthur Jack). III. Title.
Z286.S37P33   1997
080.5'72 – dc20   96–23397   CIP

ISBN-13   978-0-521-44137-7 hardback
ISBN-10   0-521-44137-4 hardback

ISBN-13   978-0-521-02768-7 paperback
ISBN-10   0-521-02768-3 paperback

Contents

Figures

Tables

Preface

Many people are involved in journal publishing. This book has been written with their needs in mind, particularly the needs of those with relatively little publishing experience. We have aimed to cover all major aspects of the subject, discussing commonly occurring problems, and have tried to answer the most frequently asked questions. We give background information to show the context in which decisions are made and we have tried to alert readers to matters which might not be self-evident but which may be important for the success of their journals.

Journal publishing does not exist in a vacuum. It responds to changes in its environment, in the economics of publishing, in its customers and in technology. We believe that the learned journal is sufficiently flexible to adapt to changing circumstances. New technology is enabling publishers to produce and distribute papers reporting research more efficiently, and is opening up exciting possibilities. What was good practice ten years ago may no longer be so. Following fixed rules can be a route to disaster, and most journals benefit from a critical evaluation of their policies and practice. We suggest some ways in which publishers can conduct such evaluation.

In 1987 we published a book under the title *Journal Publishing: Principles and Practice* with Butterworths, for an earlier generation of the readership envisaged for the present book, which is based on that 1987 edition but which significantly revises, updates and extends it. The response to the first edition was encouraging and helpful. We have acted on the many suggestions and experience from teaching in preparing this new edition. The structure of the contents is similar to the first edition but all the chapters have been completely rewritten, chapter 10 has been replaced by a longer and more general treatment of managing a list of journals, and there is a new chapter 11 on electronic publishing. Appendix 1 and 2 and the glossary are also new. Overall there is more emphasis on good practice but we hope that those outside publishing such as serials librarians will still find the book of interest.

We are grateful to Ian Bannerman, Michael Bodinham, Leo Walford, Edward Wates, Allen Stevens, John Strange and David Hibberd for comments and information, and for the contributions from friends and colleagues over the years and the forebearance of our families.

1   Introduction to journals

What is a journal?

The *Oxford English Dictionary* does not recognise the word 'journal' in the sense we use it in this book. It informs us – as would many librarians – that we should be using either 'periodical' or 'serial'. Definitions vary, but librarians – the people most concerned with these divisions – would generally accept something like the following specifications:

Serial: a publication issued in successive parts, bearing numerical or chronological designations and intended to be continued indefinitely.

Periodical: a publication appearing at stated intervals, each number of which contains a variety of original articles by different authors.

Our main concern in this book is with learned (sometimes referred to as 'scholarly') journals. These are periodicals, or serials, which contain a significant proportion of articles (often called 'papers' in scientific journals) based on original scholarship – sometimes referred to as 'primary communications'. From the readers' viewpoint, such journals blur with other types of serial. Singleton examined the holdings list of a large scientific research library and found that half of all the serials it acquired were not learned journals in terms of the definition given above (see Curwen, 1980). However, in terms of information handling, it is useful to treat 'journals' as a specific group, distinguished by the fact that the input of material to a journal is not usually predetermined. This contrasts with magazines, such as *New Scientist* or annual review volumes, where nearly all the material is commissioned (or written in-house). At the same time, some other types of publication – newsletters, for example – are dependent on input from readers. This produces some similarity in information-handling terms to journals, although newsletters are less likely to contain original research. So the boundary between serials, periodicals and journals serving the research community can, in practice, be rather hazy. Consequently, although this book is devoted to journal publishing, it is intended to say something across a broader front.

Why publish journals?

In times past, the typical reason for publishing journals was because groups of enthusiasts wished to record and circulate information concerning their work and activities. Traditionally, the printed record was a by-product of meetings between such enthusiasts, who typically joined together to form a society. The link between societies and journals is strong: most societies at least consider the possibility of publishing a journal. More recently, and especially since the Second World War, commercial publishers have become important producers of journals. In part, this has been a reactive process to cater for groups of authors and readers whose needs, for one reason or another, are not entirely satisfied by existing society-published journals. Increasingly, commercial publishers have become more proactive, and are taking the initiative in determining where there may be gaps in journal coverage. Even so, this is typically on the basis of proposals coming from individuals and societies (a well-established journal publisher may receive ten to fifty proposals a year).

Commercial publishers are necessarily concerned in the first instance with the question of financial return. (Although it should be added that they have sometimes taken a charitable attitude to worthwhile journals. The record may be held by Macmillan, who supported *Nature* for thirty-five years before it broke even.) In these terms, journals have a number of attractions for publishers. Today, most major publishers ask for payment in advance so that the kind of financial uncertainty involved in book publication is absent. Overheads are much lower than for books; the value of sales per member of staff is generally much higher. Some costs, such as for building up mailing lists, can be shared between books and journals. Moreover, journals are a continuing business, and one providing contacts with authors, which may lead to new books for publishers who produce both journals and books. At the same time, the great expansion of academic and professional activities since the Second World War has provided many opportunities to launch new titles. Commercial publishers, such as Pergamon (in its heyday) and Elsevier, have produced hundreds of new titles over the past forty years.

The market, however, has become much more difficult as shown in figure 1.1. A survey of journal publishers in Britain carried out by the Publishers Association (Oakeshott, 1995) showed that in 1994, 10 journals out of the sample of 861 were closed down although there was still a net increase over 1993 in the number of titles, particularly in medicine and the social sciences. This trend appeared to continue through to 1995. The survey also showed a decline in total circulation of 4 per cent with the institutional subscriptions declining 6 per cent, but this varied from subject to subject with the social sciences remaining unchanged.

The differences between society and commercial publishers have tended to diminish in recent years, as societies have become increasingly concerned with the profitability of their publications. This is reflected in the many co-operative publishing agreements that now exist between learned societies and commercial publishers. Societies often use profits from journals to fund other activities, while publishers will build up reserves to invest in new publications. The investment required in the first two or three years of a new journal can be considerable, as is shown in figure 1.2. However, differences in approach and infrastructure, which can affect the economics of journal publishing, remain. A study carried out in the USA (Moline, 1989) indicates how this may be reflected in terms of journal pricing. (See tables 1.1–1.3.)

The differences due to subject matter in table 1.1 have been included because it is important to remember that the mix of subjects is not the same for commercial and society publishers. Nevertheless, this and other studies do indicate an underlying difference in pricing between society and commercial publishers. One factor to be taken into account here is the greater amount of voluntary help given to society publishers, especially in terms of editorial assistance. An example of the importance of this is provided by a small modern-language research journal published in the UK. For some years this was produced by a commercial publisher. In 1979, the university editors were told that the price must be increased from £12 to £20 in order to break even. The editors took over the

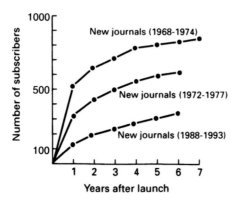

Figure 1.1 Growth in circulation of new STM research journals which are launched independently of any society, showing the decline in the market. Each graph is based on an average of three titles. Where a society is involved, the circulation is usually greater due to members taking copies.

title and produced it themselves using desktop publishing, with the result that throughout the next decade its price was kept at £15 p.a. In effect, the editors and, to some extent, their institution were subsidising the publication.

Another important difference is that society members may be expected to take copies of the society journal, or journals, as part of their annual subscription to the society. This provides a base level of sales, which a commercial journal does not have, and is important not only as a direct subvention, but also for such spin-offs as advertising revenue. In the USA, a number of other factors also favour society publishers. For example, there are tax breaks and lower postage rates available to not-for-profit publishers, and they may also be able to introduce page charges.

Some of these differences have been eroded over the past few years. Journal editors are increasingly requiring compensation for their efforts, whether from commercial or society publishers; so, too, are the institutions that house many of them. In an increasing number of societies, receipt of the journal as part of the membership requirements is no longer compulsory; so the base number of subscriptions is no longer ensured. Hence, differences between society and commercial publishers of journals appear to be diminishing.

The costs of paper, printing and binding for a journal usually account

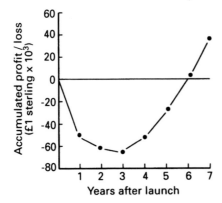

Figure 1.2 Graph of accumulated profit or loss of a well-produced STM research journal launched in the late 1980s. The size of the investment required explains why new STM journals are mainly launched by large publishers. With the support of a society the graph is usually flatter and generally new journals in the social sciences and humanities do not require so much funding.

for rather less than 35 per cent of the subscription price; for books, they may come to 20 per cent or less of the cover price. There are a number of reasons for this difference. The trade discount on academic books (other than school texts) is rarely below 25 per cent and may be 40 per cent or more; on journals it is sometimes zero, often 5 per cent and rarely more than 10 per cent. Each book requires special attention and design (if only of the cover), so editorial and production overheads are generally higher. Journals enjoy continuing sales; books generally need more spent on promotion. In addition to providing publicity, book publishers often need to employ representatives and agents overseas, while journal publishers can usually manage without a permanent overseas sales force, nor do they need representatives who can call on booksellers. It is easier to predict the sales for an established journal than for a book, even one in a series. The price of the book has to allow for the possibility of copies not being sold or, at best, being remaindered. Finally, journal publishers demand payment in advance and charge for cancellations; book publishers have to give credit (which may be for as much as 180 days in far-flung markets) and allow booksellers to return unsold copies.

Any publisher who has attempted to launch a single book title in a new subject area will know the problems this involves. Journals are different. An analysis of the journal holdings at the British Library Document Supply Centre (BLDSC) shows that many publishers produce only a single title. This is not too surprising. As we have seen, many journals are owned and published by a society or similar organisation, and are aimed at the membership. For a small or medium-sized society, a single title will often suffice to cover all of its needs. A journal published by a commercial organisation, which has to pay for all its services, is in a different position. It usually forms one of a number of titles from that imprint: economies of scale are generally necessary to achieve financial viability. This dichotomy is reflected in the data from BLDSC. A clear majority of the inter-library loan requests are for articles from scientific, technical or medical (STM) journals, and a considerable proportion of these requests can be supplied from journals produced by a small group of international STM journal publishers, primarily in the commercial sector.

The structure of the journal publishing community is also indicated by David Brown's analysis using the reported turnover with the subscription agents B. H. Blackwell (BHB) (Brown, 1993). He came up with three categories: (1) 117 publishers with a turnover of more than £50,000 with BHB producing 7177 titles in total; (2) 987 publishers with a turnover between £50,000 and £5,000 with BHB producing 4047 titles, and, (3) 16,429 publishers with a turnover of less than £5,000 with BHB producing 23,700 titles.

The importance of a few commercial publishers on the international journal scene is reflected in the holdings of most research libraries. This can be seen from the proportion of titles from a given country that actually emanate from a single publisher. For example, one US university library in the latter part of the 1980s subscribed to 253 journal titles from the Netherlands and 194 titles from West Germany. In terms of publishers, this can be restated as meaning that it subscribed to 229 titles produced by Elsevier and 101 titles from Springer Verlag.

Co-operative arrangements between societies and commercial publishers vary greatly in terms of who has overall control. However, the society typically provides the editor(s), so day-to-day editorial policy is in the society's hands. When no society is involved, the editor is still usually responsible for editorial policy, and expects this right as part of the job.

Table 1.1. *Average annual journal subscription price by subject*

	1973	1985	Increase
Science	$24.36	$197.46	711%
Social Sciences	$12.63	$64.66	412%
Humanities	$7.92	$32.81	314%

Table 1.2. *Average annual journal subscription price by publisher type*

	1973	1985	Increase
Commercial publisher	$27.93	$188.69	576%
Society publisher	$16.26	$96.21	492%
Other scholarly publisher	$11.10	$63.11	469%

Table 1.3. *Average cents per page by publisher type*

	1973	1985	Increase
Commercial publisher	3.7–4.0	19.3	400%
Society publisher	2.9–3.2	10.4	240%
Other scholarly publisher	3.0	8.9	200%

Publishers of learned journals (apart from some review journals) rarely pay contributors, which weakens their ability to exert much influence on what is published. However, they will certainly watch for signs of falling quality. One of the truest sayings in the business is that good articles sell subscriptions.

Authors

Clearly, journal publishers are looking to recruit eminent, well-known authors, just like any other publisher. Where scholarly journals are unusual is in the often appreciable overlap between their authors and their readers. The high-priority journals for reading may also be the preferred journals in which these readers publish. The extent to which this is true varies with audience. The overlap is important for many scholarly journals, less so for professional ones and hardly at all for semi-popular publications. In general, academic readers are more likely to be potential authors than readers working in other types of institution. For example, it has been estimated that 28 per cent of American scientists work in the academic world, but they account for some 70 per cent of US-authored scientific papers. Commercial or security considerations form a particular barrier to journal publication. Previously this has mainly affected potential authors in industrial or commercial enterprises, but current research pressures on universities mean that it is now an increasing concern there, too.

Within each subject area, journals can be listed in terms of the prestige that authors assign to them. In the sciences, such comparisons are made internationally; so, if the journal with highest prestige is published in (say) the United States, its prestige will normally ensure that papers are submitted to it by authors from Europe and elsewhere, as well as from North America. Such ranking of journals is not immutable. It changes – although usually fairly slowly – and, in any case, the exact order of precedence is often a little hazy. Some points are clear. The journals with most prestige have typically been established for some time – decades, or even centuries. This means that society journals are preferred, although a number of commercially-published journals have now reached the top. Prestige and subject specialisation (alternatively expressed in terms of readership outreach) always come out top in terms of why authors choose to publish in a particular journal. These factors relate to the research community which the author wishes to reach. Some way behind, though not to be ignored, come a cluster of personal factors, such as having published in the journal before, or knowing the editor. Other factors, such as speed of publication, usually rank lower still. Hence, in attracting good authors to a specific journal, prestige is of crucial importance.

The best way of finding how authors rank a particular journal is to talk to experienced authors in the relevant subject area. Another way is obviously to look at relative circulations of journals in the same field, if the information can be obtained. It can also sometimes be helpful to examine the references attached to papers in journals covering the same topic. The higher the prestige of a journal, the more likely it is to appear frequently in the references. Garfield has estimated that 21 per cent of the

4,400 journals analysed in the *Science Citation Index* for 1988 received 83 per cent of all the citations processed. (The method must be applied with some caution – because, for example, most journals preferentially contain citations to themselves.) Probably the simplest way of inter-comparing prestige via references is to use the 'impact factors' for each journal (described below); but these are still somewhat subject-dependent, so comparisons should only be made between journals in the same discipline.

The question of prestige naturally affects new journals. They are, almost by definition, likely to have a lower prestige; so authors are less likely to be attracted to them. One way around this is for the editor to invite distinguished authors in the field to contribute papers. Such a 'call for papers' is best done by a personal letter. (This approach underlines the fact that a highly ranked journal is actually one that publishes work by highly regarded authors.) The response to requests of this type is usually somewhat better for society journals than for commercial journals. One problem is that eminent authors are likely to consign their less important work to a new journal. Other factors that can attract (or deter) authors are the general philosophy of the journal, the editor, the refereeing policy, speed of publication and, to a lesser extent, design and offprint policy. The existence of page charges is frequently seen as a deterrent, even though journals may be flexible in their imposition.

Authors actually employ a range of strategies when deciding where to publish their work. A short report of important scientific work might be sent to a journal such as *Nature*, or to a relevant letters journal. A longer report might be submitted to the journal with most prestige in the specialism. Less important, but still useful, work will be despatched to journals of lower prestige. Some of these journals may also provide homes for review-type articles. As a result of this discrimination, there is scope in any subject area for journals of different levels of prestige. This fact provides an opening for new titles which, if they survive, may subsequently grow in reputation.

Various studies over the past twenty years have shown there are systematic differences in rejection rates between different subject fields. The sequence runs from low rejection rates in journals covering the physical sciences, through the life sciences, to high rejection rates in humanities journals. In terms of actual figures, the rejection rates for well-established journals may range from 20 per cent in the physical sciences to 80–90 per cent in the humanities. These variations reflect both subject differences and market forces. In subject terms, agreement on acceptability between referees (and editors) decreases along the sequence; sciences – social sciences – humanities. Equally, the potential financial rewards to publishers typically decrease in the same sequence. The overall result is that scientists can much more readily find a good journal in which to publish than can authors in the humanities.

Many researchers nowadays are under pressure to maintain a good publications record, which means they normally try to publish anything of reasonable standard which they produce. In response, those involved in the administration of research try to determine whether the published work is significant in terms of quality as well as quantity. One common approach is to assess the standard of the journal in which the work appears. At the simplest, this may be by posing the question – does this journal employ referees? More sophisticated measures look at the impact of the journal. For example, the 'impact factor' can be derived: this effectively measures the average number of times each paper in the journal is cited in other papers. (Correspondingly, various attempts have been made to exploit the number of times the publications of an individual or group have been cited by other authors as a measure of their research quality.) The use of citations for quality judgements has often been criticised, but publishers would do well to be aware of the practice, since the application of such assessments to their own titles may help attract, or deter, potential authors. In addition, publishers can themselves use citation measures of various kinds to identify which individuals and institutions are most widely recognised in particular subject fields. This is potentially useful information when launching a journal. Listings of citation measures (including impact factors) are published regularly by the Institute for Scientific Information (ISI) in Philadelphia.

Contributors to scholarly journals are mainly concerned that their work should be noted by their peers. Hence, they are willing to put considerable effort into preparing articles for publication without compensation. They are not too worried if readers make copies of their work: as readers, they often do the same. Hence, it is mainly publishers who have made the running in discussions of journals and copyright. One aspect of this has concerned the effect of photocopying on sales of journals. The evidence remains ambiguous. Librarians seem to be generally correct in their assertion that, if there are frequent requests by readers for photocopies of a particular journal, then it will normally be considered for purchase. Nevertheless, publishers point to the fact that the circulations of many titles have decreased by 1 to 4 per cent per annum in recent years, whilst the demands on document supply centres have continued to increase. The questions of copyright and copying are taken up in chapter 7.

One final point publishers should keep in mind is that different subject areas have their own traditions for the handling and presentation of journal material. For example, articles in the humanities typically have footnotes (and endnotes), whereas scientific articles do not. Again, the form in which references are given in articles varies with subject. At a less obvious level, the form of an author's name may differ according to the journal. A paper in a scientific journal might have 'J. Smith' as the author; in a social science journal, the same person might appear as 'John Smith'. Scientists usually expect more rapid publication of results than other researchers; whilst the demand for offprints differs dramatically between different research fields. A publisher venturing into a new field is well advised to investigate existing journals in order to pick up some of these distinctions.

Marketing journals

Not surprisingly, there is no single answer to the question – who buys journals? Purchasing habits vary from country to country. For example, the proportion of individual subscriptions to institutional subscriptions is significantly higher in the USA than in the UK. Habits also differ according to the subject. Thus, journals in the humanities tend to have a higher proportion of individual subscriptions than those in the sciences. Purchasers' expectations based on such traditions can affect journal marketing. For example, in a field where individual subscriptions are common, a publisher may feel limited in terms of the highest price that can be charged, since the individual pocket may prove less elastic than the institutional purse. One answer, commonly adopted, is to have different subscription rates for individuals and institutions. However, as will be noted later, this solution is itself under attack from librarians.

Many publishers – society as well as commercial – now expect their main customers to be institutional (most often some kind of library). It is therefore important for publishers to know how librarians go about selecting, or retaining, journal titles for their stock. The attitude of librarians will be discussed further below, but the first point to note is that selection and retention of titles usually involves joint activity between library staff and their customers. There are exceptions. Some major research libraries rely primarily on the advice of subject specialists on their library staff. At the other end of the scale, academic librarians in a country such as Japan typically have little delegated authority for journal purchasing. But, normally, if librarians suggest changes in journal subscriptions, these will be scrutinised by the readers in their institutions, and vice versa. In these days of tight budgets, it is common-place for librarians to demand that a new subscription can only be started if an existing title, costing the same amount, is cancelled. It is then up to the readers to decide which new subscriptions should be taken out, and which old ones cancelled. The librarians often retain a final veto, since it is their duty to maintain a balanced collection suitable for all their readers. Some attempts have been made to find 'objective' methods of deciding on a journal's worth, and so the need to subscribe to it. For example, citation measures have been suggested, but such methods are not yet widely implemented.

The prime journal targets for cutting in recent years have tended to be those for which (1) the library has more than one subscription (2) the title is available through resource sharing between libraries (3) the contents of the journal are relatively ephemeral, or do not link closely with current research and teaching programmes (4) the subscription price is very high. In addition, libraries in English-speaking countries have tended to cut subscriptions to foreign-language journals; cover-to-cover translations seem to have been particularly at risk.

The dominance of English-language journals is illustrated by one major British scientific library which tries to hold copies of less-used overseas journals. Even so, over 60 per cent of its holdings in recent years has consisted of journals published in English. Many journals nominally produced in languages other than English will accept papers written in English. This even extends nowadays – after considerable debate – to a number of French-language periodicals.

For the purchase or retention of a title, the prime requirement for a librarian, or a reader, is obviously that the journal should be used. This is nearly always a more important criterion than the cost of the journal. Readers are attracted to journals which carry high-quality information. However, the position is by no means always straightforward. Some journals have considerable historical prestige, although they may not now be extensively read. It often takes much heart-searching to cancel subscriptions to such journals. Again, when an institution owns a long back-run of a particular journal, librarians may hesitate before cancellation. It is only fair to add that the general financial squeeze of recent years has led them to hesitate less. Another factor is obviously cost. A low-priced journal can be absorbed more readily within an institutional budget, and so may have a greater chance of being retained. However, all journals incur handling and accessing costs: librarians are becoming increasingly aware that no low-usage journal can really justify its acquisition, whatever its price.

Journal publishers have only two basic ways of expanding their publications: (1) by increasing the size of existing titles (2) by launching new journals. Both ways forward are currently under pressure. The rate of appearance of new titles has been falling in recent years. For example, Elsevier launched forty-eight new titles in 1979, but only twenty-six in 1983 and ten in 1988. Moreover, all the journals launched in 1979 survived, whereas a quarter of those launched in 1983 have already disappeared. For science journals, specifically, the number of new titles appearing each year over the period 1945–88 is shown in figure 1.3. According to this, the rate of increase peaked about 1970.

It is an obvious point, but one worth emphasising, that any continuing expansion of journals depends on the availability of readers who wish to read them. Huth (1989) has pointed at that, though the number of medical journals rose sharply between 1960 and 1975, so did the size of the US medical community. He found that the ratio of medical journals in the National Library of Medicine to 1000 physicians/dentists/nurses

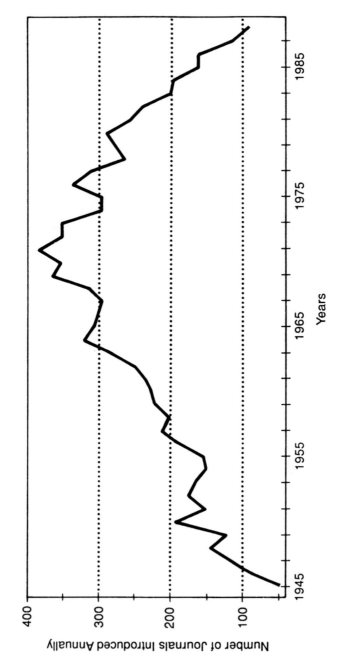

Figure 1.3 The number of science periodicals introduced annually from 1945 to 1988 based on data from *Ulrich's International Periodicals Directory*.

in the community only rose from 15.5 to 17.3 over this period. Here, again, the ratio seems to have peaked in the 1970s. It has been estimated that, in US science and engineering, there were 0.110 articles per person in 1965; 0.155 in 1977; 0.114 in 1985; 0.104 in 1990 (King and Griffiths, 1995).

Journal growth occurs not only by the appearance of new titles, but also by the expansion of existing titles. Figure 1.4 shows the growth in size of a leading British geological journal in terms both of number of papers appearing each year and of the number of pages published annually. Clearly the scale, and so the cost of producing the journal, has changed greatly over the past thirty years. The cost increases because the growth in the number of pages reflects a corresponding growth in the number of articles published. (Individual articles have not increased in length.) This requires extra effort in editing and refereeing, as well as extra production and distribution charges.

The rate of addition of new titles has not been constant across all subject areas. For example, new Elsevier titles in the 1970s appeared in such areas as physics, chemistry and the geosciences. By the early 1980s these areas were less popular, but growth in health science titles continued until at least the mid-1980s. Growth in some areas, such as business and engineering, survived to the beginning of the next decade. By this time, Elsevier was publishing more than 600 titles, or over three-quarters of a million pages per year. These trends at Elsevier reflect what happened more generally across the journal publishing scene (although individual publishers are naturally still cultivating their own particular gardens). Elsevier's experiences during the 1980s may be compared with Butterworth's. At the end of the 1980s, Butterworths produced 93 journal titles (76 in the UK and 17 in the USA). One-third of their journal business was in Europe, one-third in the United States and one-third in the rest of the world. Of the 60 journals started before 1980, 21 had circulations of more than a thousand, whereas only two of those started since 1980 reached this figure. The circulations of most of the older journals had peaked, and were now tending to decline. Nevertheless, the titles, as a whole, were providing a net profit of half a million dollars on a ten million dollar turnover.

The decreases in circulation noted by Butterworths are now

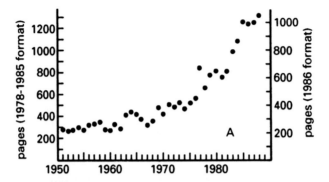

Figure 1.4 (A) Growth rate of a leading British geological journal: *Journal of the Geological Society*. The annual number of pages published since 1950 is plotted. The page size was increased in 1986. Before then each page averaged 900 words; since 1986 the page size has averaged 1200 words, hence the two scales shown.

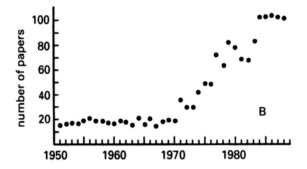

Figure 1.4 (B) Growth rate of a leading British geological journal: *Journal of the Geological Society*. The annual number of papers published in the journal since 1950 is plotted. When compared with figure 1.4(A) it is seen that the number of pages and the number of papers provide similar measures of publication growth.

widespread. This is a major factor in the survival of new titles: they are usually paid for by cancelling subscriptions to established journals, which therefore decline in circulation. Figure 1.5 contains data from the Institute of Physics in the UK on the circulations of seven core journals. The long-term decline is evident (and continues, see figure 1.6), although with these physics journals it is less marked for North American subscrip-

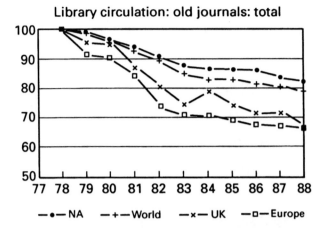

Figure 1.5 The decline in the percentage of institutional subscribers to seven core journals in physics.

tions than for European. Of course, not all subscriptions are falling and there has been some indication that journals in the physical sciences have declined more than in other subjects. Medical journals seemed particularly buoyant at the end of the 1980s although the latest Publishers Association survey (Oakeshott, 1995) suggests a recent decline (9 per cent drop in average number of subscriptions to 97 medical journals from 1993 to 1994). At the same time, increased efficiency of production and particularly 'desktop production' working from authors' disks has made it possible to publish journals with smaller print-runs than before. Until they reach a lower limit of a few hundred, journals can therefore often remain financially viable. Though production costs are not the only factor at work, this has helped permit the continued growth in the number of journal titles.

Journal publishing tends to be concentrated into a relatively few countries. Correspondingly, library expenditure on journals targets publications from these countries. Table 1.4 shows the journal subscriptions from one US university analysed in terms of the country from which the journal originated (Hamaker, 1988).

Table 1.4 contains only titles costing more than $80 p.a. In fact, many journal subscriptions are relatively low: most library expenditure goes on a few expensive titles. For this particular university library, it was found

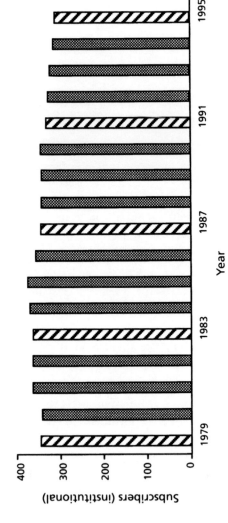

Figure 1.6 The number of institutional subscribers to a journal in biomedicine from 1979 to 1995 showing a slight but steady decline since 1985.

Table 1.4. *Journal subscriptions analysed in terms of the country from which the journal originated*

Country	Number of Titles	Total Cost
USA	1105	$403,741
UK	680	$208,634
Netherlands	253	$113,182
West Germany	194	$118,520

Table 1.5. *Average price increases recorded by one library*

Year	Cost per subscription	Index	Average increase in the index (%)
1977	$51.31	100	0
1978	$57.06	111.2	11.2
1979	$63.31	123.4	11.7
1980	$73.37	143.0	14.3
1981	$86.38	168.3	17.1
1982	$102.87	200.5	20.1
1983	$112.72	219.7	20.0
1984	$125.57	244.7	20.7
1985	$137.92	268.8	21.1
1986	$151.77	295.8	21.8
1987	$169.36	330.1	23.0
1988	$180.67	352.1	22.9
1989	$199.22	388.3	24.0

that, of the 13,000 titles taken, 20 per cent accounted for more than 70 per cent of the journal expenditure. Among serials librarians there is a rule-of-thumb which reckons that 50 cent of their acquisitions budget will be expended on 10 per cent of the titles stocked.

These figures, in themselves, do not present a problem to librarians. The difficulty is that journal prices have, for a number of years, been increasing more rapidly than library budgets for acquisitions. The more expensive titles have often gone up more rapidly in price than the average, so aggravating the problem. It is quite hard to obtain accurate figures on average price increases, not least because over a period of time samples

Table 1.6. *Average periodical prices*

Field	Year	
	1989	1994
Humanities	£51.64	£88.24
Medicine	£123.77	£225.84
Science and Technology	£214.48	£402.55

alter as individual titles combine, split up, or disappear. The results in table 1.5 come from a carefully monitored set of journals (about 3800 titles) in a US veterinary library, and provide reasonably trustworthy figures (Anderson, 1989).

Estimates in 1993 for a group of representative libraries suggested there had been an increase in subscription costs by over 50 per cent since 1988. This represented a fairly steady increase of 8 to 9 per cent per year, except for 1991 when a dramatic decrease in the strength of the dollar led to a jump of some 15 per cent. In terms of subject matter, there have been consistent pricing differences as indicated in table 1.6 (LISU, 1995). The rapid increase in journal subscriptions compared with library budgets means that an increasing fraction of budgets is now devoted to journals at the expense of books. One campus of the University of California spent 40 per cent of its library acquisitions budget on journals in 1987, 51 per cent in 1988 and more than 60 per cent in 1989. The Association of Research Libraries in the United States has noted that funding support for its member libraries rose by 234 per cent from 1973 to 1987 (compared with a corresponding rise of 183 per cent in the US Consumer Price Index). The average expenditure on stock rose from 29.2 per cent to 33.1 per cent, but with an accompanying shift in the amount devoted to serials from 40.4 per cent to 56.2 per cent. During the same period, the average serials holdings of a library are estimated to have fallen from 32 per cent of relevant titles to 26.4 per cent. Figure 1.7 compares British university book spend and periodical spend in actual and constant pounds. These spends are also compared with the growth in number of staff and students.

The librarians' complaint is not simply that such increases exceed their

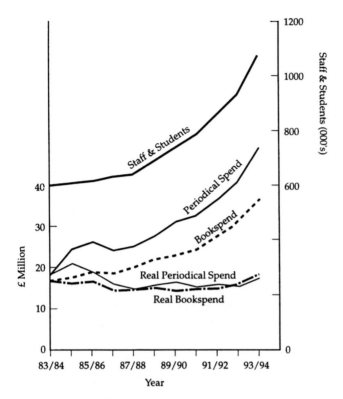

Figure 1.7 University libraries material expenditure in the UK from 1983/4 to 1993/4.

budget, but that they cannot be justified in terms of price increases in general. Publishers retort that theirs is a special case. Publishing is a labour-intensive industry, and the cost of skilled staff has increased more rapidly than inflation. Moreover, inflation is only one element affecting price increase. The other main ones are increases in journal size, currency fluctuations and increases caused by a reduction in the overall number of subscriptions. Some publishers, too, are incurring considerable costs in coping with new electronic developments. Depending on the circumstances, inflation may only account for a third or so of the price increase. For an economic analysis of journal pricing practices, see Peterson (1992).

Apart from the basic question of how journal prices are decided by publishers, the debate in recent years has expanded to cover two types of differential pricing. The first concerns differential pricing by geographical region. For example, in 1988, a Butterworths scientific journal published in Massachusetts cost $160 in the USA and $190 elsewhere, whilst one of their scientific titles published in London cost £100 in the UK, but £130 elsewhere. Publishers point to postage and handling as the main reason, though other factors – such as currency exchange coverage and higher overseas marketing costs – may play a part. Librarians argue that publishers are exploiting this device to derive further profit, and a number have tried to avoid the extra charge by 'buying around'.

The second form of differential pricing relates to subscribers. A survey of scientific, technical and medical publishers (completed in 1990) indicated the ways of charging differentially for journals shown in table 1.7. Much of the debate about differential pricing relates to individual discounts. When the publishers were asked what the average ratio of their subscription rates (institutional/individual) was, 41 per cent said 1.5:1 or less, 35 per cent said 2:1 and 24 per cent reported more than 2:1. This may be compared with what librarians regard as reasonable. In a contemporaneous survey, 70 per cent of librarians felt a ratio of 1.3:1 should be the maximum imposed by publishers. Some publishers are introducing a different approach to this two-tier pricing structure. Subscribers affiliated to institutions are offered a highly reduced subscription (in one case, a reduction of nearly 6:1), but only if their institution subscribes to the title concerned at the full rate.

Publishers in the 1990s will need to take into account a new abrasiveness on the part of librarians (especially in North America). American librarians have now begun to explore whether action can be taken against publishers whose journals experience 'exorbitant' increases in price. The Association of Research Libraries has envisaged two steps in particular: to develop subject-specific cost indices for critical serial titles, followed by identifying problem publishers, and co-ordinating protest actions by the library community. Their proposed longer-term aim is to orchestrate actions to introduce greater competition for commercial publishers. By this they mean the transfer of material for publication from journals produced by commercial publishers to existing non-commercial outlets, and the encouragement of new non-profit alternatives to traditional commercial publishers. The Association's analysis has been criticised by

Table 1.7. *Methods of charging differentially for journals*

Categories of subscription	Percentage of total journals
Institutional only	40%
Institutional and society member	16%
Institutional, society member and non-member individual	22%
Institutional and individual	22%

commercial publishers on the grounds that it is based on partial data. The Association's response is naturally that the publishers should provide them with more data. The debate will obviously continue.

One area where some progress has been made is with firm pricing. It is a habitual complaint of librarians that many titles do not have firm prices set for them by September, when many libraries start taking purchasing decisions for the coming year. Publishers, of course, point to the problems involved, especially in terms of the need to anticipate fluctuations in exchange rates. However, the situation does seem to be improving. An analysis in 1993 found that some 90 per cent of the titles produced by major STM publishers had firm prices set by September. Unfortunately, this was only true for a third of the small and medium-sized journal publishers.

All the foregoing topics are debated in detail between librarians and publishers in the (electronic) *Newsletter on Serials Pricing Issues*. This is available online and free of charge from Marcia Tuttle at the University of North Carolina. Journal publishers who are interested in feedback from librarians should certainly access it.

The variety of journals

During their development, journals have gradually expanded and specialised their functions. The basic entity remains the primary journal, publishing new material for the first time. However, it has come to be surrounded by various other types of publication whose main function is often to call attention to the contents of primary journals. The obvious example is a review journal, which typically summarises recent advances in limited subject areas. Other examples are newsletters and abstracts journals (some prefer to use the singular – 'abstract journals') which are described briefly below. Along with these, which are journals in their own right, there are items such as offprints, which represent forms of spin-offs from the primary journal.

Abstracts journals

These first appeared in the nineteenth century as a method of tracking down relevant items in the expanding literature. Scanning collected abstracts made it easier to decide which articles in one's specialism needed to be studied in detail. At the same time, such scanning provided a quick way of keeping up with developments in adjacent specialisms. Abstracts journals are still supposed to fulfil both these functions today. It may be some indication of their success that few librarians, however hard pressed, would think of cancelling subscriptions to the leading abstracts journals. (This refers to single subscriptions: librarians have been quick to cancel duplicate subscriptions to abstracts journals wherever possible.) It is only fair to add that librarians' assessments of their importance do not always coincide with those of scientists. Although *Chemical Abstracts* (say) is certainly used extensively, there are some areas of science where the abstracts journals are relatively little used. Current problems of higher editorial costs and of those publishers who still need to decide whether to change from hard-copy to machine-readable form make the future of some abstracts journals less than certain.

The growth of abstracts journals has been accompanied by the publication of individual abstracts as part of each original paper in the primary journals. These abstracts, normally prepared by the author, may be taken over unchanged into abstracts journals; though, owing to a variety of problems (including queries regarding copyright), several publishers of abstracts journals actually produce their own abstracts. There are a number of guides to abstracting services that can be consulted to see what abstracts journals are being published in any particular field. The most widely useful of such guides is probably *The Index and Abstract Directory* (EBSCO Publishing).

Indexes are often mentioned alongside abstracts journals. Many primary journals produce an index to their contents, usually annually. Some also produce cumulative indexes at (say) five- to ten-year intervals. In addition, some publishers produce indexes covering a number of different journals which have related subject matter. For example, Butterworths in the UK produce a quarterly *British Humanities Index* covering articles in a wide range of the humanities articles which appear in British journals and newspapers. Most indexes record titles/authors in a simple alphabetic sequence, but some attempt to make things easier for a user. An example is the keyword-in-context (KWIC) index. This uses a computer to cycle the keywords in the title of each article, and then presents them in alphabetical sequence with the rest of the title laid out round the keyword. This gives the user several chances of finding a relevant article, rather than one only. Another example of a user aid is *Current Contents*, which reprints the contents pages of recent journal issues in a particular discipline. This not only eases the reading task of users; it also allows them to identify relevant articles in journals to which they may not normally have access. It is now one of the most popular means of scanning journal contents amongst scientists and engineers.

Newsletters

Newsletters were typically associated with societies, but over the last decade they have been heavily developed by commercial publishers. As the name implies, newsletters are especially concerned with reporting events; they often also summarise important research findings, papers at conferences and even information from press releases. Modern methods of production and a strong market for the latest information in easily assimilable form have led to newsletters becoming an important publishing medium. Occasionally, they may become the precursor of an informal electronic journal or communication network. In some cases, the newsletter and the online service are run in parallel, when they may carry different sorts of information. (For example, print may be preferable for longer articles and electronic communication for rapidly updated news.) Newsletters available only online are increasing rapidly in number (see the final chapter).

Newsletters are so easy to start that it is difficult to keep track of how many titles there are. The 1989 *Oxbridge Directory of Newsletters* includes 17,500 newsletters available in hard-copy. Of these some 600 are aimed at investors alone, which indicates the importance of the financial sector in this type of publishing. In the Preface to the *Oxbridge Directory*, it is claimed that this is the age of the newsletter: 'Simply produced, quickly distributed, they bring their readers new ideas fast. While they are still fresh enough to be useful and profitable — Magazines can't afford to offend their advertisers. Newsletters don't need to worry about that.' If publishers are considering launching a newsletter, they should check in this directory first; many subject areas seem to be crowded with titles.

Successful newsletters have made exceptionally high profits, as production costs are low in relation to the subscription price. These titles are usually industry-based, giving latest market information and analysis, news of new products and trade gossip. There have been several newsletters in medicine, some aimed at the general reader, that have achieved very high circulation at low subscription rates. In the medical area particularly, there can be a fairly hazy dividing line between newsletters and free newspapers. If successful, there are opportunities for the latter to convert themselves into charged-for versions of the former.

A large number of newsletters are published by not-for-profit organisations and academic societies as a service to their members, sometimes complementing the society's primary journals. With desktop production these have become less expensive to produce; an attractive publication can be brought out in days. Indeed, some newsletters are claimed to appear in a day: the editor sends in the text by telephone line in the morning, the copy-editor goes through it, sets it up into pages, then transmits it to the printer, for making film plates, then printing; bound copies are despatched in the afternoon post. As will be noted in a later chapter, electronic newsletters are now produced and disseminated with even greater speed.

The problem with subscription-based newsletters is the relatively low renewal rate; around 60 per cent is typical, especially when the subscribers are in industry and may move jobs or change their information requirements regularly. This means that the publisher must budget for a sustained marketing programme including every effort to persuade lapsed subscribers to renew and a range of special offers. The high publicity and marketing cost is one of the reasons why specialist newsletter publishers tend to bring out titles in clusters, for overlapping markets, so enabling them to spread these costs over several titles. Some techniques, such as linking newsletters to meetings and seminars, could spread to the marketing of primary journals. The other main reason for clustering is that publishers can use market knowledge to plan new titles and one editorial office can provide copy for several newsletters, as many of the sources of information will overlap.

The Newsletter Association of America has produced an excellent practical guide. In Britain the best source of information is the UK Newsletter Association, which produces *The UK Newsletter Directory*; this annual publication is made up of a list of newsletters plus articles on various aspects of newsletter publishing. Unlike academic journals many newsletters have a relatively short life with the peak circulation being reached in two or three years; they are often sold on, merged or closed after five or six years. Moving from publishing journals to newsletters is not easy.

Other types of journal

Besides abstracts journals and newsletters, various other types of journal with specific purposes can be identified. One example is the letters journal. This sort of journal is published more speedily than an equivalent ordinary journal, and contains short preliminary communications rather than full-length articles. The original intention of such journals was to allow a new advance to be announced quickly: this could then be followed up at leisure by a full article in an ordinary journal. It has been found, in practice, that many of the contributions are never subsequently expanded. So letters journals are typically seen as channels for brief, rapid communication of new results.

Another type of journal is that which concentrates on reviews. (Many learned journals publish occasional review articles.) Such journals often have distinctive titles, e.g. 'Advances in . . . ', 'Progress in . . . '. In times past, a typical review journal might appear annually (or irregularly), but several now appear more frequently. During the past few years, review journals seem to have survived well, though, unlike primary journals, they often have to pay contributors.

A third category of journal is that which involves translation. A typical example might be a cover-to-cover translation of a foreign-language journal into English, issued at regular intervals like the original journal, but obviously with some delay. However, some journals provide a selective coverage of foreign-language material instead. The main problem, after deciding which material deserves translating, is to find translators with both the subject and language skills necessary. There are, for example, relatively few English-speaking computer specialists who are also fluent in Japanese. Those that do exist have to be paid reasonably well to do translation work. Translations journals tend to be fairly high priced and are often prime candidates for cancellation by librarians. Consequently, they have not represented a growth area of journal publishing in recent years.

One type of journal that was pushed hard for a time, but is little heard of now, is the synopsis journal. In this, the printed journal contains only a synopsis of the article's contents. The full text can be supplied by the publisher on demand, either as an offprint or on micro-form. Though this form of publication has some advantages for publishers and librarians, it is not well regarded by authors, who generally prefer that the whole article appears in hard-copy, rather than just a synopsis.

Similar opposition from authors has faced attempts to publish journals in micro-form rather than hard-copy. ('Micro-form' is the generic term for all forms of micro-publishing. It can be used to cover micro-film, micro-fiche and mini-print, though much the commonest for use with journals is micro-fiche.) A few publishers produce hard-copy and micro-form versions of their journals simultaneously. Though occasional libraries may like to take current issues in this form, most journals on micro-form are purchased by libraries which have decided to acquire a back-run of a particular title.

Offprints and preprints

Whereas abstracts journals have continued to grow in importance since the Second World War, the same is not generally true of another ancillary to journals – the offprint. ('Offprint' is now preferred to the older term 'reprint', since the material is rarely reprinted in the strict sense of the term.)

Once, scholars who wanted a copy of a paper in a learned journal wrote to the author for an offprint. Today, it is generally quicker and cheaper for them to make a photocopy, so authors are, on average, requiring fewer offprints than previously. The small number of free offprints provided to authors by many journals often proves adequate. The extent to which this is true varies with subject field. It depends, in part, on the number of people working in the field, but other factors are also at work. For example, contributors to journals in the biosciences (including medicine) may still commonly ask for several hundred reprints. The reasons for this are probably that plates (especially electronmicrographs) do not photocopy well; material of interest to any one research worker may be scattered over a number of journals not all readily available in a single library; and *Current Contents*, which is used especially by bio-scientists as a source of information, may increase awareness of such articles. Researchers in developing countries may also find that their only way of acquiring a particular paper is by asking the author for an offprint, so that some copies are needed for this purpose. In addition, authors may need a number of copies for such purposes as grant applications.

In part, the role played formerly by the offprint has been taken over post-Second World War by the preprint. In this case, copies of the paper are circulated prior to publication in a journal (and frequently nowadays prior to acceptance by a journal for publication). This activity is normally carried out by authors, rather than publishers and increasingly the World-Wide Web is being used to make available a 'preprint' to colleagues. It is often regarded with suspicion by editors, who fear that preprint exchanges may be circumventing the traditional, properly refereed channels of communication. In the social sciences and humanities, documents are circulated in an analogous manner, though they are not usually referred to as 'preprints'. In the social sciences, for example, much research information is circulated in report form prior to publication via more formal outlets.

Journal publishing and developing countries

Journal publishing is an international pursuit, but that does not mean that it can be pursued with equal ease everywhere. Developing countries, in particular, face a whole series of problems in trying to establish an indigenous programme of journal publishing. For example, the number of active authors in a developing country may be too small to support the publication of journals except in a very few specialisms. Countries with an adequate number of authors may, for a variety of reasons, have a fragmented approach to scholarly publishing. In Brazil, for example, the universities alone produce 300 different journals. Few journals published in developing countries receive much international recognition. Authors who wish to have their work read as widely as possible often prefer, therefore, to publish important research in journals produced in developed countries. But this necessarily depresses the quality and prestige of journals published in their own country. The problem of attracting sufficient significant contributions has a number of facets. One is the question of language of publication. Publications in the local language have the advantage not only that it is easier for the author to write them, but also that it is easier for the reader to understand them – an important point where research is aimed at practitioners (e.g. as in agriculture). But, if the local language is not also one of the major world languages, contributions in it are likely to be ignored elsewhere. Hence, editors and publishers face a difficult choice as they seek to attract both authors and readers.

Most learned journals in developing countries have low circulations. The prices that can be set are limited by the low salaries of potential readers and the limited acquisitions budgets of libraries. (One of the reasons for the proliferation of journal titles in developing countries is the need for an institution to have a medium of exchange with which to obtain copies of journals published elsewhere.) Consequently, such journals are rarely financially viable. Subsidies may either be via direct funding, or may simply involve the provision of labour and overheads. This subsidisation implies that most journals are organisation-based, typically in an organisation funded directly or indirectly by the government.

Production and presentation of the printed material is often poor, due either to the quality of the materials and equipment, or to a lack of local expertise. Distribution is a slow process and losses of stock may be serious. Marketing is rarely supported to the extent common in developed countries and is, in any case, made difficult by communication problems, currency restrictions, and so on.

Altogether an expansion by developing countries into the international journal publishing market might seem a rather hopeless proposition. However, many of these difficulties are not unique to developing countries. Thus Scandinavian journals face the problem of serving small research communities which use languages little recognised internationally. Similarly, most Australian journals have quite low circulations, usually need some form of subsidisation, and experience marketing problems. The difficulties for developing countries, as compared with developed countries, typically relate to the infrastructure. In particular, apart from resources, slow and uncertain communication stands in the way of development. It may be that electronic information-handling can help here. At first sight, the advent of information technology might simply be expected to make a bad situation worse. However, if the hurdles can be surmounted, access to networks may help both authors and readers in developing countries to have immediate access to current research activities in developed countries – a point which will be taken up again in the final chapter.

The future for journals

With so many academic publishing companies and societies financially dependent on their journals, the question 'how long can it last?' is often asked. Clearly academic library budgets are under pressure but to some extent publishers have compensated for a decline in institutional subscriptions by selling more individual subscriptions (often through links with societies) and developing non-subscription revenues (see chapter 6). Recently technology has become available that will enable publishers to offer 'electronic subscriptions', typically access over the Internet to a journal held on a server through a password issued to the subscriber. The extra cost to the publisher of an established journal is not great provided that the production is properly organised (see the section on 'The neutral database strategy' in chapter 3 and figure 3.3) and certainly less than the cost of manufacturing and despatching hard-copy. Electronic publishing may well therefore be an opportunity rather than a threat (see chapter 11).

There have been various attempts to predict the future of journals as we now know them. The usual view is that hard-copy will continue to be sold for some decades although it may only be one form of the published work, with perhaps the digital version dominating the publishing process. In North America, the Association of American Universities and the Association of Research Libraries set up three task forces in 1994 to look at issues of acquiring journals from overseas, intellectual property rights in an electronic environment and a national strategy for managing scientific and technical information. The task force looking at the third issue broke down information transfer into three models:

1 the classical print-on-paper publication
2 the modernised model in which electronic technology is used instead of traditional methods (sometimes called 'parallel publishing')
3 an emergent model that by-passes traditional print methods and includes 'collaboratories' in which scholars work together regardless of time or space, creating new methods of communication for their readers and themselves.

The task force concluded that no single model would be dominant over the next few years and predicted that by 2015 about 50 per cent of scientific and technical information will still be in print, about 40 per cent in the modernised model and 10–15 per cent in the emergent model. They would expect some variation between disciplines. Bernard Naylor in a study based on views of university librarians in the UK predicted a sharp drop in subscriptions to hard-copy journals around 2005. Publishers may just have time to develop new systems to cope with ever more research output alongside ever more limited library budgets.

2 Editing

Introduction

Editors are responsible for the selection and preparation of material for publication. There are at least five distinct editorial tasks in journal publishing though often one person will perform several. Firstly, there is the person within the publishing organisation who has responsibility for acquiring and developing journals: the 'publisher's editor'. Secondly, there is the editor of an individual journal, concerned primarily with its content as a whole: the journal editor. Journal editors may have the support and assistance of associate, assistant or regional editors, or editors for particular topics or sections. Fourth, the copy-editor, sub-editor or desk-editor (sometimes 'redactor') sees that the material to be published is presented as well as possible, and that the copy can be followed easily by the typesetter. Then there may be a 'managing editor' or 'production editor' looking after the flow of typescripts and proofs; that job may be done by a person specially designated, or by any of the other editors, or their staff. This chapter considers the role of each. A managing editor may have other responsibilities, for instance for business management and liaison with colleagues responsible for non-subscription revenue; these are discussed in other chapters. There is inevitably some overlap with chapter 10 on the management of a list of journals.

The publisher's editor

Within a larger publishing house there will be several grades of editor. The editor-in-chief, or editorial director, is responsible for formulating editorial policy and often for acquiring books, journals and electronic publications in a particular area. Commissioning editors acquire publications within the scope of the overall editorial policy. Some firms publishing both books and journals in print and electronic formats will have separate divisions for each, but since ideas for one kind of publication often emerge from discussions about other kinds, close communication between commissioning editors in different media is encouraged. In other firms, an editor will be responsible for all acquisitions in a given subject area (monographs, text books, reference material, journals, electronic publications). To be effective, that approach requires someone with a general overview of the journals business to co-ordinate policy and procedures for both print-on-paper and electronic output.

Looking after a journal

Journals today generally require a substantial investment over at least five years before they become profitable. A book which fails can be quietly forgotten, pulped or remaindered. Many books are out-of-print or remaindered two to three years after first publication; at that stage, a new journal may still be two or three years from breaking even. It follows that a major concern of an established journal publisher is nursing the existing list and the editors and sponsors of those journals. Publishers who fail to do that will, at best, miss opportunities to enhance their journals or their sales; at worst, they risk losing their journals, or journal editors or contributors, to other publishers. (See chapter 10.)

Regular contact with editors and sponsors is reassuring and should give the publisher early warning of any worries or concerns that they may have about the journal or the publisher's handling of it. Editors and sponsors should always know who within the publisher they are dealing with; sudden, unannounced staff changes are unsettling. It is helpful if they can meet not only the person in charge of that journal but others dealing with it. Regular reports on sales, promotion, income from advertising (if appropriate), production and production delays are appreciated and suggest that the publisher cares about the journal. Meetings should be minuted and points raised followed up promptly. Editors commonly complain that they thought it was agreed that the publisher would take some action but nothing happened. If suggestions from editors or others are not practicable they should be told so at the time or after investigation.

Editors or editorial boards usually monitor the number of typescripts received from different countries and how they fare (accepted, rejected, returned for revision); the number of papers received and published on different topics and the time from receipt of typescript to publication. If the time is too long, authors may submit their more interesting papers elsewhere. Both editors and publishers are interested in the 'impact factor' and the ranking of their journals by the Institute of Scientific Information: this is a measure of how frequently articles in the journal are cited in the journals scanned by ISI for their Citation Indexes (see chapter 4).

Some publishers have a regular audit of all aspects of each of their journals. However positively a publisher reacts to opportunities as they present themselves, some things may be missed. It is also desirable to look ahead: where should the journal be in five or ten years time? The lists in chapter 10 offer a framework for such a review.

Acquiring existing journals and starting new ones

Most commercial and university press journal publishers, as well as some learned society publishers, continue to seek out additional journals to publish. Major journal publishers receive numbers of unsolicited proposals each year and seek out other ideas in discussion with outside advisers and contacts. Secondly, the publisher may develop proposals for new journals in-house, probably with the assistance of outside advisers. Thirdly, existing journals may need new homes: a journal may have outgrown the capacity of the organisation that currently runs it, or the editor of the journal or its sponsor may be unhappy about the performance of the present publisher.

Journals are long-term ventures. A new journal is a major investment; the promotion alone will probably cost more than publishing a book. Consequently, a publisher enquires more deeply into the potential of a journal than of a monograph. If a journal is misconceived, or badly executed, it can be a problem for many years. Effecting changes of editorial policy, marketing strategy, or pricing policy can be slow and expensive. The aims of the journal and how to achieve them must be rethought, and fresh promotion will be needed. Vigorous efforts may be needed to acquire the sort of material that the editor really wants to publish. If the price is too low (perhaps because the potential demand was overestimated), it may not be possible to bring it to an economic level in less than three or four years.

There are many reasons for starting a journal: the publisher has to be sure that they are sound. It is sometimes said that a learned society with a membership of between 500 and 1000 will begin to feel the need for a journal. A society, an individual, a university department, a research institution, or a group of scholars may see a journal as a way of promoting their image, enhancing their power, expanding their influence, publishing their work, or of making money. It may be that there is no journal on the subject produced in the area of the world they happen to inhabit. But this is not sufficient reason for a publisher (be it a commercial publisher, university press, or learned society) to put money into it.

Unless a journal can attract enough good papers, it is unlikely either to contribute greatly to scholarship or to find enough subscribers to make it commercially viable. New journals compete with existing ones for contributions and for subscribers. So the publisher will want to know where the work is currently being published, and why the existing journals are unsatisfactory. They may be produced too slowly, take too restricted a view of the subject, or there may be no one journal embracing all aspects of the subject. What advantages can the new journal offer authors over the existing ones? (See section on content of journals below.)

A good reason for starting a journal is that an existing journal is getting too large and could either be split into two or twig off another journal. There may be a perceived need for a specialist journal to provide a focus for a growing subject, or the existing journal may be more than the editors wish to cope with. Provided that is done with the blessing of the parent journal, the new journal should start with a good base of potential contributors and potential subscribers. Sometimes subscribers to the original journal will be sent copies of the new journal for the first year without charge to help get it established.

Completely new journals are more risky. For the long-term health of their businesses, most publishers launch new journals in promising subject areas; they are also conscious that their competitors have the same objectives. To pre-empt competition, a publisher may start a journal before the market is really large enough to support it, hoping that as the subject grows their journal will be the leading one. In some cases, their hopes may be fulfilled; in others the subject may not develop as expected, leaving the journal to languish. Even if it is eventually successful, the low circulation to start with will result in either a very high price for the journal, or to a loss for the publisher, or, more often than not, both of these in the early years.

Many publishers prefer to increase their lists by acquiring existing journals rather than starting new ones. A journal that has not flourished with one publisher may do better with another. A publisher may decide to jettison (or sell off, sometimes for a good price) some of their journals in order to concentrate on other publications. Existing journals produce immediate sales revenue, usually with less work than a launch. If a publisher is starting in journals, the acquisition of a few established journals can be very helpful editorially; learned societies and others are understandably cautious about entrusting their journals to a publisher with no track record.

Any serious journal proposal needs appraisal. The first stage is in-house: some publishers use a scoring system. Are the subject matter and the type of journal appropriate to that publisher's list? Is it likely that the journal would attract enough material to publish and subscribers to purchase it to make it a viable proposition? What are the competing journals, and their relative strengths and weaknesses? Have they been growing in extent, or are they static? What sort of prices are charged for them? Are they appearing regularly? What is the time from receipt of typescript to publication? Do rough costings suggest the journal would make a profit or a loss in the first two or three years. If it looks like a loss-maker, how many years might it be until the journal begins to break even and then until it has paid back the initial investment? Is the subject one in which interest can be expected to grow over the years, or is it gently declining? What is known of potential (or actual) editors and editorial board members? Would they be good people to work with?

If the journal passes these hurdles, the publisher will canvass outside opinion. Whereas with books it is customary to consult only a few people (often there will be two referees), many more may be asked about a journal. It is not uncommon to approach 100 to 150 people and get a 60 per cent to 80 per cent response if the names were well chosen. In addition to the publishers' usual advisers on the subject, the editor and potential members of the editorial board will be able to suggest names. Ideally those approached will be from a number of countries, and represent different schools of thought.

If the journal already exists, then those consulted may be assumed to be fully aware of it; if they are not, that suggests something seriously wrong with either the journal or its publisher. If it is only a proposal, then each adviser can be given a full brief on it. Questions may include the need for a journal on the subject; the planned scope and content; the proposed editor; the likely market; whether the respondent would want to contribute to it, or to encourage colleagues to do so; and if they would expect their library to subscribe. Usually no fees are paid for advice, unless the adviser has clearly gone to a great deal of trouble.

These enquiries can have secondary uses: they make the journal known, and establish the publisher's interest in the subject. They may also suggest further candidates for the editorial board or associate editors. The risk is that another publisher might learn of the proposal and decide to start a similar journal though the first publisher should have a good start. But some publishers prefer to keep their plans as secret as they can until the journal is ready to be launched. Sometimes, two publishers come up with ideas for similar journals at the same time; one may learn of the plans of the other in time to withdraw or modify their proposals so that they are not competing head on for the same authors and the same audience.

Content of journals

The basic content of most primary academic journals is original papers, the first publication of research results. Many learned journals contain nothing else. Once established as leaders in their fields, publishing reasonably quickly and treating authors decently, most academic research journals have little difficulty in attracting all the papers they need. Indeed, the number of acceptable papers received may continue to grow each year, producing a steady increase in the number of pages and frequency of issues. Assessment procedures that take account of the number of publications put pressure on academics and researchers to get as many papers published as possible.

New journals or journals with a change of editorial policy are not so fortunate; editors often find it difficult to get enough good papers. For journals in applied fields, business and management, politics and international relations it may be a continuing problem. 'Calls for papers' set out the aims and scope of the journal and its attractions for authors; they explain how to prepare and submit a paper for publication there. The attractions can include rapid decision-making (so the author can submit to another journal without great loss of time if the paper is rejected); speedy publication; more appropriate readership; a high impact factor (see chapter 4); good quality reproduction of illustrations; attractive production; or more free offprints than competing journals.

Established journals can draw attention to their readership, citation rankings and to how widely indexed and abstracted they are; authors would rather be published in journals that feature in *Current Contents* and the appropriate major abstracting services to those that do not. In surveys, scientists responded that they prefer journals with high prestige, but this is circular: prestige comes from publishing high-quality papers by well-known scientists and that depends on attracting papers in the first place by offering the sort of advantages outlined above.

Printed calls for papers usually have little effect unless accompanied by a personal letter from the editor or a member of the editorial board. The editor will also want copies of the instructions to authors to mail to friends and colleagues. A guaranteed distribution of the first issue may encourage submissions; generally well-established authors are more willing than those beginning their careers to send a paper to an untried journal. The publisher might pay the expenses for the editor to attend a major conference to promote the journal to both authors and potential readers. Sometimes conference organisers will know of papers presented at the meeting and seeking a publisher. Mailings to promote sales of new journals can also include encouragement to potential contributors. Once the first issue is published, copies can be sent to prominent people in the subject with a further call for papers; and that might be followed up on the telephone.

Some journals may reprint (perhaps in translation) articles that have appeared in other journals if the editor thinks that they are of exceptional quality and that there is little overlap between the circulation of the two publications. Permission must of course be obtained to do this, and a fee may be levied. In addition, the costs of getting a decent translation of technical articles may be very high.

In addition to original research papers, journals may publish short notes and preliminary communications or letters and comment; these tend to require rapid publication which is difficult if the journal is published less than six times a year. Journals in the humanities and social sciences occasionally publish documents (original source material). Some journals offer editorials written by the editor or by a contributor, either named or anonymous, raising topics of current concern.

Many journals welcome review articles on the present state of a particular topic. These tend to be more frequently cited than research papers and so increase the impact factor of the journal, while readers find them useful for reference and for teaching. They may also lead to spin-offs, being included in books of readings or translated into other languages. Probably more journals would carry them if they could find good authors ready to spend the necessary time to write a lively, informed and informative commentary. Unfortunately for editors and publishers – and readers – review articles carry less weight than original papers with bodies awarding promotion, tenure or research grants.

Sometimes an invited review turns out to be unsuitable for publication when it eventually reaches the editor's desk. The contributor may well be aggrieved if, after having spent a great deal of time on it at the editor's behest, his review is then rejected. While most contributors to academic journals receive no fees for their contributions (indeed sometimes they pay; see section on page charges) some journals pay authors of review articles whether or not the article is eventually published. A hard-pressed journal editor may decide to nominate someone else to commission and handle review articles.

Shorter items can add interest. If they are not time-sensitive, they can also be used to keep the journal to an even working and so reduce production costs (see chapter 3). Book reviews are the most common additional feature, though they are labour intensive. It is not always easy to find willing reviewers who will produce a review within a reasonable time and to the right length. Often much chasing is needed once a reviewer has been found. Some journals have an editor specifically for book reviews. Reviews of new products raise the same problems.

Brief notes on recently published papers of note on a particular topic are also welcomed by readers, particularly if the selector and commentator is a well-known authority, and they are much less demanding to produce. *Cardioscience* may have been the first journal to introduce this. Correspondence may be difficult to generate and may not be topical by the time it is published. Historical accounts of major developments in the subject and how they came about are particularly valuable when written by those involved in them. Abstracts of papers recently published in other journals are another possibility. Medical journals may publish case-history reports if they are of particular interest or significance. Other items could include information about recent and forthcoming meetings and conferences, lists of books received, notices of scholarships and fellowships that might be available or of prizes.

Editorials and articles on other matters of concern to those who might be expected to see the journal for, for instance, problems of teaching the subject, the ethics of experimentation and of the treatment of patients can add interest and encourage people to look at the journal.

If the journal is the main means of communication between a society and its members, then there may be more society news or the proceedings (in abstract form) of recent meetings. The journal may also publish the text of lectures sponsored by the society or presidential addresses – though one hopes that these will be genuine contributions to the subject and not just a collection of platitudes.

Special issues and supplements

Journal editors are sometimes anxious to publish special issues on particular topics either instead of, or in addition to, a regular issue (i.e. a supplement). There are arguments for and against them. Special issues can help to establish a position for the journal in a particular field and may bring in distinguished authors who would otherwise not contribute to it. They can help to bring out opposing views on controversial topics. Some enjoy a sale to non-subscribers, either as single issues or occasionally as books. In that case, their origins should be made clear; librarians regard being asked to pay for the same thing twice as sharp practice. For medical journals they can also be a useful source of income (see below). If the journal is short of material, a special issue may help to fill the pages.

Hopes of reaching new audiences with a special issue, either as part of the journal, or as a book, are often disappointed. The necessary promotion will cost money; and booksellers are unwilling to order, let alone stock, publications that do not carry a reasonable discount. The pagination needs watching. The text of the book should begin on page one, but two page ones within the same volume of a journal confuses citations, so repagination may be necessary.

Plans to publish special issues should be laid well in advance. If they are to be paid for by the subscribers, then the cost should be included in the annual subscription (which may be announced some eighteen months before publication of the special issue or supplement); it is usually difficult and sometimes impossible for subscribers to find extra money later on. Naturally, subscribers with no interest in the subject of the special issue will resent having to pay for it at all. Special issues are also unpopular with those authors whose papers are held over until the next issue.

Editorially, special issues can pose problems. What is to be done if one of the principal authors has not delivered a contribution before the deadline and seems unlikely to do so? There may be clear overlap or inconsistencies between contributions but little chance of getting any of the authors to revise their papers in time. What should be done about invited papers of marginal quality in which the author has clearly invested a good deal of effort? Other management issues are considered in chapters 3 and 6.

Supplements for medical journals are a special case for they frequently receive sponsorship from a drug company and are distributed to subscribers without charge; for more on possible arrangements see chapter 6 on non-subscription revenue. The questions then are not financial but editorial. Contributions to supplements should go through the same review procedure as that for other issues. There should be no bias towards the products or line of approach of the sponsor. The journal may insist on a member of the editorial board being a co-editor of the sponsored supplement. The sponsor benefits from its association with the good name of the journal, automatic distribution of the supplement to major libraries and research people in the field and from extra copies of the issue for their own promotional purposes.

Language

Another question to be considered is the language of publication. For high-level scientific journals produced in English-speaking countries, the answer is obvious: English is the language of science and printing in other languages costs more. There appears to be little demand for abstracts in other languages in English-language STM journals at this level. Scientific journals in other countries are also often published wholly or partly in English to make them more accessible to an international readership; in that case, an abstract in the local language may be appropriate. Papers in other languages are less frequently read or cited; insistence on using the local language encourages contributors who seek an international audience to publish elsewhere. Scientific journals publishing in languages other than English sometimes provide an English summary or abstract; this can be helpful.

Journals in applied science, and those intended for professional groups or businesses, are more likely to be in the local language; doctors, paramedics, farmers, lawyers, or scientists and technologists working in industry may not be able to cope with foreign languages.

A few journals lend themselves to translation into other languages, either in whole or in part. *Scientific American* in its non-English editions is bought by thousands who would never have looked at the English-language version. Journals consisting of translations of selected papers from the *Lancet* and the *British Medical Journal*, both weekly publications, are put out in various languages in monthly editions by publishers licensed to do so. The Spanish translation of the *Lancet* is one of a number of translations of journals into Spanish published by Ediciones Doyma.

The prominence of English is less marked in the humanities and social sciences. A scholar working on the history, literature or institutions of a country can be expected to have a working knowledge of at least one of the languages used there; they may not however be able to cope with the whole range of languages. Some journals in the humanities will accept articles in any major European language that uses a roman alphabet.

The journal editor

The journal editor is responsible for deciding the editorial content of the journal. The editor's tasks are well set out in Maeve O'Connor, *Editing Scientific Books and Journals*. Though this is particularly concerned with scientific and medical publications, much of it applies equally to journals in the humanities and social sciences. In the space available here we can only outline the main principles.

Once the decision to publish the journal has been taken, an editor must be appointed. Often the decision and the appointment go hand in hand, for the editor of the journal will be involved in discussions of editorial policy, and the publisher will want to be assured of a competent editor before commitment. For Society journals or journals with outside sponsors, the Council or some similar body is likely to make editorial appointments. For an established journal, that might be on the nomination of the editorial board or publications committee. Publishers often look to the editorial board for nominations, though retaining the right to veto a candidate whom they think is unsuitable.

If the journal has assistant or associate editors some pattern of succession may be built into the system. Since it is important that the editors should work well together, the existing editor is likely to have a significant role in picking editorial colleagues and hence successors. With most STM journals that is not likely to be a problem, but a journal in the social sciences may become the mouthpiece of a particular group and reflect only one approach to the subject. That may not be a bad thing; but the publisher should be aware of the possibility of a narrowing of approach over the years. Editors have to feel committed to the journal and so appointments are usually for at least three and often five years in the first instance, renewable at least once. In any case, there are costs in moving an editorial office and good editors may not be easy to find if the change is too frequent.

The editor needs to be both enthusiastic and clear-headed about the journal, and to recognise that it will take much time and effort to get a new one established or to make much impression on the content of an existing one. They must be liked and respected by their peers. Editors have to battle with the vagaries of authors and referees, with whom they must be simultaneously firm and tactful, take hard decisions, be efficient and work to deadlines. While editors are better paid than they once were (those of some learned society journals were often honorary, being paid no more than their expenses) few journals can afford generous editorial payments.

The ideal editor will have a wide knowledge of the subject and of those working in it. He must be able to find referees who will produce helpful and pertinent reports within a reasonable time. It helps if there are colleagues who can provide quick opinions and suggest referees in those areas where the editor is not an authority. It is also an advantage to have a secretary or research assistant to deal with some of the more routine tasks and keep the paperwork in order. Editors who regularly attend international conferences may be able to attract authors there, as well as keeping abreast of research trends. Happily for publishers, such paragons do exist.

Is one editor enough? Some prefer working on their own; others like to involve colleagues or people from other institutions. A second editor will spread the workload (though time will be spent on communication between the two). An editor may feel the need for some permanent back-up, so that he can take a sabbatical or go on leave without taking the journal with him. It is always advisable to have someone or a group of people who could take over at short notice in the event of an accident or the editor becoming ill.

The editorial workload may be divided by broad subject area, or by type of contribution – for instance, theoretical or experimental, original papers and review articles, pre- or post-1800 literature, history or politics. There can be senior and junior editors, associate editors and assistants; sometimes they are appointed with a line of succession in mind. Some journals have editors in more than one country (who may be called regional or local editors), each dealing with papers of local origin. Some journals have a large editorial team, co-ordinated by either an editor-in-chief or the publisher's office. Sometimes any member of the board may be empowered to accept or reject papers. For the role of editorial boards in general, see below.

If a journal has more than one editor, it is important that they should each respect and trust the others. If they are in separate institutions, provision has to be made for frequent communication between them. Telefax and e-mail help with day-to-day business, but meetings from time to time are highly desirable.

The dividing line between what is done by the editor and what by the publisher varies from journal to journal and publisher to publisher. Commonly, the editor passes the copy to the publisher after it has been approved but before copy-editing. Some publishers play a more active role: the contributions go to them and they take care of acknowledgements and refereeing. Others leave the editor to deal with copy-editing and marking up for the typesetter; unless there are any problems, the editor will be responsible for seeing the journal through the production process.

Refereeing or peer review

Most respectable learned journals send every original research paper seriously considered for publication to referees for comment. This process is known as refereeing or peer review. No editor can be expert over the whole range of subjects covered by a journal, and few will have time to read every paper submitted for publication thoroughly and advise the author on how to revise it.

If a contribution has been solicited then refereeing may be rather cursory. Letters, invited editorials and other items may be reviewed by the editor alone. If a contribution is in the editor's own field it may not be thought necessary to consult an outside referee, especially when the editor proposes to reject it.

With those exceptions, articles that are candidates for publication are usually sent to one referee, with a second referee being consulted either simultaneously or subsequently, unless the first report convinces the editor that a second referee is unnecessary. A few editors use three referees simultaneously but act on the first two reports to come back to them. If the verdicts are contradictory others may be consulted, though further opinions do not always clarify matters. Sometimes a referee may suggest that someone else should be consulted on some area of the paper, for instance the methodology or treatment of statistics.

The referee is the guardian of publication standards. The referee's primary function is to advise the editor on the suitability of the paper for publication in a particular journal, and to discourage the publication of material that is not original, does not contribute to the subject or is of poor quality. By helping the editor to ensure that what is published in the journal is of a good standard and will not harm its reputation, the referee provides protection for other parties in the publication system. Many authors have been saved by referees from making embarrassing mistakes or publishing a paper in a form that might damage their reputation. The higher the standards of its referees the more attractive the journal will be both to authors and to potential readers and purchasers.

To save time and annoyance to all parties, many editors check that a potential referee is willing to referee a particular paper within a reasonable time. That avoids sending papers to people who are currently abroad, too occupied with other activities to respond quickly, or who for some reason would not wish to referee that paper. Some people refuse to referee papers if they have not been asked in advance if they would be willing to do so. e-mail can speed up enquiries about the willingness to referee a paper, but since it is not secure, should not be used for either papers or referees' reports.

Major points on which referees might comment include the interest and significance of the paper, its soundness and validity, and its originality. Is it a useful contribution to the subject, or simply a confirmation of something already known? Does it merit independent publication or should the results be incorporated in some other paper after further work? Has the author taken into account previous work on the topic or other sources of information, archives, etc.? Is there a proper description of the methods used, documents consulted, experimental techniques, use of controls or the sample studied? Are the conclusions fair ones to draw from the evidence given in the paper? If they conflict with received opinion is the case well argued?

Some editors have questionnaires or notes for referees drawing attention to points on which they want an opinion. They should be as simple as possible; a list that is too daunting may deter a referee from reviewing a paper for that journal again. Referees may be asked to divide their comments into those which they would be happy for the author to see and those which are for the editor only. They may also be asked to note deviations from the journal's instructions to authors.

Academics are under great pressure to publish to further their careers; in some subjects an author who does not publish several papers a year may be considered an underachiever. Naturally some take short cuts, so referees also have to watch for multiplied publication (using the same material – or even the same paper – several times); the minimum publishable unit (spreading ideas out very thinly); piracy (stealing someone else's paper), fraud (falsifying the evidence), plagiarism (stealing the ideas of others), and data torturing (see Mills, 1993). These may be more rife in the natural sciences and medicine than in the humanities where the pressure to publish is less acute, but they are found in every field.

If the content of the paper merits publication the presentation might still need improving. Is the order logical and the writing clear? Is the length right for what is being said? Does the author gloss over difficulties or go into excessive detail on trivial points? Are the figures and tables and other illustrations clear and to the point? Is the author consistent? Is the title fair and descriptive, and does the abstract accurately reflect the content? Is the use of language good, remediable or hopeless?

Most referees will be asked to consider the paper as a whole, but some may be consulted about a particular aspect of it, for instance, the handling of statistical data or the validity of a given technique in the circumstances in which it was used. Was the sample sufficiently large? Are there unexplained anomalies in the data? It is customary to pay technical referees, but, in return to expect them to handle a large number of papers if need be.

Sometimes the referee will give the editor a strong indication that the paper should either be accepted as it stands or rejected, but sometimes the advice is less clear cut. Many papers need minor amendments or major revision by the author. Most authors will undertake minor amendments, but papers needing large-scale rewriting may be put on one side or submitted to a journal with less exacting standards. Sometimes a referee will offer to work with the author to develop a publishable paper out of a half-baked one.

It is clear that the editor of an academic journal needs a good stable of referees to draw upon. Choosing suitable people and persuading them to referee a paper is not easy. Referees need sound judgement and to be up-to-date with what is happening in the subject, but should not be rivals of the author. Some editors ask authors to suggest at least four possible referees or to indicate people to whom they would not wish their paper to be sent. Apart from the technical referees (see above), the work is usually unpaid. Competent and helpful referees may find themselves overburdened with papers. While editorial board members may be expected to do some refereeing, it is generally unwise to use them exclusively. The load is too great; their range of expertise may be too narrow; and it is against the principle of anonymous refereeing.

Referees should be thanked for their services; some journals print a list of referees from time to time as a mark of appreciation. They feel more involved if they are sent the comments (anonymous, of course) of any other referees on the same item (*after* making their own) and are told the editor's decision.

Databases make it possible to record referees' interests in depth (including extra-curricular ones), to ensure that no referee is asked to tackle more than a given number of papers in any period, and to avoid using referees who have been slow or unhelpful in the past. This can be part of a computerised editorial management system (see section on office procedures below).

Many countries have laws allowing individuals access to information held about them in computer files. Comments on referees should therefore be restricted to the objective record: for instance, the actual time taken to send in a report, or points not considered, rather than remarks such as 'slow and incompetent'. Editors are advised not to delete incompetent referees from the records; if they do, they may forget they have already used them. Contributors may have the right to see the computer records for their own papers, so it is advisable to identify the referees by a code rather than by name in these files.

Referees' reports are confidential to the editor and possibly the editorial board, unless otherwise agreed between the editor and the referee. Some referees are happy that the author of the paper should know who refereed it, and indeed may be willing to work with them to improve it. Others may wish to be anonymous. If the paper needs revision, the editor may have to dress up the referee's comments to ensure anonymity and consistency between them. For their part, referees should treat the contribution as confidential until it is published; in principle they should not allow it to affect their own work or discussions with others, though that is sometimes difficult in practice.

Refereeing has its critics: complainants say it is slow, cumbersome, expensive and open to abuse (plagiarism or suppression of the competition). With a refereeing system it can take six weeks to two months from receipt of the paper to an editorial decision. Often referees disagree with each other indicating that there are no agreed standards. Even the best journals have accepted papers that turned out to be fraudulent or rejected papers that later enjoyed high repute, or that even, in the case of Sir Hans Krebs, led to a Nobel Prize. But no reasonable alternative to refereeing has yet been put forward. Daniel (1993) in his study of submissions to *Angewandte Chemie* concluded that 'reviewers' suggestions for improvement have had a significant impact on a large fraction of published manuscripts'. Many authors are grateful for the help which they have had from referees. The willingness of academics and research workers to continue to referee articles without payment suggests that they regard the system as valuable.

Some believe that it is fairer if the referee does not know the name of the author or the institute to which he is affiliated (blind refereeing). It is not always easy to remove all indication particularly as only a few people may be working on the topic at any one time. Others suggest that to encourage more responsible refereeing the names of the referees who recommended acceptance should be published with the paper, or that authors should be given copies of referees' reports as standard practice.

Once it was considered unnecessary to referee contributions to the journals of some national academies or scientific societies since all papers had to be submitted by a member of the academy. If an academician were the author, it was taken for granted that the paper was of high quality. If it was by someone else, it was assumed that the academician had read and approved it. That led to the publication of some sub-standard work, for academicians grow old and out of touch. It is now common practice for the publications of national academies to follow standard peer review procedures.

Anyone with an interest in the refereeing process is encouraged to join Locknet. This is an international network for research into peer reviewing, named after Stephen Lock, a former editor of the *British Medical Journal*, who was a pioneer in this field. Enquiries to Ms Alex Williamson, BMJ Publishing Group, BMA House, Tavistock Square, London WCIH 9JR.

Acceptance & rejection

Referees make assessments and recommendations; editors make decisions. They are concerned with the balance of articles and the journal as a whole. They are responsible for seeing that papers which cannot be published in a 'reasonable' time (which might be a few months for microbial genetics, or a year or more for history) are not accepted. Decisions to publish, or to reject, may be influenced by plans for the future development of the journal. The editor is also concerned with ethical considerations (did the investigation, perhaps in biology or the social sciences, cause undue suffering?); can the patients or the subjects be identified and will that lead to difficulties; the possibilities of libel or defamation and even obscenity (if in doubt check with the publisher or a libel lawyer). There may be financial restraints on the amount of foreign-language material, mathematics, or illustrations. So the editor decides what should be accepted, what rejected, and what returned for revision.

An editor is likely to receive a few excellent papers which should obviously be published, and a larger number of poor papers to be rejected. But many papers fall between these two: decisions about papers which are not clearly acceptable or rejectable as they stand are not easy. Sometimes the editor may make minor changes and submit them to the author for approval. In other cases, major rewriting or restructuring may be needed. Frequently, papers can be shortened without loss of content. Some editors ask for revision of almost every paper they publish; others rarely do so. Many editors have had the experience of getting back a revised paper and then finding further defects which had been masked in the earlier version. It is kinder to reject immediately than to encourage the author to put more work into something of doubtful value.

Letters of acceptance are easy: those asking for revision or rejecting the paper are more difficult, for they must be both firm and tactful. If the paper is being rejected, the letter should try to say something good about the submission while discouraging further correspondence or re-submission to the journal without giving offence. Standard letters can be used. Authors who are asked to revise their papers need concrete guidance on what should be done. In some cases it may be advisable to add that the journal is not committed to publishing a resubmitted paper. When the revised papers come in, it may be sensible to send them to the original referee to check that the changes have been made without throwing up other defects. If too long a time elapses between the original and the revised submission it may be treated as a new submission.

Suggestions that authors should 'improve the English' are usually unhelpful since authors use the best English they can muster. Sometimes an editor or editorial assistant will virtually rewrite a paper by a contributor who has done a good piece of work, but who has difficulties with the language; this is particularly so with contributions from developing countries. Journals published in English from non-English speaking countries may employ editors to help with language problems, as do some scientific institutes. Some editors may be able to suggest a colleague in the author's institution or an 'author's editor' who is known to have good language skills and who might be willing to help.

Acceptance rates vary with subject, and depend upon the basis of calculation: if a paper resubmitted after revision is treated as a second submission the acceptance rate will be lower than if it is considered as a continuation of the first submission. In the humanities rejections may be as high as 80 per cent to 90 per cent, while in the sciences and mathematics they may be 50 per cent or lower, with large variations from subject to subject. The high rejection rates in the humanities may be because of price restraint; that makes it difficult to increase the number of pages, so the editor must either reject a great many papers or lengthen the time from acceptance to publication. A common cause of rejection is that the paper has been sent to an inappropriate journal. Most papers submitted to STM journals arise from a research project; the authors will already have gone through a refereeing process to get funding for the work.

Editorials, book reviews, etc.

An editor has to deal with all the items published by the journal, not just research papers. Of these, book reviews are the most common.

Some editors consider a book review section to be an important part of the journal; others, that it is more trouble than it is worth. There may be an editor whose sole concern is the book review section. To cover the literature effectively the editor needs to scan publishers' lists of forthcoming titles, and ask for any books that are pertinent. He must then find a suitable reviewer who is prepared to deliver the review within a reasonable time. Reviewers often need chasing, particularly those preparing long review articles. The editor should keep a note of the bibliographical details of the book, including the publisher's address; reviewers often mislay the review slip on which it is recorded. Prices of books published abroad may have to be checked. Reviews are usually unrefereed, but the editor should make sure that they are not offensive, do not appear too long after publication, and are appropriate to the journal.

It is useful to have a checklist or standard letter to go out with review copies indicating the expected length of the review, the points the editor particularly wants covered, style and so on. (Do not begin the review with 'This book . . . ', or even, as one reviewer, 'Beautifully bound in blue, this book . . . '.)

Topical items such as letters and editorials are a problem for journals that are not published frequently. A hot topic may be decidedly cool by the time the issue reaches the readers. Editorials, either written by the editor or invited from others, may be a regular feature or very occasional; they may be signed or anonymous. They may comment on recently published or forthcoming contributions to the journal, or on topics of current interest. If they are very controversial the editor may want to add a comment that the editorial does not necessary reflect the views of the journal. Invited editorials that turn up late or are unsuitable for publication (because they do not address the issues, or are poorly argued, for instance) need tactful handling.

Correspondence can be a regular feature or very occasional. The decision whether or not to publish any item must rest with the editor, but he might sometimes feel it proper to give the original author the right to reply. News of society activities will as a rule come from the secretary, and should give no trouble provided that deadlines are met. Society lectures or invited addresses may sometimes be embarrassing and the amount of editing that can reasonably be done, limited. It may be possible to publish a synopsis or insert them in the journal as a separate publication.

As well as deciding what to publish in the journal, the editor is also responsible for determining the content of individual issues and the sequence of material in an issue. Papers may be grouped by subject or printed in order of receipt. Other items may be used as fillers to make up even workings (see chapter 3). Some features may be printed in smaller type to save space. In more prosperous countries this gives the message that the material is of less interest. However, in countries where paper is in short supply, the more important contributions may be in the smaller type on the grounds that people will be prepared to work hard to read those.

Editorial boards

Most learned journals have editorial boards, and the board usually has several roles. Members advise the editor on policy, strategy, and style, including directions in which a journal might develop, the balance of topics and approaches to them, series of articles, additional features, how to attract the best papers in the field and so on. They assist with refereeing, either doing it themselves or advising on suitable referees. In addition, they may encourage others to submit suitable papers to the journal, or advise the editor of people who might be approached. Often the members will be well known; they show that the journal has the support of leading people in the field and give it respectability. If a society is involved, the board may be expected to ensure that the journal reflects the needs and interests of that society, or the appropriate sections of it.

There are few rules about the size of an editorial board: as many people as are needed to do justice to the subject, without the numbers becoming unwieldy. If there are meetings of the editorial board, they are easier if at least six people turn up, but not more than fifteen. The number may be increased to take account of new areas of interest, or a vacancy left if there seems to be no very good candidate. Some so-called editorial boards may consist of fifty or more people; usually they will in practice act as a refereeing panel rather than a board.

The editorial board should reflect the range of interests of the journal. Those on it should be well respected and willing to give time and thought to the journal. There should be both continuity and change among the members; open-ended terms of office are not recommended. Terms of three years, renewable twice, or five years, renewable once, are common. If anyone is particularly useful and still interested in serving after the nine or ten year period is up, they can be given a year off, and then brought back for a further cycle. Appointments should be staggered so that the whole board does not come up for renewal at the same time.

For a journal published under the editorial direction of a learned society, the editorial board will usually consist of a mixture of members who are there *ex officio* and those who are selected on other grounds, including being representatives of other bodies or non-members whose contribution would be useful to the journal.

Many journals seek to be international, and to reflect that in the composition of their editorial board. In practice, this is not always as successful as hoped. It is expensive to bring overseas members to meetings, though it may be possible to hold some meetings during international conferences. If overseas members are to be involved in the running of the journal they need to receive regular editorial reports, minutes of board meetings and letters encouraging activity on their part from the editor; without that, any initial enthusiasm will wane. Some learned societies restrict board membership to their own members, but others take a broader approach, particularly if they aspire to international status. Indeed, some formal international recognition schemes (as that of the European Physical Society) have the requirement that editorial board members should be drawn from more than one country.

Sometimes the publisher will have a representative on the board, and/or may provide the secretariat for board meetings.

Editorial boards need chairmen. That may be the editor, but it can be easier to conduct editorial board meetings if someone else is in the chair. A chairman who is not the editor can be helpful in the search for a successor when the editor's term of office is up, and as an arbitrator or provider of a second opinion in the case of a dispute between editor and author or publisher.

Editorial boards are not only useful for defining editorial policy, refereeing, and window dressing. They may have ideas about promotion of the journal and access to useful mailing lists. The board can be helpful in the selection and appointment of future editors. Even if they do not make the appointment, the society or publisher may rely on them to advise on possible editors, and perhaps to sound out or interview them.

Editorial office procedures

The editorial office of the journal may be in the institution in which the journal editor works; many are based on university campuses, though some work from home. Alternatively, the office routines may be taken care of by the publisher or the offices of the sponsoring society. As already mentioned, the workload may be split in a variety of ways. Some editors feel it essential that they should be able to communicate with the printer; others want no part in the production process. The division of labour will depend upon the publisher's practice with other journals, the editor's temperament and experience, and the resources that the parties have at their command. In what follows, the word 'editor' is used to describe the person doing the work. It may be the journal editor, a junior editor, a managing editor, or their assistants or secretaries, but everyone working on the journal should understand that they are part of a chain and appreciate the importance of keeping to schedule.

There must be some basic office procedures, if only to keep track of material submitted to the journal. For many journals, a simple manual system will be adequate, with records kept according to article (a sheet for each), backed up by a filing cabinet. There may be issue-by-issue records, too. There are a number of PC-based systems on the market which can save a lot of time and trouble, particularly for larger journals: the RMTS system (produced by consultants, Dales, High Street, Didcot, Oxfordshire OX11 8EQ) is used by over 300 journals, and the University of Chicago Press system is available to other publishers. Whether a manual or a computer system is used the principles are the same.

The receipt of each article must be recorded and acknowledged (a printed card will do). Most journals assign a number to each. Records must be kept of the referees to whom it was sent and when, so that reminders can be issued as necessary. These records can also be used to see how quickly individual referees respond. All subsequent correspondence with the author and the referee needs filing and recording. The letter of acceptance may be accompanied by the copyright assignment form (see chapter 7).

The date of despatch to printer or publisher must be recorded. If the editorial office is handling proofs, their scheduled and actual dates of receipt and despatch will be noted, as should the date of publication; this is to monitor the production programme and the total time from receipt of typescript to publication. If either is lengthening, action may need to be taken. Similar records are needed for book reviews and for any other items which the journal may publish. We have already mentioned records for referees.

If possible, records and correspondence should be kept for some years after publication or rejection of an item. Queries can arise later, and will be more easily dealt with if the papers are to hand. Rejected items may be returned to the author, but, to save postage costs, some journals will only do so on request, or if the author pays the return postage.

Most editors need some secretarial help; one estimate is that a journal needs about one-and-a-half to two-and-a-half hours of secretarial time per paper, plus a further 60 per cent for general matters relating to the journal. Obviously, there are wide variations, depending upon how broad the editor's responsibility is; whether a word-processor is available; and how much work the editor delegates to a secretary. The time taken for different processes should be analysed: that can suggest more effective ways of working. It would be difficult to run a journal without access to a typewriter or word-processor, a photocopier and a telephone, and a fax machine is very useful particularly if there are a lot of overseas contributors or referees. Access to e-mail is also helpful. If the journal office cannot be manned full-time, a telephone answering machine is invaluable.

Style manuals, instructions to authors, notes for typists

Items accepted for publication need copy-editing and unless the journal uses camera-ready copy either the insertion of typesetting codes or marking up for the typesetter to ensure comprehensibility and consistency. Copy-editors need style manuals or style sheets setting out how to present the copy for the typesetter. The publisher or the printer may have a manual that is suitable or the journal may follow the style of a leading journal in the field.

Less copy-editing is needed when authors (and their typists) have clear instructions for the preparation of typescripts for the journal and follow them (see also chapter 3). Most journals have some brief instructions of their own, often printed in every issue of the journal, but they may refer the author to some more general style manual for more details. These include the Royal Society's 'General Notes on the Preparation of Scientific Papers'; the detailed 'instructions' from some major scientific societies; the style manuals of the Modern Humanities Research Association and the Modern Language Association, the Council of Biology Editors, and the 'Uniform Requirements for Manuscripts Submitted to Biomedical Journals' (Vancouver Style) which are available from the Editors of *The British Medical Journal* and the *New England Journal of Medicine,* and in both English and French from the *Canadian Medical Association Journal.*

Editors complain that authors themselves appear to pay attention neither to the instructions nor to pass them on to the person who types their papers. If most of the journals in a subject have the same style there is a better chance that it will be followed. That is also helpful because a paper rejected by one journal may not need much alteration before being submitted to another. The more accessible and briefer the instructions are, the more likely they are to be used: many journals find it convenient to print them on the inside back cover of each issue. Even so, contributors from developing countries may not have access to the journal to which they are contributing their paper.

Notes for contributors (also called a style sheet or notes for typists) should include a statement of the editorial policy of the journal; the editorial address; instructions on the form in which material should be submitted (e.g. two copies, double-spaced, whether or not articles are accepted on disks or by e-mail); the usual length of contribution acceptable; and the languages in which material can be published. Authors should be asked to warranty that the paper has not been accepted for publication elsewhere nor is it under consideration by another publication. It should also be made clear that they are responsible for getting permission to publish any material in which the copyright belongs to some other body.

Advice should be given on preferred spellings, abbreviations and punctuation, the systems used for references, abbreviations, units, special symbols, transliteration and so on. The instructions should explain what kind of illustrations (if any) can be accepted, and how they should be presented. If an illustration is enlarged or reduced, a scale should be indicated on the illustration itself: a statement of magnification will not hold true if it is enlarged or reduced to fit the page. If an abstract is required it should be clear, informative and self-contained; some journals require structured abstracts (e.g. background, methods, results, conclusion).

Some editors ask for papers which are not properly presented to be retyped, sometimes returning them with a list or a marked copy of the instructions to authors highlighting the matters that need attention. Badly prepared copy is costly to edit and typesetting is slower; the chances of errors and misunderstandings are greater. Errors will have to be corrected in proof, which is expensive and time-consuming, or they may slip through; neither is satisfactory.

If a journal uses author-prepared camera-ready copy it is particularly important that authors follow the instructions: for more on this see chapter 3.

Copy-editing

Copy-editing (sub-editing, desk-editing) may be done in the journal editor's office; in the publishers' editorial or production departments; or by freelancers. Each has advantages and disadvantages. An editorial assistant working with the journal editor, perhaps on a part-time basis, can handle office routines and the correspondence with authors, deal with the proofs, and build up specialist knowledge of the subject and the people who work in it. The editor is at hand to advise on technical questions. The institution in which the editor works may provide office space and facilities free or at low cost, though more and more are imposing hefty charges. On the other hand, the publisher may find it easier to monitor and control copy-editing done in-house and to keep down the cost of corrections. The in-house copy-editor can also monitor the flow of copy and see the journal through production, making sure that it keeps to schedule. Back-up is available to cover holidays and illness. Experienced freelance editors offer the advantages of flexibility and low overhead costs.

In this section we can only indicate some of the more important tasks of the copy-editor. More detailed information can be found in *Copy-editing: The Cambridge Handbook* by Judith Butcher, or the *Chicago Manual of Style* (see further reading). Notes to contributors or style manuals from other journals on the same subject are also helpful.

The copy-editor's task is to ensure that the material which goes to the typesetter is clear, consistent, unambiguous and well organised; to make it easy for the reader to follow and understand, while changing as little as possible of the author's text. This obviously requires some acquaintance with the subject matter. Copy must be marked so that the typesetter can follow it without hesitation, differentiating between the different type-sizes and fonts to be used.

The extent of copy-editing varies greatly from journal to journal. With journals produced from camera-ready copy, there is sometimes only a cursory check to make sure that everything is there, though experienced publishers would caution against this. At the other extreme, the journal editor may himself go through every paper tidying up sloppy wording. This can apply as much to mathematics as to journals in the humanities.

All illustrations should be mentioned in the text, and any illustration mentioned should be there. Some may need redrawing. Captions must be checked. Are the scales indicating the actual size correct? Will they be affected by reduction or enlargement? References must be checked for consistency with the text. Quotations, particularly literary ones, may be spot-checked. If there is extensive use of material published elsewhere, or of material in archives, has the author obtained permission?

References provide particular headaches for the copy-editor, for authors have been known to make mistakes even in citing their own work. One survey (Satyanarayana & Ratnakar 1989) found error rates ranging from about one in six references to over 40 per cent in major international and highly respected journals; one paper has been listed in the Science Citation Index with twenty-two variations of author's initials, volume, page and date of publication (St Cyr, Domelsmith and Houk 1980). More recently McLellan, Case and Barnett, (1992) checked the references in one year in four journals of anaesthetics; over half had at least one error. It is usually impracticable to check the information in every reference, but some of the apparently implausible may be looked at more carefully. A copy-editor with long experience of a particular journal or subject will often recognise a wrong reference. Some journals build up computer bibliographies of previously cited articles; that enables some references to be checked very quickly – and turns into a database on the subject.

Many of the references will be to other articles in learned journals. The minimum information they should give is: (1) author(s) (2) year of publication (3) title of article (though this is not always included in some subjects, e.g. chemistry) (4) the journal in which the article appeared (5) volume number (6) pagination of the article (some give only the first page, but it is helpful if both first and last pages are given). Punctuation, capitals, bold type and italics can be used as required, depending upon the system of typesetting and the whim of the editor. References to classical texts, the Bible and legal publications follow rules of their own (see Butcher). Chinese authors may be a particular problem; the best advice is not to attempt to abbreviate them (Zhao Ran Xu and Dan H Nicolson, 1992).

Journal titles are sometimes given in an abbreviated form, but many now recommend giving them in full; the small extra cost can save author, editor and reader much time and trouble. Scientific, technical and medical journals usually print references at the end of the text, either in alphabetical order by author (the Harvard system), or numbered according to their position in the text (the Vancouver system). Correspondingly, the reference in the text will be either 'It has been observed (Meadows 1991) . . . ' with the former, or 'It has been observed (4) . . . ' with the latter. In many journals in the humanities and some social science journals, references are often given in footnotes: with conventional typesetting methods that was expensive, but it is not a problem with many computer-aided typesetting systems.

Other matters copy-editors deal with include the checking of foot- or end-notes, headings and sub-headings, and the use of symbols and abbreviations. Is the title clear and to the point? Is there an author-prepared abstract or summary, and does it give a fair account of the paper? Do key-words need to be indicated? If the journal gives authors' affiliations and addresses, or the date of receipt of articles, have they been provided? Are any catchlines needed? What about the running heads? Are the acknowledgements in good order?

If an article has undergone extensive copy-editing it may be returned for the author to check that the edited version is acceptable, particularly if there were ambiguities in the original text.

The copy is marked so that the printer can follow it easily. Capitalisation, indentation, italics, bold-type and special sorts (characters other than normal ones for the language) must be indicated, and the position of headings, tables and illustrations made clear. Typesetter and publisher should agree in advance how much of this should be done by the copy-editor, for it is pointless to duplicate what the typesetter will do – and will charge for doing. As well as the individual items for publication, the typesetter will need an order of make-up for the issue, details of changes to the cover (date of publication, volume and part number for instance), a contents list, and any other material needed to appear in that issue, such as advertisements, title pages and indexes. The journal is now ready for production – the subject of the next chapter.

Some copy-editors are happy to edit on the screen and the practice has grown widely. Others find that editing on paper is faster and more efficient and they are less likely to spot errors on the screen. Editing on screen is often preferred if there is extensive rewriting. Some word-processing and DTP packages adapt to this practice better than others. Some online editing systems allow both the original and the changes that have been made to be seen, either on the screen or on paper. That is helpful, particularly if copy-edited papers are sent to authors for checking before they go to the typesetter.

Editorial costs

Historically, editorial costs for academic journals have been low. Many universities, colleges and research organisations have been happy for members of staff to edit journals using the facilities which the institution can offer. Editorial work has been seen as a proper function of the organ-isation which has been proud to have the editor of a leading journal on its staff. Budgets today are not always so flexible, and publishers may be asked to make some contribution to the costs of the institution in which the editor is working. The sums vary from the nominal (perhaps postage on review copies of books sent out) to the grasping; there is sometimes scope for negotiation. In addition, the editorial office may need PCs, fax machines, modems, telephone answering machines and photocopiers, and the publisher may have to provide some of this equipment.

Many editors in the past were honorary, or accepted purely nominal fees; today some expect higher amounts, though still less than they would receive from, say, consultancy. The sums paid depend upon what the journal can afford; publishers, particularly of small circulation journals, must consider the effect of a given fee on the price of a journal. It will also depend upon how much work the editor is expected to do; a journal editor who monitors the progress of papers through the press and deals with most of the editorial correspondence clearly deserves more than one whose involvement ends once a paper has been accepted or rejected.

Editors of journals with few pages and small circulations may receive no more than five hundred to two thousand pounds or (say US $800 to $3000) a year. At the other extreme, for a very few, very large and success-ful journals, the level may be determined by the editor's tax position. That consideration can also affect editors who are medical consultants with substantial private practices. Rather than substantial fees, some editors prefer to have more secretarial support, or help with travelling expenses to overseas meetings.

Probably the majority of established journals pay the editors a sum about equal to something between 3 and 5 per cent of receipts from subscription sales; this is to cover expenses as well as any fees or honoraria. If the editor was responsible for founding the journal, the rate might be higher: perhaps as much as 8 or 10 per cent. There are various methods of calculating editorial fees. Royalties are not unknown. An agreed annual sum is common. A variation is a fixed sum per page published, index-linked to the cost of living or some other measure. The disadvantage of that is that it may encourage the editor to accept marginal papers and discourage editorial effort to reduce over-long ones. Some editors, particularly in North America, are paid on the basis of the number of papers that they process.

Editorial board members are generally unpaid, though the expenses of travel to editorial board meetings is usually refunded. It is rare for referees to receive a fee, though one or two journals make nominal payments to them. Contributors of original articles to learned journals are usually unpaid though most are given some offprints, or, in some instances, copies of the issue containing their article. Book reviewers are usually allowed to keep the books they have reviewed. Authors of review articles are sometimes paid: this makes it easier to reject an article that turns out to be unsatisfactory.

Freelance copy-editors and indexers are customarily paid by the hour or by the page. Of course, there are variations in rates of work between individuals, but the time needed to copy-edit will also depend upon the subject, the state of the copy, the amount of detail to be covered, how heavily the publication is edited, and whether or not the copy-editor also reads the proofs and checks the author's corrections. Estimates of the average amount of work per day that a copy-editor can cope with range from around 3000 to around 9000 words. Rates paid for freelance work vary considerably from publisher to publisher and subject to subject and, of course, country to country.

3   Production

Introduction

The emphasis of this chapter is on production management. There is little technical detail as this is often best obtained from suppliers; in any case, it changes quickly, leaving a description of current equipment and systems out of date.

The weakness in the journal market has underlined the need to reduce or at least hold costs in relation to inflation. Fortunately, the cost of typesetting and composition (origination, or 'plant' in the USA) has dropped in real terms through improved software, lower computing costs, higher productivity, taking articles on disk (thus cutting out the rekeying stage) and in some cases lower wages. With the rapid development of information technology, improved communications and the widespread availability of suitable equipment, the options available to whoever is managing the production of a journal have increased. These will be outlined, with emphasis on the relationship between the publisher and the publisher's suppliers.

Another feature of the weakening market is the concern for the appearance of a journal. There is competition for good articles and a journal with the right image, helped by an attractive design and high quality printing and paper, will attract these. Good articles sell subscriptions and maintain circulation. The conflict between economy and image is more apparent than real: apart from quality and weight of paper good design should cost no more than bad design.

Many journals are typeset, printed and bound by the same firm; but there has been a trend towards using specialist typesetters who will produce proofs, make corrections, make up the pages, and send the final image on film to a printer. Once the production process is split between suppliers, it is possible to typeset in one country, perhaps close to the editorial office, and print and bind in another where costs may be lower. Some journals are now typeset in the Far East where costs are often lower and manufactured (printed and bound) near the distribution facility to save time and costs in transport, i.e. specialist typesetting very often travels while printing usually remains at home. With high circulation journals, distribution costs are a major item and the choice of where to print should relate to the final destination of issues. With higher circulations, say over 10,000 subscribers, spread internationally a publisher may split the printing with North American and European editions. That can also be done to suit advertisers who may only be interested in certain market areas.

The search for lower costs can create problems. The overheads involved in preparing the copy for an inexpensive typesetter and keeping to schedule with stages carried out in different places, will usually be higher. Indeed, savings in suppliers' charges may be lost in increased overheads. This assumes that professional staff are employed throughout, but many journals rely on unpaid or unaccounted help. Where people are willing to spend time preparing copy, making up pages or even producing camera-ready copy (see page 82) for little or no payment, suppliers' charges, rather than overheads, will dominate the thinking on production strategy.

With a short print-run publication (say under 2000), the typesetting costs offer most scope for savings as these constitute a large part of the total costs. Across a list of journals origination can make up 47 per cent of the costs (editorial 22 per cent, page make-up and correction 25 per cent), manufacturing 30 per cent, paper 8 per cent and distribution 15 per cent. Savings on presswork (i.e. printing) and paper that might be achieved by using, say, a cut-price printer will be small in relation to the total costs, and may adversely affect the appearance of the journal. There may be little scope for savings on production costs with short-run publications, yet these small savings may be vital for survival. With the weakening market print-runs have been getting shorter.

Printing and publishing are going through a period of rapid technological change. It can be difficult for publishers to keep informed of the latest developments and their potential for journals, but there are organisations which can advise them, such as PIRA (the Printing Industries' Research Association, Randalls Road, Leatherhead, Surrey KT22 7RU) in Britain, GATF (Graphic Arts Technical Foundation, Pittsburgh) in the USA and FOGRA (Deutsche Forschungsgesellschaft fur Druck- und Reproduktionstechnik, Streitfeldstr. 19, Munchen) in West Germany. The major factors influencing change have originated outside the printing and publishing industries; these include computers, micro-processors, lasers, digitisation of information, screen-based technology and telecommunications.

The classic general text on the subject is Williamson (1983). Another standard reference text is *Bookmaking: An Illustrated Guide to Design/ Production/Editing* by Marshall Lee which is good for North American practice and terms. Much of *Book Production Practice* (PA & BPIF, 1984) is relevant to journal production and it includes a comprehensive index. *The Print Production Handbook* by David Bann (1986) is a concise intro-duction to the whole production process from origination to bound copies and concludes with a useful chapter on working with suppliers. Clear advice is given on such aspects of production as format, presen-tation and binding in *Serials Publications: Guidelines for Good Practice in Publishing Printed Journals and Other Serial Publications* (UKSG, 1994). The only book devoted solely to the production of academic journals is Campbell (1992c); much of this chapter is based on it.

One of the best ways to learn about the processes is to visit typesetters and printers and see their equipment in action. Some understanding of these processes, and where the expense lies, is essential to successful journal production management. For example, if the typesetter can be sure of receiving well-prepared clean copy on schedule, corrections at the proof stage should be reduced. A typesetter may also argue a case for higher charges if the supply and standard of copy is erratic.

Design and format

General strategy

The design will normally be dictated by economic considerations and publishing strategy. More might be spent on the cover and page design of a periodical aimed at individual subscribers, than of a specialised research journal aimed at the library market. Personal preferences of the editorial team may be catered for at the detailed level (i.e. choice of type-face, use of italics, range of sub-headings and presentation of references), but the decision on format and layout should relate to estimates from suppliers and to the overall aims of the publication. The old adage should be borne in mind: 'good design costs no more than bad design'.

There is a useful summary of 'what makes a good journal' (Meadows, 1991) based on experience of judging for an award for good practices in journal design and production sponsored by the Charlesworth Group, the Publishers Association and ALPSP. The items weighed most heavily in the judging are: the ease of handling and using the journal (materials), typography, legibility, layout and balance (text), graphics and how they are used to convey information, and how easy it is to move about the text including the cover (navigation). Common faults are: failure to implement a good design, poor navigation between typically text and graphics, too much or too little text on the page and inappropriate materials.

The length of the print-run will influence decisions on design and materials. The format and page design are discussed at length below, but other factors should also be considered. For example, elaborate covers and colour work will be a financial load on a short print-run, while a heavier and more expensive paper will hit a high circulation journal yet have relatively little influence on the finances of a short print-run journal.

The range and capacity of formats

Some journals have kept to a traditional format, the old crown quarto size (246 × 189 mm), on the grounds that this is a convenient size for library shelves and yet offers sufficient width for a double-column layout. With the demise of letterpress trim sizes were altered to fit the new litho presses. The royal octavo format of 234 × 156 mm is a bit narrow for double-column setting, although some journals are produced in this size. Publishers have favoured the slightly larger size of 244 × 172 mm; this takes two columns more comfortably and gives scope for improved layout with single column formats. The size of 244 × 172 mm was arrived at

Table 3.1. *Some common European journal formats. (The trimmed sizes are for sewn binding; with unsewn binding where the fold is cut off for gluing the final bound page width will be about 3mm less.)*

Standard sizes	Trimmed page size in millimetres	Trimmed page size in inches
Demy 6mo	216 × 185	8½ × 7¼
Metric Crown 4to	246 × 189	9¹¹⁄₁₆ × 7⁷⁄₁₆
Metric Demy 4to	276 × 219	10⅞ × 8⅝
Metric Royal 8vo	234 × 156	9³⁄₁₆ × 6³⁄₁₆
Royal 6mo	234 × 209	9³⁄₁₆ × 8³⁄₁₆
Large Royal 8vo	244 × 172	9⁹⁄₁₆ × 6¾
A5	210 × 148	8¼ × 5¹³⁄₁₆
B5	250 × 176	9¹³⁄₁₆ × 6⅞
Narrow Demy 4to*	276 × 210	10⅞ × 8¼
A4	297 × 210	11⅝ × 8¼

*Also called Short A4

since the maximum sheet size of the new presses tended to be either 1,000 × 1,400 mm or 720 × 1,020 mm. Allowing the standard 6 mm extra for trim on the height of the folded page and the 3 mm extra for the width, it is possible to print 64- and 32-page sections respectively on these sheets. The official B5 format at 250 x 176 mm is too big for these presses to make the optimum use of the paper. The standard page sizes are given in table 3.1.

Keyboarding costs will be based on the total 'ennage' (i.e. the number of characters set) which will be the same whatever the format, but there is a relationship between page layout and costs. We can consider, for example, a journal of 800 pages with a conventional single-column layout (type area 197 × 130 mm) in a B5 format and a print-run of 4,000 copies in four issues with a sewn binding. If the same B5 format is used, but the layout changed to double-column (type area 206 × 133 mm) with one size smaller type (9 on 10½ pt), each page will carry approximately 25 per cent more text. Many readers will prefer the short line, especially for scanning. The disadvantages with such a page layout are the increased number of word breaks, the problems in presenting long mathematical and chemical equations, and the necessity for setting some tables across the whole page (i.e. both columns), which can be confusing. Making up each page will also be more expensive; but, as the extent of the whole journal is reduced, total costs can drop by around 10 per cent, because the charges for machining (printing), paper, binding and postage will all be less.

The economic advantage of a large number of words per page must be weighed against aesthetic factors (the 'economic format' can look cramped), the capacity of the typesetting system, the available page make-up skills and the complexity of the material. A single column format with 10 pt type is still often, for example, preferred for mathematics, chemistry and physics in order to get a complete equation on the one line. This simpler page design is also more suitable for handling text in machine-readable form (see page 87).

With the B5 format the average number of words per page ranges between 400 and 900 depending on the type area, the size of type and interlinear space. There has been a trend in recent years towards the 'A' sizes for periodicals and magazines. The standard quad sheet is known as RAO (860 × 1220 mm), and this will provide 32-page sections (16 pages to view) of A4 (297 × 210 mm). With A4, double-column layout is essential to shorten the reading line. Compared with the first example above (single column, B5 format), using the same type size (10 on 11½ pt type) 45 per cent more text will fit on a page and the presentation of tables and figures is usually easier.

With longer print runs the large page double-column formats show clear economies, but there is another problem. A4 is not a traditional book size and few presses in Britain fit it perfectly (although the situation is better on the Continent). For a better fit with the presses, some publishers use a slightly smaller and squarer size than A4, known as demy quarto (276 × 219 mm) or even 'squat A4'. Librarians may prefer this, as it fits the shelves more easily. A seminar on journal design revealed a clear preference for the old quarto size of 245 × 173 mm as opposed to A4 and the avoidance of narrow columns which lead to poor word spacing and too much hyphenation. In France a common format is 270 × 210 mm which is also used for magazines.

The popular North American trim size in STM publishing is 11 × 8½ inches (276 × 210 mm). In effect it is a slightly narrow demy quarto (often written as '4to' – just as octavo is often abbreviated to '8vo') and it can therefore be run on presses in Europe although the size is not ideal. It will fit a small web press quite economically. This larger format gives greater visibility on the library shelf and allows better display of illustrations. This format is not suitable for single-column text, but is ideal for double-column giving a long enough line to reduce word breaks. It can also take three columns which is an effective layout for references, short entries and notes. If a three-column layout is used, ranging left (with ragged right-hand margin) is preferable to avoid problems with spacing and word breaks.

The choice of format

It can be misleading to pursue these technical considerations in isolation. Printers should be consulted before making a final decision on format and layout. A company may have invested, for example, in a large press and will be looking for appropriate contracts; it may be possible, there-fore, to negotiate a favourable price for an A4 format. The supply of copy should also be borne in mind. With new journals a common problem is the shortage of good papers, and a compact layout will exacerbate this situation by 'eating up' the copy.

One strategy is to start with an attractive, generously spaced design which will spin out the copy and appeal to readers and contributors. As the reputation of the journal and the supply of copy builds up, the publisher can switch to a more compact design. But reasonable page margins should be preserved as when issues are bound up into volumes some of the margin will be trimmed off. Changing format half-way through a year or a volume should be avoided as it creates problems in rebinding. A significantly larger format could mean reshelving a whole run of volumes and altering all the relevant catalogue entries.

Other considerations are the nature of the copy and the competition. Large formats are appropriate for heavily illustrated papers, while smaller formats are more suited to solid text. Journals in the humanities, say philosophy or literary criticism, tend to be published in smaller formats such as Royal 8vo with a single column to give a comfortable length of line. In North America formats of 10 × 7 inches or 9 × 6 inches are popular in these fields. Footnotes are easier to handle with single column formats. Journals in the sciences and medicine tend to be published in larger formats as they usually carry more illustrations and are often scanned rather than read. If the market is dominated by one journal, a different format and design will give an individual image.

A publisher with a group of journals may standardise the format to give a stronger negotiating position with the printers; some will offer a lower price for a 'batch printing' contract. A standard format and design should also make it easier for a copy-editor working on a group of journals.

For a new journal, it might be worth considering some of the criteria evolved from readability studies. For example, there is a case for printing abstracts in larger type than the text, rather than in the customary smaller type; and there is evidence that the eye cannot take in easily more than seventy-two characters on a line.

Cover

Even with a specialised research journal, appearing perhaps twice a year, it is worth taking some trouble over the cover. Ideally the design should be instantly recognisable and attractive without costing too much. The trend is towards more lively, high visibility cover designs.

The traditional cover is of coloured paper or card. The text and perhaps a simple design is printed in black, or another colour, which gives a good contrast with the background. A coloured paper can give the illusion of three-colour printing. More commonly, the background colour is printed as well, which gives a greater range of colour and enables the designer to reverse out some features in white. Screens or tints can also be used to get away from the standard two-colour designs.

Some librarians prefer a lightish background with an area kept clear of printing for a circulation stamp, but white covers, unless laminated, can look grubby very quickly. Blue ink does not always photocopy well; if it is to be used for the contents list on the back cover, it should be borne in mind that some organisations photocopy and circulate them. Another potential problem with blue ink is that it is unstable and printings can vary more than with other colours. 'Light-fast' inks should be specified for outside covers.

To save costs with lower print-run journals, the basic cover design should be constant throughout the year, so that a number of copies of the cover can be printed and stored for overprinting for each issue. If over-printing is kept to a minimum (i.e. just the issue number, date and list of contents on the back), scope for errors will be reduced. As overprinting each issue has to be done, it does not cost much extra to carry a different photograph on the front of each issue, a feature of trade journals which is becoming more common with scholarly journals. Where a different full-colour illustration is printed on the front cover of each issue, there is no point in printing 'blanks' for the volume. When overprinting, a single-colour advertisement can be printed on the outside back cover at virtually no extra cost. If the same cover advertising is booked for more than one issue, printing all the covers at once should be considered, especially if the advertisement is four colour.

It should be noted that laminated or very glossy covers do not accept library stamps readily and they curl very easily. Some readers complain that light reflection from glossy covers makes the printed material on them difficult to read. Hence, they are disliked by some librarians. Lamination, however, is becoming more widespread as publishers of major journals compete to attract top papers and advertisers as well as readers. Even without lamination (glossy or matt), which can add four or five pence to the unit cost, there is a trend towards using lighter boards for the covers to save materials and mailing costs. Lamination can add one or two days to the production schedule as few printer/binders have a lamination facility on site. Alternatively, covers can be given a gloss finish to seal and protect the printed surface. This can be done by printing a varnish on the normal printing machine or by 'spirit varnishing' on a special machine. A very high gloss can be achieved with an ultraviolet (UV) cured lacquer; the lacquer is applied by a roller and then dried with UV lamps.

In North America it is common with longer print-run journals to print the cover on a six-colour press: four process colours for the advertise-ments and/or the front illustration, a PMS colour for the standard front matter and a press varnish as the sixth 'colour'.

It is worth taking some care over limiting the data included on the covers to enable the designer to lay out the text attractively with the main points easily seen. It should be remembered, however, that many readers prefer the contents list on the outside back cover for quick browsing. As each volume nears completion, the inside front cover should be checked for changes to the editorial team (or the officers of a society if one is involved and such information is published) as well as price, dates of publication etc.

Text

The layout of the page should relate to the typography. With a new journal it is usual to ask the typesetter to prepare a few sample pages, so that all concerned can comment on the proposed layout and typography. Specimen pages are expensive to produce, and typesetters may charge for these if they are not awarded the final contract. Many publishers now use DTP to prepare sample machine designs. The first page of each paper often presents most of the design problems: title, authors, authors' addresses, summary or abstract, sub-heading and straight text with the necessary use of bold and italic, capitals, large and small typefaces can look a mess. Sometimes this problem is reduced by placing some of this, e.g. the author's address, at the end of the article.

One approach is to submit an existing journal to the typesetter with instructions on any modifications. The full range of material should be given to the typesetter along with instructions for the sample pages, in order to test every eventuality (i.e. a large, complicated table, a half-tone with poor contrast, some equations, small and large illustrations, long and short sub-headings and various references). In choosing the typeface, remember that chemistry, mathematics, physics, linguistics and foreign languages all demand special sorts.

The decision process

The design of a journal is frequently the subject of much discussion by editorial board or publications committee members. A decision may have to be deferred until a compromise design, usually a hybrid between those submitted, is accepted. The process can be speeded up by finding other journals whose design they like before any roughs are produced. A member of the committee, often the chairman or editor, can be delegated to work with the publisher on the final design, having got the feel of the opinions of their colleagues. Everyone will have had a chance to air their views, and the publisher will be able to get on with the detailed work with one person who has the confidence of their colleagues.

The basic principle of good design is to keep it simple: there will be less to go wrong, costs will be lower, and the journal will probably look better.

Typesetting

Input

All text material which appears in journals is keyed at least once: the only alternatives at present are optical character recognition (OCR) of manuscript, a slow and not totally accurate process, and voice recognition, which is still in development. Some text is keyed only once, on a typewriter or word-processor, and printed using as camera-ready copy the output produced from the typewriter or word-processor printer, or used as the input for computerised pagination.

Equipment that can 'read' text, i.e. optical character recognition, is well established for input from typescript, but there are difficulties in detecting hardware errors and correcting errors in recognition. Its use in the newspaper industry is declining; most journalists input directly. The recently introduced lower-cost OCR scanners, used with word-processors, have potential but some recognition problems remain.

Of text material which appears in typeset (as opposed to typewriter) form, most is keyed again on a typesetting keyboard, following the original typescript or word-processor output, to which have been added editorial style marks and amendments (scheme 2 in figure 3.1). The remainder, a growing percentage, is typeset from the original keying (see p. 87, and scheme 3 in figure 3.1) using the word-processor or computer data already captured, and adding editorial amendments and style instructions by means of a visual display unit (keyboard plus screen).

It is useful to distinguish between keying online to a computer system and keying offline. Schemes 2 and 3 use online keying in the correcting stage, and may use online keying in the editing stage. Scheme 2 usually uses offline keying for the keyboarding stage.

Inserting typographic instructions, generic codes

Whether keying on or offline, generic codes (instructions to the output device to identify headings or footnotes, for example) can be inserted by the operator. It is usual to do this as early as possible in the composition process, but where the material has been keyed with no specific publication in mind, it can be more convenient to insert them at the editing or correction stages, usually online.

General practice

Keying is now generally treated as a function separate from typesetting (the output of type); it is common for offline keying to be done by people working from home, or by companies set up to supply keying only, using stand-alone equipment. This allows flexibility of supply and (sometimes) low wage costs. Central control, to provide consistency, can be achieved through online keying of codes and corrections at proof stage. The exception is complex setting, which requires more central control and central programmes than straight setting, so keying remains integrated with the whole setting process. As computer power and the programming for it is more readily afforded, together with advanced output devices, the online/offline distinction is likely to blur, with remote keying carried out on more effective stand-alone systems.

Typesetting systems

The 'first generation' photosetters were based on some of the principles of hot metal systems, but they employed 'photo-matrices' through which light was exposed, rather than matrices which formed the moulds for type-casting in metal. The early photosetters were usually typographically inferior to the systems they were designed to replace, largely due to the insensitive adaptation of metal faces. The major drawback was that

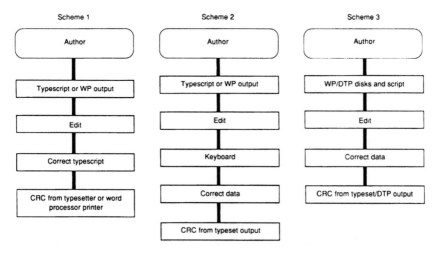

Figure 3.1 Three schemes of origination. Scheme 1: production from CRT (camera-ready typescript). Scheme 2: the traditional production stages based on rekeying by a supplier. Scheme 3: typesetting from the author's keying.

the need to move the photo-matrix into position for each exposure limited the speed of output.

'Second generation' photosetters gave greater output speed, partly as a result of technological advances in computing. The type image is digitally recorded in the machine's electronic memory, and output on to film or paper via a laser beam or cathode-ray tube (CRT). The characters are built up as a series of either vertical or horizontal lines from the pattern of electronic signals retained in the computer's memory. The visual 'solidity' of these characters is the result of an optical illusion and, under a magnifying glass, the jagged profile of the letter can be discerned.

The frequency of output scan lines (or 'resolution') is important for the visual success of such characters. On a good quality paper, the curves and diagonals of letters at low resolution show the jagged profiles of the scan lines or pixels (picture elements – the basic units into which the digitising process converts a character). The most common resolution is between 1000 and 1500 lines to the inch; the finest resolution at present is 5300 lines to the inch. A resolution of 2000 or more is thought to be preferable, especially if small type or mathematical setting is involved.

The typographic excellence of the best letterpress or hot-metal printing can now be achieved by computer-aided photocomposition. However, the choice of typeface and materials still remains a matter of skill, and the quality of work offered by different suppliers, even with similar equipment, varies enormously.

Hyphenation and justification

Computerised typesetting systems can give uncomfortable-looking word spacing, especially with short lines in double columns. The computer hyphenation dictionary stores word breaks so the performance improves. Hyphenation dictionaries are required to cover different subjects; therefore a typesetter specialising in science texts, especially an area of science covering the subject of the journal, will have a more appropriate computer 'memory'. This technicality is worth bearing in mind when deciding on a typesetter; it can make a marked difference to the appearance of the text. (Well-known examples of unfortunate word-breaks with early computer typesetting include: 'the rapist', 'not able' and 'fig urine'.)

Composition/page make-up

Once the text is typeset and prints are made of the illustrations at the final required size, the page is made up. With a simple single-column format this can be done relatively easily by the computer, which is instructed by the operator to leave the right space in the text for inserting the prints of the illustrations by hand to create the final camera-ready copy. Page make-up, however, is still done by hand (although less commonly) using a solid column of text which is cut up and pasted to fit the page. With more complex formats, such as double column, the layout of the text and illustrations by hand requires skill. The paper onto which the text and illustrations are pasted is usually printed with a pale blue grid so the compositor can make up the pages to the exact design. The pale blue lines are filtered out when photographed.

Computerised full page make-up gives complete pages of text and illustrations by electronic data processing. This is now fairly standard. There are differences between batch and single-page interactive pagination: what suits a book or journal (a flow of information through several pages) will not suit a newspaper or magazine. It should be borne in mind, for example, that a change to one page in a journal article can have a knock-on effect throughout the article. These systems have become economic for journals, with correspondingly exciting prospects for electronic publishing. Once the complete pages are stored in digital form, they can be displayed on demand either for viewing on VDU screens, or output via a line printer to obtain 'hard-copy', or photoset.

Another advantage of text storage in digital form is that it should be possible for publishers to make corrections via terminals linked to their typesetter's database. With improvements in telecommunications and data compression techniques, digitised and formatted pages can now be transmitted by land line or satellite to remote printing operations. In academic publishing the time saved does not usually justify the extra cost involved. Normal post or courier services are sufficient for film, disks or tapes. For example, *Nature* with a weekly overseas printing in both the United States and Japan sends film by air. A clean regular rented spot is needed on a satellite to ensure that there is no interference, and this is still costly.

The typesetter's expertise is still important; a good typesetter will see that all the material for a journal is handled consistently and, if possible, by the same staff. Some of the traditional rules for economy, however, have changed. For example, vertical lines in tables are no longer expensive. But despite the sophistication of modern computer typesetting systems, there remains an element of hand work. For example, final corrections are still sometimes carried out by setting a new strip of text, cutting out the incorrect text and pasting in the new strip. This is fine for camera-ready copy for printing, but leaves the original typesetting files with errors which create problems if they are converted for full-text online searching and electronic document delivery.

The database approach

In future the hard-copy edition may be only one published form of a paper. To enable other versions to be produced with minimum extra cost publishers are preparing their material as a neutrally structured database. One analysis has suggested that the cost of publishing a journal breaks down as 60 per cent for the base cost (editorial and origination) and 40 per cent for the manufacturing (printing, paper and binding) and distribution of the hard-copy. This 40 per cent drops to 30 per cent for the preparation and delivery of an electronic edition. As expertise and systems develop this reduction is likely to become greater. Currently this analysis might be used to justify a price of 130 per cent of the hard-copy subscription for a combined (hard-copy and electronic) subscription.

The first step is to use SGML (Standard Generalised Mark-up Language) (Bryan 1988, Herwijnen 1990). SGML is an ISO and ANSI standard (International Standards Organisation and American National Standards Institute) adopted, for example, by the American Association of Publishers. This is a text mark-up system in which codes (or tags) are placed around most (or all) elements in a document. These elements could be a paragraph, a title, an abstract etc. The tags usually indicate the structure of the document and not the style or format, such as founts, column widths etc. A stylesheet is required to translate the logical structure into a presentation on paper, for example. As a generic mark-up, the tags remain constant and device independent. The SGML tags can readily be converted, for example, to field codes for database creation for online access, and can be validated (parsed) to eliminate errors.

The tags can be input in-house or freelance which will add to overheads or by the typesetter for a premium, currently around 10–15 per cent of basic typesetting costs. After final corrections the typesetter can 'reverse engineer' (translate) the typesetting codes to SGML tags.

SGML provides a means of unambiguously representing electronic documents so that they can be interchanged between dissimilar computer systems, but the ease of transfer, reproduction and manipulation of SGML documents brings with it issues of copyright control (Maguire 1994). Cryptographic techniques will, therefore, be needed to link licensing agreements with controlled access.

The next step is for journals to follow an internationally agreed DTD (Document Type Definition). A DTD is used for defining text structure; presentation rules in the form of a style sheet are used to translate the structure of a document to typesetting instructions. The DTD describes and names the SGML tags which will identify the different elements in a document. For example, if there is no defined tag for an author's address it would be impossible to pull this information out at a later stage. There is parser software for validating a document's adherence to the DTD.

The development of SGML for the requirements of the humanities has been led by the Text Encoding Initiative (TEI). This is a major international project sponsored by the Association for Computers and the Humanities, the Association for Computational Linguistics and the Association for Literary and Linguistic Computing. It has defined a common encoding format for interchange and for encoding new texts, which is intended for the humanities and the language industries more generally. The TEI DTD's are built on the assumption that all texts share some common core of elements to which features for any specific discipline or theoretical orientation may be added. The user chooses a base tag set (prose, verse, drama, spoken words, dictionaries, terminology), which automatically also includes the core and documentation tags, then selects whatever additional tag sets are required, for example critical apparatus, hyper-textual mechanisms, names and dates.

The TEI proposals also include a document header which is probably the first systematic attempt to provide in-file documentation of an electronic text file. The header consists of a set of SGML tags which are divided into four sections. Of these the file description is the most important. It contains a full bibliographic description of the electronic file, which can be used for creating catalogue entries or bibliographic citations.

Publishers are also increasingly setting up articles in Postscript files, indeed occasionally authors will submit articles in Postscript files. Post-script is widely accepted as the standard page-description language which handles both text and illustrations equally well. To print Postscript files requires a laser printer or imagesetter that is Postscript capable, but almost all are now. Part of its flexibility is that it is resolution indepen-dent, i.e., it will print at the resolution of the output equipment. Some digital non-print products that preserve the look of the printed page on the screen will require Postscript files. If articles are set up in Postscript as part of the origination process, proofs can then be sent to authors for checking via Internet as when compressed by Acrobat software to a Portable Document Format (PDF) transmission is relatively quick and not limited by the type of hardware. For example, a 1.5 megabyte text document including a bit-mapped half-tone can be compressed down to 20 kilobytes by PDF conversion.

Some publishers are using a subset of SGML called HTML (Hypertext Mark-up Language) which is the World-Wide Web's electronic format and thus opens up applications on the Internet. HTML uses tags (or codes) embedded in any document that inform the Web browser how to display the information (i.e. what is a headline, what is a link with another document, what is a link with an image, what should be boldface etc.). HTML has been approved by the International Standards Organisation (ISO). It allows the creation and editing of HMTL documents to be done by any text editor on any computer and transferred over networks by almost any e-mail or file transfer system (Aronson 1994).

In the 1995 survey of members by the stm Association, in response to the question 'How do publishers code/parse/store their material – now and in three years?' Postscript came out as the favoured format although SGML is expected to be more widely used in future (figure 3.2).

With the neutral database approach, a range of products can be generated from the articles held in, say, Postcript as shown in figure 3.3. In this diagram the origination phase is assumed to be fully digitised which is the aim of many journal production managers. The production of electronic forms alongside the hard-copy is sometimes referred to as 'augmented print' or 'parallel publishing' but these terms do not really indicate the potential of this approach. A journal in effect becomes an electronic journal with hard-copy available to those who still want to read the contents in this format. With recently introduced short print-run technology it may be economic to produce hard-copy at several locations to save on mailing costs and delays.

Camera-ready typescript

CRC/CRT/DTP

In the 1960s and 70s with the widespread availability of high quality typewriters a number of journals were produced from what was known as 'camera-ready copy' (CRC). The term 'camera-ready typescript' (CRT) is

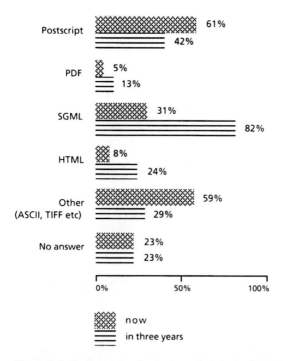

Figure 3.2 The response in the stm Association's 1995 survey of members to the question, 'How do publishers Code/Parse/Store their material – now and in three years?'

used more commonly now as CRC is also used to describe the finished typeset product in bromide form, or any other final form of the copy from which film can be made, such as output from desktop-publishing equipment. With the rapid development of desktop publishing (DTP) and typesetting from authors' disks it is likely that production from CRT will fade out but it has enabled a number of specialised journals to emerge and survive.

Procedures

Production from camera-ready typescript does not look as good as properly typeset text but it should save on costs and time. The text is typed on good paper using a good quality electric typewriter or daisy-

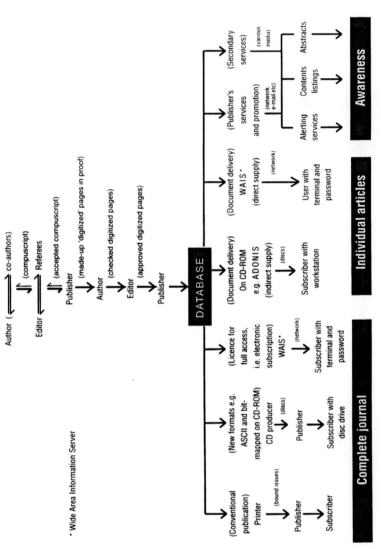

Figure 3.3 The scheme for producing a journal based on a database of articles rather than the hard-copy edition. The hard-copy can still be easily generated from the database but there is also the potential to deliver the journal on disk or give online access to it (an electronic subscription). Articles can be supplied either indirectly via a service such as ADONIS or directly from a server in electronic form. The database can also be used to run awareness services.

wheel printer. Word processing has improved the quality of copy in terms of presentation (indeed improving word processing is blurring the line between CRT and DTP). Appropriate gaps are left in the text for artwork to be pasted in, and headings may be added using transfer lettering. There may be fewer words on the page than with a typeset journal, but this is less costly for short-run publications. A skilled typist may be able to work to two- or three-column compact formats; a task made easier with word processing. About 90 per cent of CRT will be output from a word-processor rather than a typewriter.

The copy is sent to the printer, who makes the film (often with a reduction in size to sharpen the image) then plates from the film for printing. If the plate making is good, and a decent paper is used, the final result is likely to be acceptable. Current charges for typesetting, however, are so competitive that publishers might well find little real saving over a typesetter.

A more radical approach is for the authors to prepare the CRT. This way, several large journals have been able to keep their subscription price down; and smaller, more specialised journals have been launched where the market may not have supported a more expensive conventionally-produced journal. As suggested above, however, savings may not be as dramatic as expected. A greater number of pages may be needed, thus increasing machining, paper and possibly postage costs – since CRT, even when reduced by the camera, is not as compact as typeset material. In compensation, author-prepared CRT should give quicker publication, as the time taken in typesetting is eliminated and proofreading is reduced.

Instructions for authors preparing CRT

Camera-ready typescript transfers some of the production costs/time from the publisher to the author. This is acknowledged by some journals; for example, *Journal of Geophysical Research* charged authors US$140 per page if the publisher has to typeset but only US$72 if the author supplies CRT. If the instructions to authors (and, more especially, to their secretaries) are not clear and simple, the potential savings in time and cost may disappear. Contributors resent demands for extensive retyping of CRT although this is less of a problem with word processing. Publishers therefore allow authors to submit their papers initially in ordinary typescript, though laid out in the style required for the final version. Authors are then asked to correct both the points raised by referees and any significant deviations from the desired format.

Anyone preparing instructions should refer to *Model Guidelines for the Preparation of Camera-ready Typescripts by Authors and Typists* edited by Maeve O'Connor. A more recent article (Tibbo 1994) reviews specifications for the preparation of CRC using word-processing and desktop-publishing programmes.

Instructions for camera-ready typescript should be aimed in the first place at the typist (who is often not the author). The initial emphasis should be on the physical properties required of the typescript. The minimum requirements should be specified (e.g. an electric typewriter with a new black plastic carbon ribbon and using good quality white bond paper). Publishers can save considerable in-house effort by supplying their own standard paper, with a grid marked in blue, to authors. Layout, capitalisation, etc., obviously have to be spelt out in more detail in camera-ready instructions than for traditionally produced journals. Special mention should be made of the layout of tables and the positioning of diagrams.

Instructions that affect the authors, themselves, tend to refer to non-standard items. For example, the insertion of characters that do not appear on some typewriters (e.g. Greek letters, mathematical symbols) may be done by the author, rather than the typist. They should be instructed to use readily available methods for these (e.g. a mapping pen and a stencil). They should also be informed whether specific text items – such as notes – are, or are not, permissible.

Some items must be left for the publisher to complete. For example, pages should be numbered by the typist in blue pencil, and final page numbers inserted by the publisher; again, spaces must be left for the copyright statement, date of receipt, etc.

A list of basic guidelines from a printer used to taking CRT is given below.

1 Base sheets for CRT should be on stock of 80 gsm or more. CRT should be presented as single pages.

2 All lines, whether on CRT or artwork, should measure at least 0.1 millimetre wide; in the case of artwork, this means the width after any reduction.
3 No instruction or position marks, even in blue pencil, should appear within 10 millimetres of image area.
4 Any base grid should be in the faintest possible blue.
5 Character density should be consistent throughout the CRT and should not have a streaky or furry appearance. Mixing of dark and light density copy within a page should be avoided if at all possible.

Some practical aspects

The thought of having to prepare camera-ready typescript may deter potential contributors, so some publishers retype in the editorial office. It is worth remembering that some authors (e.g. in Third-World countries) may not be able to produce CRT. Occasionally, publishers have resorted to a mix of CRT and typesetting; this looks acceptable if CRT is limited to tables, or to certain sections of the journal such as brief reports of talks given at a meeting, which is still a common application of CRT. This section usually looks rather untidy although keeping all reports to a standard half page or full page can help.

Typesetting from 'papers' in machine-readable form

Advantages and disadvantages

Any author with access to a word-processor can now prepare a 'paper' in electronic form, sometimes called 'compuscript'. The disk or tape which is produced can be used with compatible equipment to drive a photo-typesetter. There are some clear advantages in this:

1 by-passing the conventional rekeying of the manuscript should mean that a proof can be produced in which no new errors have been introduced;
2 the elimination of keyboarding should remove a costly element in the process of composition and speed up production; and,

3 the manuscript can be delivered by a telephone link (modem), for example, thus avoiding the sometimes expensive and time-consuming process of sending a manuscript through the mail.

The disadvantages include the need to train staff to edit and code files, made worse by the tendency for such staff to move to other jobs, and the problems with incompatibility between systems. It can take almost as long to hunt through the file, clean up and add codes as to rekey; there may be charges for disk translation. When a paper is transmitted via a modem, interference can cause problems and the charge may be high if the author does not have access to Internet. As with camera-ready typescript there is also the problem of getting what is required from the authors.

Ever-improving software, standardisation and hardware is making it much easier for publishers to take papers on disk and some journals now receive nearly everything in this way. The proportion of material on disk depends largely on the attitude of the editor. If the editor encourages authors to prepare their final version in the light of referees' comments on disk in a form suitable for typesetting, most will do so. Some journals offer the inducement of lower page charges and others demand disks without apparently driving away contributors.

In the 1995 stm Association's survey most respondents accept electronically submitted manuscripts which are usually delivered on disk. Files produced with Word or Word Perfect are sent in most frequently and are gladly accepted in most cases. 30 per cent of respondents offer macro packages ('style files') mostly LATeX and TeX but also for Word and Word Perfect.

There is a clear introduction to the basics of typesetting from authors' disks in John Peacock's comprehensive text on book production (1989). Diehl (1990) offers some practical advice from personal experience.

Standardisation and practical issues

Although many typesetters are now able to work from disk and tapes produced on a wide range of equipment and employing a variety of commands, some measure of standardisation is required to make the best use of the new technology. Various guides have been prepared. These are not intended to provide an exhaustive system of coding, but are seen as interim measures for use while work on developing a standard generalised mark-up language (SGML) is carried out at an international level.

While the electronic manuscript has been used extensively in book publishing, it has only recently gained ground in scholarly journal publishing. There is some standardisation in that virtually everyone uses an IBM-compatible machine or a Macintosh. This has led to reasonable uniformity in the use of disks. Data conversion systems such as 'Inter-Media' take a wide range of formats and convert them for text processing. Most editorial offices can manage with equipment that can take disks prepared on a Macintosh or an IBM-compatible machine backed up by an outside service for conversion of more unusual formats. A recent survey showed that 80 per cent of the contributors to several ecological journals use three word-processing packages: Microsoft Word, Word Perfect and Macwrite.

The availability of desktop-publishing (DTP) equipment has enabled the publisher to receive disks, edit them, paginate and get to CRC at reasonable cost. The commercial typesetter will now take papers in machine-readable form for final page make-up or simply to output CRC at high resolution. Their charges have also fallen, partly as a result of technological advances which have enabled specialist typesetting units (often in the developing world) to be established with low operating costs. For example, a manuscript may be typeset conventionally for less than using an author's disk. Currently typesetters usually give a discount of around 20 to 30 per cent per page for papers on disk if they are styled and edited by the publisher.

Within several years most journals are likely to take papers on disk or by telephone. Some authors prefer this option; it makes proofreading easier and reduces editing and production time. Already some journals are pushing this service in their promotional material. To quote, for example, from a leaflet for *Nucleic Acid Research*: 'Taking full advantage of the recent developments in disk conversion technology, manuscripts will usually be typeset from authors' disks'; and lower down the first starred feature is 'Typeset from disk'.

Some practical aspects of taking disks are dealt with in the section on DTP. With the number and variety of authors contributing to journals it is not possible to brief each of them. To achieve the required quality, the publisher has to intervene with the author's file. Advice on instructions to authors is given on page 98. Authors mailing disks from one country to another should state NCV (No Commercial Value) on any documentation or custom declaration. Some use special safety packets or wrap foil around the disks in case the package is X-rayed.

A useful, short introduction to preparing text in machine-readable form for publication aimed at authors but giving plenty of practical advice for journal producers is available from the Publishers Association (Denley 1989).

Using TeX

The TeX computer typesetting system was written by Donald Knuth, Professor of Mathematics at Stanford University, and can be used on micro-computers. It is designed for setting mathematics but that requires some skill; it is relatively simple for straight text. Mathematicians and physicists have taken up the system.

It is under constant development; for example, the American Mathematical Society has developed the AMS founts for Computer Modern maths output. At the front end a proprietary package called LaTeX provides authors with predefined macros to assist them in formatting their text.

Various specialist typesetters such as the printing division of Cambridge University Press have been active in the development of TeX and LaTeX and can advise publishers on its use. With some of the journals of the Royal Astronomical Society, for example, CUP has developed macros to enable the author to load in the complete content of the paper in its final typographical form. The macro files are available electronically to authors through the UK TeX archive at the University of Aston. When a paper is accepted, it is sent to the copy-editor who marks up the hard-copy which is then returned to the author for amendment and with instructions to load the revised version into a TeX and LaTeX macro. This is returned to the copy-editor as a disk together with hard-copy printout in the exact typographical style of the journal. Authors do not receive proofs. The overall saving in production time is about a month.

Computer viruses

Computer viruses are self-replicating programs. Once introduced they can install themselves in a computer and usually cause damage – generally hard disk erasure or file corruption – and infect other programs, floppy or hard disks by copying itself on to them (particularly on to components of the operating system or 'boot' sectors of the disk). Some university computer systems become 'infected' through multi-access by floppy disk users. There is, therefore, a chance that an article submitted on disk will be carrying a computer virus which could infect the publisher's equipment or even the commercial typesetter's system. A publisher set up to accept disks might consider taking insurance cover. Lloyd's of London offer policies. The PC platform has always been the prime target of the virus author.

A list of precautions was published in *Learned Publishing* (vol. 2, no. 3, 1989, 'Computer Viruses'); see Ball (1995) for a good recent review with some useful anti-virus hints and comments on the standard packages that will serve well in the fight against viruses. The first rule is never boot up a micro-computer using a 'foreign' disk or with a 'foreign' disk in the non-active drive. Ball recommends that users write protect then scan all incoming disks – including those from shrink-wrapped software and new, blank pre-formatted disks – before performing any other operation on them.

Desktop publishing

Relatively inexpensive packages consisting of software, a laser printer and a standard micro-computer, enable the user to produce pages that look professionally typeset. This is described as desktop publishing or DTP although 'desktop production' would be a more accurate term. The laser printer is really a photocopier without a camera. Instead of scanning the page photographically, it reads the stream of data from the micro-computer.

Early desktop production was little different from production from camera-ready typescript but newer DTP systems are changing the way journals are produced. They can turn out camera-ready pages for newsletters, reports, manuals, books and many other types of printed material. They have full-page layout capabilities, eliminating the paste-up of columns or pieces of text. Indexes, tables of contents, page numbers and cross references can be automatically generated, and different type founts and sizes can be used in making up the pages.

DTP packages allow an editorial office to get to the camera-ready (i.e. ready for printing) stage quickly and at relatively low cost. Quality is improving rapidly. It is difficult to discern whether a journal of straightforward design was originated on a desktop system or if the camera-ready copy has been output through a commercial typesetting system. Before making a final decision on which package to use all eventual applications should be considered. For example, Quark Xpress is a successful package that has been widely adopted, but although articles made up with this software can be saved as fully integrated Postscript files that can be distilled to produce Acrobat files, it is difficult to get SGML out of them for other electronic applications.

Using DTP

The role of DTP in producing a journal is shown in figure 3.4. Usually the text is entered via a word-processing program; the DTP system converts the text into one of a selection of typestyles and flows it through as many pages as are necessary. Half-tones and line diagrams can be scanned to convert them to digitised images to be positioned on the pages either automatically or by the operator. Simple graphics can be generated on the micro-computer using standard programs such as Apple's MacPaint and MacDraw. The text is then flowed around the illustrations. Images take up a lot of computer memory (especially half-tones) and are time consuming to print; even if the quality is thought to be adequate, it is often better to leave blank spaces on the CRC for illustrations to be dropped in by the printer although this is changing as more powerful computers become available at lower cost.

The made-up pages can be proofed through a laser printer which can

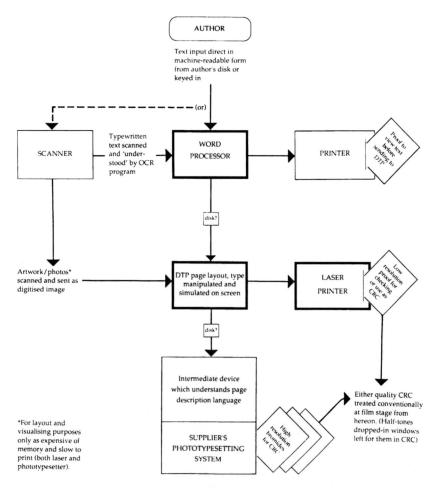

Figure 3.4 Diagram of DTP work flow with options of input by scanning and output direct for CRC or through a supplier's typesetting system for higher quality CRC. Equipment shown in bold outline is the heart of the DTP system; other hardware is optional or suitable for adding later.

also be used to produce the CRC if the quality is good enough. Laser printers commonly print out at a resolution of 600 dpi (dots per inch); much finer resolution is achieved if the pages are printed out through phototypesetting equipment at around 1200–1500 dpi. As complex illustrations, particularly half-tones, take so long to print out they can be very expensive to play through a typesetter. A modem can be used for sending work to a typesetter.

A DTP set-up is easier to use if the copy is generated in-house, but it should be possible to get contributions in a form which can be used by the DTP micro-computer. As most authors produce their papers on a limited range of word-processing packages and translation software is readily available, papers can often be input directly from disk giving the advantages outlined above. Another option is to use an electronic mail-box. This reduces the text to a simplified format which can be collected and used easily.

When taking on the responsibility for the final typesetting, many difficulties need to be anticipated. Typesetters of academic journals are usually highly trained to cope with the finer points of spacing, hyphen-ation, layout, avoidance of widows and so on. If material is produced in-house, this becomes the responsibility of the publisher. It is surprising how often a piece may be rerun to correct errors or improve typographical detail. Users of DTP must become editor, typesetter, designer, proof-reader and paste-up artist all in one. Training is required not just in the system but also in the related disciplines. Turn-over of staff with this expertise can be a tremendous problem.

Ideally a file being prepared for DTP in-house should have codes or tags added by the operator so that the typographical styling can be done auto-matically. Although styling can be done piecemeal at the make-up stage, that does not use the set-up to its best advantage. Coding, on the other hand, should not be difficult to introduce gradually. If generic coding is used for all the text, the styling programme for each design/journal can convert the codes accordingly. This way the keyboarders need simply to code consistently.

Tables can be difficult; they depend on compatibility between word-processor and make-up software. Mathematics and chemistry can also present problems and may require special packages (see section on using TeX). A standard graphics program can cope with small mathematical equations thus avoiding the problem of TeX files which cannot be handled by most DTP programs.

Equipment

Alongside the basic equipment several extras can be helpful. A large screen (A3), although more expensive, is almost essential to view double-page spreads at a reasonable size.

An optical character reading (OCR) program may be run in conjunction with a scanner so that hard-copy can be 'read' into the system without keying. These programs are not infallible; for example, the numeral 1 may be entered as lower case el. Checking for errors, although time consuming, is usually less arduous than keyboarding which itself will need to be checked.

Other less essential items include a tape streaming device for storing the files of back issues and a modem for transmitting and receiving information over the telephone line.

Illustrations

Introduction

In some journals these are an important feature. High quality reproduction of illustrations should attract readers and potential authors. Line drawings and half-tones (photograph) are handled in different ways, but, on receipt from the authors, they should all be checked for completeness and clear identification. Comprehensive guidelines for the publication of illustrated scientific material, including an excellent chapter on half-tones, are given in a book published by the Council of Biology Editors (1988).

Line drawings (artwork)

Redrawing for reproduction is expensive and time consuming; most journals use the author's artwork. Some editors accept only figures that are suitable for direct reproduction and return unsuitable artwork for redrawing. If this is the policy of the journal (and it certainly saves on costs) the editor should be briefed on what is acceptable and what should be redrawn. Authors should be given clear guidelines in the 'Instructions to Authors' on preparing figures for reproduction. As a general rule, artwork should be able to take a 50 per cent reduction.

Increasingly, authors are using micro-computers to prepare illustrations; these are often of a much higher standard than illustrations drawn and lettered by hand. Where a standard computer graphics package has been used it is often possible to take 'electronic artwork' to reduce errors and costs.

Where there is a policy of redrawing the figures, or at least relettering, the production schedule must allow for this; the cost can be considerable when there are complicated diagrams. Most publishers use outside artists. There are some large teams of artists with full facilities for producing the final bromide prints (or 'photo-mechanical transfers' – PMTs) ready for the camera. Their charge for prints is sometimes less than the printer's; it is worth checking this. A bromide is a print from a negative. A PMT is usually less expensive; the image is copied directly onto a light sensitive paper without going through a negative.

When costs are kept down by only redrawing when necessary, the production assistant will have to decide whether each figure is suitable for reproduction, i.e. the size and quality of lettering, thickness of lines and consistent symbols. If acceptable, the author's artwork can be sent straight to the printer or print-maker with instructions on the reduction necessary to fit the page, column of type, or whatever. The guidelines for CRT should be followed. Occasionally, a publisher will lose any savings made in using the original artwork by reproducing the figures too large, giving an ugly appearance and taking up space needlessly.

Line drawings in two or more colours involve greater costs. Sometimes the author is able to supply separate artwork for each colour, but this will require more camera work, and printing and proofing costs will be higher.

Half-tones

Printers are responsible for the reproduction of half-tones; indeed they may be chosen for their ability to print them. Original prints should be sent with instructions on the reduction required. A coarse screen size is used for newsprint, while a fine screen is appropriate for reproducing works of art or electron micrographs. The screen size should be agreed when the order is first placed and should be determined by the capabilities of the press. PMTs for half-tones are gaining currency in commercial journals but the best results are still achieved by letting film into the final negative.

The printer can use either a camera or a scanner to make the film from a half-tone. The camera will give a finer screen but a scanner is more controllable enabling the operator to manipulate the image and adjust the balance in colour work. If the illustration is on stiff board, it will have to be stripped to wrap it round the scanning drum (which may damage the illustration).

The cost of reproducing colour photographs depends on three factors: the need for a good quality paper; separation from a transparency or print of the basic colours (usually four) by filtering; then the actual plate making and presswork. Occasionally, authors can supply colour separations, but these should be checked carefully with the printers. It is common to charge authors for the cost of colour reproduction or at least a proportion. Some journals ask authors to supply colour slides as the cost of reproducing from these can be less. Advertisers usually supply separated film plus 'progressives' which show the densities of each colour and the final quality to be matched. Some advertisers will accept electro-static proofs, for example, Cromalins, which are made photographically rather than printed. These are cheaper, but may not provide a sufficiently accurate colour guide for reproduction. They are often the first choice for colour proofing.

Instructions to authors

General

In theory, time spent in preparing detailed instructions is well spent. Papers produced in a uniform style and exactly to the journal's require-ments, need less preparation for typesetting, thereby reducing costs and speeding up production. Unfortunately, authors rarely follow the instructions exactly; the effectiveness of the instructions is probably inversely proportional to their length. This has led to the strategy of publishing a brief notice, usually on the inside back cover, which, if followed, should give a reasonably standard typescript. The brief notice can be backed up by more detailed instructions published in the first or last issue of each volume, or in a booklet supplied on request. This can be easily revised regularly if produced on desktop equipment. Some major journals even publish a list of their standard abbreviations, but it is simpler to refer to an accepted guide such as that published by the Royal Society of Medicine (Baron, 1988).

Most of the instructions will apply to editorial style but the basic points relating to production are listed below.

1 Submit more than one copy of the paper; three copies are often requested as one might be kept on file while the other two will go out to referees.
2 The text should be well spaced out on one side of the paper, e.g. double spaced with ample margins, with details of how the first page carrying the title etc. should be laid out.
3 Ranking of headings.
4 Full postal address of the author who is to check proofs.
5 All pages should be numbered.
6 A short running title should be provided (some journals prefer to provide their own).
7 The length and presentation of the abstract or summary.
8 Preferred abbreviations and units.
9 Presentation of tables and figures with advice on preparation of illustrations for reduction.
10 Style of references.
11 Stress importance of returning proofs quickly with minimal alteration.
12 Arrangements for offprints

For submission on disk

Traditionally instructions mainly cover basic presentation and layout with some detail on style to reduce the work of the copy-editor. Instructions for submission on disk are still evolving along with the technology. They are often very detailed as the author is in effect being asked to prepare camera-ready copy, but some of the guidelines below have become standard.

1 Supply hard-copy along with the disk and make sure that the text is the same.
2 Save files in the word-processor format.
3 Be consistent with the presentation and layout, and keep encoding to a minimum.
4 Warn the publisher of any special characters, i.e. if a keyboard character has been used to represent a character that is not on your keyboard.
5 Tables may not be set from disk so it is essential that adequate hard-copy is provided.
6 Advise on any matter that you think could be a problem.
7 File name(s) should be given with the disk. Use separate files for text, references, tables etc.
8 File description form should be completed and sent with the disk.
9 State preferred disks, formats, operating system and word-processing packages.

Some journals supply authors on request very detailed instructions with a design disk (comparable to supplying blue-ruled paper to authors for the preparation of camera-ready copy) and some sample pages. This is not usually necessary if the text is straightforward, but can be worthwhile for more complex mathematical contributions where TeX can be effective.

It can be helpful to have a standard form for authors wanting to submit on disk. The author can fill it in and return it with the disk. The form can carry some of the information listed above (file name and description of contents, features which could be a problem and keys used to denote special characters), the make, model and year of computer used, operating system, size and format of disk, name and version of word-processing program, and name of any proprietary coding system used.

Handling proofs

As the production editor receives the papers from the editor (or from the author, if editing and production are carried out in the same place), they should record the date of receipt, author(s), title and number of pages of typescript, figures and tables. The publishers may give the paper a reference number, or perhaps use a reference number already given to the paper by the editorial office. Some suppliers use the same numbering system as their customers; it helps in the tracking progress and the common number can form part of the job number for invoicing. A note may be kept of when any figures are sent out for redrawing or improving (such as relabelling). The date of despatch of manuscript and artwork to the typesetter should be recorded (see figure 3.6, a sample logging card). The next dates should be for the receipt of the page proofs from the typesetters and their despatch to the authors for checking; in some cases, the typesetters send the proofs direct to the authors, when the typesetters should report the date of despatch even if they send a set of proofs to the publisher. As small computers become widespread, such data may be kept in machine-readable form. The computer can then be used to generate reports on, for example, proofs of papers overdue from the typesetters, or, at a later stage, overdue from the editor.

With large circulation periodicals, or where the publishers make up the pages, the typesetters may supply galley proofs which can be the last chance for the author to check the text. The author should also be sent proofs of the illustrations with an indication of where they will be placed in the text and which way up. Most typesetters now take the composition to the fully made-up page stage and provide good photocopies as proofs.

Typesetters often read the proofs before sending them out, so the proofs carry marks indicating inconsistencies, typesetting errors, or text that should be checked by the author. Some typesetters economise by sending out proofs unread, putting a greater burden on authors and editors; the proofs should be stamped accordingly.

When the proofs are sent out for checking they can be accompanied by a number of items, such as those listed below. These should all be supplied to the typesetter if proofs are sent direct to the author.

1 A request to read the proofs and return them within a short time, or by a given date. A return address label might be supplied. With an international journal, more time should be allowed for the 'proofs out' stage of the schedule, as proofs will take longer in the mail.

2 A list of standard proof correction marks.
3 A request to use different colours to distinguish between author's alterations and typesetter's errors. These can help settle disputes with the typesetters; publishers may suspect they are being charged for corrections to errors in typesetting as well as author's alterations.
4 A warning that alterations are expensive and that the authors may be charged for excessive alterations. If authors want to make extensive alterations, they should explain their reasons to the editor. Occasionally, publishers may agree to resetting a paper extensively only if the author contributes to the costs. It is important to establish that because of the high cost of alterations, these may not be carried out at the publisher's expense and are subject to the editor's discretion.
5 An offprint order form (see page 122).
6 A copyright assignment form if one was not sent with the letter of acceptance.

Page proofs are usually photocopies of the bromide paper output of the photo-typesetter. Some typesetters produce proofs on a laser printer to reduce costs. Half-tones proofs are normally bromide prints made from the negatives which the printers will subsequently use for plate-making, but which do not reflect the quality of the finished product. The first step is to request scatter proofs when setting up the journal contract with a supplier. Thereafter, bromides provide a means of proofing the content and position of half-tones. The quality of printing should be checked by the publisher comparing running sheets (printed sheets) with originals or the approved bromides or scatter proofs. As proofs are expensive to produce and mail – especially if schedules demand airmail – the number of copies should be kept to a minimum.

When checked proofs are returned, the production editor may go through them to ensure that only essential corrections and alterations are indicated for the typesetters. Any additions or change in meaning by an author at the proof stage ought to be checked by the editor, as an opinion or new information could be slipped in without peer review. Typesetters charge extra to send out revised or press proofs. Most publishers like to check these, or at least check revised proofs of any pages where corrections were heavy, or the typesetters have queried a correction.

Some publishers will be offering authors the option of receiving proofs via Internet. As mentioned above (page 81) this can be done relatively simply if each article is held in Postscript files. These files can be converted with Acrobat Distiller to a portable format and transmitted to authors with Acrobat Reader (now supplied by Adobe free of charge) so that it is viewable by them. The system is much the same as that used for electronic document delivery (see chapter 6).

Alterations need firm control; corrections is an area where production costs can get out of control. Traditionally 10 per cent of composition costs were allowed for corrections but this can grow to as much as 25 per cent. One advantage in taking papers on disk is that the author has less scope to make changes.

Title pages and indexes

The title page, list of contents and indexes for a journal are best included in the last issue of each volume. The indexes may be paginated in sequence after the last paper, while the title and contents pages are set as preliminaries, either unpaginated or with roman numbers. They are often printed as a separate section, so that they can be pulled out for binding at the front of the volume. This material cannot be completed until the last issue of the volume is at the proof stage, so the production schedule should allow for this. They may be compiled by the editorial office, but often it is the responsibility of the publishers. The back (verso) of the title page, sometimes known as the copyright page, may be used to give details of the editorial board, publishers and printers; sometimes all this material is placed on the title page itself.

Indexes generally consist of an alphabetical list of the authors of papers in the volume together with a simple subject listing referring to the titles of the papers. It may be helpful if someone who knows the subject devises a system of key words covering the titles. The traditional method was a set of index cards; most typesetters will work directly from these. Many indexes are now prepared on micro-computers. The print-out may be used as camera-ready copy, or the floppy disk or tape may be used to drive the typesetter. Some typesetters offer the possibility of database manipulation, and can compile author and key-word entries from the original text.

Printing

General technical trends

There are five major processes used in printing: lithography, gravure, flexography, letterpress and screen printing. These are all plate or pressure (impact) printing processes that use plates or some form of image carrier, an imaging material (usually ink), and pressure between the image carrier and the substrate, usually paper, to reproduce the image.

There are also pressureless, or non-impact processes, such as electronic, electrostatic, magneto-graphic, ion deposition and ink-jet printing which are used for short-run forms, manuals and other short run publications or on-demand systems.

An important recent development has been the appearance of new direct-to-paper digital colour presses. These accept data in Postscript and a number of other formats. A digital interface then supplies page information directly to the press, bypassing film, plate, proof and make-ready stages.

Impact printing

Lithography has become the dominant printing process. This has been due to its compatibility with photographic and subsequent typesetting and electronic composition technology and to the demand for short run work.

The basic principle of lithography is the mutual antipathy between grease and water. The lithographic printing surface is a thin metal plate coated with a light-sensitive emulsion and exposed through negative or positive film. The light hardens the image area on negative plates. For short runs, plates may be of paper; plastic plates will cope with longer runs. On a processed plate, the printing area will accept grease – in this case, ink – and repel water, and the non-printing area will accept water and repel grease. Plates can be baked to give longer life.

Single-sided printing (one side of the sheet of paper printed at a time) is preferred when there are many half-tones and solids which will require heavy inking. Journals are usually printed on 'perfector' presses which print both sides of the sheet as it runs through. Double-sided printing can give problems with heavy inking as one side is printed immediately after the other and before it is fully dry. Along with the difficulty of ensuring there is little or no variation in inking from one side of the sheet to the other, there can be difficulties with register (the accurate super-imposition of colours and the exact alignment of pages so that they back one another precisely). Journals with many half-tones may be printed on a hard surface paper on which ink will dry slowly. Single-sided printing doubles the machine time and may be up to 50 per cent more expensive.

Web-fed (using a continuous roll of paper) machines are becoming increasingly competitive in the journal printing market, once dominated by the slower sheet-fed machines. With the new, fully automated web-fed printing and binding lines offering lower prices, publishers should now be prepared to adapt their journal formats to web-fed machines. Relative costs are changing; currently web printing becomes economic at print-runs over 2000/3000 copies of a text only journal. With half-tones the minimum economic print-run is higher, e.g. 4000/5000 copies, as 'dryers' are needed on the press and these are expensive to fit and run.

The boom in magazine publishing, with more and more titles being aimed at specialist markets, is stimulating technical innovation in both computerised page make-up systems and in the development of presses. New 'short grain' web presses can increase productivity by 30 per cent; the page is arranged across the plate cylinder rather than around the circumference. Finishing on short grain can be carried out far more easily in-line because trimming of two sides – head and bottom – is in the web direction. Such innovation could eventually benefit journal publishers. Generally, press speeds will continue to rise. Printing presses will become more 'intelligent', giving higher quality with less personnel and making shorter runs more economic through faster speeds and less down-time.

Non-impact printing processes

Ink jet printers, based on the electrical control of a stream of droplets of ink, are being used increasingly. The process enables each copy to be different, if this is required. The best quality ink jet printing is at present about equivalent to good quality typewriting. Further development of both hardware and software is in progress.

New laser electrographic printers which work from instructions supplied in digital form offer the potential of on-demand publishing, as single copies can be produced at high speed and reasonable quality from a digital record. Suitable methods of binding the sheets of print so produced are already available, but they could be improved. Some publishers claim it is now economic to print editions of less than 400 copies including four-colour covers on Docutech equipment which combines laser electrographic printing with rapid binding.

The print-run

Deciding on the print-run is usually straightforward for an established journal. The print orders should be checked before each volume and ideally before each issue goes to press; for example, extra sales might be expected of a special issue, sample copies may be needed to give out at a meeting or the society taking the journal may be planning a major membership drive which could increase its requirement by several hundred copies. Although run-on copies are relatively inexpensive to produce, surpluses can build up and storage is expensive.

The general rule is to print enough copies of each issue to allow for wastage during binding, claims from subscribers for lost copies, free copies for advertisers and promotional purposes, and to fill orders for back issues. Typically, for a journal with a circulation of 1000, the print-run might be 1200 copies, while for a journal with a circulation of 5000 the print-run might be 5300. Where grace copies are sent out (copies of the first issue sent automatically to all the subscribers of the previous year) the print-run of the first issue should be about 5 per cent longer; with a monthly publication grace copies of the first two issues might be sent out.

With a new journal, the publicity effort should be taken into account. A large number of specimen copies may be given out; the print order should allow for this. If a rapid rise in circulation is expected, the print-run of the early issues should be sufficient to supply subscriptions that come in later in the year. The print-run should always err on the side of too many as run-on costs are low in relation to the cost of reprinting. If it is essential to reprint several early issues, a saving can be made by producing a combined reprint issue. If only a few copies of an issue are required to make up the volume for late subscribers, it might be cheaper to buy back copies of that issue from subscribers.

The print-run of a supplement needs careful thought. Usually a supplement is despatched to all subscribers so the print-run will be the same as that for a standard issue with perhaps an additional fifty copies to service single copy orders. There may, however, be further requirements; the supplement might be based on a meeting and the organisers of the meeting may want copies to send to all the delegates. Occasionally a company will sponsor a supplement and as part of the arrangement may require several thousand copies for promotional purposes (see section on supplements).

The publisher should check the likely requirement for copies going to society members in writing every year. If there are not enough copies, there could be a dispute over who should pay for a reprint.

Paper

Buying paper

The cost of paper has dropped in real terms over the last five years but is now rising sharply. Printers charge for supplying paper (often referred to as 'stock' in the trade), but, if the quantity needed is small, it is generally sensible to pay the surcharge. When larger quantities are required, the publisher will usually find it cheaper to buy from a paper merchant, although this ties up capital. Paper can be purchased from merchants either as stock items, or 'makings' (see below). Most merchants hold stock of their main lines in the more popular sizes, but these may not coincide with the publisher's requirements. The publisher may have to purchase oversize paper; this can be cut down, but is wasteful. The merchant's price will include a charge for storage.

The most economical method of buying paper is by 'makings'. The publisher specifies the paper required and places an order with a mill through a merchant, so there is no charge by the merchant for storage and handling. The minimum quantity for most mills is two tonnes; as the quantity increases, so the price per tonne decreases. If the publisher can standardise on one particular size and quality of paper for several titles, significant economies can be made, both in the price paid for the paper and in the costs of administering purchases and stocking different lines.

The choice of paper has a further effect on the economics of journal publishing; the weight of the paper determines the cost of despatch. As the sheet weight decreases, the price per tonne increases, but the cost per sheet is less and there should be a saving in despatch costs. The publisher must balance the cost of paper and despatch, the number of pages in an issue and the desired quality of production. Sometimes a publisher will ask the printer to produce sample pages on paper of several different weights to test the opacity of the lighter papers.

In Europe, the weight of paper is measured as grams per square metre (gsm), but, in North America, the measurement is the weight per 500 sheets of paper of a certain size. For example, a 60 pounds paper means that 500 sheets in the 'basic size' (25 × 38 inches) for book paper would weigh 60 pounds. The size of the sheets should be known. For example, if the sheets were 50 × 38, the weight of 500 sheets would actually be 120 pounds, but it would still be described as 60 pounds paper. Sixty pounds stock is roughly equivalent to 90 gsm. In North America a different terminology is used for cover stock; 10 point stock is approximately 100 pounds paper. Paper is often ordered by the 'car load' (40,000 pounds or just under 18 tons); this is usually the minimum quantity that can be bought in bulk cost effectively.

Recycled paper is improving in quality and price as the market for it develops, but paper cannot be recycled indefinitely as the fibres lose strength each time they are recycled. Perfectly adequate recycled acid-free paper for journal printing including most half-tones can now be purchased at a cost of around 10–15 per cent more than standard papers. Processing recycled paper, however, requires strong chemicals (basically to bleach out the inks in the old paper) and may damage the environment more than the processing of standard papers. Also because of the inferior quality of recycled paper, it is much harder to achieve good quality printing; thus printing costs can be higher (due to the need to stop the machine more frequently to clean the blanket). Finally, there is the criticism that one of the main properties of permanent or archival paper is that it must have long fibres; recycling involves pulping, a process which breaks up fibres.

Calculating the amount of paper required

Start by establishing the size of sheet required for the press; always check with the printer. If the journal trim size is 244 × 172 mm it will normally be printed on a sheet 1000 × 1400 mm, for example. The calculation on how this format fits the sheet is as follows:

divide the depth of the sheet by the depth of a page before trim
i.e. $\frac{1000}{250}$ (assume 250 trims to 244) = 4
this means that 4 pages can be fitted in across the sheet

divide the width of the sheet by the width of the page before trim
i.e. $\frac{1400}{175}$ (assume 175 trims to 172) = 8

Therefore there will be 4 × 8 = 32 pages to view with no wastage of paper, and the sheet will take 64 pages when printed on both sides.

If there are 192 pages per issue and each sheet of paper takes 64 pages then a bound copy will use 3 sheets and 2000 copies will use 6000 sheets plus 5 to 10 per cent for wastage. A greater safety margin should be used for colour or if there are many critical half-tones or for single-sided printing.

As mentioned above, however, merchants often prefer to sell by weight. Using the example above, to estimate how much paper will be needed for four issues for an annual volume is fairly simple. Multiply 1 by 1.4 (i.e. 1000 × 1400 in metres) to give square metres, multiply this by 6300 (i.e. the number of sheets), then by the weight of paper (say 80 gsm) to give total weight in grams; divide by 1000 for kilograms and then by 1000 for tonnes. If in the example above there are 4 issues in an annual volume the total weight of paper required for the year will be 2.868 tonnes, just above the minimum bulk order for most mills.

Ordering paper

The check list below covers the sort of information a buyer should consider when placing an order.

1 Quality, including colour, finish and brand name.
2 Quantity, tonnage or number of sheets or reels.
3 Format, sheets (dimensions) or reels (width, length); if ordering reels the mill must identify any joins on the reel.
4 Grammage or thickness.
5 Grain direction of sheets and preferred moisture content. For sheet-fed octavo journals it is usual to purchase paper with the grain running the length of the short edge of the sheet (short grain), but for quarto journals long grain is preferred.
6 How the paper should be trimmed.
7 Intended use, including printing process, number of colours, binding and special properties such as acid-free, fast to light.
8 Price and payment terms.
9 Method of packing, marking instructions and delivery. The merchant or mill should be advised of the hours the printer's warehouse is open.

Opacity

The usual opacity of paper for printing journals is between 92 and 96 per cent. Opacity is measured as the reflectiveness of a sheet of the paper printed in black on the reverse side. It is expressed as a percentage of the greater reflectiveness of a sheet of the same paper when unprinted and backed up with a number of unprinted sheets of the same paper. An informal way of assessing opacity is to place a blank sheet of the paper over a printed page. The quality of the pulp and other ingredients determines the opacity; any treatment that reduces the length of the fibres and packs them more tightly will reduce opacity.

Permanent papers

Paper made from pulp produced mechanically is less expensive than paper made from pulp produced chemically, but it is relatively short-lived and bulky with shorter fibres and, therefore, rarely used for journals apart from ephemeral newsletters. Journal publishers normally use so-called 'acid-free' paper (actually neutral paper at a pH of 7), as it is believed not to deteriorate when it absorbs moisture from the atmosphere. During the making of the paper, the acid in the wood pulp is removed or neutralised. If any acid remains, the paper can become discoloured and brittle (as does old newsprint, which is an example of acidic paper) as the acid attacks the cellulose polymer of paper, breaking it down into shorter and shorter pieces until the paper's structure collapses.

With the recent interest in acid-free permanent paper higher standards are being suggested and a minimum pH of 7.5 may be demanded as in the 1994 International Standard (ISO 9706) for 'Information and documentation – Paper for documents – Requirements for permanence' which also lays down minimum tearing resistance, alkali reserve and resistance to oxidation. Publications printed on papers that comply with the requirements of this International Standard may be identified by a symbol and a statement of compliance.

John Trevitt (1990) points out that permanent papers have the added advantage of being 'green'. The process of making alkaline paper reduces water consumption and facilitates waste treatment; it adapts more readily to environmental law requirements; it is cleaner and saves energy, particularly in the drying cycle. It can also be stronger, weight for weight.

In early 1989 the Senate and House of Representatives of the United States passed a joint resolution in response to the widespread deterioration of national historical, scientific and scholarly records through the self-destruction of acidic papers. The resolution includes the recommendations quoted below.

> American publishers use acid free permanent papers for publications of enduring value, in voluntary compliance with the American National Standard, and note the use of such paper in books, advertisements, in catalogs, and in standard bibliographic listings . . . The Secretary of State make known the national policy regarding acid free permanent papers to foreign governments and appropriate international agencies since the acid paper problem is worldwide and essential foreign materials being imported by our libraries are printed on acid papers.

Various organisations have acted on this and urged publishers to use acid-free papers and ideally alkaline papers for coated stock. As a result of the widespread interest in the source and quality of paper, many publishers are now including a statement on the paper used for the journal on the inside cover. This statement might include reference to ECO-CHECK; for example, 'the paper used in this journal has an ECO-CHECK 4 Star rating'. ECO-CHECK is the first environmental assessment scheme introduced into the UK paper industry measuring five key areas of environmental concern, as listed below. The maximum rating is 5 Star.

1 Fibre source, environmental management and recyclability.
2 Energy efficiency.
3 Minimisation of chlorinated organics.
4 Liquid effluent and solid waste standards.
5 Gaseous emission standards.

Binding

The range of bindings

Most printers offer limp binding facilities, but not all can provide sewn binding. Where separate binders are to be used, they must offer firm evidence that they can collect the printed (or folded) sheets quickly and deliver on schedule. If they are to despatch to subscribers, they should have full facilities for this. The ideal binding is sewn (unusual now in North America) with the covers drawn on (i.e. as in good book binding), but unsewn 'perfect' binding with the fold cut off and the edges glued is around 30 per cent less expensive. It should be borne in mind that many academic and research libraries rebind volumes of journals at considerable expense.

The problem with perfect binding is that it is less robust and trimming and roughening the back prior to gluing uses some of the inner margin, which can make it more difficult to bind the issues into volumes. Improved forms of perfect binding, known as 'notched' or 'burst' binding, are now available. With notched binding a series of slots are cut along the spine during the penultimate fold, which enables the glue to travel easily to the centre of the section thus giving a stronger binding. With burst binding a serrated wheel rips through the fold pushing some of the paper fibres out to give more surface for the glue to stick to. This leaves a bit of the fold at the back which makes rebinding easier. Sometimes there can be a difficulty with perfect binding glossy coated stock as the glue and cover adhere to the coating and not the paper fibres. One way of getting over this is side stabbing in conjunction with drawn-on covers (which is more common in North America).

Saddle stitch binding, where staples hold the sheets together at the fold through the spine, can be used for slim issues (perfect binding can present problems with issues of less than fifty-six pages of thin paper especially if coated). Saddle stitched binding fastens the pages to the cover in one operation and costs the same as perfect binding or even less. Side wire stabbing (where a staple goes across the spine) can be used for thicker issues but looks less attractive and loses about 5mm of the inside margin so the text layout should allow for this. The cost is usually much the same as saddle stitch binding.

Although sewn binding is generally more expensive, charges can vary considerably. For example, short runs with few pages may not cost much more, especially if the printer can offer sewn but not perfect binding. If reply cards are to be bound in, the charge for this 'extra' can be high; obtain estimates before ordering.

There is often spoilage in binding and agreed limits should be established with the supplier before placing the order.

Imposition

Imposition is the positioning of the pages on the printing plates so that they will appear in the correct order when the printed sheet is folded and trimmed. The imposition affects both printer and binder so the imposition scheme must be agreed before the plates are made up. One advantage in working with a printer who also binds is that this is the responsibility of the one organisation. Differences in imposition can influence the folding, inserting plates, gathering and sewing, and therefore cost.

The grain direction of the paper often determines the imposition. Binders generally prefer to feed sheets into their folders in a short-grain direction so that the grain runs up and down the page; the journal should open more satisfactorily this way. Most publishers use a very limited range of impositions to avoid frequent changeovers.

Dealing with suppliers

Good suppliers are honest, reliable, punctual and flexible. If delays are foreseen, they communicate at once. They never promise dates they cannot meet, but will help out if the publisher is running late. Their quality is excellent and their prices reasonable. Apart from that, they should be established, financially sound, with a well-organised production department and quality control, innovative, flexible, communicative.

There are obvious advantages in placing a large amount of business with one supplier. Besides the greater strength in negotiating, a large account should give greater flexibility and the traffic between publisher and supplier may justify regular collection and delivery, thus cutting out the delays and expense of mailing. The downside of such an arrangement is that the exposure to risks such as a machine breaking down, overbooking, staffing problems and even financial collapse is magnified. Publishers should watch for warning signs. Many typesetters only have one central processor; back-up facilities should be checked.

Probably around 10 per cent of journals move to a new printer each year with commercial publishers showing a slightly higher tendency to change suppliers than 'not-for-profit' publishers. Nearly all publishers hold regular reviews of production and performance with suppliers when either party can draw attention to any problems. Such meetings should also help to establish good relationships between publisher and supplier which are helpful when difficulties do arise. A record should be made of points agreed and action to be taken, and this record should be followed up.

Recently the requirement by some publishers for article files in a form that can be used for electronic access and document delivery has pushed suppliers into making rapid technological progress. A journal publisher may demand, for example, adherence to their standards for Acrobat PDF files with graphics and half-tone images compressed in a form suitable for clear display on a screen. Sample PDF files that have been produced from fully integrated Postscript may be requested. The supplier might be asked whether they can include hypertext links within the PDF file for an article to tables, figures and references. The preferred medium for the supply of PDF files should be established (for example, by FTP, via ISDN, CD-ROM, DAT tape or SyQuest cartridges). If articles in SGML are required to the publisher's DTD then this should be specified exactly.

All suppliers should be responsible for a failure or loss of work in progress and should insure against such a likelihood. The publisher is responsible for (and should therefore insure against any loss or damage) any artwork, tapes, disks, film or stock once it is received from a supplier.

Terms

It might be thought that as most typesetters and printers of academic material like handling journals, because they represent steady work with lower administrative costs, a lower charge than for book production can be negotiated. Unfortunately, this is not always the case, as the suppliers are well aware that they will have to live with their prices for some while and tight schedules can present problems. Book production prices can be lower because, for example, a printer may decide it is worth doing the job at little more than cost to keep staff busy during a slack period. For those new to the trade there is a short introduction to customs in the manufacture of books which is almost equally applicable to journal production (PA & BPIF, 1985).

Estimates will depend on whether the range of text and the proposed format will suit the supplier's equipment and on the quality of service expected. An expensive typesetter may, for example, offer better quality and time keeping and thorough proofreading. Reliability in making the corrections is also important. In some subject areas where a high standard of printing half-tones is required, the choice of printers may be limited.

In some countries, typesetters and printers conduct their wage negotiations at a particular time of year. In the UK, for example, this usually occurs in April/May, so they customarily discuss price increases with publishers then. It is possible to establish a scale of prices for a calendar year which may include a realistic allowance for expected wage increases. The same costs apart from paper will apply to every issue produced during the calendar year which simplifies the budgeting process. There may, however, be a cost in getting a price for a calendar year; the supplier may cover for the highest likely wage increase.

Such is the commercial pressure on typesetters and printers at present that publishers are in a strong bargaining position and increases can be kept to a minimum. Publishers have their own approach, but there is much to be said for maintaining supplier loyalty and amicable working relationships. Moving business to another supplier costs money.

In obtaining estimates, a clear brief should be given of what is required. The estimates should be checked that they are complete and include all items. Some suppliers will also prepare dummy invoices to show the way they intend to charge: this can be helpful, especially when negotiating with a new supplier. Care should be taken to allow for all 'extras', such as the cost of additional sets of proofs, posting proofs, sorting, packing and consolidating for post, PDF files, offprints and the freight of the residue, following subscription despatch, to the warehouse. When evaluating estimates and the service offered, it is essential to be sure that like is being compared with like. It is wise to check the effect of changing the print number on the price.

When launching a new journal, suppliers may be prepared to give extended credit on the condition that they will keep the contract for some years. If the preferred suppliers are a little higher in their estimates than another, it is worth telling them so, as they may come down in order to win the contract. They may also be enticed by the promise of further journals, if they are successful with their first contract.

Points to consider before placing an order for typesetting

(1) *Price, terms etc.* Will charges be made on the basis of the component parts of each job (e.g. so much for typesetting, so much for tabular matter, references etc.) or as an average price per page? Also, what payment terms are required, and does this fit with your own cash-flow projections? Will they produce only one invoice per job?

(2) *Corrections* How are corrections to be charged – on a fixed rate per line or as an overall average for the job?

(3) *Capacity* Does the supplier have the staff and equipment for the projected workload?

(4) *Speed* How long from despatch of copy to proofs and return of proofs to completion?

(5) *Expertise* Does the typesetting require special expertise (foreign languages, mathematics, chemistry and complicated tabular matter)? Some suppliers may offer extra services such as creating an index automatically from flagged items which might otherwise have to be prepared manually. Can the typesetter provide SGML coding and article files in Postscript? Article files in PDF (Acrobat) might also be required. What extra charges might be involved for these extra services?

(6) *Disks* Can the supplier accept text on disks? Close co-operation with the supplier can give benefits with new technology. The supplier might require the following information: sample disks, sample hard-copy accompanying the disks, a printed sample, typographic specifications, a view on the range of disk formats that might require conversion and processing, and a listing of the standard coding used for the text, headings, paragraphs and other material such as tables and references.

(7) *Page make-up* Will this be manual or automatic, and will it suit the nature of the work?

(8) *Half-tones* How are these to be originated – by printer, reproduction house or sub-contracted by the typesetter? If the typesetter is involved, does he have access to a scanner or conventional camera only? Is the typesetter able to supply film as end product (negative or positive), digitised images (in what form and at what resolution) or camera-ready copy only?

(9) *Colour-work* Can the typesetter handle more than one colour, and if so how?

(10) *Typeface availability* Does the typesetter hold the typefaces and sorts required and on the system specified (e.g. Monophoto, Lasercomp, Linotron, etc.)?

(11) *Studio facilities* Can the typesetter provide artwork where necessary, or supply more complex graphic elements (which may be machine generated)?

(12) *Communications* How are day-to-day communications to be made – by telephone, letter, e-mail, fax, etc.? Is a collection/delivery service offered? If overseas, is there likely to be a language problem?

(13) *Housekeeping practice* Does the firm seem efficient and well

organised? Is the supplier able to provide a fully updated disk or tape on completion of the job (each issue), which may be used for a subsequent archiving/database project?

Points to include in an order for typesetting

1 Buyer's name, address, telephone and fax number.
2 Supplier's name and address.
3 An order number and date.
4 Title of journal to which the order relates.
5 Description of copy to which the order relates (either part or whole hard-copy or disk).
6 Equipment on which the copy is to be set.
7 Styles for the various parts of the job: type face, type size, line length, measure etc. A layout may be needed to amplify this description.
8 Details of illustrations (line, tone, combined line and tone, colour line including number of colours, four-colour half-tone etc.) and the form of copy supplied.
9 Proofs required: galley and/or page, quantities and despatch instructions.
10 Dates for delivery of proofs and final product, i.e. production schedule.
11 Final product: camera-ready copy or film (positive or negative, right or wrong reading, emulsion up or down) plus any special requirements such as PDF files.
12 Confirmation of prices and payment terms.
13 The signature of the person placing the order.

Points to consider before placing printing and binding orders

1 *Price, terms, etc.* This should include rates for various extents (which may change from issue to issue).
2 *Press size* Is the printer's equipment suitable?
3 *Web or sheet fed* Most journals are printed on sheet-fed presses, though titles with long runs may be suitable for web printing.
4 *Colour printing* Can the printer produce satisfactory colour work? Bear

in mind that even if colour is not often required in the text there may be colour advertisements.

5 *Perfecting* Not all papers are suitable for perfecting, and many printers are unwilling to perfect work which contains a large number of half-tones.

6 *Binding equipment* Where will this be done? What binding options are available: sewing and gluing, 'perfect' (unsewn) binding, or wire stitching.

7 *Offprints*

8 *Cover printing* Can the printer print the covers, or do these need a more specialised unit? How will they handle lamination or ultra violet varnishing?

9 *Origination facilities* If typesetting elsewhere, does the printer want film or camera-ready copy? If the latter, what about the origination of half-tones? Does the printer have compatible typesetting equipment for late corrections?

10 *Paper/board* Can the printer supply suitable paper and board?

11 *Special requirements* Can the printer cope with any special require-ments, for example, tip-ins, fold-outs, loose inserts, etc.?

12 *Quality* Will the quality be adequate especially for half-tones?

13 *Despatch/delivery* Can the printer organise the mailing of journals, usually in plastic wrappers and using the customer's labels, though card envelopes may be required for larger items, or will the issues be shipped in bulk to another address for despatch?

14 *Warehousing/storage* The printer should store all film for an agreed period pending any reprint requirements. The printer may also be able to store back issues if the publisher has no warehousing – at a cost.

Points to include in orders for printing and binding

Figure 3.5 shows a sample print and bind order form which is largely covered by the checklist below.

1 Buyer's name, address, telephone and fax number.

2 Same details for supplier.

TO (Supplier) :			
TITLE			
ISSN :	Volume :	Issue :	Dated :
Trimmed size :	Total Extent :	Margins :	
Text pages :	Adverts :	Others :	
Despatch from binders :			
Delivery to			
Print & Bind quantity details :			
Advance copies :			
Subscription copies :			
Offprint copies :			
Remainder copies :			
Cover :			
Text :			
Adverts :			
Printing :			
Binding :			
Loose inserts :			
Bound inserts :			
Text paper :	Sheet size :		
Supplied by :			
Cover materials :	Sheet size :		
Other materials :			
Copy of despatch note to :			
Production queries to :			
Date of estimate or scale :			
Date of this order :	Division :		
Signed :	Position :		
SPECIAL INSTRUCTIONS			

Figure 3.5 A sample print and bind order form including delivery instructions. Note that this is where instructions for offprints and inserts (often administrative problems) are given.

3 Order number and date.

4 Title and issue number of journal.

5 Exact description of what is to be printed and bound (e.g. 96 pages in black consisting of i–iv prelims and 1–91 text, 1 blank + 4 pages cover printed in pms 300 and black on pages 1 and 4).

6 Materials to be used for text and/or cover and whether or not they are to be supplied by publisher or printer.

7 Style of binding and materials to be used (16- or 32-page sections, sewn or unsewn, square or rounded back, scoring of covers).

8 Any inserts, plates or folders to be printed and their position in the issue.

9 Style of packing (bulk on pallets, binder's parcels of 10 etc.).

10 Address to which the goods are to be delivered or arrangements for despatch to subscribers from the printer.

11 Delivery date, i.e. production schedule.

12 Confirmation of prices and payment terms.

13 The signature of the person placing the order.

Offprints

Offprints, sometimes called 'reprints', are printed copies of individual articles. Printers find offprints a nuisance, although they may be an important secondary source of income. With many journals a number of free offprints (commonly twenty-five or fifty copies of each paper) are given to authors. Offprints can be vital to the image of the publication. The number of free copies and the charge for further copies may be taken into consideration by potential contributors; the quality of production and efficiency of service can also influence the reputation of the journal and its publisher. Contributors often send out copies of a paper to colleagues. An offprint will be more effective than a photocopy, especially if the paper includes detailed illustrations, and is preferred for a job or grant application.

Printing

The actual quality of printing should be the same as for the journal; usually the appropriate number of extra sheets is run off with the main printing. If a smaller machine is used to print offprints, new plates have to be made; to maintain quality, they should be prepared from the film used for the original set of plates.

Offprint production is simplified if each paper starts on a right-hand page. Otherwise, either the offprints are re-imposed, or some will start with the final page of the previous article (and, consequently extra copies must be printed of these pages). Editors may object to what appears to be 'waste-space' – the blank left-hand pages at the end of articles. These pages may be filled with book reviews, advertisements, or other small items. Statistically, the number of extra pages required to start each paper on a right-hand page is half the number of papers per issue minus one, since the first paper will begin on a right-hand page.

Starting papers on the page immediately following the preceding paper can markedly reduce the length of a long issue made up of short papers, lowering the cost of machining, paper, binding and even mailing the whole issue. The decision on whether to start papers on right-hand pages depends on the extra charge for re-imposing each paper (if this is required), and the savings produced by reducing the extent of the journal. Generally, it is more economical for journals with longer print-runs (say over 2000) and short articles to start articles immediately after the preceding one.

An alternative is to print the offprint of the paper at the same time as the main text, then subsequently reprint the first and last two pages of each paper, omitting the parts of the preceding and succeeding papers. This gives sheets carrying only the appropriate paper; when collated with the over-runs they make up offprints which carry no extraneous text.

Starting papers on a right-hand page may be justified on other grounds. It simplifies production if typesetting is on a copy-bank system, in which papers are set as they come in (see below), rather than on an issue-by-issue basis.

Binding

Offprints are usually held together by a couple of staples down the left-hand side, sometimes covered by a tape. The tape holds the offprint together and improves its appearance. Some printers can offer strip binding without staples. This opens flat, making the offprint easier to read.

Covers without a title are worse than no covers at all. One solution, where all articles start on the right-hand page, is to head each article with the title, volume, number and date of the journal, as if no covers were being used, and bind in a plain cover with a 'window' cut to display this information. Another trick is to instruct the printer to run off special off-print covers. These are reprints of the actual cover of the issue, but with the spine taken out and the words 'reprinted from' added to the front panel. The cost of this is not large, provided that the printer accepts that there shall be only one 'printed cover' charge for all the offprints of an issue.

A low cost approach

One publisher has developed an economical method of supplying off-prints. When the printers are printing the covers for the year (in colour) they are also instructed to print light-weight simplified covers for off-prints. These covers identify the journal, the editorial board and the publisher, but are not dated to any year (so that a generous supply can be printed at one go). Then, when each issue is being printed, an additional twenty-five sheets are ordered and these are folded and then guillotined into loose pages. Since each article begins on a right-hand page, the loose sheets are simply collected up appropriately, put into covers and mailed to the authors. This system, of course, is less suitable for a journal that sells additional offprints.

Management and despatch

It is usual to send the first-named author an offprint order form with the proofs of their contribution; before then, the extent of the article will not be known. The form asks for the address to which offprints should be sent and how many additional copies are wanted (often in multiples of twenty-five). It should give a scale of charges for different quantities and extents. These charges may relate to the scale of charges from printer to publisher and should include postage by surface mail or air-speeded delivery (air mail is often extra). To reduce administrative costs, authors are usually asked to send cash with their order.

The publisher then draws up a table showing how many offprints are needed of each item and supplies that to the printer. Often printers send the offprints direct to authors (using labels produced by the publisher), but some publishers prefer to handle despatch themselves. Authors want offprints as quickly as possible, so the time from delivery of the issue to the despatch of offprints should be monitored and kept to less than two weeks if possible.

The publisher may want offprints of the book review section to supply a couple of copies to each reviewer and to the publishers of books reviewed. If the journal publishes special lectures or a society newsletter, there may be a standing order for a large number of copies.

Supplements

Most journals run on a tight schedule with little spare capacity. Supplements can be a problem especially when they do not follow the usual editorial arrangements. In some cases, for example, they are much longer than a standard issue and they may be handled by an editor appointed for the supplement rather than the established editorial team with which the publishers should have developed a smooth working relationship.

The management of supplements is covered in the non-subscription revenue chapter, but some aspects of their production should be borne in mind. A schedule for the supplement should be agreed with the editor. Where the cost is not already covered in the annual budget a separate estimate should be obtained; this should take into account any special features. If the production editor is already at full stretch, freelance help should be organised. Occasionally the sponsor of a supplement will want a reprint; sometimes a saving can be made by obtaining estimates from one or two other printers as well as the usual printer of the journal.

Scheduling

A schedule should be set up with the editor that the suppliers can work to. Most journals take about four months from despatch of copy for type-setting to bound copies. Faster schedules are likely to be more expensive, and the publisher must be sure that suppliers can cope if copy is late, or with delays in advertisements, artwork or proofs or last-minute corrections. In all cases the publisher should consult the editor over the schedule to ensure, for example, that proofs do not arrive just after the editor has left for a long trip.

Figure 3.6 is a typical form for tracking manuscripts for a particular journal. Parts could be expanded: for example, the columns for figures and half-tones could be increased from two to six to include progress of artwork to illustrator and back. Some publishers also use a separate form for illustrations (figure 3.7). With production management software this information can be called up on screen with, say, a code F for figures to give more detail on these. Below this form a facility for recording the progress of issues could be included and another column on the right could record in which issue the article is to appear.

Table 3.2 shows typical and fast schedules. (Figure 3.8 shows the time spent on each operation in more detail.) It may be possible to reduce the time proofs are with authors on the typical schedule, but this will be difficult if many are overseas. Errors may be missed if proofs are faxed, but corrections can be faxed back to the publisher. Increasingly, e-mail is being used and transmitting proofs as electronic documents will save on time; articles can be transmitted as Acrobat Reader files for the author to access on their screen or preferably as Acrobat Exchange files (Exchange is an enhanced version of Reader which allows full text searching and the clear presentation of additions and corrections for the editor to assess afterwards). Sometimes only the editor sees proofs which shortens the schedule, but most would not want the responsibility or have the time. Second (final) proofs may not be necessary, or can be supplied only on request, perhaps when there are a lot of changes to be made. They might go to a proofreader only, and are rarely sent to authors.

With conventional typesetting, it is possible to get schedules down to about six or seven weeks (see the fast schedule in table 3.2). Schedules tighter than that will probably increase overheads and suppliers' charges. Desk-top production systems allow shorter schedules, with less proofing and more work in-house.

If illustrations need redrawing, the copy preparation time will be longer, but papers can be sent for typesetting before the artwork is complete. Magazine type journals may need longer for design – though DTP can speed that up.

Table 3.2. *Typical and fast journal schedules*

Stage	Production schedule	
	Typical	Fast
Copy-editing and preparation of artwork	1 week	1 day
Typesetting	4 weeks	1 week
Proofs out	4 weeks	2 weeks
Corrections	3 weeks	1 week
Revised proofs out	2 weeks	2 days in-house
Print and bind	4 weeks	2 weeks
Total	18 weeks	6.5 weeks

The programme for the final issue of a volume should be a little longer to allow for the preparation of the volume contents list and index; the title-page can be prepared in advance. Sending them out with the first issue of the next volume is much less satisfactory.

The subscription department, or whoever is responsible for despatch, needs advance notice of the dates of publication, and warnings of any variations which could affect the despatch routine or the packaging material. Larger organisations usually have a progress monitoring system on computer; deviations from plan should be reported automatically and full reports on all issues of all titles can be produced on demand. Explanatory notes may be entered below a delayed title, e.g. 'running 3 weeks late through delays in copy from editor' or 'proofs of 2 papers delayed in mail but printers will catch up on schedule'.

Two systems: batch and copy-bank

For many periodicals, the production of each issue is treated almost as a separate unit; the copy is supplied in one batch, with the contents in a set order. With this batch process, it is hard to make significant reductions in the schedule. The publisher/editor may have to go to press without waiting for a slow author's proofs to keep to a schedule.

More frequently published and larger periodicals can use a copy-bank system. Papers are sent to the typesetter as soon as they are ready. The

JOURNAL

Ms No / Editor C/L	Author & Short Title	Date rcd at C/L	Folios		Figs		Date sent for setting	Proofs rcd & despatched		Proofs rcd from Editor		Proofs rcd from Author		Date sent to press	Published		Notes
			Mss	T/set	L	H/T		Sch	Act	Sch	Act	Sch	Act		Sch	Act	

Figure 3.6 A form for recording progress with papers through to publication.

Article	Fig. No.	Line H/T Colour	To artist	%	Originator		Notes	Article	Fig. No.	Line H/T Colour	To artist	%	Originator		Notes
					Out	r'tn							Out	r'tn	

Figure 3.7 A form for recording progress with the preparation of illustrations.

typesetter sets the papers as they come in. Corrected proofs are held in a pool, or bank. The editor makes up issues from the material in the bank (i.e. ready for press). Provided everyone involved is well organised, the copy-bank system offers prompt publication and means that issues are not held back for a laggardly author. This is especially true if issues can be of varying length; otherwise, a temporary shortage of copy can delay publication.

The extreme example is where all the copy in the bank at press date is allowed to go through to publication. This gives rapid publication, but requires some control, since the subscription price for a year will assume a certain number of pages. Typesetters who operate banks of papers may charge at proofing out stage.

Some journals are run with dual schedules. The main, or feature articles are produced as they come in, and published as space allows, while the short pieces and news items might be made up on an issue-by-issue basis to a shorter schedule.

Monitoring costs and quality

Prices and budgets for journals will be based on assumptions about production costs; computer systems can be helpful in showing variances between the forecast and the actual costs. Action should be taken if these are significant; the most common problem is publishing more material than planned. All suppliers' invoices should be checked carefully against the order and a copy of the issue concerned. Editors should be advised if they are unwittingly increasing the costs.

One common cause of higher costs, especially with a policy of publishing all that is in page proof at a certain time, is not making 'even workings' and running over postal charge weight steps. The cost of machining and binding an oddment, say 4 pages over a signature (the set of pages from a folded printed sheet of paper) of 16 or 32 pages, can be very much higher than the norm. This should be watched for when the issues are made up. Most presses print 16-page sections; to print eight pages costs 80 per cent of the price of 16 pages, and to print four pages costs 60 per cent of the price of 16. Therefore, to print a 12-page section would cost 140 per cent of the cost of printing 16 pages. If a journal

Production Scheme

(one representative issue)

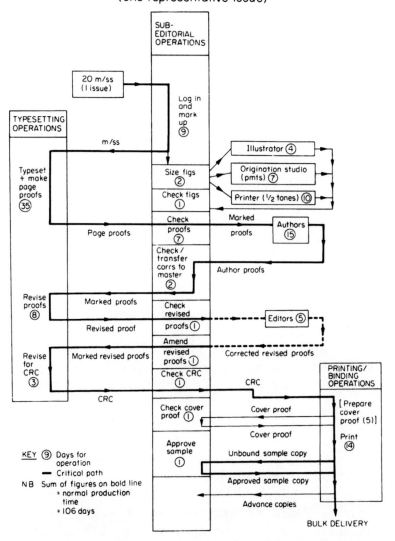

Figure 3.8 The schedule for a large (over 2000 pages per annum) scientific journal showing the time spent by the copy-editor, typesetter and printer/binder assuming all copy typeset by a supplier.

A. *Composition*

    (a) More type to given area:
        (1) reduce type size;
        (2) reuse narrower type face e.g. Times gets 13 per cent more characters
            and Bembo 22 per cent more for given area than Century.
    (b) Increase type area:
        (1) longer lines – but may require more leading;
        (2) more lines.
More type on page should mean fewer pages in total therefore lower printing, paper, binding and mailing costs, but typesetting charge per page will go up as there are more characters per page.

B. *Corrections*

The earlier in the production process the corrections can be made, the less expensive they will be.
Educate editors to make/allow essential changes only.

C. *Illustrations*

Obtain the best quality originals to minimise redrawing and reproduction difficulties.
Size to smallest possible column width, but maintain clarity.
Ask author to indicate area(s) of particular interest on half-tones to ensure best reproduction of those features.

Figure 3.9 A checklist of cost-saving tactics.

publishes only research papers, each starting on a new page, there can be difficulties here; but where there are less urgent items, such as book reviews, some juggling can usually be managed. Advertising also has to be considered in this context: if it takes the issue over an even working, it can lead to extra costs actually exceeding income.

It is sensible to obtain estimates from other suppliers from time to time; they may be able to do the job more cheaply, or quickly, or suggest ways in which they could reduce costs. Other ways of keeping production costs down are shown in figure 3.9 which is developed from a list published by Kiley and Chalfant (Drew, 1989).

D. *Paper*

Standardise sizes and bulk buy to obtain best prices.

Use lightest weight possible to reduce paper and postage costs, but watch opacity.

Mechanical papers cheaper but not suitable for journals with long 'shelf life'.

Use of printer's stock rather than publisher supplying may help cash flow and gain the benefit of printer's buying power, but will most likely be more expensive as the printer will add handling charge.

E. *Presswork*

Choose format to make maximum use of press area.

Strict control of extent to even workings to minimise oddments.

Where schedules allow, batch journals with same format and paper to reduce set-up costs.

Print year's supply of covers with base colour(s) and then overprint details for each issue as needed.

F. *Binding*

Consider cheaper forms of binding, e.g. perfect binding, but remember needs of librarians to be able to case-bind volumes subsequently.

G. *General*

Negotiate discounts for volume and early payment with suppliers.

Review prices and service regularly.

Quality should be monitored also. Advance or sample copies should be checked for evenness of inking, accurate imposition, trim alignment, any changes to cover details, tightness of sewing or strength of gluing, and how well the originals of the half-tones match the printed result. If the despatch of individual copies is handled by the printer or binder, copies can be sent to home addresses to check actual arrival dates and the condition in which copies arrive. Some publishers check running sheets before binding. Producing PDF files of articles for online access adds to quality assurance costs as the files will need to be checked before adding them to the journal database.

4   Marketing

Introduction

The essence of marketing is to have a product that people want or need, at a price they can afford, and to get a convincing message to them. Anyone developing a product should have a clear idea of how it will be sold and who will buy it. Publishing is no exception: some journals have had no more than ten or twenty subscribers six months after publication of the first issue and have folded before the end of the first volume. Although this chapter follows those on editorial and production, the market should always be considered before any decision to publish is made.

The market for learned journals differs from that for most consumer goods. Firstly, the total achievable market for a learned journal is small; it may only be a few hundred and most have fewer than 5000 non-member subscribers. Secondly, it is international. An English-language scientific journal published in the USA or Western Europe might have subscribers in fifty or a hundred countries. The geographical distribution of subscribers varies with subject, but, in rough terms, about one-third of the subscribers to an international scientific journal published in Europe might be in the USA and Canada; one-third in Europe (10 per cent in the UK); and one-third elsewhere, with perhaps 10 per cent in Japan and 5 per cent in Australia and New Zealand. Journals published in the USA often have a higher proportion of subscribers in North America.

Another difference from most products is that the purchasers are often not the users; many subscribers are libraries buying for their readers. Buying decisions are made on the basis of readers' requests. Both library and end user therefore need to be informed about publications.

Market research

The starting point for marketing an established journal or determining whether to launch a new title is market research. Market research can have a number of objectives. It will explore how the product (in this case a journal) is or will be perceived and what can be done to enhance its appeal to readers, contributors and subscribers. What points should be emphasised in promotion? What weaknesses need to be overcome? What is the potential market (who and where?) and how large is it, and how it can be reached effectively and economically? And what is the competition? Another reason for market research is to give potential advertisers or sponsors of supplements information on the readership. Methods range from the informal – a chance meeting at a conference or over a dinner table perhaps – to a highly structured questionnaire circulated to several thousand people or organisations worldwide.

Assuming that a journal proposal is within the scope and competence of the publisher, a prime question is whether it can attract enough contributors and enough subscribers to earn its keep. Market research for a new journal might start with discussions with potential board members and other advisers and an analysis of the strengths and weakness of competing journals and rough estimates of the size of the market. If that looks promising the publisher will want to explore it further; if a project looks doubtful it can be ditched before too much has been spent on developing it.

Questions about competing journals will include questions of whether there are major gaps in their coverage? Is the editorial policy heavily slanted in certain directions? What makes people submit papers to them? How do they rank for citations? How quickly do they process papers? Do they offer any features other than research papers to make them more attractive to subscribers, particularly individuals? From which institutions in which countries are their authors drawn? Do they look attractive to read and are illustrations well reproduced? What is their offprint policy? How are these journals and their editors regarded? Do the prices seem in line with the general market? What is known of their sales? How could they be improved upon?

Rough indications of the number of people working on a subject may be gleaned from the size of learned societies or mailing lists. Another guide is attendance at conferences, though that is affected by geography, weather and access to funds. Low numbers may mean that the journal is not viable, but high numbers may not mean a large number of library subscriptions if those working in the subject work in large groups in relatively few centres.

Figures for the number of subscribers to similar journals should be interpreted with care. Those in *Ulrich's International Periodicals Directory* and similar publications are supplied by publishers and may be overstated and rarely distinguish between subscriptions paid at the full rate and others. Advertising directories may be more reliable, but some specialist journals do not accept advertising or do not have audited circulation figures. Some publishers refuse to give any figures. Some volunteer their figures, or supply them to 'bona fide' advertisers, but may exaggerate the numbers. The size of library mailing lists can also indicate the likely demand, but their classifications rarely match exactly the subject matter of the journal or tell one what proportion of the list would subscribe.

For an existing journal, much can be learnt from the subscription lists. Are there parts of the world under-represented by comparison with other journals or sectors of the market which do not seem to be properly covered? If the journal sells to some, but not many, food processors, legal practitioners, departments of computer science, agricultural machinery manufacturers or water authorities, is there scope for selling to others in the same line of business? Letters or telephone calls following up cancellations or non-renewals can provide useful information about how the journal is perceived and may suggest points that should be made in promotion.

Another useful source of market information is the *Science Citation Index*. Impact factors (see below) indicate which are the strongest journals in any field. The lists of contributors to these journals (with their addresses) are likely to include many of the leading authors and the leading centres in the subject.

More formal approaches include letters or questionnaires which might be sent to anything from about fifty to several thousand people. Some-times a publisher will start with a personal approach to a selected group of known opinion formers. If that produces a positive response then a questionnaire is sent to a much larger number. The questionnaire is likely to benefit from the responses of the smaller group or from a pilot study. Questionnaires need careful design to elicit usable information. Some questions may be open-ended and allow flexibility; others should produce answers that can be quantified. They should look as though they will be easy to complete and not take much time. It should be possible to explore correlations between answers: the 50 per cent in favour of some course may be 75 per cent of one group and 25 per cent of another. Even if respondents do not give their names and addresses there should be questions to show what groups they belong to. The sequence of questions should be logical and the language clear, simple and international (check, *not* tick; please print, *not* use block capitals). Plenty of space should be allowed for replies. It is helpful to get someone unconnected with the project to try to answer the questionnaire before printing and despatching copies worldwide. The return date should be realistic. Ideally there should be a reply-paid envelope.

The questions should be aimed to help develop both marketing strategy and editorial policy. What sort of items appeal – or do not appeal – to the potential market? For existing journals it can be asked whether the format is attractive? Is it easy to find one's way through an issue? How does this journal compare with others in its field? Do librarians have any problems in handling it? In exploring an existing journal with mainly individual subscribers, it costs less to insert the questionnaire in the journal, but the response rate is likely to be much lower than if the forms were sent out separately with a covering letter. Libraries in particular are likely to overlook inserts or shake them into a wastepaper bin. If the circulation of the journal runs into many thousands, then it may be sufficient to take a random sample of subscribers.

Where a journal mostly goes to libraries it is not so easy to get a response from the individual readers. An outside mailing list – or the publisher's own lists of bookbuyers in the same field – may be useful here. It can also persuade recipients who do not regularly see the journal to have a look at it and so act as promotion.

Different questionnaires may be needed for libraries and individuals, and sometimes for different groups within those categories. As with publicity mailings, one can use a selection from a list (e.g. one in ten addresses) instead of sending out many thousands. A prize draw of entries received before a given time may encourage respondents and a covering letter from the editor may carry more weight than one from the publisher.

Some publishers find it useful to send questionnaires to new subscribers, particularly individuals, to establish why they started their subscription. If, for instance, it was because of a particular feature perhaps that feature should be highlighted in future promotion.

Publishers may also consult librarians about new journals; librarians sometimes complain they are consulted too rarely. Many publishers fear the reaction will be 'not another journal please' regardless of the merits of the proposals. In any case, the publisher usually wants responses primarily from those who might contribute to the journal or recommend its purchase. The danger of doing any market research for a new journal involving people outside the publishing house is that rival publishers will learn about it and may decide to set up a journal on the topic themselves. Some publishers announce new journals in *Nature* or other widely read publications early on in the hope of stalling off rivals before exploring the market in great depth. It should however be noted that some countries have laws prohibiting the advertising of non-existent products.

What makes a journal saleable?

The four main factors that influence whether or not a journal is bought are pertinence (or likely usage), quality, accessibility of the language and affordability. An inexpensive high-quality journal that is of no interest to the users of a library will not be bought. Libraries with tiny budgets may be unable to buy even the least expensive and highest quality journals in their chosen field. Better funded libraries will often check whether a high-price journal is available in some nearby library, particularly if they have relatively few readers working on the subject. Few libraries buy journals in languages that their users can not read.

Librarians may run user studies to gauge the value of the journal to the library. Methods include noting how often current issues need reshelving, the demand for copies of articles or the thickness of the dust on the shelves. Readers may be asked to sign a form when they use a journal, or thin cotton thread is tied round the issues in the expectation that it would be broken if anyone consulted the journal, but there are difficulties in interpretation. Readers' opinions can be canvassed by questionnaires or each can be given 100 votes to be allocated to individual titles in any way they chose. Some libraries run detailed user studies; these are expensive but can repay the costs by subsequent cancellation of unused titles.

If a reader wants the library to start a new subscription to a journal they may be asked to complete a form giving the title, the publisher, frequency, price and the nature and duration of the research project that makes it desirable. If it is to be used in teaching, at what level for which courses with how many students? They may be asked to suggest sources of funding other than the library budget or journals that might be cancelled to release funds for it.

There is no single reliable measure of quality in a journal – and what is good quality for one reader may not be to another – particularly in fields where there are differences of philosophy. The standing of the editor and the editorial board are indicators, as is that of the publisher and of any sponsor. If a journal is covered by the relevant abstracting and indexing (secondary) services that also suggests that it is of a reasonable standard.

One commonly used measure is the 'Impact Factor' a term coined by Eugene Garfield of ISI (The Institute of Scientific Information) to quantify the frequency with which journal articles are cited. The impact factor for a journal in a given period is the number of citations to the journal divided by the number of citable items published. The citations are those recorded in ISI's 'Science Citation Indexes' which cover leading journals in science, technology, medicine and the social sciences. Librarians are increasingly using the impact factor as an indicator of quality, and some subscription agents include it in their databases which they make available to their library customers.

Impact factors should be interpreted with caution. Review articles and papers on methodology tend to be more cited than original research. The journals that are covered by the citation indexes may be biased towards citation of US articles and against items in languages other than English. There is variation from subject to subject: an impact factor of 1 is low in molecular biology but high in technology. We look at the editorial implications of impact factors in chapter 2.

Another point that might be considered is whether the journal offers some unique and desirable features. Does it publish supplements; if so, are they useful and included in the subscription price? Is it printed on permanent (acid-free) paper? What is the publishers' track record with other journals? Is their service good or are there constant problems with delayed or missing issues, hefty price increases not attributable to increases in extent or other obvious causes? Does the publisher produce proper indexes, contents lists and title pages? If it is a new journal does it look like staying the course?

It is sometimes suggested that with document delivery and online services, libraries do not need subscriptions to more than a few journals; anything else can be acquired as single articles when needed. The simple view is that a philosophy of 'just in time' rather than 'just in case' will reduce the pressure on library budgets, particularly if the costs of document delivery can be claimed from other sources. The jury is still out. Some libraries are running tests comparing the costs of offering unlimited document delivery to the faculty with those of subscribing. A study at Loughborough University in 1986 (Macdougall, Woodward and Wilson) found that over the three subject areas studied, the total cost per use (including library overheads) of an article in a print-on-paper journal was much less than that of getting individual papers by other means. Other observers point out that many readers regularly scan a number of journals; they are browsers picking up items here and there but reading few papers in depth. If they are given free range to order anything they think may be of interest the cost could be very high. Will the library be so willing to pay for articles needed by students? What about items other than research papers – including advertising and book reviews – that readers also like to skim through. A more fundamental consideration is that good journals are not just collections of papers. They are part of the social structure of their subjects and the context in which an article appears is also important.

Who buys journals?

Something of the order of 90 per cent of the non-member subscribers to learned journals are libraries. There are many different types of library;

few publishers are equally good at selling to all of them. Publishers of academic research journals may be able to reach academic institutions in many countries, but might be poor at selling to industry and commerce abroad. More industry-oriented publishers may achieve high sales to industry or commerce in their own countries and a few others, but sell few subscriptions outside these regions or to academic libraries.

Academic libraries include university central, faculty and departmental libraries and college libraries. Major university libraries in developed countries may have holdings of 5000 to 20,000 serials and spend a million dollars or more a year on serial acquisitions. In developing countries they may be able to afford only a few hundred titles if they are lucky, though their holdings may be boosted by donations and exchanges.

Financial and other pressures have led to centralisation of libraries in many universities; faculty and departmental libraries usually involve some duplication of holdings, systems and staff. MacDougall, Woodward and Wilson (1986) found that members of a given department can account for fewer than half the uses made of publications taken for that department. However, if a college or university is on a split site, or spread over many sites, then several libraries may be necessary. With OPAC (Open Access) systems, the library catalogue (and indeed catalogues of the libraries of other institutions) may be networked through the campus so readers can discover where any publication is located.

Few librarians have acquisition budgets that allow them to buy everything they and their readers would like (see below). The traditional view of the library as an archive that would maintain existing subscriptions regardless of use has generally been replaced by the idea of a dynamic collection responding to changing user needs. Institutions add new departments and develop new areas of interest and so need access to publications not previously in the library. Some librarians now expect to cancel perhaps 10 per cent of their subscriptions each year and add 5 to 10 per cent of new subscriptions in response to readers' requests. This juggling of holdings and budgets adds to the library's staff costs. Not all library users are equally influential; special budgets ('squeal money') may be available for special cases.

Research institution libraries are generally smaller and more specialised than their university counterparts; they are catering for a smaller range of interests and their teaching, if any, may be limited to graduate students. Their holdings too must respond to changes in research interests. Medical libraries are a special case. They are often based on a hospital, with or without teaching facilities, and may also be used by practitioners from the locality. Industrial or commercial libraries are an important market for some journals, particularly those dealing with technology, applied science, business management, economics and law. The librarians of industrial or commercial enterprises are often also information officers, whose duties include alerting their colleagues to information which may be of value, carrying out literature searches, and circulating periodicals and other items of interest. They are more likely than academic librarians to make acquisition decisions without consulting the users. That reflects the awareness they have of the information needs of their users and the company's interests; it is also because the right information at the right time can make the business more profitable. Teleselling may be appropriate in some cases. But funds are not inexhaustible and finance departments require expenditure to be justified and are unsympathetic to price increases above the rate of inflation.

The public library market for most learned journals is small worldwide, but it should not be ignored. Some public libraries are also major reference libraries sometimes with special collections on particular subjects. Acquisition decisions will usually be made by the library staff though they will be open to suggestions from their users.

Library budgets

It is rare for a library's serials acquisition budget to have grown fast enough to meet both the increases in prices of existing subscriptions and to allow for new journals. In the US, research expenditure (and hence research results for publication) has increased much more rapidly than library expenditure. In UK universities as a whole, expenditure on libraries dropped from 4 per cent in 1980 to less than 3 per cent of the overall budget in 1994. That has to pay for staffing, heating and lighting, preservation and cataloguing as well as acquisitions, binding and inter-library loan and non-print materials, computer systems and online services. In the shortrun the acquisition of print material may be sacrificed to keep the opening hours or to buy CD-ROM materials and equipment. Over the years, many libraries have increased the proportion of the acquisition budget devoted to serials at the expense of books. In extreme cases, almost all the acquisitions budget goes on serial publications. Many librarians feel that this policy has gone too far and are trying to get a better balance.

Budgeting problems are exacerbated by currency fluctuations. A US academic library might spend more than half its periodicals budget on serials published in Europe, while one third of the subscriptions in European libraries may be to US titles. The dollar has been known to move against a basket of European currencies by as much as 25 per cent in a year. If the price of a journal is increased by 8 per cent and the value of the importer's currency falls by 25 per cent, the journal will cost 35 per cent more than in the previous year. On the other hand, if the currency rises by 25 per cent, the journal could cost about 18 per cent less. A rise in the value of local currency may allow a library to acquire new titles (provided they expect to be able to keep the subscription going for some years), to reinstate cancellations or to buy back issues; a fall may lead to hasty cancellations.

In the past, many libraries decided on subscriptions for the following year before they knew what the price would be, let alone the rate of exchange. That is unsatisfactory and librarians continue to urge publishers and agents to get price information to them in the early summer of the previous year. Larger subscription agents put out early overall forecasts, based on discussions with publishers and estimates of currency movements; these are helpful for planning, but even central banks and ministries of finance are unable to predict (let alone control) currency movements.

Strategies for reducing acquisition costs include reducing all multiple subscriptions to single copies, cutting back on the number of suppliers and negotiating lower service charges (see section on subscription agents below), buying round (from the country of origin) if that is cheaper, and greater reliance on document delivery. Journals with high subscription prices (perhaps US $250 or more) are looked at carefully. Libraries may also explore possibilities of getting journals at members' rates. Some societies welcome institutional members and are happy to provide them with publications at very reduced rates, but a publisher is placed in a false position if any library can join and then get the journal at a lower price. One solution is to make the cost of institutional membership higher than the cost of buying the publications as a non-member.

Cancellations have caused anxiety among publishers, but journal survival rates are still quite high and publishers are still starting new journals, though at a lower rate than a few years ago. Some observers suggest that the number of journals being published is now fairly constant. There have been attempts to correlate cancellation of subscriptions with the growth of document delivery, but most studies suggest that while document delivery has made librarians less unhappy about the effects of cancelling, it may not have had much effect on the cancellation rate. Still the most common reason for cancelling a journal is relative lack of interest or lack of use by library users.

Individuals

There are two main types of individual subscription. Many journals are published in association with societies whose members are entitled to the journal without further payment (some societies have charters which lay this down), or at reduced rates. Some journals are directed to an individual readership (Elsevier's *Trends in* . . . for instance) and others sell anything from a few copies to a few hundred subscriptions to individuals. A large number of individual subscribers can make it easier to sell advertising space (see chapter 6).

If the journal is a relatively modest publication, individual subscriptions do not present great problems, but there may be a conflict of interest for very large journals. Only a small proportion of any issue is likely to be of interest to any individual; the rest, for that reader, is wastepaper, yet it has to be paid for somehow. The marginal cost (see chapter 8), or even the cost of paper and postage, may be more than many individuals particularly students or retired people feel able to pay.

If a member does not want a journal for his own use, but gets it anyway, it is tempting to let copies filter through to the library, especially if that enables the library to buy another journal which the member wants. In any case, knowing that the journal is available in the institution may make the librarian less worried about cancelling the subscription.

One approach is to make the journal an optional extra, so that those members who want it pay a supplementary charge, not less than the marginal cost of their copies. A disadvantage is that the journal is no longer the society's notice-board and a newsletter may be needed to keep members informed of society activities. Another possibility is to split the journal into two or more smaller and more specialised ones, or divide it into sections, with members getting only one automatically. But that has implications for the editor and editorial policy, the development of the journal, library subscriptions and handling costs.

Many journals offer reduced rates for individuals other than members of a sponsoring society. The marketing argument for them is that individuals are only interested in a part of the journal and would not find a full-rate subscription worthwhile. The financial considerations are discussed in chapter 8. In practice, individual non-member subscribers are fairly rare for most specialist primary research journals in science and technology (often around 1 per cent of the subscription list), but more common for journals in the humanities, social sciences and clinical medicine. They are relatively more common in the US than elsewhere, reflecting the relative prosperity of the market and tax allowances and research grants which include funds for the purchase of publications.

New journals are a special case. Sometimes they attract more individual than institutional subscriptions in their early years. That may be because individuals want to see the journals, but know it will be some years before their library will find the funds to subscribe. Once the library subscribes, the personal subscription lapses. That is an argument against the practice adopted by some publishers, at least in principle, of only accepting subscriptions at the individuals' rate from those whose library also subscribes.

Offers to individuals may be without restriction or confined to certain groups, such as teachers or students or members of societies which may not have any formal connection with the journal. The society provides the publisher with a mailing list; its members benefit from the lower

prices. Some societies in the USA have a large number of such arrangements, circulating coupons to their members to be returned direct to
the publisher with payment. Most societies welcome this kind of
collaboration. Publishers are naturally anxious that copies supplied to
individuals at less than the full price should not go into libraries. They
may ask for signed statements that the copy is for personal use, and will
not go into a library, at least for a certain number of years and may
demand payment by personal cheque or credit card. Some societies overprint 'Members Copy' on the front cover and have been known to expel
members for passing on copies to a library.

Bulk purchase

Bulk purchase applies most commonly to medical journals which may be
bought by pharmaceutical firms to present to practitioners. It is not
necessary for the content to be accessible to the practitioner. In some
cases it is not; the object is to persuade the recipient that the presenter is
associated with the highest level of research on the subject. The journal
must look attractive and be in a field in which the firm currently markets
products or plans to do so in the future. Sometimes while a whole
subscription cannot be sold, a firm may want a large number of offprints
of an article. Alternatively they may be prepared to sponsor a supplement.
(See chapter 6.)

How journals are bought: the role of the subscription agent

A typical periodicals library might have between 300 and 20,000 subscriptions. The journal publishing business is widespread geographically, with
the largest concentration in the USA, the UK, West Germany and the
Netherlands. It is estimated that there are about 50,000 to 60,000 current
journal publishers worldwide, and a large subscription agent might deal
with 15,000 to 20,000 of them. Even a modest library might take journals
coming from several hundred publishers in twenty-five or more
countries. They may also be buying newspapers and magazines. It takes
time to track down the publishers, to deal with different currencies and a
multitude of invoices, or learn the differences in trade practices between

publishers. Libraries therefore generally order through subscription agents, who handle perhaps 80 per cent of subscriptions for libraries in the USA, and between 70 per cent and 99 per cent in other countries.

In some countries currency controls and import licences make it virtually impossible for anyone other than a state-buying organisation or the holder of an import licence to buy from abroad. Publishers must therefore expect to deal with subscription agents whether or not they give a discount; this point has not always been appreciated by learned societies particularly in the USA.

The largest subscription agents are in the USA, UK, the Netherlands and Japan. Most of these have offices in many countries dealing with both local publishers and library customers. A library may put all its business into the hands of one or two agents, or may use a number. Some use only agents in their own country, but many use overseas suppliers for at least some of their journal subscriptions, sometimes preferring an agent based in the country of origin of the publications.

The subscription agent collects and collates information on existing journals, particularly changes of price, title, frequency and publisher, and on new journals. This is passed on to clients in hard-copy or electronically; the information can be tailor-made for particular customers and their specific interests. Agents will search for information on particular titles. Some produce comprehensive catalogues of journals with current prices for library use. They can invoice their clients in a variety of ways, for instance alphabetically by title or publisher, by order number or ISSN, according to the department for which the journal is taken or the fund from which the payments will be made.

Subscription agents may agree appropriate invoice dates with their customers depending on when the library receives its funds. Interest can be earned on any balance in the library's account. At times of high interest rates this can stretch the library budget significantly.

Most publishers hold that the agent is serving the library and any funds the library pays to the agent belong to the library until paid over to the publisher. After all, the publisher has no choice in the selection of the agent, unless they have granted an exclusive right to sell the journal in a particular territory. On the other hand, the publisher may feel a moral duty to supply journals if the agent goes out of business.

The agent collates orders by publisher, and sends payments in the appropriate currency. The agent informs the publisher of changes of address, and acts as a buffer for claims and queries. Because agents know something of both publishers' and libraries' procedures they can help to avoid misunderstandings. Collating orders reduces paperwork; collating payments cuts down the cost of currency conversion.

Usually the publisher despatches the journal direct to subscribers and the agent never sees it. Some agents offer a consolidation service (and find this area of business is growing fast): journals are sent to the agent who checks their receipt and forwards them (by air if the library is in another country) with any necessary documentation. The receiving library does not have to bother with checking in or claiming for missing issues. A disadvantage is that the publisher may not know who the subscriber is unless he insists on having that information. Naturally, where publishers have different prices for different markets, agents want to pay the lowest possible price.

New technology is helping communication between agents, libraries and publishers. Some agents supply their customers with machine-readable invoices and other information to help with library management: for instance, serials by subject classification; serials costing more than a certain sum; subscriptions started in the last few years; price increase for recent years, and so on. Some offer major customers online access to their database which speeds up the processing of orders, invoices, claims and queries. The agent may send orders to the publisher electronically.

The agent is paid for his service by a discount from the publisher, or by a service charge to the library, or, most often, by a combination of the two. In recent years, some publishers have reduced their discounts, or stopped them altogether (see also chapter 8). The agent continues to service library orders, but will add a surcharge to the invoice sent to the library. For a fuller account of the role of subscription agents, see Cox (1991).

It will be obvious that publishers should make sure that subscription agents are kept informed of the journals they publish or will start soon, including the ISSN, prices, delays in publication, and changes of title, frequency or anything else that affects the handling of orders. If the subscription agent does not know where to send an order, or cannot give his customers information about the price, orders will be lost or delayed.

As noted above, many individuals subscribe by virtue of society membership. For the rest, a number of publishers are only prepared to accept individual subscriptions which come direct from the subscriber, so subscription agents play virtually no role here. In any case, subscription agents are not geared to supplying a single subscription to a single journal; some are reluctant to handle clients subscribing to fewer than say 25, or 200, journals. The costs of converting currency are a problem with individual subscriptions from customers in other countries; credit cards, UNESCO coupons and the international giro system can help.

Promoting journals

The principles of journal promotion are simple and the same as for any other product or service: to get the right message to the right people in a compelling way. For journals, the essential questions are: Who is this journal for? What special features does it offer its readers and what benefits might they expect from it? What is the best way (and best time) to reach potential readers and subscribers? How can the message best be presented to them?

The major component of any publicity campaign for a journal is usually direct mail; that offers the best chance of getting information into the hands of potential readers and decision makers. It may be backed up by advertising. Established journals get promotion from listings in the secondary services and from citations in other publications and they may have exchange advertising arrangements. Journals should also promote themselves – and can be promoted with and by the publisher's other books and journals.

Newly launched journals may distribute specimen copies unsolicited or run a pilot issue. If the launch coincides with a major conference on the subject it may be worth exhibiting there and either advertising or getting leaflets into the folders for participants. Review copies should be sent out for new journals and press releases may be useful for both new journals and from existing ones. National bibliographies may list the first issue of a serial title. We discuss all these means of promotion below.

What information do potential subscribers need?

Before anyone buys a journal they want to be sure that they are spending their money wisely. Here is a checklist of items for inclusion in journal promotion. A leaflet or leaflet and covering letter can include them all; for advertisements the publisher will have to be more selective.

Title, and subtitle (if any)

This should be clear and descriptive. 'Biochemistry Letters' or 'Population Studies' indicate the content; 'Transactions of the National Academy' does not. (See also chapter 9.)

Special features

Why should the recipient of the leaflet subscribe to or read this journal? What is different about it? Why is it worth noticing? What does the journal offer that its competitors do not? How will the subscriber benefit from it?

Scope and contents

This should make it clear what the journal covers, its approach to the subject, the sort of material it publishes and the languages used, unless that is obvious. For what readership is the journal intended? The reasons for starting a new journal should be explained. If the journal is established, the publisher should emphasise new features that could encourage those who have managed without it for many years to take another look.

The editor and editorial board

The list should include the affiliations of both the editor and the editorial board members to give an idea of the status of the journal. If the editor is in a widely respected institution, and the board includes people known to be sound, drawn from different institutions, it suggests that the general standard may be high. But this is not necessarily convincing unless supported by other evidence, for some editorial boards are no more than window-dressing.

Contents list

This should give authors and titles to indicate the type of material the journal will publish. With a new journal, the list may be tentative or provisional. Forthcoming articles generate more interest than those already published and 'recent articles' should be recent.

Coverage by abstracting and indexing services

If a journal is covered by the major secondary services (see below) in its field, that suggests that it is reputable – and that there could be a demand for papers from it.

Price and frequency

Subscribers need to know the cost and what they will get for their money. Does the price include postage, indexes and so on? What format is the journal? How many pages will there be per issue? When can a subscription start: at any time, at the beginning of any year, or from the beginning of any volume? Are subscriptions accepted for more than one year at a time?

Bibliographical details

Should include publisher and publisher's address, International Standard Serial Number (see chapter 9), current volume number and year of publication, or when the first volume will be published.

Order information

The address to which orders should be sent; to whom payment should be made; the currencies and methods of payment that are acceptable; any credit cards which can be used.

Special offers

These should be writ large, but always include an expiry date.

Back volumes

For existing journals give information on the availability of back volumes. This is particularly welcome in rapidly developing markets in South East Asia where libraries are building up their collections.

Order forms

It is customary to include an order/response form, though few are actually used to order a subscription. The form usually allows the respondent to request a specimen copy: sometimes the best measure of the effectiveness of a campaign is the specimen copy requests that come back. Information which appears on the form should also be printed elsewhere on the leaflet. The return address may be that of the distributor if the publisher does not do their own distribution, but most publishers want the response to come back to them.

Promotion plans

It is easier to create interest in a new journal than in one which is already established. None the less publishers have to promote older journals, partly to balance cancelled subscriptions and partly because the market for any journal changes. A library that has managed without a particular title for all the years of its existence will want good reasons to start a subscription. Changes – of editor, editorial policy, scope and content or publisher – should be highlighted, without making the journal appear so different that existing subscribers will be prompted to cancel.

It is good practice to draw up a costed promotion plan for each journal for each year. Ideally it should be based on discussions with editors and sponsors and they should certainly be asked to agree to it. Without a programme, some things that should be done may be overlooked, while co-ordinated plans may show up opportunities, for instance for promoting several titles together.

The plan should set out in detail what needs to be done when and what it will cost – and the return that is needed to cover those costs. It is a useful exercise to calculate the cost of getting each new subscriber. That figure is often astonishingly high: the cost of promoting low-price journals with a limited circulation can seem prohibitive. There is also a problem with multi-disciplinary journals which may require very large mailings in order to reach all potential readers.

Once the promotion plan is agreed it becomes an action document; it should be monitored regularly to check that everything is in hand and that the costs were as forecast. But it is not cast in stone; it may be necessary to amend it in the light of experience. Other possibilities may emerge, or test mailings may show one list producing a very poor response and another a much better one.

Publicity budgets

The publicity budget for a journal generally covers the direct cost of publicity, including postage, production, materials, mailing lists, specimen copies (at run-on cost), advertising space and exhibition fees. The cost of running a publicity department and any associated overheads is not usually costed in at this stage.

Most of the budget will probably go on direct mail (see below). This is not cheap. Postage and rental charges for lists are usually lower in the USA than in Western Europe; sometimes they are less than half. A rule of thumb for estimating direct costs (production, lists, postage, envelopes) is to double the postage costs – slightly less if the lists are held in-house, and a little more if they are bought in. It is usually more cost-effective to pay a higher price for a selective up-to-date list, than to use a larger less expensive list with a lot of wastage. Savings can be made by using co-operative mailings, or by combining the mailings for several publications, though that may reduce the response rate.

For an established journal expenditure on promotion will usually be only a small proportion of sales, particularly if the journal is high priced. 1 or 2 per cent of the income may be enough in most years. For new journals, expenditure is much higher. A commercial publisher looking for 500 subscribers after three to five years and assuming a response rate of around 1 per cent, might allow for about 50,000 mailing pieces to be sent out over this period at a total cost of around £20,000 to £30,000 (US $30,000 to $45,000). Expenditure on pre-launch publicity is unlikely to be less than £5000 (US $7500) and is often at least double that, with similar sums being spent in each of the first two or three years. A learned society might hope that part of the work would be done by members of the society, at least in the domestic market. Some publishers spend less on publicity, but allow longer for the journal to reach its full potential market.

Promotion for a single title can be expensive. It helps if several titles, books and journals, perhaps, can be promoted together, and if a single printing of a leaflet can be used for several markets.

Direct mail

The market for a learned journal is, as we have seen, relatively small and widely scattered geographically; purchasing decisions are often made by committee and on the basis of factual information; at the same time, most journals have quite low prices, compared with those of cars or computers. The market is therefore not reached effectively by national advertising campaigns, publishers' representatives or telephone selling. Direct mail is the most-used form of promotion for journals. The publisher produces a leaflet (brochure/flyer/mailing piece) giving the information listed in the previous section and sends it to those who might subscribe themselves, or who can influence a library decision. The same leaflet is likely to be sent out with the call for papers for a new journal (see chapter 2) and by the editor with letters to potential contributors.

The most important thing about the leaflet is that it should be clear and give the necessary information. Factual description of the journal, its content and aims, and lists of editors and editorial board members are more persuasive than any publisher's puff; extravagant claims may be counterproductive. Much journal publicity is, however, very boring, and does little to persuade the reader that access to the journal would be beneficial to him. The copywriter's and designer's skills lie in setting out the basic data about the journal in an interesting and attractive way without advertising 'hype'.

The design and typography should be agreeable and legible. Cramming in too much copy for the space makes for unreadability. Coated or coloured papers may look pretty, but print on them can be more difficult to read. Elaborate or idiosyncratic typography or layout may deter librarians rather than encourage them. They receive enormous amounts of mail every day and resent having to search for basic information. Commonly, leaflets are based on a quarto or A4 sheet of paper printed on both sides, and folded once to give four pages or twice to make six. In the USA, leaflets can be designed as 'self-mailers' with the address label simply affixed to the leaflet; postal authorities in most other countries require an envelope round the leaflet.

Some publishers have envelopes specially printed for promotion campaigns making it clear to the recipient that the contents are trying to sell them something. Questions that might be asked about this practice are will the intended recipients open their own mail (if not, they will never see the envelope) and will the overprinting of the envelope make it more or less likely that they will remove the contents before putting the envelope in the waste bin?

For economy, a single leaflet may be produced for several different markets, although there may be more than one group interested in the subject matter. Very often leaflets are accompanied by a letter: provided it is not too long, that usually generates a higher response rate. (Typing errors in the letters are reported to produce a better response – but do not help the publisher's reputation.) Letters can be tailor-made for different groups of recipients, drawing attention to the aspects of the journal of greatest interest to each group. For instance, a letter to academics in a particular area of the subject would emphasise the interest of the journal in that area, but might suggest that they encourage their libraries to subscribe (and enclose a card which can be sent to the library with their recommendation) and also offer them special reduced rates as individuals. It might solicit contributions.

Special offers can increase the response rate. Examples include reduced subscription rates (to 'founder' or 'charter' subscribers ordering in the first year of publication, or if the order is placed within a certain time);

special rates for two or three-year subscriptions; back volumes at cheap rates for new subscribers; second subscriptions at reduced prices. Some publishers offer recent books on the same subject as the journal to new subscribers; they may do so on condition that the subscriber pays for two years or more at the time. This seems to be particularly effective in persuading individuals to subscribe to journals in the humanities and social sciences. The books must be seen to be desirable; it is not a way of disposing of otherwise unsaleable stock.

Librarians express distaste for special offers that bear no relation to the journal. They suspect that the 'free' mugs or other offers are not really 'free' and that they pay for them in the subscription price.

Special offers should have always have a closing date (advertisers have been embarrassed to find people claiming on them ten or twenty years later). The deadline is also there to encourage a speedy response – but should allow enough time for the offer to reach everyone to whom it is being mailed.

Direct mail campaigns should not only sell journals but should also test ideas about selling them. Which of two lists works better? To what extent does a covering letter increase the response rate? Is one kind of letter more effective than another? Does including a reply-paid envelope or specimen copy request card increase the response rate? It is usually possible to test only one thing at a time.

Mailing lists

Most publishers send direct mail promotion to potential readers and contributors and to their libraries. Some libraries claim to be good at passing on mailing pieces to their advisers or library committee members, particularly if they receive more than one copy of the mailing; others keep them in the library. In some libraries the subject specialists play a significant role in the selection of materials and one cannot rely on library users to feed them with information. There is often a high staff turnover so librarians should be addressed by title rather than by name. Subscription agents need information, too. Some also pass on leaflets to their customers, though if they have large mailing lists they may charge a fee for distributing them.

Mailing lists can be built-up in-house or acquired from other sources. Outside sources usually 'rent' rather than sell their lists: they are supplied for one-time use and should not be re-used or incorporated into the publishers' own mailing lists without permission. Many lists contain 'seed addresses' which allow the list supplier to check how they are being used. List owners commonly ask to see a specimen of the material to be mailed.

It is usually possible to test a large list before buying it all. The publisher is supplied with a certain proportion of the addresses (usually not more than 50 per cent and not fewer than 10 per cent); if the mailing is successful, they can then rent the rest of the list. The response rate may be difficult to measure, particularly in the short term, since orders often take some time to mature and only those from individuals are likely to be on the publisher's order form. Requests for specimen copies are sometimes the only guide.

Most publishers at some stage buy in lists from specialist suppliers and brokers. Lists of academics and academic libraries in the USA and Canada are available from Educational Directory or College Marketing Group; the Direct Marketing Market Place (National Register Publishing, New Providence, New Jersey) gives many other sources of US lists of interest to specialist publishers. A-Mail is a useful source of UK academic and library lists. For the rest of the world, IBIS (UK-based and now owned by Mardev) probably offers the largest range of academic lists and conference participants and will seek out lists for publishers. Information on other specialist list brokers and vendors in the UK can be obtained from The Direct Mail Producers Association.

Lists of society members or participants at conferences can often be rented, either from the society or from a broker. Other journals may be prepared to rent their subscription lists, or exchange them for the list of another journal. There are snags: journals are often addressed to a processing department rather than to an acquisitions librarian or subject specialist, and increasing numbers of copies go via an agent rather than direct to the subscriber; the list will also include exchanges, legal deposit libraries and so on. A little intelligent screening can reduce wastage.

An alternative way of reaching the subscribers to another journal is to have leaflets inserted in it; that saves addressing and mailing costs. However, it is not a reliable way of getting information to libraries, for library staff are trained not to open journals, and may simply shake them over the wastepaper basket. Individuals are more likely to notice an insert in the journal, but a mention in a newsletter or bulletin may be more effective. Leaflets inserted in catalogues may or may not reach the right people. Journal catalogues are likely to be retained by a serials librarian rather than circulated.

Some publishers make their lists of book buyers available through mailing list brokers. These can be helpful in selling journals provided the lists are up-to-date and the subject classification right. Many printed directories can provide labels for the addresses they contain; it is often possible to select by category rather than having to use the whole list.

In-house lists are economic if the list will be used frequently and can be kept up-to-date; they are particularly useful if based on known buyers of other publications. Assembling lists may be slow; reference books and directories will be out-of-date by the time they are published. Some publishers of directories object to outsiders culling them for mailing lists, even for their own consumption, claiming breach of copyright; the grounds for this complaint are uncertain, but would be stronger if the list was sold on to a third party.

Many publishers have their own lists of subscription agents. Most publishers will be dealing with the major agents, but there are many smaller ones handling only a few subscriptions, or who deal with a restricted range of subjects.

Few mailing lists are perfect. If the publisher buys labels, a little time spent going through them can save money. It may be possible to cut out existing subscribers and legal deposit libraries, and to modify some addresses. If a journal subscription list is being used, the publisher may want to change the library addresses to start with the words 'serials acquisition librarian (subject)' or 'periodicals librarian', so that the leaflet is not treated as an incoming journal. Sometimes duplicates can be removed. Many lists have faulty data in them which can be corrected. There are even addresses which appear to have strayed from the wrong lists. Lists may include some institutions unlikely to subscribe to very specialist journals. Do not remove labels for editorial board members or others associated with the journal. If you do they will believe that the publisher does nothing to promote the journal.

Response rates

Response rates for journal mailings are difficult to establish, particularly outside the US. It is rare for direct mail to be the only promotion for a journal. The order may be very slow in coming (some libraries estimate that it may take up to three years for them to find the necessary funding), and orders are rarely written on the publisher's order form, unless that is a condition of a special offer. Even if the publisher puts a special code into the return address it probably will not be shown on an order coming through a subscription agent. For new journals figures of 1.5 to 3 per cent are sometimes quoted, though, on occasion, publishers have claimed rates of 5 per cent or more. For established journals it is likely to be much less. In doing costings, it would be optimistic to assume a maximum return of more than 2 per cent; 1 per cent or less might be nearer the mark. Indeed there are instances of publishers sending out several thousand leaflets and getting only ten or twenty subscriptions as a result.

It is even harder to judge response rates for established journals than for new ones. One difficulty is in distinguishing genuine cancellations from apparent ones. Some letters of cancellation are of subscriptions to be ordered in future through a different channel; the library does not want duplicate subscriptions – one through the old route and one through the new. Many who are really cancelling simply do not renew. An order with a slight change of address, a late renewal, may be treated as a new subscription, and a change of subscription agent will also affect the subscriber status. In one study, about 50 per cent of the cancellations which a sample of US publishers reported from US libraries turned out not to be cancellations at all (White, 1979). On an international scale, with addresses in many languages, the problem is much greater. A publisher may believe that he has had 100 cancellations in one year, which have been made up by 100 new subscribers; but he might have had only 40 cancellations and 40 new subscribers, and perhaps only a handful of these new subscriptions were generated by his promotion.

From the figures above it is clear that there is an enormous amount of wastage with direct mail. That can be reduced by better mailing shots and monitoring results to see what is effective. Much of the wastage is because mailings are sent to those who have no interest in the publication or who already subscribe to it. Cuts in library budgets have forced librarians to manage their acquisitions more actively; publishers are responding by putting out more promotion. The costs of wasted mailings have therefore become greater, both as an absolute sum and a percentage of total costs. Mailing lists should be tailored as closely as possible to the particular journal or group of titles being promoted and broadcast mailings which end up in the wastepaper basket avoided.

Sample/specimen copies and pilot issues

The most common response to a mailing is a request for a sample copy; few libraries will take out a subscription without seeing a specimen first. Specimen copy requests may come from individuals who want a copy in order to persuade their library to subscribe. Unless the request seems absurd or frivolous, or a copy has recently been sent to the same institution, it is customary to supply one, usually with more publicity material. Since incoming mail in a library may be opened centrally and the packaging discarded, it is advisable to stick a label to the cover with the name of the recipient; some libraries have shelves of journals for which no home has been found. The label should note that this is a sample copy sent on request.

The publisher should also note who has taken specimen copies from displays at meetings and whether they or their library (with contact name and address) might place an order. If no order follows from the specimen, then it should be followed up. With individuals, that can be a week or so afterwards, for they do not have to take it to a committee, wait for a new budgetary year, or order through an agent. With libraries it is sensible to wait a couple of months before following up. Some publishers estimate that between 10 per cent and 20 per cent of specimen copy requests turn into subscriptions. Telephone calls, if feasible, produce the most helpful responses: the caller may be able to find out the selection committee's reaction to the issue and that can provide useful feedback editorially. It may be that the library has decided to order – when funds are available. If telephone calls are not possible, a personalised follow-up letter should be sent. e-mail might also be used.

Since libraries want sample copies before taking out a subscription, the publisher may decide to send copies of new journals unsolicited to the core market. If a journal has been split off an existing journal, that might extend to sending the complete first volume or first year to subscribers to the parent journal without charge. If a new journal has no such parent, but is well funded, it may be possible to identify the key market and offer them the first year without charge. The object of either of these approaches is to gain more paid subscribers in the second year than would otherwise be possible.

An alternative approach is the pilot issue sent out free to a large mailing list with encouragement to subscribe. The publisher might decide to issue this around September (when libraries are making up their budgets for the next year) and to publish the second issue early the next year. The pilot issue should be featured as volume 1 no. 1; otherwise there is no proper bibliographical reference for the papers it contains. The editor will naturally want to include the best selection of papers that he can, and advertisers may be offered very special rates for this issue. However, librarians are conscious that journals do not always live up to their early promise and may want to see several issues published before taking out a subscription.

Other means of promotion

The journal itself

Every journal issue should help to sell the journal. An attractive cover and a clear list of contents will help. Information about its objects and editorial policy, price and frequency and how to subscribe should be clearly presented. The different types of content (if there is more than one) should be explained. Future attractions may be listed. What secondary services (see below) cover the journal? Who are the editor and the editorial board? Give their affiliations – not just name and country of the city where they work. Is the paper permanent?

Some journals, especially those which attract individual subscribers, find it useful to include cards for potential subscribers to complete and return for a specimen copy, more information or to take out a subscription; and also cards that can be used to recommend the journal to a library.

e-mail and the Internet

While academic networks are not intended for commercial purposes, editors are free to put information on the journal they are starting on a network or bulletin board. The response in terms of requests for specimens can be both fast and impressive, though in some cases the conversion rate to subscriptions has been low.

Increasingly publishers are establishing a presence on the World-Wide Web although this type of promotion is still in its infancy. The physical maintenance, capital expenses, staff training, content and design, and features needed for an effective home page must be seriously considered. Revenues generated may not cover costs yet but within a year or two the WWW could be an important means of promotion. Publishers will be aiming to build up electronic mailing lists by asking those that access their home pages to give details of how to contact them.

The Web site should be registered with the Internet 'Yellow Pages' and advertisements for it placed in all the standard promotional material. Links should be established with related sites, such as the home pages of a society associated with the journal. The role of the Web site should be thought about carefully. It can act as an online catalogue, provide general promotion for the publisher, be used as a discussion forum for the publisher's editors, authors and customers, and more specifically to promote each journal. All the standard information on a journal, such as is presented on a leaflet, should be set up for online searching but structured for the medium; individual packets of information should be small and linked in an easy way to follow with opportunities for users to interact with the site (by e-mail or by downloading information or demonstrations). There might also be information, for example, on how to submit manuscripts electronically and what papers will be published. More sophisticated systems might include the facility to order these papers.

It has been said that a 'rule of four' applies to web sites: a web site should be improved/updated in less time than it takes the average browser to access the site four times. If a browser sees no change, they will lose interest in visiting the site. Smaller publishers might find it more economical to use a third party provider rather than set up their own server. Once sufficient volume of usage has been built up the publisher can then take over with their own server.

In addition to a full review of technical issues when considering a web site, publishers should think carefully about the choice of domain name and the setting up of efficient systems to handle the information delivered to the publisher from the Web. Customers, e.g. libraries, may prefer to deal with an intermediary such as a subscription agent to enable them to browse through a range of products and to simplify ordering and payment. In this case publishers should ensure that the intermediaries are regularly updated, ideally electronically, with information about their journals.

Periodicals directories

Ulrich's International Periodicals Directory (Bowker-Saur) is the principal listing of serials and is the place that many libraries turn to first for serials information. It is available in print, on CD-ROM, online, and in micro-form and tape versions. Publishers should ensure that all their serial titles are listed; otherwise potential customers may be unable to trace the publications.

The Allen Press produces a catalogue each year of scholarly and scientific journals which goes to libraries and subscription agents throughout the world; they also circulate price information in advance of the catalogue. This may be useful for publishers with only a few journals. Publishers (whether or not they use other Allen Press services) can buy a page for basic information about each of their journals; the journals are in alphabetical order, but there are subject indexes. There are also sub-sections put out separately: in health sciences for instance. The 1995 catalogue includes 470 journals from around 300 publishers, many of them learned societies.

Many of the larger subscription agents also put out serials catalogues or make their database available to their customers. Most take advertising from publishers.

Publishers' catalogues

Publishers with a number of journals usually produce an annual catalogue or list with information on all their serials. This is primarily for librarians and subscription agents. If this is arranged so that each journal occupies one page, quick and simple leaflets can be produced by running off the appropriate page with an order form on the back. That can be useful for exhibitions, and for dealing with enquiries. Journals should be included in complete catalogues of publications, and if the publisher produces seasonal lists, new journals can be included in those; however, they are unlikely to reach serials librarians. Another useful sales aid is the subject catalogue, listing journals as well as books. Similarly, journals can be included in direct mail promotion for books on the same subject.

Other publications

Publishers with several titles can use them to sell each other. If the publisher has several journals in the same field they can be listed in a prominent position on each journal, perhaps on the cover. Many journals are sent out with a large sheet of paper giving the subscriber's address; some publishers print a simple request form for information on their other titles on the reverse. And they can always exchange advertisements (see below).

Advertising

Advertisements for journals may be paid for or exchanged. With exchange advertising, Journal A is advertised in Journal B, and vice versa. While no money changes hands, there is the cost of producing camera-ready copy and printing the advertisement. An extra page could push an issue over an even working (see production chapter) or put up the mailing costs. Sometimes arrangements are flexible enough to allow for that, but publishers should check that the advertisements for their journals are actually being published; that is commonly done by sending 'tear sheets' or voucher copies of the issues with the advertisement.

New journals can offer little in the way of circulation for an exchange and so may have to buy advertising space. Advertising is more likely to be seen if it is in a major journal that carries material other than simply original papers, particularly if it is in a publications section or a special issue on new journals (cf. *Nature*). Newsletters, bulletins and 'trends' journals are more likely to be scanned than a conventional learned journal, so the chances of an advertisement being seen there are much higher. If a journal is being launched at a major conference, the publisher might advertise in the programme. Advertisements in subscription agents' catalogues have brought worthwhile responses for some publishers; others have been disappointed with the results. Most of these catalogues are used for reference purposes only so advertising may not be noticed. With journals publishing only original research, readers usually turn direct to the items that interest them and miss the advertisements.

The publisher might also considering advertising journals in the appropriate *Current Contents* (see below); this enjoys a wide specialist readership seeking out publications of interest. This may help to win citations later on.

Conferences and exhibitions

Exhibitions at specialist meetings can be helpful, particularly in launching or relaunching a journal, but they can also be expensive. They are most significant in North America, where meetings usually attract more participants than elsewhere. They provide an opportunity for a large number of people with an active interest in the subject to see and handle copies of the journal, which can be far more convincing than any number of mailing pieces. It can also help to bring in contributions and fellow exhibitors may also be interested in advertising in the journal.

The costs of exhibiting are high. In addition to any fees charged by the organisers, there are freight and travelling costs and the cost of staff time. For established journals, exhibitions may be more highly regarded as a way of selling by academics (including editors and editorial board members) than by publishers. There are occasions when a publisher exhibits journals for political reasons, rather than because of any anticipated increase in sales. *Acta Endocrinologia* needed twenty-six new subscriptions to break even with a promotional campaign at an international conference; they actually got two (Krog and Binder, 1990).

A publisher may not be able to afford an individual stand (booth), but at most major meetings there is a co-operative stand run by a bookseller, subscription agent, or specialist exhibitions service. Another type of exhibition is the co-operative touring one put on by a single firm visiting a number of university centres, which some publishers have found successful. Publishers can also arrange to have exhibitions of their own publications in bookshops or libraries; these are generally more effective at selling books than journals. Little attention is paid to journals at most national or international book fairs.

Media coverage

Sometimes the editor or publisher may feel that an article, particularly on medical or public health issues, is of sufficient general interest to draw the attention of the media (newspapers, magazines, radio, television) to it. These work on very different time scales: magazines are put together long before the publication date, but the lead time on newspapers is only a few hours. Press releases should make it clear in lay terms what is noteworthy about the article, provide a short and comprehensible summary and give the name of the person who can provide further information and should be sent out in time for the media to respond. There should normally be an embargo on publishing so that the layman does not have information before subscribers get their copies. This is important for clinical journals; a doctor cannot be expected to advise a patient on the basis of an item in the media. The penalty for breaking an embargo is a cutting off of information in future. (Kassirer and Angell, 1994).

Telemarketing

Selling by telephone (telemarketing) is not greatly used to promote new subscriptions to academic journals, though it can draw attention to special offers and new products. Perhaps the most common use in learned journal publishing is to follow-up non-renewed subscriptions. It is most developed in the US where there is a large and prosperous market with a common language.

Subscription agents

Subscription agents include information on new journals in the bulletins they send to clients. Publishers should check what promotional material subscription agents want and in what quantities. In some countries (Taiwan for instance) the agents visit their customers regularly and are happy to have publicity material to give to them. Other agents may be prepared to do a mailing, perhaps for a fee. An agent in Japan might produce a Japanese version of the publisher's leaflet for his clients. Swets offer a number of mailing lists to publishers. For catalogues from subscription agents, see above.

Review copies

With a new journal, review copies should be sent to appropriate journals, with a review slip giving basic information about the journal, including publisher, price, and date of publication of the first issue. It is wise to check that the journal does publish reviews; *Ulrich's Periodicals Directory* gives this information. The same journals might be approached when the first volume is complete to ask if they would like it for review. Extracts from reviews can of course be used in promotion.

Offprints

Some publishers regard authors' offprints as a promotional tool as well as a service to the author. Those that do are likely to give them covers which promote the journal and to have relatively high free allowances and rather modest charges for extra copies. They argue that the more copies that are circulated of an article, the more likely it is to be cited. The more citations, the higher the 'impact factor' (see above).

Secondary services: Abstracting and Indexing (A&I)

A common preliminary stage in a research project is a literature search. Ploughing through all the journals that might have published papers on any given topic is a very tedious and time-consuming business. Abstracting and indexing services exist to help readers discover what has been published on a given topic or by a given author. They also give rise to document delivery requests.

An abstracting service scans a large number of periodicals (and sometimes conference proceedings) in its chosen field and selects those thought worthy of inclusion in their listings. They may use the author's abstract if that is clear and reflects their interests; if it is not suitable, they will prepare their own. Occasionally an outside expert may be used to write a critical abstract, perhaps comparing the paper with other published work. The edited abstracts are classified by subject and published in a variety of forms. Most are available in hard-copy (print on paper) but many are also available online, on floppy disk and on CD-ROM.

The original publisher cannot determine which papers from which journals will be abstracted. If clear and informative abstracts that can be used by the abstracting service are printed at the start of each paper, the abstract can appear earlier than if one has to be specially prepared. Journals going to abstracting services overseas should be sent by air, even if the bulk mailing does not. If a journal does not appear to be covered by an appropriate secondary service, the publisher should write to suggest it, sending some specimen copies and publicity material.

Current Contents is a much used guide to current literature, and seen by many individuals in print or electronic versions. It lists the contents of the latest issues of selected journals in different subject areas. There is much competition to get into *Current Contents* and some authors are reluctant to publish in a journal that it does not cover. Usually the publishers, ISI (see also impact factor above), want evidence that a journal has been published on a regular schedule for two years before they will consider including it.

Secondary services commonly ask for free copies; it is sensible to supply them if the request is for a genuine serious indexing/abstracting journal and/or searchable database which appears to be sound, and for which the journal is appropriate. But some requests may be for a literature listing within a single institution which hopes to build up a library without paying for it.

Coverage by the secondary services is more likely to lead in the first instance to requests for individual articles, but that in turn can lead to more citations – and ultimately to subscriptions.

Overseas agents

Many journal publishers operate happily throughout the world from a single base for their journals, even though they may have offices, agents or representatives looking after their book publishing interests in other countries. Both librarians and subscription agents are used to working in this way, and it is obviously simple and economical. But a local agent should have a closer understanding of the market and how to approach it than a publisher based many thousands of miles away. A publisher with large enough sales might think of employing an agent or using an overseas office to handle or simply promote journals in some markets. The principal areas where this system operates are the USA, Japan, India and Western Europe.

Firms which act as agents for journals may be subscription agents, journal publishers or other suppliers of services; for a few it is their only business. They may be paid a fee for their services or a percentage of receipts from their territory, or some combination of both. Payments may be higher for new subscriptions than for existing ones. The level of payment will depend upon how much work the agent is expected to do and the annual turnover. For a proposition to be attractive, there should be a reasonable existing subscription income and the prospect of increasing it. That may come from a single journal, but a list of titles is more likely to be able to generate the necessary sales income. The agent might guarantee a certain minimum income for the first few years, but as the market becomes more difficult this is less common than it was.

As well as promotion, an exclusive agent can help to speed the processing of claims (for non-arrival of copies) and queries and can investigate persistent claims. They can also speed up the collection of money, and handle much of the routine paperwork for the publisher. But the real benefits from using an exclusive agent lie in increased sales of journals; this needs to be significant to cover the additional costs.

Subscription agents (unless they are themselves the exclusive agents) tend to dislike the practice. The larger subscription agents operate world-wide, and resent being asked to pay for some subscriptions to a journal in one currency to one address, and for others in another currency to another address. If the publisher charges differently for different markets, some will try to buy round. Some libraries suspect that information from a local agent will be less current and less reliable than information direct from head office.

The USA is usually the largest single market for a learned journal. Subscribers expect good service: envious outsiders sometimes describe them as 'pampered' though US librarians might not agree. Most find it easier to work in US dollars. They like to be able to call the publisher (toll free) if something is amiss, or they need information. Publicity is more effective if written in American English, rather than English English, with American design, on US legal size paper rather than the European A4. A local agent can organise more easily participation at exhibitions and specialist conferences than someone in another country: that is particularly important in the USA. Some agents have representatives calling on libraries to discuss systems, problems, new developments, acquisition budgets and so on. In passing, they can introduce journals which the library might be interested in, but does not already subscribe to. A US agent would usually also cover Canada, and possibly Mexico and the other Latin-American countries, where the US dollar is the most familiar foreign currency.

Japan is a significant market for English-language academic publishers; for many scientific publishers, it accounts for at least 10 per cent of their total sales of institutional subscriptions. There are a number of reasons why a publisher might think of using an exclusive agent in Japan. First, it has been difficult to get good mailing lists for Japan; the lists held by publishers' local offices, agents and representatives are often closely guarded, though this is changing. Secondly, librarianship is less developed in Japan than in many other countries, and library staff may not be able to cope with publicity material in languages other than Japanese. Academics have strong control over journal acquisitions and are used to representatives visiting them to introduce new publications.

The downside of this is that costs in Japan are high. The costs of these extra services (and the long credit period libraries there are used to) have been reflected in high mark-ups on the publishers' prices. Competition with agents from outside Japan has put pressure on mark-ups and hence reduced the amount of promotion, particularly visits from representatives, that can be done. There is therefore less interest in exclusivity among Japanese agents now than a few years ago. An alternative is to use a specialist organisation to market journals. These firms (e.g. Kubota Associates International or Woodbell) can work with Japanese editorial board members and may help to establish links with Japanese learned societies.

Some publishers also employ exclusive agents in India. This is mainly because of the distribution problems there, rather than for their marketing function. That is more fully discussed in the next chapter. North American publishers in particular sometimes look for exclusive agents in Europe, but Europe is a well-developed but diverse market with long established relations between subscribers and subscription agents; customers are used to receiving promotion direct from overseas publishers and handling transactions in foreign currency. An exclusive arrangement in Europe is most effective when the publisher has their own European office, but many publishers prefer to handle the European market from their home base.

No exclusive agency will work, however good the agent, if the journals have no interest for the local market, and unless the value of sales is high enough to pay for the work of the agent. Trust, patience and understanding between the contracting parties is necessary for success. Agents sometimes seem expensive, but, in appropriate cases, a good agent can increase sales and save the publisher much paperwork. A poor agent can cause many problems. All agency agreements should be for a fixed term of years, renewable if both parties are satisfied. No agent can be expected to put effort into selling journals if he is not to receive some reward for his efforts; a minimum initial period should not be less than three years, and might well be five.

The credit-worthiness of any exclusive agent is a matter of some importance. If the publisher selects the agent to be used, that makes him responsible for supplying journals to subscribers once they have paid the agent. If the agent goes bankrupt, then the loss is the publisher's, not the subscriber's.

The best source of information about exclusive agents is probably the other publishers who are using them. They are usually willing to talk fairly freely and frankly about their experiences. The questions that a publisher should satisfy himself on include:

1 Is the agent geared to this sort of journal? Does it fit well (but not conflict/compete) with their existing business?
2 How quickly will they deal with orders, claims, queries? Will they pass claims on to the publisher, or have a stock of copies to deal with them themselves?
3 When will they transfer orders, payments, etc.?
4 What are their renewal procedures? Do they send out enough reminders? Will they telephone those who have not renewed by a certain time?
5 What promotion can they be expected to do? What assistance is needed from the publishers?
6 What reports will the publisher get on the promotion that has been done; these are needed both to satisfy the publisher and to persuade the editor and editorial board that the publisher is actively trying to promote the journal.
7 What methods of communication do they have? Correspondence is slow, and time differences can make telephoning difficult. What about fax, telex and e-mail?
8 Some duplication of effort and information may be inevitable; how can this be kept to a minimum?
9 Are these the sort of people you want to do business with? Are their present customers satisfied with the service that they are getting?

Marketing and its relation to other departments

Obviously, much of the briefing for marketing will come from editors and sponsors of journals. The publisher should treat their suggestions with respect; if they are absurd (for editors are not specialists in publishing) reasons for not following them should be explained courteously. A common complaint from editors and editorial board members is that nothing was done to follow up suggestions made at meetings, even when action was agreed by everyone present.

If the publisher has representatives at editorial board meetings it is helpful if one of them understands marketing and can speak with confidence about what has been done and what is feasible and what is not. The international conference on the subject may be taking place in Australia or Japan, but sending a couple of staff to set up and run an exhibition stand there will cost thousands of pounds or dollars. *The World of Learning* lists many academics, but it is largely out of date when published, and very tedious to work through. But editors and sponsors may be able to provide names of key people, lists of society members and persuade friends in high places to do things that they would never do for a publisher.

The flow should not be one way. Journal editors and sponsoring societies are often very concerned that the publisher should support their efforts with good marketing, promotion campaigns and displays at conferences. So it is vital not only to do the promotion, but also to make sure that everyone concerned with the journal knows that it is being done.

Unless there is some flow of information from the marketing people to those responsible for editing and producing the journal, we are talking not about marketing, but about selling. Perhaps the editorial policy should be rethought, the presentation changed, or the design re-vamped. Those handling the marketing may be the promoters of changes that will strengthen the journal. At the present time, when many subscriptions are being cancelled, these changes may make the difference between survival and failure.

The criterion of effective selling is the number of orders that it generates, and the cost of getting those orders. Those doing promotion need to be aware of where the journal is currently selling; where it could sell more, and where new orders are coming from. So close liaison is needed with those handling orders. And, if special offers are being made, it is important to be sure that colleagues know about them before any response comes in.

Summary

Good marketing cannot make a bad journal successful, but a journal can fail because of poor promotion and marketing strategy. The main means of promotion is direct mail, which can be very simple, provided that it gets the right message to the right people.

5   Subscription management and distribution

Introduction

Subscription management and distribution does not always receive the attention it deserves. Poor service is costly for publishers, librarians and other subscribers and for subscription agents. In extreme cases, librarians have been known to cancel subscriptions because of difficulties in dealing with publishers. The object is to get orders and payments from customers and journals to them speedily, efficiently and at reasonable cost, with the journals arriving in good condition. At the same time the system should produce regular, reliable and pertinent reports for accounting and management purposes.

There is no substitute for meeting one's customers. Anyone responsible for the distribution of copies of journals to libraries should visit several customers with a fair collection of journals to see what happens to journals when they reach the library, and the problems that can be caused by inadequate information, poor packaging or not thinking how journals are processed.

Good subscription management depends upon having simple but powerful systems. Everyone concerned with subscription management and distribution must understand the system, and follow it. Even in the smallest organisation the procedures to be followed should be set down in writing. If exceptions are made to general rules, then they must be recorded in such a way that anyone new to the system should be able to find them, and act accordingly. Memories are fallible, and their owners change jobs, take holidays, or get sick.

In this chapter we shall be looking at the handling of subscriptions – usually the bulk of the sales of a learned journal – and also of individual copies (single parts) and back volumes. The basic elements in the handling of orders for hard-copy or CD-ROM journals are four: getting the order from the customer (which we dealt with in the previous chapter); collecting his money; recording the order so it can be acted upon; and physical distribution. The chapter on electronic publishing looks at electronic subscriptions; the role of the subscription agent is covered in the section on how journals are bought in chapter 4.

Subscriptions

Subscriptions are a convenient way to buy and sell journals. In effect, the publisher offers to sell a certain number of issues at a certain price to those who pay in advance, sight unseen. With a single order, and a single payment, the customer can ensure that he receives all the issues of a journal on publication.

Most libraries, and most publishers of academic journals, work on a calendar-year basis and their systems are geared to this. This chapter assumes a calendar-year system; publishers whose subscriptions have a different time-span will need to make appropriate adjustments. The advantages of using the same time-span throughout the trade include clarity and simplicity. Libraries and publishers can plan their work and their budgets. Volumes and issues can be identified by year of publication. Many libraries purchase any-time start journals on a calendar-year basis. New subscribers are often anxious that their subscription should go back to the beginning of a year. The disadvantage of using a calendar year is that the workload is highly seasonal.

The minimum unit of subscription is either a volume or a calendar year, whichever is the smaller. A volume is simply a number of pages which it is convenient to bind together (along with an index and title page). Fewer than 200 pages make for a very thin volume; volumes of more than about 700 pages tend to be unwieldy (and need wide inside margins if they are to be readable).

Most volumes are issued in a number of parts (issues, or numbers). If all contributions had to wait until there was enough material to fill a decent-sized volume, publication time would be unacceptably slow for the authors who got their submissions in first, and the resulting volume might contain more than readers wanted to tackle at a time. There are no rules about the number of issues a year. It depends upon the amount of material to be published and how rapidly authors expect to be published. For some journals, two issues a year are enough, while others produce issues every few days. Probably more than half of all journals appear either quarterly or every two months.

Subscription prices and discounts

Few journals have a single subscription price. The basic price is usually that charged for a domestic institutional subscriber. A few publishers offer a special discount to subscribers who pay for several years at one time. Most British publishers include postage in the price; which makes life easier for the customer to learn the total price. One reason for their doing so was a possible complication when VAT was introduced to the UK: journals were zero-rated, but their carriage might not have been. Postage is often an extra for journals published in other countries. No discount is then given on the carriage charge.

Many publishers charge a higher price to overseas subscribers. (It should be noted that the EU is the domestic market for publishers based in any EU country and it is expected that publishers will charge the same price throughout this market.) Higher prices for non-domestic subscribers are intended to recoup the higher costs of overseas postage and marketing and perhaps the services of a local office or agent. (For comment on currency conversion costs see below.)

Higher prices to overseas customers without some extra service are very much resented (though of course this is common with other goods). They also provoke 'buying-round', when the subscriber finds a way of purchasing the journal in the country of origin rather than paying the higher price. The consequence of that is that the publisher no longer knows who is subscribing, making it difficult to target promotion or estimate its effectiveness. If the publisher has a local agent in the country concerned, then that agent loses business.

If the copies go to a subscription agent rather than direct to the customer, it may take longer for the journal to reach the subscriber. On the other hand, the agent may provide check-in services for the library (making sure that all issues are received and in good condition) and consolidate deliveries in such a way as to reduce the time that it takes to get the issue onto the library shelves. Major subscription agents report that this kind of business (consolidation) is growing fast.

Most libraries order through subscription agents. This is usually by choice since using a subscription agent removes the problem of dealing with a large number of subscriptions from different publishers in different countries and making appropriate payments to each in currencies that they will accept. The library may have access to the subscription agent's database of journals and may benefit from reports on journals supplied for different departments, from different countries, price changes in the current year and in recent years and so on. Sometimes the library has no choice: currency control or import licensing may prevent a library from purchasing direct from the publisher.

Many publishers give some discount to subscription agents. The discount may be a fixed sum per subscription (for instance, US $5.00 per subscription), but a percentage of the selling price is more usual. The percentage discount may be lower on higher-priced journals, though subscription agents claim this is unfair. Some publishers give a higher discount for payments made early (e.g. by December of the previous year). Discounts now are rarely more than 10 per cent, and are often less (see also chapter 8). If the publisher charges postage separately, then there is usually no discount on that.

Publishers' discounts overall average around 6 or 7 per cent and have been steadily declining. For lower-price journals this is not enough to cover the subscription agents' costs. Agents generally charge a supplement to their customers. This service charge will vary from customer to customer, depending on the average discounts and prices of the journals in the collection, the size of the account and the amount of work involved, the negotiating skills of the purchaser and competition from other agents. It may be shown on a title-by-title basis (more common in the UK), or added to the invoice as a lump sum covering that particular mix of titles (which is the usual practice in the USA).

When a journal is published in association with a society, its members usually have some entitlement to receive the journal, either by virtue of their membership, or on payment of a supplementary charge which is much less than the institutional subscription rate. (Husband-and-wife members sometimes ask for a reduced subscription rate on the grounds that they do not want two copies of the journal.)

Some publishers also offer reduced rates to individuals; for many journals outside the humanities, the regular subscription price is more than most individuals could countenance paying (see also chapter 8). The offer may be open to all individuals, or restricted to a particular group. It should be noted that special student subscriptions should be limited to a certain number of years and evidence may be required that the subscriber is actually a student.

Sometimes the special rates may be more to satisfy that editor (who points out that at the full price few if any individuals will buy the journal) than to meet a demand from the market. It is not uncommon to find that for an established conventional learned journal in the sciences the number of non-member individual subscribers is less than 1 or 2 per cent and uncommon for it to be more than 5 per cent, even with heavy discounting. Trends journals, scientific magazines and those with features directed to practitioners can expect a higher proportion of individual subscribers, as can journals in the humanities and social sciences.

As well as these basic subscriptions, a publisher may offer extras at a supplementary charge. These include binding cases (most common with legal journals), or a hard bound volume at the end of the year (legal journals and 'Trends' publications); simultaneous micro-fiche editions; cumulative indexes; supplementary volumes; or air mail despatch. Subscriptions to electronic versions may be standard or may be reduced if the subscriber also takes the hard-copy edition.

Some publishers quote prices in currencies other than their own. If a journal requires a mailing permit in the USA (for instance, any journal sent to the USA in bulk for onward transmission by the US mails) then it must carry a price in US dollars. Overseas prices may be definitive, that is if the exchange rates change, the publisher stands the gain or loss, or indicative, with the price in domestic currency being the firm price. In either case, if a publisher accepts payments in a currency other than the ones in which bills are paid, some allowance may be made for the cost of currency conversion. Some European publishers reduce their exposure to changes in exchange rates by selling forward their anticipated dollar receipts for subscriptions.

NAME AND ADDRESS OF PUBLISHER

(including telephone & telex numbers, email, telegraphic address & giro account number)

Journal price list for 1997

Issued: 30 June 1996

Title	ISSN	Volumes	Parts/ vol	Price/vol	Annual subscription	Trade	Single parts
Bookshop News	1234-1234	17-19	4	£60.00 US $110.00	£180.00 US $330.00	£171.00 US $313.50	£18.00 US $30.00
Journal Times	2345-6789	5	3	£50.00 US $80.00	£50.00 US $80.00	£45.00 US $72.00	£19.00 US $32.00
Publishing Futures	3456-7890	6-7	3	£100.00 US $160.00	£200.00 US $320.00	£190.00 US $304.00	£40.00 US $65.00
Subscription Agent	0123-4567	49	12	£110.00 US $176.00	£110.00 US $176.00	£99.00 US $158.40	£11.00 US $18.00

Please note that from 1 January 1987 POETRY PUBLISHING is published by Nonplus Press, 90 Utopia Road, Erewhon ZZ9 AA1. All orders and enquiries for Volume 16 onwards should be sent to them.

Prices include surface mail postage in the UK and Europe, and accelerated surface mail elsewhere. Air mail rates on request.

Please send cash with order. Cheques/money orders (in sterling or US dollars) should be made payable to:

Claims should be sent not later than three months after the month of publication.

Cancellations received after orders have been placed will be subject to £10 (US $18.00) cancellation charge.

Figure 5.1 A journal price list.

Price information to subscribers

The first stage of the subscription cycle is to inform subscription agents and direct subscribers of what will be published in the following year (which journals, how many volumes, and how many issues) and the prices. Libraries are often expected to confirm their orders to their subscription agents in September or October for these to be properly recorded for despatch of the first issues in December or January. The library may need to confer with their users about cancellations and new subscriptions, and, in academic institutions, the faculty may not be accessible in July or August. This means planning and budgeting must start before prices are announced and that libraries will certainly want information on prices of individual titles not later than early September.

Subscribers therefore need to know prices for the following year by the end of August. Publishers should therefore aim to fix their prices by the end of July at the latest, and let subscription agents have details then (by air or electronic means to those overseas). If there are delays in fixing the prices of one or two journals, it may be necessary to circulate a preliminary list in advance, with the complete list to follow.

Journal price lists can be simple (see figure 5.1): what is important is to get the information out quickly and clearly. A simple list is often all that is needed. It should give

1 The publisher's name and address with telephone, telex, fax and e-mail information.
2 The date of issue, and the year for which the prices are applicable.

. . . and, for each journal:

3 The definitive title for the journal (otherwise two journals with similar titles may be confused).
4 The ISSN.
5 The number(s) of the volume(s) to be published in the year.
6 The number of issues in a volume, and the months of publication (not season: Fall is Autumn in Europe and Spring in Australia). Are any special issues to be published? Do volumes include an index and title-page?

7 The price for a volume, a year, and an individual issue. It should give the full price, any reduced rates, and the rate after agency discount for each currency in which the price is quoted.

8 Prices for bound volumes, supplements (if extra), micro-form or electronic versions and so on if the publisher offers any of these.

9 If alternative editions are available from another supplier rather than the original publisher, details should be given of how they can be obtained.

10 If applicable, an indication that the journal is new, or new to the list, or any special points agents should notice, such as change of frequency.

11 If the journal is delayed in publication, it is helpful to indicate when the first issue of the new subscription period will be supplied.

For the whole list:

12 A statement that postage is included, or a figure for postage. Make it clear how copies are sent to overseas subscribers. Explain any arrangements for air mail, and quote the price if possible.

13 Acceptable currencies and forms of payment.

14 Terms, e.g. cash-with-order. What is the publisher's policy on claims and cancellations? How much notice is needed for changes of address?

15 Where orders and payment should be sent.

16 If space permits, it is helpful to add a note about back volumes. This is particularly appreciated by subscription agents dealing with the more rapidly developing Asian countries where libraries are being built up. What is available? At what price? Where should orders be sent?

Subscription agents need to write on the price lists before entering them into their computer systems. Publishers should allow space for notes and avoid the temptation to cram as much information on to the page as possible.

If the new subscription price is much higher than the current one, some publishers provide an explanation. Others prefer not to draw attention to the increase. But if the higher price is the result of a significant increase in the amount of material to be published, or more frequent publication, a note to that effect may discourage some sub-scribers from cancelling their subscriptions.

Sometimes a publisher (or a journal editor) wishes to issue a volume which was not included in the subscription price, and to charge for it. This should be resisted if possible. Such extras are not popular with either subscription agents or librarians, and library budgets are often not flexible enough to cover the extra cost. Some subscription agents ask their customers whether they are willing to accept such volumes and pay for them without further consultation. Publishers generally try to avoid the problem by consulting editors before fixing prices, and, if necessary, by delaying the publication of some extra material until the next year, when it can be charged for in the new subscription price.

Sales tax and supplies from overseas

Tax rules, regulations, effective rates and exemptions vary from country to country and may change without consultation. Journal publishers are particularly affected since they sell journals to virtually every country of the world and it is difficult to keep up with the changes. Another complication is triangulation: a publisher may receive an order from an agent in another country to despatch the copies to a subscriber in a third; sometimes all three are in different continents. Trade associations may draw attention to new complications and be able to advise their members on how to proceed.

Canada is a particular case. It has a goods and services tax (GST) which includes items sold to Canadian customers by suppliers in other countries. The outside supplier is responsible for registering with the Canadian tax authorities, lodging a bond with them, and collecting the tax due on behalf of the Canadian government. The goods should then carry the GST number on the package so that authorities can check that the tax has been paid. There are some exemptions – mostly for small firms or for those who can claim to have done no promotion in Canada. In most cases, journals for institutions will be purchased through major subscription agents who have registered themselves, but individuals usually order direct or get journals through society membership.

Although much of the trade in journals is on a cash-with-order basis with no invoices or receipts passing between publisher and customer, they may be required for tax purposes, particularly if the price paid by the customer includes a reclaimable tax element.

The complications of collecting tax for foreign governments are not attractive and it is to be hoped that other countries or US States do not follow suit. Optimists hope that the Canadian GST will also be repealed. Pessimists fear that the habit will spread.

Although there is progress towards harmonisation of Value Added Tax (VAT) in the European Union, the rates applicable to publications vary from country to country; in the UK they are taxed at 0 per cent (or zero-rated). But publishers or agents registered for VAT may have to charge VAT to customers in other EU countries, unless the customer is registered for VAT in their own country and has supplied their VAT number to the publisher. The publisher must then report sales to these clients to the authorities giving the correct VAT number for each client.

Getting renewals

In the previous chapter, we looked at how publishers get orders in the first place. Journal publishers hope that subscribers will continue to renew their subscriptions for many years. A publisher wants renewals as early as possible. There are two reasons for this. Firstly, interest can be earned on money received in advance. Secondly, early renewals help the publisher to spread the workload over a longer period, reducing the demand for overtime or temporary help. Many subscription agents today (especially the larger ones) have no use for publishers' renewal notices; it is wasteful to send out notices that will go straight in the wastepaper bin.

It will be obvious that the handling of price information (see above) and orders (see below) can involve a lot of paperwork and rekeying of information by the publisher and the subscription agent though both will have computer systems. That makes subscription fulfilment a good area for Electronic Data Interchange (EDI). An International Committee for Electronic Data Interchange with the Serials Industry (ICEDIS) has publisher and subscription agent members. They have developed standards for the transfer of orders by magnetic tape and despatch data which are widely used (see below). Other developments are for claims and claim responses and for order changes, and sales and pricing information (for ICEDIS members only). They also have a committee looking at EDI and tables of contents.

The larger agents now transmit their orders in machine-readable form to the larger publishers, either online or by tape-transfer. That can save a great deal of work, and ensures that the publisher's and subscription agent's records are identical. Because renewals are processed more quickly (60,000 subscriptions in an hour perhaps) the information can be supplied later to the publisher than with traditional systems. Consequently it is more up-to-date, and there will be fewer changes to be made later. The success rate so far for agents and publishers in processing orders in this way has been very high; often more than 95 per cent of subscriptions have been handled smoothly at the first attempt. But it requires a good deal of careful preparation, and there can be problems of compatibility of tapes and tape formats, and mismatches can take a good deal of time to sort out. Indeed some publishers claim that tape transfer saves them little time overall and certainly does not, in their case, justify an extra discount.

Direct subscribers and some agents need renewal notices/invoices. Those for agents and institutions can go out well before the subscription expires, for instance in September for a journal that runs on a calendar-year basis. Individuals are unlikely to take any action more than a couple of months before their subscription expires, so renewal invoices for them should be sent to arrive not earlier than about eight weeks before the end of the subscription period.

The information in renewal notices/invoices should include:

1 The publisher's full name, address, telephone and fax numbers, etc.
2 The date of the invoice.
3 The full name and address of the customer; this can be positioned so that the invoice can be put in a window envelope. In most systems there will also be a subscriber number: the publisher will want to include this. It may be in a machine-readable form so responses can be wanded into the subscription system.
4 The customer order number and/or date of order.
5 The publishers order reference, possibly in machine-readable form.

6 The name and address for the despatch of the journal, if not the same as 3.

7 The title of the journal, and its ISSN.

8 The volumes/issues concerned and the date of publication, and the format if not the print edition.

9 The full retail price before tax if applicable.

10 The price charged to the customer, if different, again before tax.

11 The number of copies to be supplied and the format if not print.

12 Extras included in the price.

13 Any supplementary charges, e.g. air-mail postage.

14 Tax, if any.

15 The total sum due and to whom payment should be made. (Is it the journal, the society, the distributor, or the publisher?)

16 The terms of the invoice. If it is a *pro forma* invoice, it should state for how long the prices are valid. If the publisher works on a cash-with-order basis, the invoice should make that clear. If payment is expected within a certain time, or if there is a discount for prompt payment, that information should be on the invoice.

17 Acceptable methods of payment and currencies: cheques, credit cards, money orders, bank transfers, giro, UNESCO coupons. Can the customer pay in the currency of his choice? Is there a surcharge for this? If so, how much is it?

The invoice should be accompanied by a remittance advice which the customer can return. This may be a duplicate of the invoice, or a tear-off portion. The remittance advice should give clear instructions to the customer (including what he should return), and have enough information on it for the publisher to identify the subscriber and the journal. If it includes a machine-readable code, that should reduce the time taken to process the subscription in the publisher's office.

Some subscribers order and pay on the first notice from the publisher, but many need several reminders. A first reminder might be sent a month or so after the renewal invoice, and a second shortly before publication of the first issue for the new subscription period. Later reminders should be sent direct to all subscribers who have not paid, regardless of whether or not the subscription came through an agent in the past. At one time, only two or three further reminders were sent; now many publishers send more, until the return is less than the cost. Ordinary reminders (or first/second/third/fourth/final renewal notices) and the remittance advices may be generated in multi-part sets. They should be sent by air (or an air-speeded service) to customers overseas.

Some publishers print the renewal notices on the paper carrier which goes with the journal giving the name and address of the subscriber. This is of course very cheap, involving no extra paper or postage, but it is ill-advised; some subscribers throw the carrier and the packaging away without a second glance. It is also poor practice to include renewal notices in the issues themselves; they will certainly be missed by libraries and probably by most other subscribers.

Many publishers find it worthwhile to send letters to those who have not renewed after receiving, say, three reminders: quite often, failure to renew is inadvertent. A personal approach may produce either a subscription, or an explanation of why it is not being renewed. Some publishers telephone those whose subscriptions have lapsed, particularly in the US, where telephone calls are relatively cheap and there is a large domestic market with a common language. Follow-up letters or telephone calls can also elicit comments on the journal useful to the editor or the marketing people. All such comments should be passed on to the appropriate person.

Before writing or telephoning laggard subscribers, it is as well to check the current subscription list. Renewals often are entered as new subscriptions (perhaps because of minor changes in the address, or in the way that the journal is ordered). It wastes time, and looks foolish to pursue subscribers who have actually renewed.

Getting payments

Most journal publishers operate on a cash-with-order basis. No copies are sent out, not even to subscribers with 'standing orders', unless the publisher has received payment. That eliminates the need for credit control, and gives subscribers an incentive to pay early.

If the publisher does not operate on a cash-with-order basis, then he must also issue invoices and statements, usually monthly, to chase up payments. Statements should give the full name and address of the supplier and the customer, the date of the statement, and list all invoices (invoice number, date and amount) and all sums received, with a total showing how much is now due. Many firms add a note of how old the debt is.

Individuals can be asked to renew by direct debit in the UK or continuous credit card authority elsewhere. The subscriber must be informed in good time of the sum to be paid for the subscription. If he or she takes no action, then the sum is debited to their account. Thus the subscriber has to act in order to stop a subscription rather than to continue it. The publisher may offer an extra discount as an inducement to subscribers: in one case, 40 per cent of them took up the offer of a 5 per cent discount.

One problem for all publishers is what to do if the payment made falls short of the sum required. Most have a cut-off point, below which it is not worth pursuing the customer. Few return money and ask for the whole sum in a single payment. This is not recommended in any case; and if the customer has to deal with currency controls or import licensing schemes he may cancel the order rather than tackle the bureaucracy again. Most publishers send a supplementary invoice if the difference is large enough to justify the cost of so doing. If the difference is small, a supplementary invoice might still be raised if the customer habitually pays the subscription for one year at the price for the previous one.

A frequent cause of a shortfall in payments is because the sum sent is not enough to meet the publisher's invoice, the cost of converting currency and recent fluctuations in exchange rates; one currency can move against another by 10 per cent or more in a month. Bank charges for converting currency are high, so most publishers try to restrict the range of currencies which they will accept. Floating exchange rates can cause problems for publishers operating in currencies other than the one in which they pay their bills, though there can also be windfall profits. Subscription agents, by consolidating orders and payments, help to keep down currency conversion costs.

Less common are subscribers who pay too much, or who pay more than once. If the sums are very small (a windfall from a foreign currency transaction, perhaps), then the publisher usually keeps them; at least it offsets the small losses from subscribers whose payments are not quite enough. Bank charges will swallow up small refunds if currency has to be converted. If the publisher has a flexible system whereby a subscription can be entered for any period or number of issues, appropriate adjustments can be made. A publisher who works on an annual subscription and cash-with-order basis will probably find it simpler to refund the surplus (however painful that may seem) than to open an account for the subscriber and issue a credit note.

Regrettably, many countries suffer from currency restrictions, import regulations and customs controls. Certain conditions may have to be fulfilled before payments can be made, or orders placed. If a customer specifies a particular number of invoices, or confirmation by telegram, or documents by a given date, the request should be met. Telexes, faxes or locally produced photocopies will not be acceptable substitutes. Failure to meet the requirements by the given date may mean that the order cannot be placed, or payment cannot be made.

Keeping subscription records

Subscription systems may be either publication based or subscriber based. The latter is more common when the publisher has a number of journals with overlapping readership; data relating to the subscriber then needs to be entered only once. It is also helpful in suggesting marketing opportunities.

Whether a publication- or subscriber-based system is used, adequate and accurate records are needed for each subscription. The ideal subscriber is one who orders before the subscription period begins, and sends the right money with his order. The publisher records the subscription, and despatches each issue on publication. Late subscriptions will be recorded in the same way, but it will be necessary to send subscribers any previously published issue to which they are entitled, and to note when that was done.

In many countries data protection laws require that the only information held in a computer should be that required to carry out a particular, specified activity. Individual subscribers should be given the opportunity to indicate that they do not wish to receive promotional material on other products, services or publications. Publishers must also be careful that their subscriber records do not include information about individuals that is not pertinent to supplying the order. Most subscription management systems would contain:

1 The title of the journal.
2 The subscriber number.
3 The address for despatch.
4 The subscriber's telephone and fax numbers.
5 The sum paid, the date it was received, and the issues and formats it covers.
6 The number of subscriptions (if more than one).
7 The address to which invoices should be sent, for instance the subscription agent, or an accounts office, with telephone and fax numbers.
8 The subscription price which applies (e.g. full rate, trade rate, special discount, electronic subscription, micro-fiche, with or without bound volumes, free copy).
9 Any special despatch instructions (e.g. air mail, registered post).
10 The customer's order number and date of order.
11 The date on which an order was first entered for the customer.
12 Records of any claims made and how they were satisfied.
13 Previous addresses if any and the dates on which amendments were made.
14 Any other information that the publisher needs. For instance, individual subscribers may indicate that they should not receive mailings on other products.

Unfortunately, not all orders give these details clearly, so the publisher will have to edit them before or while entering them in the records. Which volumes are wanted? What is the exact postal address? How many copies? Sometimes a little detective work will provide the answer, but there will be times when it is necessary to check what is required with whoever placed the order. Despatch addresses may have to be abbreviated to fit the addressing system, and the country may have to be added. Every subscription department needs access to a good atlas. List of post codes (zip codes etc.) for some countries can also be very useful, particularly for the USA.

However the records are arranged, it is necessary to be able to get quickly to any subscriber's record. Subscribers and subscription agents who want to know the current status of a subscription often reach for the telephone; it obviously saves everyone time if the query can be answered then and there. But in many systems, even manual ones, records are updated in batches, rather than as orders or amendments come in. Orders which are awaiting processing should be kept in a logical sequence, by customer or by journal, depending upon whether the system is customer based, or journal based, so that queries that come in before the order has been processed can be dealt with easily.

Access to subscription records is needed for changes of address, and when packaging material is returned without its contents. Unless the publisher has only one journal, and keeps all records in a very simple sequence, each despatch address should include a code so the subscription can be traced quickly and an indication of which journal it relates to. Publishers using computer systems usually give a number to each subscriber or each subscription: on manual systems one might include a couple of letters to identify the journal, and two or three to indicate the subscriber. Subscribers can be asked to return a current address label when notifying a change of address, and to allow adequate time for the change to be recorded.

Some publishers find it helpful to include in their record the date the subscription was started: that allows them to check the turnover of subscribers, and promote back volumes to the newer ones. It is necessary to record the date of despatch of each issue, so that claims and queries can be handled with confidence. This can be done by manual recording, tagging the computer record of each subscriber, or running off a duplicate set of despatch addresses when the lists are produced for the mailing of each issue.

Subscription records can be kept in a number of ways. The fall in the real cost of computers has made it possible for even quite small societies and publishers to use a computer-based system. Address labels, invoices and reminders can be generated easily, and much tedious recording can be avoided. Useful management and promotional information can be generated as a by-product. If the addresses are entered in a standard format, then they can be sorted automatically in various ways. For instance, subscribers in the USA could be printed out in alphabetical order, by State for checking against lists of those who might be expected to subscribe, and in zip code order to facilitate despatch.

Computer systems for journals are not foolproof, and there are many tales of disaster. But there are now systems which can be bought more or less 'off the peg'. The market is changing rapidly: the best advice is to talk to publishers actually using different systems and see which best fits your needs. Many are very willing to show their systems to others, but it should be remembered that they will not necessarily point out the shortcomings. In practice, different publishers make very different demands on a system. It is also sensible to check claims of marvellous service with a large subscription agent, or some libraries; publishers are not always the best judges of their own performance.

Before embarking upon any computerised subscription system, it is necessary to define clearly what it should be expected to do, and what management information it should provide. A simple mailing list system is unlikely to be a suitable starting point. How many different subscription rates might there be to a single journal? How does the system link with the accounts department? What listings of subscribers will be required (e.g. by country, by agent, by year, by despatch method, by type)? Will subscriber lists be used for other purposes, for instance as mailing lists for other publications? How frequently will updates be required? Is it necessary to have access to the system at all times during the working day? Would it be better to use a computer bureau in the first instance? If so, is the bureau's system one which the publisher could take over later on, if he wished?

In spite of the computer, many small publishers and publishers in developing countries may have no alternative to manual or mechanised systems. One relief for those whose mechanisation does not stretch beyond a typewriter and a photocopier, is that, if the addresses are typed on sheets of paper in a suitable format, they can be photocopied onto self-adhesive labels. That means that one typing of the address can be used to produce the labels for a year's despatch and for renewal invoices and reminders.

If a mechanical addressing system is used, it is possible, by careful construction of the lists, to make the address plate double as the subscription record. With such systems, one can usually print the address directly onto the packaging material, which avoids the need for separate labelling.

The addresses and packaging for any despatch should be ready as soon as the production of that issue is complete. If they are produced too early, there may be changes between the time they are run off and the actual despatch, particularly in the early part of the year; it is not unknown for a publisher to scrap a list that was produced prematurely. Few journals always keep to schedule. Those responsible for producing the address lists therefore need either a trigger to prompt them to act at the appropriate time, or regular information from those responsible for the production of the journal, so they know when to update and run off the labels or address carriers.

Gracing subscribers

When a new subscription period begins it is usual to find that a significant proportion of subscribers have not yet renewed their subscriptions. Some publishers continue to send one or two issues to these subscribers; that is known as gracing. Others cut them off and send nothing until they have been paid. There are arguments for both positions.

Those who grace subscribers claim that they are giving a service to their customers and saving themselves from having to send out the previously published issues when they eventually get a renewal. Those who cut them off point out the costs of printing and despatch of copies to those who are not going to renew. They suggest that if the customer knows the subscription will be graced they will delay renewing, and that the receipt of copies can lull subscribers into thinking that they have actually renewed. It is also a problem for libraries that have cancelled their subscriptions. They may feel obliged to return grace copies and resentful about doing so. The print number needs to take account of grace copies.

Cancellations and refunds

Cancellations are not always what they seem to be. Most subscribers who decide to stop subscribing to a journal do not bother to tell the publisher; they simply do not send any payment. Paradoxically, the publisher may be asked to cancel subscriptions by subscribers who are continuing their subscription, because they plan to order the journal through a different route: a change of subscription agent perhaps. These subscribers do not want to receive (or be charged for) two subscriptions in future.

Another type of cancellation is that which arises midway through the subscription period, accompanied by a request for a refund. Some publishers will not refund unexpired subscriptions; others are willing to make some payment. The maximum refund is a proportion of the subscription: if the subscriber has received only half the issues, half the sum is refunded. This is rare, and might be restricted to cases of genuine hardship: death of an individual perhaps. Sometimes a handling charge is deducted, or the issues which have been already supplied are charged at the higher single copy price, and the difference refunded.

If the journal ceases publication, subscribers have a moral claim to a refund on any outstanding subscriptions. If the journal is continuing in some modified form, they might be offered a generous credit towards the new subscription (as an inducement to take it up). If they still demand a refund (and the cause of cessation is not bankruptcy), then they should be paid off.

Claims for missing and damaged issues; quality control

Claims are a major concern to both publishers and librarians. The automation of library systems has made claiming more immediate (sometimes premature) and more comprehensive. Claims are time-consuming for publisher, librarian and subscription agent; publishers should aim to reduce claims to a minimum, and to respond to them speedily and efficiently.

However good the publisher's system, there will always be some claims. Post Offices are not infallible, and not all packages arrive in decent condition; India and Nigeria often present problems. With inexpensive magazines, relying largely on advertising for their income, it may be economic to replace issues claimed as missing, damaged or faulty without much question. But learned journals are frequently expensive, and some claims arise because the journal has been misplaced in, or removed from, the library.

Journal publishers usually put a time limit on claims, which may depend upon the distance the journal has to travel, and the frequency of issues. A nearby library might be expected to spot quite quickly that an issue of a monthly journal has not arrived, but it will take longer for a library many thousands of miles away to realise they have not received a quarterly journal, particularly if it is despatched by surface mail. Time limits for claiming should be included in price lists and on invoices; many agents record the information in their databases. Locals might be expected to claim within three months; those further afield might be allowed six.

There are various reasons for claiming. A subscriber may believe that he has paid when he has not, or perhaps the agent has not passed on his order. The subscriber's address may not be correctly recorded. A few packages do get lost in transit. Sometimes the packaging material is not robust enough, and the contents and their wrapper become separated, or the label is detached. The journal may arrive so damaged that the customer asks for a replacement. Pilferage is sometimes the problem, either in the mail, or in the library. Occasionally the receipt of an issue may not be properly recorded in the library's records. Probably about 50 per cent of claims arise because the journal is published late, or the subscriber has simply not allowed enough time for the issue to arrive.

More dramatically, mailbags may be stolen or destroyed by accident and whole consignments can go astray. If the whole despatch is lost, then the publisher will probably have to reprint and send the issue out again. Sometimes only a few are known to have been lost, but it is not possible to identify from the records which subscribers are affected. In this case, the publisher should write to all subscribers who might be affected and their subscription agents positively soliciting claims.

Another hazard is using the wrong labels; this is more likely where the lists (as for instance with some society members) come from outside. It underlines the need to identify carefully all labels and to check for which journal they are. The risk is greater where there are journals and societies with similar names or where a society publishes more than one journal.

Otherwise, on receiving a claim, the publisher should first check that the subscriber is correctly recorded and that the issue was despatched to the correct address, and when it was sent. He then either sends a replacement, or informs the claimant (who may be either the subscriber, or the agent through whom the order was placed) of the position. Where there is doubt, the subscribers may be asked to wait a little longer and claim again if the issue does not turn up, or to have another look and claim again if they are still sure that they never received it. If the claim is long after the publication of the issue, then the publisher will assume that it arrived originally, but has since been lost. Many claims can be dealt with by a standard letter (for an example, see figure 5.2).

If a subscriber who has been asked to wait a little longer, or to check again for the missing issue, claims again, it is customary to send a free replacement. When the original claim is too late, then the publisher may send a *pro forma* invoice for the issue concerned, so the subscriber can acquire replacement copies with the minimum delay. Most journal publishers do hold stock for some years after publication. Allowance for missing issues should be made when fixing the print number.

Claims are expensive to handle, so it is worthwhile trying to reduce their numbers. Records should be kept of all claims: otherwise claims from the same subscriber for the same issue may be duplicated but the publisher will add to the confusion if the response is also duplicated. The records should also show if a subscriber is generating a large number of claims. At the same time, monitoring claims is a practical way to check on the efficiency of the distribution system. Subscribers commonly claim through their subscription agents and the major agents record the number of claims made on each publisher. They can therefore indicate how well a publisher is doing; if the publisher's journals generate a great many claims, that may be used as an argument for a higher discount.

Sturdy packaging and clear and accurate addresses, including postal codes, will help to reduce claims. Many larger publishers produce regular information for subscription agents giving information on delayed issues – and also new journals, changes of frequency and so on. Not all agents have been entering the information in their records but it is hoped that

Dear

Thank you for your claim of (date) for (title, volume, issue, date of publication).

[Then as appropriate:]

This journal is not published by us. Orders and enquiries should be sent to:

We cannot trace your subscription from the information given. Could you therefore provide us with (old address/new address/subscriber number (if known)/title of journal and issue numbers claimed/details of your payment to us).

This issue was despatched to you on ..... If you have not yet received it (have not received it by [date]) please claim again.

This issue has been delayed: it will be despatched on publication which we hope will be (date of expected despatch).

We regret that we cannot honour claims made more than x months after publication.

Figure 5.2. The content of a standard claim letter.

the system may improve with electronic transfer of data from publisher to subscription agent.

India, as we have remarked, is a special problem; some publishers have found the rate of claims there perhaps twice that of most other countries. Accurate and complete addresses including postcodes (PIN numbers) are essential. Some subscription agents in India offer a consolidation and distribution service, and will handle subscriptions for publishers on an exclusive basis. Publishers using such services have seen their claims decline.

Other forms of quality control of distribution include regular or occasional inserts in the packaging to check that the contents arrived in good condition. If there is a problem, the recipient can return the form with comments. Points on a checklist could include damaged wrapping, bent covers, broken spines, bent corners or water damage and the date of receipt so the publisher can verify the transit time.

Back volumes and single parts

Orders for back volumes and single parts require different treatment from subscriptions. Not all customers will send in a firm order: many will want quotations or *pro forma* invoices. The publisher must make it clear for how long the quoted price is valid, and whether it includes postage and packing. Sometimes the publisher will not be able to supply all the volumes requested. Some may have been licensed to a reprint house, or may be unobtainable except through the secondhand market. Others may have been passed on to a specialist dealer in back volumes. A few customers are only interested in complete sets (see chapter 6).

When the publisher has a firm order, and either payment or sufficient guarantee of it to persuade him to part with the goods, the journals have to be looked out, packed and despatched according to the customer's instructions. An agent may want the journals sent to the ultimate purchaser, but will need confirmation of despatch from the publisher; or perhaps the journals should be sent to an intermediate point for consolidation. If the invoice is not sent with the journals, an advice note should be enclosed; this should give sufficient reference to the original order (e.g. order number and date) to allow it to be traced.

Entries have to be made in the records for both stocks and sales, for the information will be needed both for accounting purposes and for making decisions about stocks. If back volumes are selling fast, a reprint may be called for; more commonly today, excess stock of slow-moving journals may be sent for pulping.

A common problem is the large amount of storage space which back volumes require. Although there may not be many copies of each issue, there may be a large number of issues, each of which has to be stored in an accessible location. Some stock control system will be needed, however rudimentary, to reconcile stocks and sales, and to detect shortages or surplus copies. It may be wise to insure the stock.

Packing

Journals are costly items, easily damaged in the mail. Customers rightly expect issues to arrive in good condition. Damaged copies may be returned to the publisher for replacement. If the journal becomes separated from the address of the intended recipient, it is unlikely to reach its destination. Economies in packaging material can prove very expensive.

In the USA, a publisher can stick an address label on a journal and mail it unwrapped, but that is not acceptable to most postal authorities. The ideal packing material is cheap, light, easy to address and robust. It must be easy to put the journal into it and for the recipient to extract the journal from it. The traditional manila envelope is usually unsatisfactory for a heavy and fairly rigid journal, particularly if it has to travel great distances. Cardboard envelopes are more expensive, but are more robust, and can be packed fairly fast by trained operators. Padded bags are usually proof against the worst that post offices can do, but they are expensive.

Many publishers use plastic film wrapping. The film needs to be of a fairly heavy and even gauge. The journal must be packed loosely; otherwise, it is more likely to suffer damage in the mail, and may be further damaged when the package is opened. Wrapping in plastic film is usually done by machine; inserting copies in other forms of packaging is usually a manual job. If all copies are wrapped in film as the final stage of binding, they will remain clean. The film is light, which helps to keep down postage and freight costs. Another advantage of clear film is that pilferers can see the contents; most are not interested in learned journals.

Plastic film has two further advantages. It can be overprinted with advertising and looks more attractive than paper envelopes treated the same way; and it is possible to put in other pieces of paper separately, rather than inserted in the journal. For instance, a readership survey, a notice of some change in the journal, or announcements of other publications, can be separately enclosed in their own envelopes, and addressed to the librarian or to the subscriber. They may still be over-looked, but are a little more likely to reach its intended recipient than an ordinary insert in the journal.

A few libraries keep the packaging material tucked inside the journal until they are sure why the issue was sent to them; they have had problems with self-seal packaging which will lift the print off any page to which it adheres.

One disadvantage is that the plastic is slippery (that, indeed helps to keep the contents undamaged), so handling large quantities together in a bundle, or on a pallet, can be tricky. The cost of machinery needed is beyond the reach of a small publisher, but many printers are equipped to pack journals in this way.

Addressing

The address must be clearly printed in accordance with the instructions from the subscription agent or subscriber. Subtle changes of address may be important to the recipient. The name of the publication and the publisher should be clearly indicated; then, if the contents do get separated from their packaging the recipient at least knows what they should have received from whom and can then claim for it.

Addresses can be printed directly onto manila or cardboard envelopes with some mechanical addressing systems. But typewriter or computer output is more likely to be in the form of labels. Self-adhesive labels are readily available in a variety of formats and can easily be applied to paper-based packaging materials. Not all stick firmly to every type of plastic film: many journals have gone astray because of this so they should be tested first. The alternative is to print each address on a separate sheet of paper (the carrier) which is inserted between the cover and the trans-parent film. The whole process is mechanical, but care must be taken then to make sure that only one carrier is inserted in each package. The verso of the carrier can be used for a variety of purposes, including promotion of other titles, back volumes, or changes of subscriber address (but not renewal notices: see above).

It is sensible to test any packaging material before investing in it. Sample journals can be sent to some friendly body overseas to report on the condition on arrival, and perhaps return them so the condition they arrived in can be seen.

Postage and freight

Learned journals are normally distributed to addresses scattered through-out the world in relatively small packages. Consequently, most learned journals are despatched by post. Postal services are labour intensive, and postal costs have risen more rapidly than other prices in many countries.

Postal charges, (and some freight charges, too) usually depend upon the weight of the individual items, and, unless special terms have been negotiated, increase stepwise rather than continuously. An extra page can move a journal into a different weight step. That can result in a considerably higher postage charge, which is a heavy burden for relatively low-priced, long-run journals. It is therefore worth finding ways to keep the weight down.

Weight-reducing methods which can be considered include:

1 A lighter weight of paper: but it must be reasonably opaque and not so light as to slow down printing.
2 Narrower margins, so as to get more words onto the page (but still wide enough for some to be trimmed off if the journal is rebound).
3 A smaller type size, allowing more words to be got onto the page (but without making the journal difficult to read).
4 Lighter weight packaging material (but still offering good protection).
5 A close watch on the number of pages. Varying the extent so that issues are always towards the top of the weight-step they are in (while keeping to an even working, i.e. using whole sheets of paper) can save money.
6 Illustrations, including electron micrographs, if printed by litho instead of from half-tone plates, can be reproduced at least as well on a text paper as on a heavy coated one.
7 Making sure that inserts do not take the journal to the next weight step (or else that the advertiser pays any additional postage).

Another way of keeping down the costs of distribution (and binding) is to publish the same number of pages in fewer issues; but there may be editorial or marketing reasons for not doing so. It should also be remembered that concessionary postage rates (e.g. US second-class mail) may depend upon a certain number of issues being despatched each year. If two journals go to substantially the same subscription list, and their publications dates coincide, it may be possible to mail them together, but in practice that is very rare.

Surface mail is satisfactory for some journals, but, particularly in STM subjects subscribers want them faster, though most are reluctant to pay to get them by air mail. There is little point in rapid publication if the issue then takes six weeks or more to reach the reader. Ordinary airmail is expensive, though some subscribers are prepared to pay a surcharge. Some libraries in Asia or Australia have a collecting point in Europe or North America; journals are air freighted to them from there.

Air freight charges depend upon many things, including the distance and the surplus capacity available on flights on any particular route. It is often cheaper for a European publisher to send journals for North American subscribers by air freight in bulk to a distributor, and have them mailed out from a US address, than to send them by surface mail: it is certainly quicker and more reliable. Because of higher European postage rates, there may not be any saving in sending US journals to European subscribers that way. Each case has to be considered on its merits: one factor is whether the journal is eligible for concessionary rates in the USA.

Many publishers despatch overseas copies by air-speeded printed paper services. The journals then go by air between countries but are treated as surface mail within the countries concerned. In principle it should not take more than two to three weeks to any destination, and the cost is much lower than air mail. The service has various names in different countries, for instance SAS (Surface Air Surface), or ISAL (International Surface Air Lift), or 'Printflow Airsaver' (in the UK).

In many countries, discounts are available for large users of postal services. Some apply nationally, but there is sometimes scope for local negotiation. Such arrangements usually require the publisher to sort the mail by destination; often subscription lists can be arranged so that this involves no extra work. The saving can sometimes make some manual sorting worthwhile. The largest discounts go to the largest users;

consolidation services allow smaller publishers to benefit from bulk rates.

Using distributors

Journal publishers do not necessarily need to have in-house facilities for distribution; there are other organisations providing distribution services. Some printers are happy to handle packing and despatch using address labels provided by the publisher, and some can undertake the whole subscription fulfilment operation. Computer bureaux will keep subscription records and generate invoices and reminders. Publishers, both commercial and learned society, sometimes have surplus distribution capacity which they are willing to sell. There are also organisations specialising in the distribution of journals and handling of subscriptions.

A publisher who decides to sub-contract some or all of this work should examine several possibilities, choose contractors with care and check with current customers about the service that they are getting. Systems and costs depend upon the type of subscriber and their geographical location, the price of the journal and the number of subscribers. Magazines (especially closed circulation ones) are not the same as learned journals. If the staff do not recognise the names of the major subscription agents the organisation is clearly not familiar with the learned journal business. It is common sense to check what other publications the firm handles and how satisfied their clients are.

Subscription fulfilment houses and distributors have many ways of calculating costs; sometimes there are surprising extras. Do the proposed charges include stationery and postage on invoices and notices of price changes? If charges are based on a percentage of sales, does the percentage vary with the number of subscribers and the subscription price?

Cost and suitability are not the only considerations in selecting a distributor. Others include:

1 How fast is the turnaround of orders; how promptly do they deal with queries?
2 What credit arrangements do they have? How long credit do they

allow, or do they work on a cash-with-order basis? Can they accept credit cards?

3 How quickly will the publisher receive income from subscribers, and when will he have to pay the distributor's charges? What might appear to be identical figures from two organisations can look very different if the timing of payments is taken into account.

4 How many renewal reminders are sent out and when are they sent? Can reminders go to libraries and individuals on a different timetable? Is it possible for the publisher to send a letter to the most laggardly subscribers?

5 What kind of packaging material can they offer? Is it right for your journals?

6 What methods of despatch do they use? Is there a choice?

7 How frequently do they report on sales and income received? Can you easily get up-to-date lists of subscribers?

8 How are receipts for your journals held? What would happen if there was a calamity and the firm went into liquidation?

9 Can they accept orders electronically?

10 What management reports do they produce (cash flow forecasts, subscription trends, subscriber analysis, renewal rates, and claims for instance) and how meaningful and intelligible are they?

11 How good is their stock control?

12 Warehouse conditions: is stock satisfactorily housed?

13 Who makes good damaged copies?

14 Do librarians and subscription agents find their service satisfactory?

15 Do you feel them reliable and trustworthy, people you are happy to work with?

A publisher who does his own distribution obviously has greater control over it than one who sub-contracts the work. However, the latter may be spared a number of headaches, and, if he has only a few journals and little voluntary help, a distributor should cost less than an in-house system. In either case, at least one person from the publishing house should be included in the main despatch of the journal as a check on when copies were despatched, how long they took in transit and their condition on arrival.

Distribution in relation to other publishing functions

Distribution should not be isolated from other aspects of journal publishing. Accounts, editorial and production departments will need regular reports of numbers of subscribers, and will want to know who these subscribers are. Few learned journals get many comments from readers or subscribers, and these may well be addressed to the subscription department. Any comments or suggestions should be passed on. The subscription department should be kept aware of marketing plans – and used to monitor their success.

Money received for journals should be paid in as quickly as possible, and reported to the subscription section, so that the order can be processed without delay. Whoever handles the subscriptions will need information on the expected publication date of each issue of the journal, and to be kept up to date on programme changes. Changes in the page size or extent will mean changes in the packing material. Any special offers made in promotion campaigns should be discussed with those looking after distribution.

In addition, editorial and marketing people need reliable and meaningful information and reports at regular intervals on numbers of subscribers of different types (new, renewed, individual, institutional, special rates etc.) in different geographical areas, of income generated, sales of back volumes and so on. Too little information is frustrating; too much is overwhelming. It is better to produce reports that encourage further enquiries than to swamp the user, provided that their further questions can be answered. Weekly reports of changes in the number of subscribers in every country will generally be less informative than reports less frequently issued and by larger regions.

The publisher is likely to want more frequent reports or access to information for new journals, particularly in the first year or two, than for established journals. Some systems allow other departments to access the subscription fulfilment database to get information as required. Even so, reports are still helpful in crystallising information and in drawing attention to points that may need looking at: a sharp decline in subscribers in one country, a suspiciously low (or high) renewal rate and so on.

It may also be sensible to build in precautions against unauthorised access to information that the publisher might wish to keep confidential. Publishers have been known to telephone their competitor's distribution centres and, by giving the impression that they are in-house staff, obtain sales figures for titles of information to them.

6   Non-subscription revenue

This chapter is devoted to sources of revenue other than subscriptions, sometimes called special sales. With some journals the profitability of these revenues is vital to the journal's financial success. In all cases it should be borne in mind, however, that these other revenues involve additional costs. Even collecting a permission fee will involve raising an invoice and checking on payment. Storing and insuring back issues is expensive, and organising advertisements, offprints, mailing lists, page charges, establishing arrangements with document supply organisations and copyright collection agencies, and licensing directly with customers all add to overheads. Apart from offprints, which are often offered as a service to authors without any expectation of extra profits, all these items should help to improve the journal's financial position; but they will only do so if realistic rates are charged and procedures are well thought out and followed carefully.

Outside the usual sources of non-subscription revenue there is the possibility of obtaining grants to assist publication. Such funding is generally only obtainable for specific projects: these may include reducing a backlog of papers, publishing papers given at a meeting sponsored by the grant-giving body, inserting colour plates or the distribution of free or low-priced copies to a specified group (for example, certain libraries in the Third World or East Europe or favoured customers of products from a company). Usual sources are national academies, foundations, UNESCO and commercial concerns. Pharmaceutical companies, for example, may pay for the distribution of medical journals to people working in an area where they are trying to promote a drug; the free copies might be accompanied by a letter from the company. Some publishers may refuse such deals on the grounds that the financial involvement with a commercial organisation could diminish the perceived status of the journal and its editorial integrity.

There is also the controversial question of whether medical journals should publish supplements based on meetings sponsored by pharmaceutical companies (Bero, Galbraith & Rennie, 1992). The extra income for the publication of the supplement and run-on copies for distribution by the company can be considerable (indeed several journals are dependent on this income), but it can affect the reputation of the journal. Some journals insist on a member of its editorial board being a co-editor of the supplement to ensure that reasonable standards are maintained.

A special sales manager can do more if he has access to the contents of the journal as it is assembled by the editorial office so that, for example, a favourable mention of a product can be brought to the attention of the manufacturer who may then be persuaded to advertise in the journal and buy offprints of the article. Again, however, this raises the issue of editorial integrity as the commercial value of such deals could sway editorial judgement. Some leading medical journals separate very clearly their editorial functions and special sales, with the latter having no access to the contents until publication, to establish beyond doubt editorial independence.

When publishers compete for publishing contracts from societies or societies weigh up the relative merits of using a commercial publisher or 'self-publishing' the potential non-subscription revenue is a major factor. This can be an area where a major publisher with specialist departments in each sector of special sales may do better than a small publisher where one person may be handling all aspects of non-subscription revenue.

Advertising and inserts

With most scholarly journals there is relatively little revenue to be gained from selling space to advertisers; indeed, some journals do not accept advertisements. This source of revenue is discussed first, however, because in some cases it is as important, or even more important, than the subscription revenue.

In the most extreme cases, a professional periodical, as opposed to an academic one, may be entirely financed by advertising revenue. A large number of so-called 'limited', 'closed' or 'controlled' circulation (give-away) publications have been launched in the last three decades and some have achieved a reasonable reputation. Potential advertisers need to be assured that the publication is actually read when it arrives in the mail free of charge and not just thrown into the wastepaper basket along with other publicity material. There is therefore every incentive for the publisher to include good copy of wide interest. The managing editor will also plan the contents to attract advertisers; special or thematic issues may be scheduled months in advance with details sent to relevant advertisers and followed up by telephone. Special issues may be tied into major conferences and distributed to all the delegates; those companies exhibiting at the meeting are likely to agree to buy space.

Occasionally, a limited-circulation journal has such status that the publisher can switch to charging a subscription. The new subscription revenue and the reduction in costs through the inevitable drop in circulation can more than balance the loss in revenue from advertisers. The independence of editorial policy from immediate commercial interests should be made clear.

What lessons about selling advertising space can be learnt from such periodicals? Apart from efficient service and sustained pressure on potential and existing advertisers, the job advertisements are an obvious feature. They can make up a high proportion of the advertisements and are often the first thing that readers look at. Indeed as Gordon Graham, the editor of *Logos*, once said, a trade journal such as *The Bookseller* appeals mainly to backward readers! Many people start with the jobs at the end of the periodical and then work backwards. A survey carried out by *Nature* also revealed that the job advertisements were the single most-read item. One society discovered that if they really wanted their members to read something, they had to put it in the vacancies section. Unfortunately, many journals cannot exploit this source of revenue, as it requires frequent and rapid publication. If a publisher is considering to change to, say, fortnightly publication the potential here should be exploited.

Because controlled-circulation publishers decide to whom to send their periodical they can provide advertisers with enough subscribers in specified subject areas to attract their orders. On the Continent of Europe a number of hybrid journals have developed where to keep up circulation to the right people for the sake of the advertisers the publisher gives away issues as well as sells subscriptions. The free distribution might be to members of a society but more often it is done on a changing basis which might also lead to subscriptions. The publisher might, for example, give two issues to a part of its mailing list then switch to another part following up on the recipients of the free copies with a letter asking them if they would now like to subscribe, perhaps at a special discount. In the United States the mailing list might be created by first sending out promotional material asking whether the recipient would like to receive sample copies of the periodical.

Finally, controlled-circulation periodicals often look more attractive than learned journals and advertisers respond to this. When publishers decide to redesign a journal they should bear in mind this potential added benefit, and that an unusual format will put off some advertisers as they will have to produce advertisements of a special size. There are many examples of a change to a larger standard format, colour cover and more interesting typography leading to an increase in advertising revenue.

Advertising information

To sell advertising it is essential to get out the information on what the journal has to offer at what price. Many advertisers in learned journals, besides some publishers, book space through advertising agencies. The agencies select the journals, recommend the scheduling, prepare the advertisement and book the space on behalf of the client. They should therefore have up-to-date information on the rates, type areas, technical specifications, frequency of publication, copy dates, etc. For the UK this information is published in the monthly *British Rate and Data (BRAD)*, and any publishers hoping to attract advertising to their journals will make sure these details appear in *BRAD*. Media departments treat it as a bible: if a journal is not listed, it will quite likely be overlooked when advertising schedules are planned. In the USA there are regional and industry directories rather than one dominant, national directory.

BRAD is the first place in the UK where information should be sent. It is important, however, not to leave it at this point. A rival publication has developed called Willings Press Guide; information should also be sent to this. *BRAD* is a huge publication and a new entry will not be spotted without some back-up from the publisher to the agencies. Printed circulars announcing the journal, telephone calls to media staff in the agencies, e-mail messages, sample copies to selected people involved in media planning (the space buyers usually), all serve to increase agency awareness of the journal.

The agencies receive their instructions from firms who intend marketing certain products in particular markets, and therefore they have to be kept informed of the possibilities of advertising. Regular contact with the major firms' marketing or advertising departments is advisable, especially as marketing managers and advertising policy change frequently. When an agency has full responsibility such contact may not be necessary, but since firms give quite specific instructions covering the placing of their advertisements it can be fruitful. A telephone call to the marketing manager may bring to light the firm's intention to launch a new product which is entirely appropriate to the journal. A sample copy and a letter may also be effective.

Many journals have printed rate cards giving all the necessary data. If the publisher has a large number of journals in one field, however, it can be more cost effective to have a catalogue presenting them all with notes on editorial policy, readership and so on; then, if an advertiser wishes to cover the field thoroughly he may choose several titles in which to advertise. Wherever the rates are given, potential advertisers should be warned that the publishers reserve the right to reject any advertisement thought to be unsuitable without having to give reasons. An advertising manager usually refers any suspect advertisement to the editor before accepting it. With a medical journal, for example, the editor may object to some advertisement for a drug – because of the way the advertisement is worded, because it may be felt that the drug is suspect or because publication of the advertisement could be taken to mean that the journal approves of the drug. In other cases it may be felt that advertisements of a trivial nature are not appropriate for a learned journal. Other publishers might be encouraged to buy space with a special discount (often 10 per cent) as such advertisements will be of particular interest to readers.

As well as putting out information, knowledge of what is happening in the commercial world that relates to the journal can be helpful. A standard source of information for those selling space to the pharmaceutical industry is *Scrip* which covers most of the industry from market analysis to the latest in molecular biology as it relates to new therapies. This is often where a space seller may first learn of a new product which could be relevant to one of his journals. Editors should also be encouraged to feed back information on commercial interests and new developments which might help the publisher sell space or similar services such as an insert of a leaflet.

Selling space

Close contact with the agencies is important as should be clear from the previous section. The agencies usually operate on the basis of a budget agreed with the advertiser. In the UK media buyers expect a commission of 10 per cent; in the rest of Europe, and in North America, they expect 15 per cent with occasionally a small discount, say 2 per cent, for prompt payment. In North America the publisher will often use an agent to sell space on a commission of 15 per cent; these agents often have specialist knowledge and will call regularly on the media buyers, something which a space seller for a learned journal can rarely afford to do.

The advertising sales people should build up a comprehensive list of potential advertisers, together with information about their products. Each journal requires a basic mailing list for advertising: this should cover firms who like to keep up to date with the rates and who may at some time place advertising. A firm may not book space for a while and then surprise with four-colour double-page spreads; as mentioned above, marketing managers and policy change.

Many firms send out press releases to editors of journals, and if these can be intercepted by the advertising department they may provide information about a new product, who is controlling the firm's budget, who is responsible for sales, etc. A follow-up letter together with a sample copy of the journal may encourage them to advertise. Usually they warrant a friendly telephone call, but the success rate is low, as companies going to the expense of issuing a press release are looking for 'free publicity', such as a mention in a product news section (a common feature of a controlled-circulation periodical).

In some subjects the editor can help and they should be encouraged to do so. As editors should have an intimate knowledge of their journal's specialist field and some standing in that field, they can not only provide names of marketing managers that might be approached but they may also be persuaded to make approaches themselves, at least on an informal basis such as at a conference.

Trade directories contain masses of information, which should be used selectively. It is easy to waste money by sending material to people who are only vaguely concerned with the placing of advertising. Nevertheless, they and advertisements appearing in journals covering the same subject from rival publishers can be extremely useful guides to potential advertisers. The aggressive space seller will telephone the company that has placed a new advertisement in a rival publication and try to persuade them that his journal would be more appropriate and offer a deal on price.

Another way of identifying potential advertisers is to attend major meetings that include exhibitors. It is worth going to all the stands to get an idea of what advertising the companies might undertake and, if possible, to meet or find out the name of the marketing manager. If the cost of attending is too high in relation to the likely return, every effort should be made to obtain a list of exhibitors and their addresses so that they can be contacted afterwards.

It is often possible to glean from the papers awaiting publication the names of firms whose products are specifically being considered (in technical notes, apparatus reviews, etc.) in the journal and who might therefore be interested in advertising. For this to be of use, quick action is essential, since the firm will wish to brief its agency and have the required artwork prepared before the issue goes to press. It should be added that failure is more common than success with this approach.

New journals can obtain some measure of advertising by offering free space for a number of issues, followed by a relatively low rate while the circulation is rising. The idea is that this establishes the habit with the advertiser and encourages others to buy space as they see their rivals already supporting the publication. Advertising in a new journal is often a good proposition to an advertiser, since large numbers of copies are given away to potential subscribers. An inflated initial print-run can consequently be presented as an advantage to the advertiser.

Advertising rates

The most common mistake is not to charge enough. The total costs of producing and distributing a journal in a year can be divided by the number of pages published in that year to get a basic cost per page. To this must be added the overheads involved in selling space and organising the printing of the advertisement. Since advertisements are usually included to cover some of the costs of publishing the text, a reasonable level of profit is obviously required. A standard rate might therefore be around two and a half times the basic cost. This allows for discounts agents who book space regularly, take a large number of pages in one issue, etc. VAT charges should be made clear.

Extras include bleed charges and special positions – such as the back cover, or facing text or even on the envelope or wrapper in which the journal is sent. Some advertisers will demand to see where their advertisement will appear, particularly in relation to the advertisements of competitors. If more special positions can be agreed to with the editor (such as amongst the text near the front) the space seller's job becomes easier. Many learned journals have a policy of only allowing advertising before or after the text. Some publishers demand camera-ready copy for advertisements and will charge extra for any setting.

Charging for each extra colour is more complicated. Where the advertising section carries a number of colour advertisements the extra printing costs per advertisement are reduced, and a further charge of £150 to £200 (in 1995) per extra colour for a full page would be reasonable. Where, however, a journal may only be able to attract one or two colour advertisements per issue, a realistic charge would be more in the region of £250 per colour, which would, of course, deter most potential advertisers. A publisher may offer a lower rate in the hope that this will encourage a build-up of colour advertising. With most learned journals the potential for this is limited, and there is little point in subsidising the occasional colour advertisement out of subscription income. With the trend towards more colour on the front cover, however, it can be possible to offer attractive rates for space on the rest of the cover. The same is happening with some journals, particularly in medicine, where more colour is being included in the text; as much or all of the issue is being run through a colour press the cost of reproducing colour advertisements drops.

The dilemma of selling advertising in learned journals is that most advertisers want a large national readership, whilst what most publishers of learned journals can offer is a relatively small, international readership. There is, therefore, a limit on what can be charged. Most advertising agents get paid by their clients on the basis of what they spend, so their commission on an advertisement in a learned journal is likely to leave them out of pocket. Consequently, the main source of advertising revenue for many scholarly journals is other publishers.

Where a national society publishes a bulletin for its membership as well as one or more research journals it might be able to exploit advertisers' preference for national circulation. There are various examples of societies gaining considerable income from advertisers happy to support their bulletin which appears sufficiently attractive to be read by most of the members, but who see little attraction in a high-level, specialised research journal. Some investment in the editorial development of a society bulletin or newsletter can pay off with greater revenues from advertisers. Some of the features of controlled-circulation magazines might be used such as a special issue for the annual conference of the society.

Handling the advertisement and conditions of acceptance

Advertisers who have booked space should be reminded of the copy date. Artwork or film sent in should be checked on receipt to make sure that it is the right size and that the copy is not likely to be rejected by the editor. With many journals all new advertisements have to be approved by the editor. Policy on this in medical journals is covered in a statement by the International Committee of Medical Journal Editors (1994). This committee recommends that editors must have full editorial responsibility for advertising policy and readers should be able to distinguish between advertising and editorial material. The recommendation that advertising should not be sold on the condition that it will appear in the same issue as a particular article would be difficult to follow for some controlled circulation journals.

Advertisers who do not supply artwork or film should be asked to submit copy earlier to allow time for the publishers to prepare the copy and, if requested, submit a proof to the advertiser for checking. With a repeat booking, the advertiser should be asked to confirm each time that the right copy is being used and a replacement is not on its way. If the advertiser sends artwork or film there is no need of a proof. A copy of the published issue should be sent, usually with the invoice. Bad debts are unusual, but the status of advertisers should be watched in case an agency goes into liquidation. Occasionally, there are problems over payment through the advertiser claiming that an order had been cancelled or the wrong advertisement had been used. This is why careful checking at the copy date stage is essential. All orders and cancellations should be in writing.

Some problems can be avoided if the conditions of acceptance of advertisements are made clear. A full statement of these conditions should be printed in any media data catalogue sent to potential advertisers and ideally a condensed version on the back of individual journal rate cards.

A list of conditions that might be considered is given below.

1 All advertisements are subject to acceptance by the publishers.
2 The publishers cannot be responsible for any error or omission, or damage to the film or artwork.
3 The publishers reserve the right to change the position of the advertisement.
4 The publishers reserve the right to require an advertisement to be amended to meet their approval.
5 The publishers shall charge the advertiser for any changes to the copy made at the advertiser's request.
6 The publishers shall specify the copy dates.
7 Placing an order does not confer the right to renew on the same terms.
8 The publishers may increase rates at any time, but in such event the

advertiser has the option to cancel the balance of the contract without surcharge.

9 If the advertiser cancels the balance of a contract, unless in the circumstances of (8) above, all unearned series discounts will be charged.

10 The publishers may surcharge if a series of advertisements are not completed within the agreed period.

11 The advertiser warrants that the advertisement does not contravene any regulation, is not defamatory and does not infringe any other party's rights; and will indemnify the publishers against any claims arising from the advertisement.

12 The advertiser submitting an advertisement will observe national codes of practice and standards.

13 The placing of an order will constitute acceptance of these conditions.

Inserts

Inserts are leaflets, or similar material, slipped into a journal before despatch. The problem with inserts is that they can annoy subscribers, so most journals limit them to two or three per issue. It should be remembered that they are a fairly low-cost form of promotion, since they enable an advertiser to send out a leaflet or card without the cost of envelopes, addressing them, inserting the material and postage. The charge, therefore, should be reasonably high; a typical rate would be the same as that charged for a full page of single colour advertising (say around £400) plus a premium for any extra sheets. It needs to be in this region, as the publishers must ensure that the insert arrives at the right place at the right time, and the publicity material must be inserted in each copy before despatch. Printers or binders in the UK charge about £80 per 1000 in 1995 for inserting a leaflet. The publishers must also check that the insert will fit into the journal and does not raise the weight of the total package into a higher mailing rate. If the insert requires folding this should be charged for. The conditions of acceptance should be as for a printed advertisement. Series discounts are not usually offered.

With journals that go mainly to libraries, advertisers might feel that not enough inserts will reach potential customers; librarians may empty the inserts into a bin when the issues are unpacked. Many advertisers are aware of this problem and look for periodicals which mainly go to individuals. A society's bulletin distributed to members would therefore seem to be a better vehicle for an insert than the society's scholarly journal. Societies may be able to develop this source of revenue to offset the cost of producing and distributing their bulletins or news-letters.

Back issues

For many learned journals the sale of back issues is still the largest source of revenue outside subscriptions; this is particularly so for long-established journals in the law and humanities. Almost all back-issue sales are to libraries, who usually buy through agents. Where a library is considering a major purchase it usually asks agents to tender for the supply, but such orders are becoming infrequent and other media might be considered. For example, when the Kuwait University library wanted to replace its lost back issue sets after the war it decided on micro-fiche rather than hard-copy. The market for hard-copy probably peaked in the 1970s and has declined markedly since the mid-1980s. Back runs in the publisher's warehouse can certainly no longer be considered to be an asset worthy of inclusion in the balance sheet.

Most agents treat supplying back issues as a service rather than a 'profit centre'. Two agents, Dawsons and Swets & Zeitlinger, still have large stockholdings and have become in essence wholesalers, supplying other agents at a discount. Many publishers now sell their back issues over three years old to one of these agents or give them what stock they require and lease the right to trade in these on their behalf for a royalty (usually 10 per cent); they estimate that the revenue from selling older issues does not cover storage costs and the overheads involved. As publishers have become much tighter on claims for older issues, agents sometimes have to buy single issues from these wholesalers to supply their customers.

Where the rights to older issues are sold or leased to a specialist agent, details such as the number of volumes involved, period between publication of a volume and moving it to the dealer, micro-form rights, royalties or commission, charges for existing stock and termination will need to be covered in any arrangement. The rights to any machine-readable form should be kept by the publisher, as it is possible that compact disks carrying back runs in digital form will be used by libraries.

Up to the 1970s reprint specialists were active in the field of journal back issues. At that time, around 50 per cent of the back issues market would be in reprints. Now micro-forms dominate the market (Ashby & Campbell 1979) and can be used as a back-up. If a whole run has been filmed, 'difficult' issues no longer available from the trade, or the original publisher, can be produced from a reader-printer (i.e. a photocopier which gives paper sheets from micro-film).

Around 90 per cent of the business is in copies published within the last three years. Once issues are bound up as volumes, and become less frequently referred to, there is rarely any need to replace them. Some libraries may have a policy of, say, clearing out volumes over ten years old to save on space and using inter-library lending document delivery to deal with requests for older issues; this is more common in commercial concerns than in universities. When a library takes a new journal it may buy back two or three years or to the first volume so that they have a complete run, but such orders are much less frequent now that library budgets are under pressure. Sometimes a publisher will offer the previous volume free of charge to new subscribers as a 'premium'.

An important factor which creates a market for recent issues is the difficulty librarians have in budgeting for price increases. There have been clear examples of marked increases in subscription prices of journals published from a particular country, usually resulting from changes in exchange rates or inflation, leading to some loss of subscribers in one year followed by a good year for back-issues as libraries catch up on the previous year. The library generally buys the back issues through the agent who handles the current subscription. The dealer is unlikely to have built up any stocks of the previous year's issues, so the order will usually go to the original publisher. 'Missed issues', as opposed to back issues, might be a more appropriate term for this type of business.

Most publishers advertise high prices for their back issues; for example, the current price for a volume of single issues is commonly around 15 per cent higher than the full volume subscription price. If, however, there is the possibility of a large order, a discount may be offered: otherwise the order may go to back-issue agents. Occasionally, publishers, particularly in the legal field, offer to supply back issues in cloth-bound volumes. Some publishers supply cloth-bound volumes to current subscribers for an additional charge.

Publishers' prices for back issues may sometimes seem high but, when the overheads, finance charges, storage and insurance costs are considered, they are working to a reasonable margin. Indeed, where large numbers of back issues are still being stored the real costs are probably reducing the operation to a loss. Publishers should analyse their holdings carefully and dispose of any surplus, especially now that the market for older issues has diminished. For insurance purposes, the back issues might be valued at replacement cost but, since the reprinting of a back-run would cost so much more than the market value, this is unrealistic. Some publishers insure at a value somewhere between, while others simply insure at an estimated market value, or not at all. Usually, in any accounts the stock of each issue is given no value as soon as the issue is published, i.e. when it no longer counts as work in progress.

Today's back stock is yesterday's surplus. Now that circulations of established journals are fairly static, most publishers are not overprinting to cater for strong demand later. The standard policy for a typical learned journal is to print enough copies to allow for replacement, and to give a small back stock of around 100 copies. This stock might be trimmed down to 25 copies when three years old if it is not passed on to an agent. Publishers are likely to make more use of the new printing equipment which produces one copy at a time (see chapter 3) to deal with orders for older issues and keep print-runs very tight.

Mailing lists

Many publishers rent out the list of the names and addresses of subscribers to a journal for rates at around £80 per thousand addresses. Occasionally, publishers may exchange mailing lists. Some publishers use list brokers to help them develop this source of revenue.

The problem with releasing a mailing list is that it can then be sold on, and eventually subscribers to a journal could find themselves being mailed leaflets about life insurance schemes, credit cards and so on. With academic subjects the usual customer is a publisher, who may use the list repeatedly for several years to promote books and journals including, possibly, a rival publication. The list should usually be rented for one-time use only, therefore, (ideally with the use agreed) and should not be undervalued. Some publishers insist on seeing a copy of what will be mailed before agreeing to rent out their list. Another common restriction is for the mailing to be completed within a maximum of, say, six months of receiving the list. Supplying a list in machine-readable form will make it very easy to reproduce; supplying labels will make it a little more difficult to copy.

Some publishers, especially societies, refuse to rent out their mailing lists, as they feel that their members and other subscribers may not want their names given to advertisers. If names and addresses of subscribers are being rented out, i.e. being used for a purpose other than supplying subscribers with the journal, then in some countries clearance should be obtained from the subscribers and the list should be registered (for example, in the UK with the Data Protection Registrar). There is also the sound commercial argument that releasing the mailing list can reduce the sales of advertising space in the publication.

One way of controlling the use of the list of subscribers is for the publisher to carry out the actual mailing, perhaps inserting the advertiser's leaflet with other material. A typical charge for mailing a leaflet to the subscribers would be around £400 for 2000 names plus £50 for each additional 1000 names plus a handling charge of around £40 per 1000 plus postage. As with advertisements acceptance of a mailing piece is usually subject to editorial approval. If the list is to be rented out, some publishers slip in an address specific to that copy of the list, so that they can monitor the use made of the list.

Supplements

Supplements are collections of papers that deal with related topics, are published as a separate issue of the journal or as a second part of a regular issue, and are usually funded by sources other than the journal publisher (certainly in medicine). Occasionally a journal will take one on to cover what is felt to be an important topic and the cost is carried by the overall subscription revenue. A few journals actually budget to publish special issues or supplements alongside the scheduled issues. More usually, however, a supplement will be at least partially funded from an outside source such as the organisers of a meeting who want the proceedings published. The charge may well be negotiated between the publishers and the organisers on the basis of an estimate of the costs involved including a contribution towards the overheads.

With some medical journals, for example, supplements may actually contribute much of the final publishing profit. Because of the funding sources the content of supplements can reflect biases in choice of topics and viewpoints. A list of principles was published by the International Committee of Medical Journal Editors. The essence of these are: the journal editor must retain complete control and authority, the sources of funding should be clearly stated, advertising should follow the policy of the journal, the funding organisation should not be involved in the editing, the journal editors and supplement editors should not receive excessive compensation from the sponsors of the supplement and redundant publication should be avoided (International Committee of Medical Journal Editors, 1994).

If the editorial policy allows the taking on of sponsored supplements the deals can involve tens of thousands of pounds; the sponsor will usually have to pay for the production and despatch of copies to the subscribers as a condition of acceptance, and may also wish to purchase a number of run-on copies for their own distribution. Very occasionally run-on quantities of 10,000 or more might be involved. In such cases, the publisher might seek quotations not only from the existing suppliers but also from other suppliers who may offer better prices for longer runs. In medicine around 40 per cent of the business comes through agencies handling the promotion of a product (often new) on behalf of a company; sometimes they will be putting together a tender to win the contract from the pharmaceutical company. The company will not necessarily base its decision on price; it will be looking for high standards of production and editing, often a fast schedule, status and appropriate readership.

For those planning to take on a supplement some guidelines are given below.

(1) Clear the project with the editor. Provisional approval is usually sought on the basis of an outline or programme (sponsors often need to set up publication well in advance). Approval should be on the understanding that it is subject to an assessment of the final copy.

(2) Discuss carefully with the organisers/editor of the supplement what is exactly required, how much copy will be supplied and in what condition, the arrangements for copy-editing and proofing, and the schedule.

(3) Establish a charge on the basis of quotations from suppliers and the requirements of the organisers and sponsors. A special binding and cover might, for example, be specified for the run-on.

(4) Arrange for extra resources such as copy-editing and brief the suppliers to ensure that the extra workload can be borne without jeopardising the schedule of the standard issues.

(5) Check that extra paper will be available and that the binding and delivery instructions are clear.

(6) Establish an agreement with the organisers or sponsors at least by exchange of letters to cover price, editorial input, specifications, schedule and delivery instructions. Normally editorial policy dictates that the editorial and production standards must not be lower than those for regular issues of the journal. Where a sponsor has invested heavily in a meeting, gathering first-class contributors and paying for extra editing and rewriting, the standard of the supplement can compare very favourably with the rest of the journal.

In some European countries it is required that a doctoral thesis is published, and this may be done as a supplement to a journal. Some journals do this as a service to the academic community and charge as little as possible to the author; this policy may even allow for lower production standards and in some cases production from CRC. Occasionally the author may be allowed to organise their own production provided certain minimum specifications are followed; such journals supply special instructions on the preparation of supplements. DTP has helped here.

Offprints

The use of offprints varies greatly between subjects. Often in medicine and the life and earth sciences authors require one to two hundred copies to distribute to colleagues. In the humanities and some pure sciences, authors are usually satisfied with the free allowance, though they may sometimes also use a photocopier. Smaller budgets, the photocopier and improved document-delivery services have all served to reduce demand. Pressure on authors to distribute copies widely is also less now, although requests still come in from East Europe and the developing countries, where there may be limited access to the original journal.

Review journals vary greatly in their offer of offprints. Some journals publishing mainly primary articles give more free offprints of review articles to encourage authors to submit these. (It is thought that one or two review articles in each issue adds to the appeal of the journal.) Large-circulation journals usually deem it sufficient to send authors one copy of the issue in which the article appears. A few journals treat offprints as a fee, i.e. an author is offered payment or offprints. Reviewers of books might only be given two or three copies of the journal, although longer essay-type reviews in the humanities may be treated like normal papers.

Offprints are thus mainly supplied as a service to authors. Where, however, authors wish to purchase further copies over and above their free allowance publishers tend to set their charges to make a small profit, since the overheads involved in dealing with orders for offprints are considerable. For certain large scientific, technical or medical journals – especially where companies may buy quantities of particular papers if they include, for example, a favourable mention of a product – offprints can add up to £20,000 or more to the total revenue and make a net profit of around 25 per cent. With one of these journals the offprints manager will actively sell to industry. This might involve looking for a mention of products in papers at the proof stage and contacting the company. A special sale of this nature might include a cover for the offprints similar to that of the journal with perhaps a statement or advertisement on the back from the company. In medicine and allied health, orders for 50,000 copies and even more are occasionally won. When negotiating a price the use of the reprinted article should be borne in mind.

The revenue from offprints for an established journal in medicine, biology or geology may be similar to that for back issues. Where the journal has a policy of encouraging colour illustrations, perhaps by publishing them without extra charge as is happening more often in medicine or at a reduced charge, authors tend to order more offprints as ordinary photocopies will not be so useful; this can push up offprints revenue significantly and meet some of the cost of printing the colour plates. With journals in the social sciences and humanities, however, the revenue from offprints is unlikely to be as much as 10 per cent of the revenue from back issues, so they are a loss-making item.

As there is competition for good papers some editors demand larger quantities of free offprints to attract authors. Whether this will attract authors depends in part on the subject area. Most journals give 25 copies free of charge, but many give 50 and some 100, or even 200. The problem here is that someone has to pay for those free copies, and usually the rates for further copies are increased to compensate. It is difficult to analyse the financial effect of this, but it seems that most contributors, or their institutions, have a certain amount to spend on each paper published, so they simply receive more free copies and buy fewer at a higher price. Other institutions seem to require a certain number, so again they only need buy fewer at a higher rate if they receive more free of charge. The general result is that institutions pay more and individuals less, which is often the financial outcome in journal pricing. If a larger allocation of free offprints reduces the profit made on the service it may be justified on the grounds that the larger number attracts better contributors, and an improvement in the quality of the papers published in the journal will lead to an increase in the subscription revenue. In some cases where a society publishes a journal it may give free offprints only to members; other contributors may receive no free offprints, or a smaller allowance of free offprints.

Offprints are in competition with the photocopier. If they are too expensive, contributors will prefer to photocopy unless the quality of, say, the photographs is vital to an understanding of the paper. Obviously, photocopies are also no use to an organisation which decides to distribute copies for prestige or promotional purposes, but in this case they must be well printed (see chapter 3).

As explained in chapter 3, the printers' charges for offprints vary widely. They should be established for each journal to set against revenue, and to make sure that, where possible, a profit is made. Larger publishers may employ a standard scale for all their journals. This could mean that some are overpriced, but it does avoid excessively high charges where printer's rates are very high for a particular journal, and should simplify procedures.

The overheads in organising offprints are considerable and should be allowed for in the pricing. Another problem is the money lost through authors, or their institutions, not paying for the offprints. To avoid this loss (which leads to high prices to compensate) and to reduce overheads, many journals ask contributors to pay for their offprints before receiving them. When this policy is introduced there may well be complaints but, although some individuals may argue that their institutions will not pay until the offprints are received, practically everyone does agree to pay in advance. The offprint revenue increases, since losses through bad debts are avoided and the overheads involved in chasing slow payers are also cut out. Bad debts can also be reduced by accepting payment by credit card which has the added advantage of eliminating currency problems for overseas contributors.

If the policy of advance payment is followed it should be explained on the scale of charges and order form (best produced as a simple card with a tear-off business reply card addressed to the publisher). The form of words might be: 'In order to keep the cost of offprints as low as possible we must have payment in advance.' The reply card should enable the author to fill in how many copies are required over and above the free allocation, the title of the paper, the address for the despatch of the offprints and the name and address to be invoiced. The author should be asked to ensure that the total number of copies required are given on the reply card (i.e. for all the authors, if there are co-authors) and the authors' institutions, as further copies cannot be supplied after publication at the same rates. It should also be made clear that there is only one lot of free copies for a paper, however many authors are involved.

Another way to simplify matters is to give automatically 25, or even only 10, offprints of each paper free of charge, and leave the author to photocopy, thus avoiding the overheads involved in organising offprints. This tactic is fairly common with the North American 'trade' journals. Another tactic of such journals is to give several copies of the journal to the author, and only offer offprints with a high minimum number, say 500, and at a high price which makes it well worth the publisher's handling the order and organising the printing. It is more difficult for learned journals to get away with this.

Offprints involve much paperwork in relation to income, and often create irritating problems in production and despatch (such as authors saying that their offprints have not arrived), so perfect record keeping is required to sort these out. Any means of simplifying procedures, such as charging in advance and using a standard reply card attached to the rate card, should be employed. Provided administrative errors can be kept to a minimum, and the scale of charges (usually around twice the supplier's charges) is right, there should be a reasonable profit in relation to the work involved for subjects where offprints are commonly purchased.

Document delivery

For centuries libraries have lent each other material, but with the advent of photocopying they were able to supply each other with copies of chapter and articles, i.e. individual documents. Some organisations within the library community specialised in document delivery but as it is based on the fair or personal use limitation in most copyright legislation it cannot be conducted commercially without paying copyright fees. This has meant that 'not-for-profit' organisations have dominated the field. The volume of business in now enormous with OCLC in the United States switching millions of requests per annum to the appropriate source and the British Library supplying over three million documents per annum. Estimates of the number of documents supplied by one library to another in North America vary but OCLC has suggested that inter-library loans in the United States rose from 21 million items in 1981 to 27.9 million in 1993 (a rise of 33 per cent); the volume in Western Europe is thought to be similar.

As was predicted in the early 1980s the volume of document delivery worldwide is increasing. A figure of 5 per cent per annum is often quoted. The decline in library budgets in real terms, the cost of storing back-runs and the potential of new technology to enable users to identify an article and order it quickly have all driven up demand. Typically, an academic library in the UK spends around 8 per cent of its acquisition budget on document delivery and 35 per cent on journal subscriptions. Publishers have received a minute fraction of the money spent on document delivery. A number of studies agree that the 'transactional cost' of document delivery (without any copyright fee) is of the order of US$30 per item (mostly library staff cost). Many librarians have been assuming that reducing their journal holdings to 'core titles' and using current awareness services, linked with document delivery/inter-library lending to cover the rest, will use their budgets more effectively. However, David Baker (Librarian, University of East Anglia, UK) concluded after a careful financial study of the use of document delivery in his library that: 'In many subject areas – and especially where average journal costs are relatively low – the room for economy through use of document delivery and 'contents page' services – whether manually or digitally based – is very limited' (Campbell 1992a).

The BLDSC (British Library Document Supply Centre) claims that its service to some extent complements rather than competes with the supply of journals on subscription. A study in 1995 of the institutional subscribers to a journal in molecular biology showed that 25 per cent of the libraries also purchased copies of articles from the journal from the BLDSC. Presumably these libraries were using the BLDSC for articles in recent issues on circulation (the peak of article requests is generally two or three weeks after the article is published) or otherwise not immediately available (Russon & Campbell 1996). This study also indicated that industry makes relatively much greater use of document delivery than academic libraries.

Some commercial organisations, particularly in North America, have paid copyright fees to RROs (Reproduction Rights Organisations) and recently the BLDSC has paid a standard negotiated fee on copies of articles sent to North America and under their copyright cleared scheme to the CCC (Copyright Clearance Center) and the CLA (Copyright Licensing Agency) respectively. Some national RROs have made progress in collecting copyright fees and distributing them (for example, Kopinor in Norway has persuaded the Norwegian government to make a per capita payment to it to cover photocopying) but this has been largely outside publishers' control. Distribution of fees by RROs has usually been on a fairly arbitrary basis (sampling) and publishers have not been able to establish their own copyright fees internationally although the International Association of STM Publishers has pressed for this.

New technology, however, could transform the situation for publishers. One of the problems in trying to claim copyright fees from photocopying was that it was virtually impossible to monitor. The CCC tried hard to collect on a transaction basis but only made progress when it implemented annual negotiated licences based on sampling. New systems such as the ADONIS service (Stern & Campbell 1989) have shown the way: subscribers to the service print out copies of articles from compact disks on a workstation which records usage. These records are then used to charge the subscriber every quarter; each publisher receives royalties on the basis of the copying charge that they have fixed for each journal.

This new technology offers such greater efficiency for document delivery services that some of them are switching to, say, ADONIS even though this means that they have to pay copyright fees. The BLDSC, for example, from the end of 1993 started using its ADONIS workstation for all requests for articles on the ADONIS database even when they were for personal use and therefore not requiring copyright clearance. For the first time publishers were receiving royalties from this area of secondary distribution of their material.

The next step for organisations such as the BLDSC is to offer electronic document delivery. At present this term is sometimes used inaccurately to describe services which take orders electronically, often linked to a database of tables of contents of journals accessed through a network. These orders are usually serviced by mailing photocopies or for a higher charge by fax. Bit-mapped images of pages can be transmitted but with normal bandwidths this is slow. Developments such as ATM (Asynchronous Transfer Mode) will speed up transmission and new software such as Acrobat from Adobe Systems offers a huge improvement. Journal articles held in Postscript files (see chapter 3) can be compressed by Acrobat using Acrobat Distiller into portable files which are platform independent, i.e. can be used on any hardware. Adobe supplies the Acrobat Reader software (which enables a user to receive the document file, decompress it and set it up on their own screen) free of charge. Adobe also supplies more powerful software which enables the user to browse the document files.

Organisations moving into electronic document delivery will have to obtain a licence from the copyright holder. Most copyright legislation is clear on this. When a publisher is approached over this they should bear in mind the potential of electronic delivery. Some of the issues are discussed in more detail in Campbell (1992b) and Hunter (1993). One concern of publishers is that efficient electronic systems will give such easy access to their journals that giving up the hard-copy subscription and their local availability on the library shelf is no hardship for the library's users. The response to this is that publishers cannot hold back technical progress, but they should charge enough for copies of articles sold through these systems to compensate for lost subscription revenue.

A simple model analysing what revenue might be required from document delivery to compensate for declining hard-copy subscription revenues indicated that charges should be double what they were and this would still not be enough on the basis of what is collected by RROs and the few document supply services that pay publishers direct (Bodinham & Campbell 1992). The model showed, however, that this extra revenue in combination with the savings in origination costs from type-setting directly from authors' disks could maintain current levels of profitability.

Publishers should support their RROs, especially those that are trying to uphold publishers' rights. Copyright revenues from RROs, however, are subject to delays and overheads charges, and there is the risk that RROs will be used by some countries to operate compulsory licensing. It is usually more effective to negotiate direct arrangements with document delivery services; the points to note in making such arrangements are listed in chapter 7. Some organisations will try to negotiate a discount for high volume and early payment. With fully computerised systems it should be possible to obtain usage reports along with the royalties down to the level of the individual article; these data are valuable feedback for the journal editors, indeed they could influence editorial policy. A deal may be linked to supplying tables-of-contents and abstracts in machine readable form for a fee as some of the larger services also run current awareness databases. Within a year or two it should also be possible to supply services with the full article in machine-readable form (say in Acrobat), which should be worth higher charges.

Ultimately some publishers will want to supply documents themselves as well as through secondary services, indeed several have begun to do this. In some cases the secondary services may simply route orders from their customers (using the service's current awareness database) to the publisher for a commission or discount. The publisher then supplies by mail, fax or through a network. Within several years such a facility could be part of an electronic journal subscription (see chapter 11) with the customer subscribing to a service made up of a title database, perhaps abstracts, and full articles all held on their local server backed up by access to the publisher's server for titles not held locally. Some information scientists (see Brown 1993 for an analysis of the rise and expected decline of document delivery) already predict that document delivery will reach a peak within five years then slowly fall back as full electronic journal subscriptions become available through broad-band networks.

Material for secondary services

Secondary services offering databases of abstracts and tables of contents of journals have traditionally rekeyed this text, sometimes using elaborate systems based on faxing photocopies of article headers (the first page of an article giving title, author and abstract) to parts of the developing world for low-cost keyboarding. As publishers move towards producing articles with SGML coding, they are able to supply article headers in machine-readable form that can be fed into the secondary service's database with relatively little manipulation (see figure 3.3). In theory, therefore, secondary services have the opportunity to assemble their databases more quickly and without keyboarding errors. Unfortunately, as these services have often invested heavily in a system based on their own keyboarding it can be difficult for them to adapt to this new source of material. As more publishers organise their production to be able to supply article headers in machine readable form, the secondary services should find it worthwhile to adapt and pay the publishers a charge per article head. This should make this a useful additional source of income as well as ensuring that users of the secondary services get timely and accurate information.

Permissions

Requests for permission to reproduce material from a journal vary from someone wanting to photocopy some pages for handouts to students on a course to an editor compiling a volume of 'readings' or a database on, say, CD-ROM who may want to reproduce several articles or even the whole journal. In the latter case there are major issues involved (discussed at the end of this section), in the first case it may be worth finding out just how many copies are required, and whether the material is actually sold to the students. The overheads involved in obtaining a small fee probably amount to more than the fee itself. Usually it is simpler to return the letter stamped with, say: 'Permission granted provided full acknowledgement is made to the source, and the author(s) also agree. Journal Publishing Co. Date . . . Rights Manager . . . ' Such a stamp can save a tremendous amount of time over the years. This can only be done, however, if the letter clearly states what is being requested; otherwise, a reply asking for full details and an exact description of the use to be made of the copyright material will be required. The Copyright Clearance Center (CCC) and its counterparts in other countries are an important development in the efforts of copyright owners to control photocopying and make it easier for users to obtain permission to copy material (see chapter 7).

When someone wants to reproduce, as opposed to give away material for teaching purposes, a fee is usual. Publishers may charge per paper, per thousand words or per page; typical rates per page range from £10 to £25. With any lower charge it is scarcely worth the time spent in raising an invoice and collecting payment; justification must be in terms of copyright control, rather than finance. Some publishers charge more for 'world' rights than for, say, just USA and Canada, or UK and British Commonwealth. Another option is to vary the charges for quoted text according to whether the material is being reset or not, i.e. there is one charge for the matter and another for the typesetting.

Sometimes a request will come in from an institute which reproduces in its annual report, or a separate volume, all the papers written by members of its staff. Several hundred copies of the volume might be produced and the exercise might be seen as promoting the institute, but usually no reproduction fee is demanded, as it is of indirect benefit to the author and the journal and not a directly commercial enterprise. The same argument can apply to a request to reprint an article in another journal; if the other journal is a scholarly specialised publication the extra exposure through a clear statement of origin is often considered sufficient, but where the article is to be reprinted in a commercial magazine a charge similar to that appropriate for an anthology might be acceptable.

Most requests are for permission to reproduce figures. A number of publishers charge for this, but most academic publishers in Europe do not, as they, in turn, may wish to reproduce figures first published by another house. Charging each other would simply add to costs all round; few would be better off. As mentioned in chapter 7 there is now an arrangement amongst stm Association publishers whereby they do not charge each other. Such blanket schemes are complicated by the fact that, in some cases, the publishers do not own the copyright.

Some periodicals, such as *Scientific American*, demand a high reproduction fee, but their artwork is usually of a high standard and produced by professional illustrators. With most journals, the small revenue from reproduction fees is kept as an addition to the revenue for the journal; sometimes part of it is passed on to the original author. There is, however, no clear principle on the copyright of figures. Since it is generally accepted practice that less than 50 words of text can be reproduced without infringing copyright (excluding poetry, of course), a publisher could argue that simply redrawing a figure with a few small changes should render the figure free from the original copyright. This will be even easier when authors can download an article from a database and manipulate the material on their computer – an issue of some concern to publishers.

To simplify office procedures most authors or publishers requesting permission to reproduce material send two copies of their letters, asking the copyright holder to sign both copies and send one back. They should also seek clearance from the original author, even if the copyright appears to belong to the journal, as the copyright position is confused (see chapter 7). This may be difficult if the article was published some time ago. Where only one copy of the request is received, the simplest procedure is to rubber stamp the letter, sign it and return, keeping a photocopy for the files.

Basically, therefore, there are two approaches to permissions. Either one should charge enough to make the procedure of dealing with requests in detail and raising an invoice worthwhile or keep the procedure as simple as possible to reduce overheads to a minimum.

Occasionally, a publisher will be asked if an article, or even a whole issue, can be translated. The response to such a request is usually related to the translator's purpose. Where it involves a book or journal issue to be published at a profit, a fee similar to a reproduction fee, or a little lower, may be demanded, but where there is some other purpose, with no commercial gain, there is little reason to charge. Further exposure of the journal through another language could be beneficial and will please the original authors.

In some cases a publisher will license another publisher to produce a translated edition, for example, in Japanese or Spanish. The problem here is that the translating publisher may only be able to afford to translate a selection of papers, which may be against the wishes of the editors. These projects are usually limited to medicine and can be linked to selling advertising space or even single sponsorship by a pharmaceutical company who may try to influence the selection of papers. The editors will probably insist on a senior colleague vetting the selection and translation.

The largest reproduction fees are negotiated for the licensed right to reprint an article, or even just part of it, such as a figure or table, for promotional purposes. A drug company might, for example, want to include a favourable mention of a product in a brochure that will be circulated to thousands of addresses. In terms of the total budget for such a publicity effort, a reproduction fee of $1000 or more might be insignificant, yet the researcher's findings might be central to the publicity. This sort of opportunity to negotiate a large fee can also arise in other applied areas such as engineering. This type of use might not always be apparent in the request for permission; it is well worth examining the letters carefully.

At the beginning of this section permission to reproduce material in database was mentioned. If the usual run of requests are dealt with by standard procedures at a clerical level, there should be a mechanism for picking up requests for use in a database perhaps involving electrostorage and referring them to a higher management level. As discussed in chapter 7 licensing for electronic reproduction is more complex as these new systems of electrocopying and storage are in effect means of secondary publishing and linked to a network could give widespread access to copyright material with little or no control. A more comprehensive agreement will be required by the publisher or the RRO (Reproduction Rights Organisation). The RROs are looking hard at this field of electronic licensing and testing various forms of agreement. Some publishers prefer to handle these arrangements themselves rather than leave them to a third party such as an RRO.

Micro-forms

In the 1970s it was thought that micro-forms would play an important role in journal publishing. The concept of a synopsis journal backed up by the full paper and all the data in micro-form was of interest, as it appeared to be a solution to the problem of handling research material. (An approach now revisited with new technology which offers much higher storage capacity and quicker access.) In practice, however, such schemes failed to attract good papers, and without them the substitutes could not gain a viable circulation. Some libraries did decide to store back-runs in micro-form, and a small market has developed for these. Unfortunately, the market has not settled on one standard format; some libraries order micro-fiche, but enough prefer roll film to make it necessary to offer this format as well.

In most developed countries it is possible for a publisher to prepare its own micro-form edition by finding a bureau to carry out the filming of issues and make duplicates. Many of these suppliers, however, are used to handling other materials, which do not require the same high archival standards. It is usually safer to go to one of the companies in the UK or USA that specialises in the production of micro-forms for publication. The cost is not high unless a long back-run is to be filmed, but the overheads involved in organising the production of the various formats, marketing and distribution in relation to the revenue has deterred most publishers.

234 | Journal publishing

Consequently, they commonly license a specialist micro-form publisher or UMI who now dominate the market. The agreement will usually involve the publisher supplying the hard-copy without charge and the licensee not publishing the micro-form edition until each hard-copy annual volume has been published so that customers will not take the micro-form edition in preference to the hard-copy. The licenser should receive an annual sales statement and royalty, and perhaps a free copy of the micro-form editions.

Some publishers organise their own micro-form editions, supply them direct to the few regular customers they pick up and sign a non-exclusive licence with the main micro-form publishers, who will carry the titles in their catalogues and pass on any orders for a discount. The master micro-forms are usually held by the production bureau, who will duplicate the required quantities and despatch to customers direct. This approach is probably only worthwhile if the publisher has enough large journals to create a sufficient volume of business to justify the overhead. Revenue from the sale of micro-form editions tends to be considerably less than that from the sale of back issues in hard-copy.

There is a chapter on journals in *Microform Publishing* (Ashby & Campbell 1979); the subject has not changed much since this was published.

Page charges and submission fees

A number of North American journals charge authors a fee on the basis of the length of their contribution (as measured by the final printed pages). The justification is that learned journals are giving a service to the author and require the financial support either to survive or be published at a price that the academic community can afford. Certainly, the subscription rates of these learned journals compare favourably with those of their counterparts published in other parts of the world. Several commercially run journals also employ page charges, but traditionally it has been the right of 'not-for-profit' publishers, such as societies and university presses.

With the more highly regarded journals authors are prepared to pay page charges, rather than publish in a journal of lower status. The actual charge is usually met by the author's department or out of a research grant; indeed, again, the institution as opposed to the individual is the source of revenue for the journal. Where the author does not have any financial support for publication the editor of the journal may waive the page charge, or at least reduce it. In some cases, where a society publishes a journal, members of the society need not pay page charges. With National Science Foundation grants, which provide the funding for most of the page charge payments in the United States, page charges should only be paid to 'not-for-profit' journals, and, even then, only if they are voluntary; mandatory charges may not be met.

The practice of charging for publication may be declining slightly, partly because editors are concerned that it might be driving away good papers. The journals usually stress that payment of the charge is not a condition of publication, and separate the business of collecting charges from the editorial office, so that its decisions may not be prejudiced. Most charges vary from $25 to $75 per page, sometimes rising after a certain number of pages. It is significant that one major North American scientific journal, *Proceedings of the National Academy of Sciences*, can charge considerably higher than this range plus the cost of extensive changes in proof, colour reproduction and any other special items. As a general rule, journals that have low page charges are strict about charging, while journals with high ones are fairly free with waivers. A few journals offer faster publication for articles covered by page charges and slower for those not paying.

In a Royal Society (Coles 1993) report on research journals the introduction of page charges was recommended, but this received little support. Page charges are uncommon in Europe, and their absence may help to attract good papers from North America and elsewhere. Occasionally, when a journal is in financial difficulties the introduction of page charges is considered but usually rejected, as it may reduce the number and quality of pages offered for publication. Sometimes page charges are brought in for papers over a certain length (for example, twelve pages). The intention here is to give the editor a chance of 'persuading' authors to reduce the length of their contributions rather than to generate much revenue. The problem with this strategy is that it could encourage authors to split their papers in two, so that each is below the page charge limit.

It has been argued that it is unfair that those whose papers are accepted for publication should contribute to the cost of refereeing papers, while those whose papers are rejected make no contribution. Some journals therefore introduced a submission fee: but this may put off some authors who do not want to risk paying something for nothing. Several journals charge a submission fee to those who send in papers and who are not members of the society behind the journal. The submission fee can be the same as the membership fee. With several other journals the submission fee is the same as the individual subscription rate. In these cases the fee can be seen as an incentive to join the society and/or subscribe rather than as a deterrent to submission. Another practice is to employ a submission fee, sometimes termed a 'handling charge', and deduct this from the page charge should the paper be accepted.

Page charges and submission fees can produce useful revenue, particularly for major medical and scientific journals published in the United States. Such revenue, however, usually does little more than contribute to editorial costs and its collection adds to the overheads. With one European journal it is used to keep down the length of papers, and any payments received are not added to the publishing revenue but put into a fund to help younger members with the cost of attending the society's meetings. As it is sensitive issue, where a society's journal is published by a commercial company the page charges are usually administered by the society's editorial office.

Many publishers employ a form of page charges to cover the cost of including colour plates; the author is usually expected to pay for all the extra costs involved. Several older academic societies have special funds to assist with the publication of colour plates. Occasionally, an editor may press the publisher into meeting some of the cost of the colour printing if it is felt that the use of colour is sufficiently important. There is a trend in medical journals to include more colour and it can be argued that this makes the journal more attractive to advertisers.

Now that many journals can take papers in machine-readable form, thus saving on origination costs, there could be a case for charging for papers set from hard-copy but not those set directly from disk. This could, however, be seen to discriminate against authors who do not have access to the appropriate equipment. A more complex issue is copyright. When an author contributes towards the cost of publication the publisher is in a slightly weaker position to claim copyright. When an author supplies the paper on disk in the correct format and meets the page charges, the publisher's position is weaker.

The debate over the potential of electronic publishing has produced the suggestion (Harnad & Hey 1995) that publishers should rely solely on page charges for their revenue if only online access (as opposed to hard-copy) is offered. This is discussed in more detail in chapter 11.

Site licensing

The practice of licensing software on the basis of a site or specific group of users is being explored by journal publishers (see chapter 11 and Hemingway & Campbell 1995). The current trial of a national site licence for all the British Higher Education Institutes (HEIs) involves the supply of hard-copy, electronic access, electronic document delivery and the right to copy material from the journals for class use. The arrangement is unusual in that it covers such a large community of users; it is likely that licences with single organisations or small groups of organisations will become part of marketing journal material. To a large extent they will be electronic subscriptions, a concept discussed in chapter 11. The concept of a site licence will evolve with experience and changing technology, but some of the key points to be borne in mind when negotiating such an arrangement are listed below.

1 The parties to the agreement with registered offices.
2 What material and service the agreement covers.
3 The rates for the supply of hard-copy.
4 The use to be made of the hard-copy.
5 The rates for electronic access and the specifications of this access.
6 The use to be made of the electronic access with limitations on site and/or users (both should be clearly defined)..
7 The licensee cannot alter the material or sell it on.
8 Details of arrangements for supply and access including use of identity and access codes.
9 Warranties such as the copyright of the database of journal articles.

10 Undertakings of licensee to respect copyright.
11 Schedule and terms of payment.
12 Termination and rights after termination (has the licensee purchased or leased copyright material).

The complexity of managing such a licence on both sides are obvious. There may well be a new role for subscription agents in handling such agreements on behalf of the licensee which could also simplify matters for the publisher. If they have not done so already, publishers should ensure that they have staff who understand and can manage this new way of marketing intellectual property.

CD-ROM

As mentioned above there is a steady if limited demand for back-runs of journals in micro-form. Increasingly publishers are offering issues published in the previous year or larger collections on CD-ROM which is probably more attractive to most users. Several publishers have upset some librarians by supplying CD-ROM editions without asking whether they were wanted. Librarians generally would prefer to be asked whether they wish to order a CD-ROM edition and told what the extra charge will be rather than have it automatically bundled in with the hard-copy subscription. If the database production strategy is followed (figure 3.3) the cost of preparing a CD-ROM edition based on articles in PDF is relatively low. Scanning the hard-copy and storing bit-mapped files of the articles uses up more space on the disk and does not offer the same functionality.

The CD-ROM edition should be supplied with a short licence agreement so that the publisher has stronger legal protection. Some of the points that might be included in such an agreement are listed below.

1 Statement that the licence is a legal agreement giving the registered office of the publisher.
2 Description of what is on the disk and that it is the copyright of the publisher.
3 By purchasing the disk the licensee is entering into agreement with the licensor.

4 Use limited to one copy; the licensor might consider a higher charge for more than one concurrent user (i.e. networking).
5 The licensee cannot alter the material or sell copies on to a third party.
6 The licensee acknowledges that there is no warranty but is given some weeks to return the disk if defective.
7 No liability for the licensor.
8 Conditions of termination of the agreement.
9 The laws of the country that govern the agreement.

7　Legal and ethical aspects

Copyright

The purpose of copyright legislation is, on the one hand, to reward the author and the publisher (the originator and the financier/distributor) for their efforts and to fund further creativity, whilst, on the other, to allow access to their published material. Until recently, such legislation was designed to deal primarily with printed material. The development of photocopying technology already presented it with problems, and the effects of the computer-based information revolution of the last few years have been to leave some copyright legislation lagging far behind. The USA was one of the first countries to recognise the need for new legislation. Unfortunately, its copyright act of 1978 was introduced before the full implications of information technology had been recognised. The Copyright, Designs and Patents Act of 1988 in the UK is more satisfactory in this respect, and gives a fair indication of the way in which current thinking on copyright is going. Two general introductions to copyright worth consulting are Strong (1993) and Cavendish and Pool (1993). The former is particularly concerned with the USA, and the latter with the UK. *Learned Publishing* produces a regular column on copyright which is useful for keeping up to date; see, for example, a review by St. Aubyn (1995).

International agreements

The oldest international copyright agreement, the Berne Convention (the International Convention for the Protection of Literary and Artistic Works), was concluded in 1886. Even today, after many revisions, it is still far from universal, but it was given a significant boost by the adherence of the USA in 1989. The basic purpose of the convention is to protect the rights of authors in their literary and artistic aspects in as effective and uniform manner as possible. The standard term of protection is for the life of the author and fifty years after his/her death.

To solve the problem of conflict between national laws the principle of national treatment was introduced; foreign works and authors are treated within each country in the same way as national ones. States following this convention must grant a certain minimum level of copyright protection to all. The situation is confused, as some states have stayed with earlier versions of the agreement while others give the higher level of protection of authors' rights of the more recent revisions, especially those agreed in Paris (1971).

The important part of the Paris revision – Art. 9(2) – which relates to photocopying reads as follows: 'Permit the reproduction . . . in certain special cases, provided that such reproduction does not conflict with normal exploitation of the work and does not unreasonably prejudice the legitimate interests of the author.' This, in effect, allows photocopying, an issue discussed later in this chapter. The inter-American copyright conventions followed by seventeen Latin American states and the USA provide for reciprocal national treatment.

The Universal Copyright Convention (UCC), promoted by UNESCO, is a compromise between the Berne Convention and the American view. Formalities are reduced to a single notice of claim of copyright – the symbol ©, the name of the copyright holder and the year of publication. The main feature is that the work is protected in other states in the same way as the works of authors of the particular state.

National legislation

In the UK, the Copyright, Designs and Patents Act of 1988 came into operation on 1 August 1989, replacing the existing Copyright Act of 1956. The legislation is not retrospective, so questions concerning copyright may hinge on the date of appearance of the work. For example, copyright legislation in much of Europe includes the principle that authors have moral rights in their products, which cannot be transferred. The UK Act of 1988 introduced the idea of moral rights into British legislation (though it allowed the rights to be waived in particular circumstances). However, such rights cannot be claimed in anything done before the new act came into operation.

Like legislation in other countries, and like the previous UK Act of 1956, the UK Act of 1988 allows limited copying of works under a 'fair dealing' provision. More especially, copies can be made for the purposes of research or private study. No explicit definition of 'fair dealing' is provided, though multiple copying is clearly excluded. The British legislation draws a distinction between copying a part of a work and fair dealing. US legislation, more reasonably, combines them under the concept of 'fair use'.

As indicated by its introduction of moral rights, the UK Act of 1988 has blurred some of the previous differences in approach of the Anglo-American tradition and that of Continental Europe. At the same time, the tradition in the latter countries has never been homogeneous. Thus copyright legislation in Germany and France may be similar in (say) preventing an employer from assuming the copyright in an employee's work, but they differ in (say) their use of 'fair dealing', which is carefully defined by the Germans, but not by the French. The position is beginning to change now that the European Commission has become concerned with the harmonisation of copyright legislation between member states. Much recent discussion has stemmed from the *Green Paper on Copyright and the Challenge of Technology* published by the Commission in 1988. As the title suggests, the Commission is particularly concerned with material in electronic form, but some of its proposals range much more widely. For example, it has been agreed that copyright protection in all EU countries should, from 1995 onwards, be extended to seventy years from the author's death.

Most countries require publishers to deposit copies in one or more libraries; in some, printers are required to do so. Sometimes, deposit is a necessary step to establishing copyright, although, in the UK, legal deposit is independent of copyright requirements. Publishers in the UK are required to send a copy of every journal issue, free of charge, to up to six legal deposit libraries; some of these libraries need only be supplied if they make a specific request. The national library is generally the source of information on legal deposit practice in each country.

Under the US copyright act, there are five fundamental rights of the copyright owner – reproduction, adaptation (including translation), distribution, performance and display. However, there are limitations on the copyright owner's exclusive rights under 'fair use'. The definition of fair use depends on the purpose of the use (i.e. commercial or non-profit education/research), the nature of the copyrighted material, the amount used and whether such use affects the potential market or commercial value of the copyrighted material. As in the UK, a copyright owner can transfer rights; work created in employment is considered to belong to the employer. In the USA, as in some other countries, it is necessary to register copyright. Registration of publications with the US Copyright Office is no longer mandatory for copyright purposes, but it still remains important in order to gain full protection.

The USSR adhered to the Universal Copyright Convention (UCC) in 1973. Its approach to copyright was along typical European lines (e.g. including moral rights), but with a very broad interpretation of what was meant by 'fair use'. No agency for commercial transactions existed when the USSR started to follow the UCC. The Copyright Agency of the USSR (VAAP) was therefore set up to negotiate with publishers and collect licensing fees for foreign copyright holders for the reprinting or translation of their works in the USSR. The break up of the former USSR led, in 1992, to the new Russian Federation setting up a Russian Agency on Intellectual Property (RAIS) to replace VAAP. The new agency is expected to develop copyright law within the Federation.

The People's Republic of China for many years lay outside the international copyright conventions and was involved in extensive copying of complete journals. Document delivery systems in the country remain rudimentary, but it now adheres to both the Berne Convention and the UCC. Japan also belongs to both copyright conventions, and its approach to copyright is, in principle, similar to that of Western countries, though there is doubt whether, in practice, it is strictly following the guidelines relating to the copying of journal articles. A number of Asian countries adhere to neither convention. The piracy of foreign books in such countries is financially significant, but most journals do not offer sufficient sales to make their piracy worthwhile.

Assigning rights

Publishers are sometimes lax over copyright in that they assume that a statement in the notes to contributors, such as 'on acceptance of a paper for publication it becomes the copyright of the journal', is sufficient. New information technology and the growth of Reproduction Rights Organisations (discussed later in this chapter) and other fee-collecting agencies now require the copyright in journal articles to be established more clearly. Some publishers have for many years asked authors to sign a form assigning copyright to their journal or its publisher, but there are still publishers who do not follow this practice. Usually 'free' offprints and, occasionally, the editorial work put into the article, or just publication itself, are mentioned as the consideration, i.e. payment, for the rights, although whether these are legally acceptable as 'considerations' has not been examined in the courts.

Publishers who ask authors to assign their copyright have apparently experienced no problems from authors, except where they are not able to sign because they are employed by an organisation which insists on retaining the copyright to all work produced by its staff. Where a fee is charged for reproduction of journal material in other outlets the publisher will need to decide beforehand on the proportion (if any) to be passed on to the authors. It is customary to allow authors to reuse their own material in later publications with due acknowledgement, but without having to seek prior permission from the publisher. A sample copyright transfer form is shown in figure 7.1.

It should be added, that several journals published by societies carry a statement that waives fees and grants permission for single photocopies for personal use subject to some limitation to 'encourage the use of primary research material within the educational system'. They usually stress that this is a policy adopted to clarify the confused situation over copyright and photocopying, and should not be taken as a permanent measure.

Despite note 2 in figure 7.1 (B), publishers often allow authors to use copyright material elsewhere without prior permission. In note 4, publishers should insert the name of their own Reproduction Rights Organisation and country. For example, in the UK the 'Copyright

Clearance Center' would be replaced by the 'Publishers Licensing Society' (which collects through the Copyright Licensing Agency – CLA).

By transferring, or assigning, the copyright to the journal the author is allowing the publisher of the journal to use such copyright in the best interests of the journal. If anyone wishing to reproduce material from a journal had to contact each and every author, it would clearly act as a deterrent. This would act against the interests of the authors, who normally wish to see their work disseminated as widely as possible.

One of the many unresolved copyright questions concerns the reproduction of abstracts or summaries prepared by authors as part of their paper. The use of these abstracts or summaries by abstracting organisations is generally regarded as publicity for the original publication; but, strictly speaking, the abstracts are often being reproduced without permission of the copyright holder (although when a publisher provides a journal free to the abstracting service or 'secondary publisher' this can be considered to be consent). In the USA, the reproduction of abstracts requires the permission of the copyright holder, whilst science and technology abstracts in the UK can be reproduced without permission according to the 1988 Act. The text of the Act seems to indicate that medicine, like all other subjects apart from science and technology, is protected, but it is far from clear where the boundary between science and medicine is to be drawn. Such issues can easily lead to dispute, especially as profitable online abstracting services are developed.

Many publishers feel that charging another publisher a fee to reproduce a figure simply adds to the paperwork for both parties without any net financial gain. A growing group of STM publishers have signed an agreement known as the STM Permissions Guidelines, whereby they allow each other to use their figures free of charge subject to the permission of the publishers and the author and a full acknowledgement to the original source. This does not apply to the reproduction of whole papers or substantial parts of a work.

The licence to reproduce, say, a whole paper is usually related to the nature of the secondary publication. Where an institute wishes to include it in a collection of work published by its members, which might be duplicated for internal use and not sold, publishers would not normally charge. Should a drug company wish to reproduce some text in a

COPYRIGHT ASSIGNMENT FORM

Your paper No .... has been received *and if accepted* will be published in the ....

....

Copyright assignment

Please read the note overleaf and then fill in, sign and return this form. A duplicate is enclosed for your retention. Please use BLOCK LETTERS.

1   Name ....

     Address ....

     ....

     Article title ....

     ....

2   *To be filled in if copyright belongs to you*

     By signing this form you certify that your contribution is your original work, has not been published before and is not being considered for publication elsewhere; that you have obtained permission for and acknowledged the source of any excerpts from other copyright works; that to the best of your knowledge your paper contains no statements which are libellous, unlawful or in any way actionable; and that you have informed any co-authors of the terms of this agreement and are signing on their behalf.

     In consideration of the publication of my contribution in the above journal, I hereby assign to the Publisher (acting as agent for the owner of copyright in the journal where different) the present and/or future copyright throughout the world in any form and in any language.

     Signed ....   Date ....

     (to be signed by corresponding or senior author on behalf of all authors)

3   *To be filled in if copyright does not belong to you*

     (a)   Name and address of copyright holder ....

            ....

            ....

     (b)   The copyright holder hereby grants the Publisher non-exclusive rights to deal with requests from third parties in the manner specified in paragraphs 3 and 5 overleaf.

            ....   (Signature of copyright holder)

            Date ....

PLEASE RETURN WITH THE FINAL VERSION OF THE MANUSCRIPT (AND DISK IF AVAILABLE)

TO ....

Figure 7.1 (A) Copyright assignment form.

Copyright Notes for contributors

1 The journal's policy is to acquire copyright for all contributions. There are two reasons for this:

(a) ownership of copyright by one central organisation tends to ensure maximum international protection against infringement;

(b) it also ensures that requests by third parties to reprint a contribution, or part of it, are handled efficiently and in accordance with a general policy which is sensible both to any relevant changes in international copyright legislation and to the general desirability of encouraging the dissemination of knowledge.

2 In assigning your copyright you are not forfeiting your rights to use your contribution elsewhere. This you may do after obtaining our permission (only withheld in exceptional circumstances) provided that the journal is acknowledged as the original source.

3 All requests to reprint your contribution, or a substantial part of it, or figures, tables or illustrations from it in another publication (including publications of the Publisher) will be subject to your approval (which we will assume is given if we have not heard from you within four weeks of your approval being sought).

4 The journal is registered with the Copyright Licensing Agency (London) and the Copyright Clearance Center (New York), non-profit making organizations which offer centralized licensing arrangements for photocopying. Any income received through these arrangements will be used to further the interests of the journal.

5 It is understood that in some cases copyright will be held by the contributor's employer (for instance the British or U.S. Government). If so, the journal requires non-exclusive permission to deal with requests from third parties, on the understanding that any requests it receives from third parties will be handled in accordance with paragraph 3 above (i.e. you and your employer will be asked to approve the proposed use).

6 In addition to reproduction in conventional printed form your article may be stored electronically and then printed out (e.g. from CD-ROM under the ADONIS document delivery scheme) to meet individual requests. Your assignment of copyright signifies your agreement to the journal making arrangements to include your paper in such document delivery services and electronic journal databases.

7 **By signing this form you certify that your contribution is your original work, has not been published before and is not being considered for publication elsewhere; that you have obtained permission for and acknowledged the source of any excerpts from other copyright works; that to the best of your knowledge your paper contains no statements which are libellous, unlawful or in any way actionable: and that you have informed any co-authors of the terms of this agreement and are signing on their behalf.**

Figure 7.1 (B) Copyright notes for contributors.

widespread publicity campaign a charge of several hundred pounds might be reasonable; in either case, the author should be consulted. The licence to reproduce material should never be given on an exclusive basis and may reflect the size of market: for example, the fee for a licence to reproduce an article in a volume of 'readings' should be higher for the whole world than just for the USA. Licensing to a secondary publisher or document delivery service is becoming a major issue, not least because of the republishing potential of electronic systems. It is likely that Reproduction Rights Organisations will have a role here (see the next section). In this connection, any request to reproduce articles should be examined carefully: electronic storage may appear in the small print.

In recent years, universities have become increasingly concerned with the question of assignment of copyright. In its simplest form, the argument is that authors in universities present their work to publishers 'free of charge', and then their universities have to pay the publishers handsomely for the privilege of obtaining access to it. It is therefore concluded that authors and/or their institutions should retain the copyright. The discussion of this proposition has been particularly intense in the USA. In 1993, one group (set up by the Triangle Research Libraries Network) produced a model copyright document. This suggested that academic authors should seek to support not-for-profit journals. If this were not possible, authors should use an 'authorisation to publish' form which allowed the publisher to reproduce an article, but did not transfer copyright.

Publishers have naturally responded, more especially by emphasising that their organising of the supply of information adds value to it, and that this added value itself requires protection. They are arguing, in effect, that there exists a 'publisher's right', which should run in parallel with authors' rights. However the debate develops – and the growth of interest in electronic publishing is only serving to accentuate it – it is likely to require some rethinking of author/publisher relations.

A number of journal publishers license their micro-form rights to a specialist micro-form publisher. Agreements are usually based on the original publisher's supplying the hard-copy free of subscription charges to the micro-form publisher and receiving a royalty based on net receipts from sales of the micro-form edition.

Reprography and RROs

Although photocopying is still of major concern to publishers, the discussion of copying now tends to revolve round the wider question of reprography. Reprography refers to any facsimile process, such as fax transmission and micro-form versions, as well as photocopying. For years, journal publishers have been concerned that the practice of photocopying has cost them if not journal subscriptions, at least some return by way of fees. Their fears are now focusing on the further possibilities of electronic copying. In principle, apart from 'fair dealing' concessions, reprography requires permission from the copyright holder. In practice, it has proved very difficult to monitor what copying is occurring. The solution in recent years has been seen to lie in the creation of licensing bodies, called Reproduction Rights Organisations (RROs), in each country.

In the UK – and it reflects common practice worldwide – a licensing body is defined as, 'a society or other organisation which has as its main object, or one of its main objects, the negotiation or granting, either as owner or prospective owner of copyright or as agent for him, of copyright licences, and whose objects include the granting of licences covering works of more than one author'. Reproduction Rights Organisations, such as the Copyright Clearance Center (CCC) in the USA or the Copyright Licensing Agency (CLA) in the UK, thus act as intermediaries between potential users and the copyright holders. Currently, they are mainly concerned with the control of photocopying, but are already exploring the need to control copying of information in electronic form.

The CCC has consulted widely with the publishing community in devising a trial licensing scheme for electrocopying and document delivery based on royalty rates set by the publishers, non-exclusivity, 'user-controlled' networks (i.e. a limit on onward cascade copying) and an initial two-year period with ninety-day termination. The proposed CCC pricing structure is based on an access royalty for a single location. This covers the right to store electronically, a discount on the access royalty if the hard-copy subscription is maintained, a transactional fee for downloading and printing out, and a 'sizing' factor relating (say) to the number of employees. As this scheme has the acceptance of most of the major journal publishers, it is likely to be an important model for other RROs.

The RROs typically aim at the collective licensing of photocopying to particular groups, more especially in education, industry and government. The CLA, for example, licenses Local Education Authorities in the UK so that the schools and colleges under their jurisdiction can photocopy onto paper a specified amount of any journal or book covered by the agreement. For journals, this is one article for each member of a class on one course each academic year. If a school wishes to do more than this, it must approach the copyright holder in the usual way. Where a publisher can claim copyright in the typographical arrangement (i.e. design, layout and typeface), this is covered by the RRO agreement as well as the contents.

Typographical copyright lasts for twenty-five years in the UK (and this is likely to become the EU norm). The stm Association of publishers have produced a draft checklist of common standards for collective licensing in electronic publishing. Its main headings cover: scope of licensing; terms of licensing; distribution requirements; reasons the licence is not individually contracted.

Nearly thirty countries now have some form of Reproduction Rights Organisation, sufficient for them to have formed their own association, the International Federation of Reproduction Rights Organisations (IFRRO), which is growing steadily as more countries set up RROs. The association acts as a focus for discussions with copyright holding groups, such as authors and publishers, on such matters as worldwide policy on the collection and distribution of copyright revenue. The national organisations both license photocopying in their own countries, and co-operate concerning the fees charged in one country for the use of copyright material from another. A number of the RROs (including those in the USA and UK) have negotiated agreements so that publishers only need to register with their own RRO in order to be covered as regards licensing in all the countries concerned. The funds so collected are distributed to the copyright holders as indicated by some kind of survey or sampling exercise (after top-slicing for the RRO's overheads). An alternative approach, which seems to be growing in favour, is for the copyright holders to devolve the direct dealing with users to the RRO, but to continue to decide on conditions – such as the charging of variable fees – themselves. Such a 'permissions clearance' service, with the conditions fixed by publishers individually, has been set up for photocopying by both the Copyright Clearance Center in the USA and the Copyright Licensing Agency in the UK.

The RROs are a heterogeneous community as they have been set up by widely different governments with varying aims and ideas of control. For example, the CCC has a number of publishers on its Board, and tries to reflect the interests of publishers: its charges for copying are based on rates set by publishers (in conjunction with the amount of copying measured by sampling). Several European RROs receive their revenues from the government (in Norway on a per capita basis; in Germany from a tax premium on imported copying equipment). Their main role lies in deciding how to distribute funds to copyright holders, rather than in the problems of collection. Given this variation, the publishing community's hope that IFFRO will protect its interests throughout the world will take some time to fulfil. For example, the STM publishers' proposed basic requirement – that the RROs pay publishers directly, on the basis of their copying charges, rather than indirectly via the RRO in the country where the publisher is based – poses some difficulties when the funding comes as a block grant from the government.

Reproduction Rights Organisations vary greatly in their role and policy. Kopinor in Norway, for example, simply receives an annual grant from the state: its role is to distribute this. Part of the grant received by Kopinor is allocated to publications from the United States, but it has not been possible to divide this between individual publications, or even publishers. The Board of the CCC, therefore, with the approval of Kopinor, decided to use these funds to support the defence of copyright in the courts. This led to the 1992 Federal district court case, American Geophysical Union v. Texaco, Inc.

It was established that much journal material is now distributed as individual articles. Texaco argued that an article is only part of a copyrighted work (the issue of the journal), but the court held that copying an article constituted copying an entire copyrighted work. In consequence, the court ruled that photocopying of copyrighted journal articles by a scientist employed by a for-profit organisation was not fair use. The decision has huge implications for copyright holders as it means that all copying by researchers employed by a commercial organisation requires copyright clearance.

Unlike previous plaintiffs, such as Williams & Wilkins, the American Geophysical Union (with the support of other publishers) successfully argued that they had suffered substantial harm to the value of their copyright through photocopying. Texaco could have paid for copies at a reasonable cost: for example, by paying royalties to the CCC, or buying articles from document delivery services which had licence agreements with the publishers. The existence of the CCC as a means of enabling people to pay copyright fees easily was vital to the publishers' case.

Texaco took the case to appeal and, in October 1994, the Second Circuit Court of Appeals upheld 2:1 the district court's decision that Texaco's unauthorised photocopying of eight journal articles did not constitute fair use. The majority opinion characterised the copying as primarily 'archival' (done for the primary purpose of providing the Texaco researchers with their own copies of each article without Texaco having to purchase another original journal) and not 'transformative', since it does not add some new contribution of intellectual value. The majority also found that the publishers demonstrated substantial harm to the value of the copyright primarily because of the licensing revenue that would be lost if Texaco's claim of fair use was upheld. It also confirmed the decision that an article is a discrete copyrighted work and supported the role of the CCC in creating a workable market for individual articles.

Texaco filed a request for a rehearing by the Court of Appeals and indicated that, in the event that this might be denied, it might seek review of the decision by the United States Supreme Court. The Second Circuit denied Texaco's petition for a rehearing, and Texaco then agreed to settle out of court. Under the terms of the settlement Texaco paid a seven-figure sum to cover retroactive licence fees from 1985 through 1994 and legal fees incurred by the CCC in connection with the litigation. Texaco also entered into a standard licence agreement with the CCC. Publishers registered with the CCC during the period of the retroactive licence will receive a distribution for each journal.

The role of the RROs in making it easier to obtain permission to reproduce copyright material is important, therefore, in generating copyright revenue and in establishing legal support for the copyright holder's position as electronic publishing gains momentum. The CCC is leading the way in the development of new technology for the rights management challenges of the future. It has launched a new database with online access known as The Transaction Factory, a low cost, highly flexible processing system, designed to handle large volumes of rights transactions for any type of work – print materials, photographs, illustrations, graphics and video.

The collection of fees for providing copies of journal articles is not, of course, restricted to RROs. A variety of document delivery services also provide photocopies of articles to customers. Some work closely with publishers. For example, the Uncover service, set up by CARL (Colorado Alliance of Research Libraries) and provided in the UK by Blackwells, negotiates agreements with individual publishers concerning which journals can be copied and what fees must be paid. For a number of years, the photocopying service provided by the British Library Document Supply Centre (BLDSC) was the target of complaints by publishers, because they felt its services were depriving them of possible income, but recently the British Library has made some effort to deal with the concerns of copyright holders. In 1991, BLDSC started its Copyright Cleared Service, for which users pay a flat copyright fee. This is passed on to the CLA. In 1993, a further agreement was reached with the CCC regarding photocopies dispatched to the USA. The US publishers involved would be paid royalties at the rate they themselves set. It should be noted that not all document supply services fully accept publishers' views on copyright, so some bones of contention still remain.

An alternative approach to the collection of fees is obviously for publishers to supply copies directly to customers. For some years past this approach has been followed in the ADONIS project, which brings together major journal publishers and libraries in Europe. The contents of a range of current issues of scientific journals are regularly placed on CD-ROM, and the disks supplied to the libraries. Articles can be printed out from this disk as required by library customers. Records of the articles so produced can be recorded automatically, and the fees – set by the publishers – can then be levied. Arrangements based on supplying customers with a database for printing out articles need to be supported by a tight licence agreement covering access, reporting and restrictions on distribution of the database.

Electronic publishing

The need for new laws regarding intellectual property rights has been urged primarily because of an extremely rapid growth in the handling of information in electronic form. The problem for publishers is the greater flexibility that such handling offers, and, consequently, the loss of control over their material that both publishers and authors may suffer. This flexibility means that it is difficult to prevent unauthorised copying from electronic sources, especially when these are networked. It is equally difficult to prevent the modification of their contents and their onward transmission with no attribution to the original creators. A further complication is that information can be stored in electronic form for a number of purposes and in a number of ways. These can affect how copyright applies. In addition, copyright in paper-based and electronic works cannot necessarily be dealt with separately, since an increasing number of items are being published in parallel in both media. (This may well be a preferred route for primary publications in the next few years.)

The words 'digital' and 'electronic' are often used interchangeably as descriptors. It is actually possible for information to be in an electronic form, but not be digital. The distinction is unlikely to be important for journal publishers, but it may be worth noting that copyright acts typically use the broader 'electronic' term. In a similar way, it is normally acceptable to use 'machine-readable' interchangeably with 'digital'. A computer program (spelt in this way in both English English and American English) is a set of instructions in machine-readable form which, when inserted in a computer, instruct it how to carry out a specific task. Computer programs, presuming that they contain sufficient originality, are considered as literary works, and are covered by copyright as soon as they have been stored on an appropriate medium.

An electronic database is a collection of material in electronic form, usually collected from a variety of sources but with a specific theme. One example is a collection of journal abstracts dealing with a particular subject area. The word 'databank' sometimes appears, often as a synonym for database, but it can be used to distinguish databases which contain numerical/quantitative data. So long as it has sufficient originality, a database can claim copyright separately from the individual works it contains. The legal protection of databases is currently under investigation by the EU. One important proposal is that, even where there is insufficient originality to claim copyright, databases should be protected from wholesale copying.

A distinction needs to be drawn here between open systems and limited-access systems. An online database is an example of the former, whilst a CD-ROM is an example of the latter (though, inevitably, technology is blurring this distinction, e.g. by networking CD-ROMs). Protection against copying is usually more difficult for open systems than for those with limited access. To set against this, online access typically provides a direct and continuing link between the provider and the user in a way that CD-ROMs do not. This allows publishers to establish contracts with their users, prescribing conditions for online access to their databases. They can then pursue unauthorised use under contract law, which is a good deal easier to enforce than copyright law.

Electronic information is increasingly being provided in multi-media form (i.e. including text, sound, still and moving pictures). This media mix can create problems, since copyright law has traditionally varied according to the medium concerned. For example, the 'fair dealing' principle applies to text, but not to sound recordings or films. Correspondingly, creating a multi-media publication can require complex copyright negotiations. (The same is true, conversely, when publishers are approached for permission to use material they have published.) Once multi-media material is in electronic form, it can be as readily manipulated and transformed as purely textual material. The more complicated the copyright negotiations, the more temptation there is to modify any adapted graphical material to the point where its source is no longer distinguishable.

Clearly, the publishers' main concern at present is with the possibilities for electrocopying (the electronic equivalent of photocopying printed documents). Most attention currently focuses on control via licensing, etc., with computers used as a back-up, e.g. for counting the number of accesses by customers to a particular information source. However, considerable effort is also going into possible technological solutions. One approach is to provide the information, but to monitor its use in a more sophisticated way. This may involve embedding some form of coded identification within the transmitted electronic information, or developing software that tracks the transmitted information, so identifying access to it. The alternative approach is obviously to control access from the start. For example, some use is already being made of smart cards (i.e. cards containing computer chips) to allow access to information and to provide automatic payment for it. One useful input here is the CITED (Copyright in Transmitted Electronic Documents) project which has involved publishers and others from Belgium, France, Spain and the UK. It was set up to develop a model for providing copyright protection for digital information. This CITED model suggests ways in which use can be monitored, and compensation given to copyright holders. It is likely to influence future EU thinking on this topic.

It is likely that there will be new copyright legislation to cover electronic publishing. Proposals are being considered by the European Union and in the United States a Presidential study group set up in 1993 published a report entitled 'Intellectual Property and the National Information Infrastructure' in late 1995. This said that the nation's growing computer communications system would not flourish without safeguards against theft and recommended changes to bring copyright law into line with current technology. The report, however, suggests an exemption for libraries and archives, allowing them to prepare a limited number of copies 'for purposes of preservation'; the concept of an 'electronic fair use' will need close attention from the publishing community. The recommendations include the proposal that the Government should prohibit the manufacture or distribution of any device that would circumvent electronic tags that might be used to protect copyright on electronic networks.

Publishing agreements

Most journals are owned entirely by publishers or a publishing society. In this case a legal contract between publishers and editors should require the latter to use their best endeavours to avoid libel, obscenity and breach of copyright. It may further stipulate that the editor provides a certain amount of copy on a given schedule; in return, the editor might receive expenses and an annual fee, or a royalty, or occasionally a share of the net profit. In some cases, the share of the net profit made by the journal might go to the editorial board, or even to a trust representing interests within the subject area (i.e. the publisher is giving back to the subject some funds, in return for papers to publish, editorial advice and refereeing of papers).

A problem with some agreements between editor and publishers is that there may be inadequate provision for replacing the editor should editorial policy, loss of interest or overall inefficiency start to jeopardise the journal. This oversight can happen, for example, when an editor brings an idea for a new journal to the publisher, who might well fail to look to the future when drawing up a publishing agreement in the general enthusiasm for the venture. With magazines, the editor will expect a standard type of employment contract, and will be looking to establish editorial freedom as well as financial compensation. With academic journals there should be a clause giving ultimate editorial authority to the editorial board, who can replace the editor, if an initial warning has not been heeded. (Provision should be made for arbitration in case of a dispute.) This degree of authority would be claimed by the publishers with a more commercial publication. To reduce this problem for an academic journal, editors and editorial board members should be appointed for a fixed (but renewable) term of years; procedures should be laid down for the appointment of both, e.g. on the nomination of the board and subject to the approval of the publishers and/or the society. In some cases, the founding editor moves on to become chairman of the editorial board; this post might command a small fee and some expenses. Agreements with editors should always include a clause making it clear that material submitted to the journal is the property of the sponsor or the publisher.

Editors, and particularly founding editors, should not undervalue themselves when negotiating an agreement with publishers. A successful journal can become a major asset for the publisher, and launching a journal will take up a huge amount of time and effort for the editor.

Editors should look, therefore, not just for fair financial compensation, but also sufficient expenses to employ a secretary/assistant (perhaps part time), to run an editorial office (i.e. postage, telephone and stationery), and perhaps to travel to major meetings where they can identify and talk to potential authors and generally promote their journal. They might also insist on a certain level of promotion, or a set promotional budget. The publisher, in turn, would be unwise to limit such payments too severely; it is in the interests of the publisher to have an active well-supported editor and, occasionally, dissatisfied editors have moved the journal to another publisher, or left and created a rival. One way of eliminating difficult negotiations over fees and expenses is to agree on a budget for the editorial office and editorial expenses as a percentage of the total revenue of the journal; the amount will therefore automatically go up with the growth of the journal.

As mentioned above, there is always the chance that a disaffected editor might leave to set up a rival journal, taking papers with him. The publisher might try to include a clause precluding the editor from doing this, but it could be difficult to enforce.

Where journals are published by a publisher on behalf of a society, arrangements vary from the publisher taking financial responsibility, and paying a royalty or share of profits to the society, to the society taking ultimate financial responsibility and the publisher receiving a share of revenue for its services. Such services may only involve the collection of non-member subscriptions and distribution. In most cases the publisher will be closely involved in the whole publishing process, advising on pricing and carrying out the copy-editing, production, distribution, marketing and general day-to-day management. The financial aspects of the different arrangements are discussed in the next chapter.

The range of publishing agreements and their relative merits have been reviewed in a booklet by Alan Singleton (1980). Societies about to sign an agreement with a publisher sometimes take legal advice, but few lawyers have any experience of a journal publishing agreement. Though Singleton's booklet is now somewhat out of date, it might still be worth using as a basis for discussion. Members of the editorial board, or publications committee, with experience from other journals should also be consulted.

The main points to watch are as follows:

1. Ownership should be established. Where a publication is jointly owned by a society and a publisher there should be a clause outlining how one party may buy out the other and in what circumstances. This may involve a formula for establishing the value of the journal (such as a multiple of the average net profit over the last three years), or consulting a recognised authority along the lines of an arbitration clause.

2. As already mentioned, a journal may be owned by the society, but be the financial responsibility of the publisher. This requires some safeguards for the publisher; for example, some control over pricing and the budget in general, the right to have a say in the use of copyright material in relation to the finances of the journal and a guarantee that the society's editorial team will supply copy on time. The publisher also requires from the editor some commitment to achieving and maintaining high editorial standards; this is difficult to cover by contract, but a separate statement of editorial aims and policy could be agreed upon and used as an addendum to the publishing agreement.

3. Neither party can actually claim copyright in the title of the journal, but the society can insist that on termination of the agreement the publisher shall not publish another journal with the same title, or one likely to be confused with it. The society can claim copyright in the design, arrangement of material and typography, but not in the papers, unless the authors have transferred their copyright to the society or journal, as outlined earlier in this chapter.

4. The control of editorial policy, the appointment of the editor and the selection of the editorial board are rights that normally belong to the society. Nevertheless, there should be some provision for the publisher to advise on policy, if the publisher feels that the journal is being adversely affected, or could be improved by changes in the editorial team, or in subject emphasis. Editorial control over advertising material is also usually specified.

5. The exact duties of both the editor, on behalf of the society, and the publisher should be spelt out. In some cases, societies insist on a guaranteed maximum period for the publication of copy and even specify times within that period (e.g. four weeks for typesetting and despatch of proofs to authors for checking).

6. The frequency of publication, the number of pages to be published per annum and the standard of production should be established, subject to change by mutual agreement. For example, extra pages will increase the publisher's overheads, whilst the publisher may be committed to supplying members at a fixed price based on a certain number of pages and quality of production, thereby reducing profitability. Occasionally, the society may agree to contribute towards the cost of publishing extra pages in a year, even though the financial responsibility rests with the publisher.

7. Where members are to be supplied with the journal, the society should undertake to supply a list of members and their addresses in good time, and to update this at regular intervals, though publishers may sometimes prefer to maintain the list themselves. The supply of address labels in a form suitable for the wrapping and labelling equipment of the publisher may be stipulated for the supply of members' copies, especially if large numbers are involved. The society should also give due warning to the publisher of any foreseeable changes in the number of members to enable the publisher to adjust the print-run accordingly.

8. A procedure for excess stock should be established. In some cases the publisher agrees to store this at no extra charge for two years, after which the stock is transferred to a back-issues dealer. Where the publisher stores all the back issues for a society it is usual to agree on charges for storage and insurance.

9. The financial terms should be defined in full along with the procedures for payment. Where a net profit is to be shared out, what is meant by 'net profit' should be stated clearly. The discount to subscription agents and, where appropriate, advertising agents should be laid down. There has been a slight trend towards agreements which give a society a royalty, rather than a share of net profit. The reason is that royalties can be predicted more accurately than the net profit, so the society's treasurer can work to a more reliable budget.

10. The society may require a certain number of free copies for officers of the society and the editorial team; the total allowance of free copies (including copies for other purposes, such as legal deposit libraries and abstracting services) should be stated. The number of offprints supplied to authors free of charge should also be agreed upon.

11. In most cases, the costs of publicity are included in the costs of producing and distributing the journal, but sometimes the publisher takes responsibility for these costs as part of the justification for charging a commission, or taking a share of profits. The allocation of publicity costs should be established, and, if the society has financial responsibility, it will need a procedure for controlling these costs.

12. The allocation of editorial costs should also be specified. Where a society takes financial responsibility, it usually pays the costs direct. In some cases, the publisher pays them in the first instance, then includes them in the accounts when submitting a statement at the end of the year. There needs to be some flexibility here, since the editorial costs may change with the editor.

13 Publishers sometimes include a clause to cover copyright infringement, libel and obscenity, whereby the society warrants that the copy from the editor will not cause any of these offences. It is possible for publishers to take out insurance cover in case a libellous item gets past the referees and editors and is published. A provision for such insurance cover might be mentioned in this clause.

14. To enable both parties to plan in advance and establish budgets, a procedure should be set up for regular reporting and close liaison. Ideally, there should be a formal meeting at least once a year to assess developments and decide on prices and a page target for the following year.

15. It will sometimes be appropriate to insert a clause stating that the agreement does not constitute a partnership between the two parties.

16. Towards the end of the agreement, there may be a clause stating what laws (e.g. Laws of England) in which country, or state, will apply in the event of a dispute.

17. Finally, there should be clauses outlining the procedure for arbitration and termination of the agreement. The ownership of back issues, the list of subscribers and their addresses and, where appropriate, the list of purchasers of advertising space should be established. The society should have the right to decide on whether the list of members and their addresses should be made available to any outside party. Most agreements run initially for three to five years, and are then automatically renewed annually subject to one year's notice. The end of a calendar

year is usually specified for such notice, since subscriptions and volumes are normally run on a calendar-year basis.

There can be some confusion over copyright when a journal moves from one publisher to another. This is not a problem if the copyright has been held by the society throughout, but the position should be clarified if the society allows the publisher to hold the copyright. The publisher that has lost the journal is unlikely to want to have to handle copyright permissions for the back issues they published, and for a small consideration they will usually transfer the rights along with the back issues to the new publisher. This can involve messy negotiations unless a formula for calculating such a consideration is given in the agreement.

Occasionally, the publisher will have a fairly loose arrangement with a society whereby members can take out subscriptions at a reduced rate, but the society has no direct editorial involvement, or at most a representative on the editorial board. In this case, an exchange of letters is usually sufficient to define the arrangement.

Inevitably, agreements in the electronic publishing field are still at an exploratory stage. There can be differences in terms of the parties to the negotiation. For example, software houses and database hosts may be involved. Equally, the position of the authors regarding electronic rights needs to be defined clearly. In general terms, publishers should try and ensure that they have at least covered all the following points.

1. The granting as copyright holder of the right to market the work online, on CD-ROM, or by whatever other computer-controlled means is agreed. Limit to non-exclusive licence, and define media and market area (usually worldwide).

2. Control over pricing.

3. A reasonably detailed outline of what the vendors will do to market the database.

4. A clear statement of how the text is to be supplied in machine-readable form, who is responsible for the conversion to a searchable form and at whose expense, and the ownership of this version of the machine-readable form; this might relate to who pays for the conversion.

5. A schedule for the supply of the machine-readable form and its publication online, or by whatever other means defined earlier.

6. The right of the original publisher to access the database and to

make use of it in demonstrations to potential customers without royalty charges.

7. The royalty to the original publisher. As vendors have to compete more for databases they are likely to offer better terms; the publisher should have the right to renegotiate terms after a set period. The different modes of charging used by the vendors should be established in defining the revenues on which the royalty is to be based.

8. A schedule for payment of royalties.

9. Confidentiality over usage and market data.

10. Term of the agreement including rights to the database created during the period of the agreement.

Data Protection Act

Most developed countries have legislation covering data held on computers. In the UK, the Data Protection Act became law in 1984. Broadly speaking, the Act is designed to ensure that personal data (that is, where the named individual can be recognised from information stored) held on a computer are secure, accurate and not misused, and that the subjects of the data can have access should they so desire. This has relevance to journal publishing, as lists of individual subscribers are usually now held on computer. The editorial office might also, for example, hold the names and addresses of referees on a micro-computer.

The requirements define the 'data user' as a person who controls the contents and use of data and 'personal data' as information by which any individual person or sole trader can be directly or indirectly recognised. Some of the requirements are as follows:

All personal data and the users thereof shall be registered.
Personal data shall not be used, disclosed or sent abroad except in accordance with registered particulars.
Every computer bureau handling personal data shall be registered.
The person about whom data are held (the data subject) is entitled to be told what these are.

Information on the more detailed requirements and on how to register is available from the Office of the Data Protection Register, Springfield

House, Water Lane, Wilmslow, Cheshire SK9 5AX. Contravention of the Act could result in both the institution and the individual responsible being subject to an unlimited fine.

Ethical considerations

In recent years, there has been a growing concern with some of the ethical questions raised by scholarly publishing. This has focused particularly on the publication of falsified data, mainly in the biomedical sciences. Major falsification of results is probably fairly rare, if only because its detection has very severe consequences for the culprit's career. But it is far from clear how frequently more minor adjustments to data – some of them probably justified – are made. Along with this concern with accuracy of reporting, the discussion touches on a number of different aspects of scholarly publishing. In essence, the activities of authors, referees and editors have all come under scrutiny.

For authors, the prime ethical requirements remain that both the methods and results reported in published papers should properly reflect what actually happened. Deliberate misdirection of readers is probably much less common than unrecognised errors. For example, many biologists and psychologists have problems in using sophisticated statistical techniques. It is known that this can easily lead to inaccurate analyses of the data appearing in the literature. Something which may be easier to control is the natural tendency of authors to exaggerate the significance of their research. This is sometimes accompanied by a tendency to play down the importance of previous work, which may lead, in turn, to the omission of relevant references. Authors are correspondingly disinclined to point out all the problematic aspects of their own research.

A less important, but often more bitterly contested question is who should be included as an author. In principle, authors should only be included if they have contributed significantly to the research. But the word 'contribute' can be ambiguous. Suppose a member of staff obtains the funding for a piece of research, but does not actually become involved in the research itself. Should he, or she, be regarded as a contributor? Again, should the technicians, who set up and maintain a piece of equipment, be considered as contributors? The answer, in both cases, may depend on the circumstances.

Another source of contention, in a multi-authored paper, is the order of the authors' names. The first-named author of a paper tends to receive more recognition than the other authors. This is partly a result of information-handling procedures – citation indexes, for example, cite papers in terms of their first authors – but it is also because the order of the authors' names is often assumed to reflect their relative contributions to the reported work. This is sometimes circumvented by listing authors in alphabetical order, but conventions vary from subject to subject.

Many of the ethical problems in the research arena arise from current pressures on authors to publish. This can have two particularly undesirable results from the viewpoint of journal publishing. The first is that authors are tempted to publish their research as a series of short papers – the so-called 'least publishable units' – rather than a smaller number of papers which treat the topic in depth. The second is that authors may decide to send their paper to more than one journal simultaneously, to try and speed up the publishing process. These two problems lead on to a third, where authors publish essentially the same material in more than one journal under different titles. Not all these activities are necessarily unethical. For example, where material has to be conveyed to two different audiences – such as, researchers and practitioners – it may be sensible to write it up and publish it through two different channels.

Some of the foregoing problems can be tackled as part of the refereeing process. Competent referees should certainly be able to detect authors who allot excessive significance to their own work. They should also be able to spot papers which contain a bare minimum of research content. But other serious problems, such as errors in analysis or falsification of results, can be difficult to recognise without access to the original raw data. One virtue of electronic publication is that it has fewer storage problems than paper, so original work in electronic form can be accompanied by the raw data without difficulty. Unfortunately, this will not entirely solve the problem, since re-analysis of the data may often take more time than a referee can afford.

Where authors have the greatest suspicion of referees, however, is over the question of bias. This is not so much a question of whether referees are more or less severe in their assessments, though this sort of variation certainly annoys authors. It relates rather to whether referees have an in-built bias against certain methodologies or research groups. Alongside bias, another author worry relates to the possibility of plagiarism. Since referees are typically working in the same field as the authors, they will often gain early access to useful information by virtue of their refereeing activities. It would obviously be unacceptable for referees to incorporate this newly acquired knowledge into publications of their own before the publication of the original work.

Editors are faced with constraints similar to those of referees, but more stringent. It is, for example, a considerably more serious matter if editors of journals show bias in their judgements, than if an individual referee does so. Editors must be seen as undoubtedly independent: potentially conflicting links, financial or otherwise, with publishers and advertisers need to be avoided.

Editors are the main line of ethical defence in handling material from authors. In carrying out an initial review of submissions, they must ensure that the author has revealed all the information that should be known. For example, sources of funding for the research must always be reported. In addition, editors must check that the research has followed any ethical guidelines that apply to the subject. This is especially important for work that involves animals, human beings, or the release of genetically altered material. Some journals try to ensure that the language used in papers satisfies particular requirements, e.g. that it should be gender-free. Such requirements are acceptable if offered as guidelines, but become more questionable if made compulsory.

Since editors usually choose referees, they have the duty of ensuring that papers are reviewed without bias and with reasonable speed. They must also decide on questions of confidentiality. Obviously, referees must not show submitted papers to colleagues without permission, but, equally, the names of referees must not be revealed to authors without permission. Editors must publish corrections to papers in a prominent position, and with proper bibliographical control, so that they are as readily available to readers as the papers they correct.

Ethical conflicts between editors and publishers are best avoided by establishing what are the rights and duties of each party at the time they start working together. Some of the trickiest situations can arise for journals that accept advertisements. Conflicts are potentially possible not only over the acceptance or rejection of papers dealing with advertisers' products, but also over such matters as the positioning of advertisements relative to articles in the journal.

Ethical questions are often far from simple to resolve. In the past, publishers have typically felt that, though they should be aware of good ethical practice, they could leave the handling of any problems that arose to the editor. The main exceptions have been some society journals, where ethical guidelines have been included as information for authors. The continuing ethical debate may suggest, however, that those publishers who produce journals dealing with particularly controversial topics might find it useful to provide ethical guidelines for authors and editors.

One topic that is now surfacing as a significant issue, especially in North American medical journals, concerns conflicts of interest. 'Conflict of interest' is here typically understood to mean support (usually financial) to journal participants from external bodies (usually commercial organisations). The question, which continues to be debated, is whether a journal should have a written policy on such matters. If so, should it expect not only authors, but also editors, members of editorial boards and referees to sign statements regarding conflicts of interest? The advocates of such a move see it as one way of ensuring that any potential bias in a journal's publishing activities can be publicly scrutinised.

Libel and obscenity

Libel can be defined as a statement in print, or some other permanent form, concerning any person, which exposes that person to hatred, or ridicule, or which might injure that person in their profession, trade or calling. In the UK, the printer, publisher and author are jointly responsible for all libel in printed published form. Ignorance is no excuse, but the Law Reform Act 1935 allows judges to discriminate between the various parties who might be responsible. An indemnity against the publication of a libel is lawful unless the person indemnified is knowingly a party to the publication of the libel. Libel is actionable without the plaintiff having to prove pecuniary loss, whereas the plaintiff in an action for slander must, as a general rule, prove such loss.

There is a range of defences to an action for libel; the two main ones, apart from 'privilege', are 'justification' and 'fair comment'. In a defence of justification it must be established that the words in question are true in substance and in fact. In a defence of fair comment, which only protects statements of opinion, the plea is that the words in question are a comment, based on actual facts, on a matter of public interest and are not malicious.

A new defence in cases of unintentional defamation was introduced by the Defamation Act 1952. This Act provides that anyone who publishes a libel may offer to publish a suitable correction and apology; if this offer is not accepted, it is a defence to prove that the words in question were published innocently. Words are regarded as published innocently if the publisher did not intend to publish them concerning the allegedly wronged person, or the words were not defamatory on the face of them, and the publisher exercised all reasonable care in their publication.

Editors should therefore be warned to watch out for any obvious libel. Reviews of books and letters are sources of potential trouble; these should be checked for libel and returned to the reviewer for revision if comments may not be justified. Remarks that might throw the author's honesty into question, for example, should obviously be removed. The general principle of libel law throughout the world is that it applies only to the living, and truth is usually sufficient as a defence.

In the UK, an article is deemed to be obscene if its effect is, taken as a whole, such as to tend to deprave and corrupt persons who are likely, having regard to all relevant circumstances, to read, see or hear the matter concerned or embodied in it. The standard defence is to show that publication of the article is justified as being for the public good because it is in the interests of science, literature, art or learning, or other objects of general concern.

As loss levels are difficult to predict, libel and slander insurance is unattractive to insurers on a stand-alone basis, and where they do insure, substantial minimum premiums apply. Many insurers will only give cover as accommodation business (i.e. where they have a substantial account in respect of more profitable classes, such as Material Damage and Business Interruption, or Public and Products Liability). Claims arising in North America will often be excluded. Libel and slander insurance usually includes liability arising from injurious falsehood, slander of title, slander of goods, infringement of trademark, registered, design copyright or patent right, negligent statement and passing off.

Electronic publishing could introduce new problems with as yet little legal precedence. In the USA the recent Prodigy case should be borne in mind. Prodigy conducted an electronic discussion forum and exercised some control: the discussion leader was entitled to delete messages posted to the forum which were obscene or otherwise in bad taste. The leader did not act to delete a message which turned out to be libellous. The Supreme Court of the State of New York decided that since Prodigy has made some effort to supervise, then Prodigy was a publisher of statements concerning the plaintiff. Insurance policies should be checked to ensure that they cover publishing over the World-Wide Web or by any other new means.

8   Financial aspects

Introduction

A journal may be brilliantly edited, beautifully produced, with a large subscription list, and yet be a drain on the resources of the publisher. If a journal, or a list of journals, is to survive financially, the income must be greater than the expenses. There is no way of ensuring that, but disaster is less likely if proper costings are done before prices are fixed; if the figures are monitored regularly; and action taken when actual figures differ from the budget, particularly if they are worse than forecast. This chapter is primarily concerned with journal subscriptions: policy and pricing for other sales are covered in chapter 6.

Some terms and definitions

This section is a beginner's guide to some of the terms commonly used in discussions of journal finances. More experienced readers may wish to skip to the next section. Estes' *Dictionary of Accounting* is a useful reference for accounting terms.

It should be noted that different businesses, even in the same sector, do not always treat the same items in the same way. Comparisons of the figures for two publishers, or two journals, are meaningless unless they follow the same practice both for accounting and for the running of the business. For instance, low overhead costs or high 'sales per employee' may reflect efficiency; but they could also be the result of sub-contracting all editing, production and subscription fulfilment. A publisher who buys paper ahead of requirements may have a lower bill for materials, but will have the cost of financing it.

The explanations which follow are simple ones. We are not concerned with discussion of such matters as capital allowances, depreciation, stock valuation or taxation. These are important to journal publishers, but vary from country to country, and from year to year. We have tried to put the various terms into a logical rather than an alphabetical sequence. Though this may make it a little more difficult to find the one you are looking for, it makes the explanations easier to follow.

Net revenue, (or, in the UK, *net income*) is the total receipts from sales, and from any other income (e.g. grants, permission fees), after allowing for deductions such as the costs of converting foreign currency, bad debts, commissions to credit card companies, discounts to agents and so on.

Gross profit, or *gross margin*, is the net revenue less the direct costs (see below). Gross profit is needed to pay the overheads, as well as providing a net profit. *Net profit* (or, in the US, *net income*) is the gross profit less the overheads. *Direct costs* are costs of goods and services which can be related to particular products; they are sometimes referred to as the cost of sales. For instance, production bills, postage and salaries which are directly attributable to journal publication would count as direct costs for a journals business. Costs which cannot be allocated in this way are called *indirect costs*, or *overheads*, or *operating expenses*. They include rental, heating, lighting and other service charges, salaries which cannot be allocated to a particular product, and so on. It is not always possible to make hard and fast distinctions: payments to freelance copy-editors working on a particular journal are direct costs, while the cost of employees whose duties include in-house copy-editing of books and journals may be included in overheads.

Fixed costs are those costs which do not vary with the volume of sales, or with other variables. They are sometimes described as *first copy* costs, for they would be incurred if only one copy of the journal was produced and sold. For journals, they include the editorial costs, the cost of producing an image from which copies may be made, of setting up systems for handling subscriptions and accounts, and of promotion. The cost of an editorial board meeting, a system to handle subscriptions, or the printer's make-ready, will be independent of the number of copies sold, the number of pages or the price. *Variable costs* are those which change with the volume of the business. If the journal adds another 1000 subscribers, or publishes an extra issue, the costs of paper, printing, binding, packing and despatch will all be increased.

The *marginal cost* of a subscription is the difference in cost between the first subscription and the second, or between n subscribers and n+1 subscribers. It includes both the cost of printing the additional copies (the run-on cost) and the cost of handling the subscription.

The *break-even point* for a journal is the number of subscribers needed at a given price if the publisher is to 'break even', that is, to make neither a profit nor a loss. If a journal is at break-even, then the net receipts from any further sales, less the marginal cost, are contributions to the gross margin.

The *unit cost* of production is the total production cost, divided by the number of copies produced. The unit cost of sales is the total cost of sales, divided by the number of copies sold (or, in a forecast, expected to be sold). Since a publisher cannot sell more copies than are printed, the unit cost of sales is always higher than the unit cost of production.

Cash flow is the money coming into and going out of the business and its timing. It has been said 'cash is fact; profit is opinion'. Established subscription-based journals enjoy a strong positive cash flow, with subscriptions being received many months before some bills are paid.

Return on capital is the profit expressed as a percentage of the capital employed in the business. Historically it has been an inappropriate measure for journal publishing where the capital invested was often negligible, or even negative, with subscriptions being placed in advance. However today it requires capital to develop a new journal to break-even point and journals are traded between publishers for a price. Many firms have considerable investments in hardware and software. The publisher whose list is static may have a very high return on capital; a publisher who is developing journals that should provide a future for the business may have a much lower return.

Industry figures

There are very few figures available on the finances for the journal publishing industry as a whole, or for 'typical journals'. It would be helpful if one could give a clear indication of the percentage of income contributed by each item of income, and similarly with costs, for a typical journal. Alas, this is not possible. There are economies of scale from which larger circulation journals benefit; there are differences from subject to subject; there are journals with page charges (commonly those of large US scientific societies) and those without. Journals in the humanities and social sciences and in medicine often benefit from permission fees. Journals such as *Nature* may get as much income from advertising as from subscribers and clinical medical journals find it easier to sell advertising than those in philosophy. Some very approximate numbers in figure 8.1 give a very rough picture; they should not be taken as a guide or a target for any particular journal.

Annual periodical price surveys are published in the Library Association Record (based on data from Blackwells) and by the American Library Association (with data from Faxon). The Blackwell survey looks at the subscription prices (expressed in pounds sterling) of about 2000 journals. Not surprisingly, journals in the humanities and social sciences are the cheapest. The 1996 figures give an average price of about £104 or US $158. Medical journals on average were more than twice as expensive, at about £276 (US $420) and those in science and technology more than four times as expensive at about £500, or US $760. The most expensive journals were those in biophysics, biochemistry and microbiology and chemistry at about £1200 (UK). US published journals generally cost less than European based ones.

Overall, prices of journals in the Blackwells index in 1996 were about twenty-seven times those of 1970, an average annual increase of nearly 13.5 per cent. Prices in the humanities and social sciences have increased by rather less (about 12 per cent a year), but the science journals in this sample have increased by more than 14 per cent a year on average. Prices of US published journals increased by an average of about 9.6 per cent a year between 1986 and 1996.

More revealing is the price per page, but this can only be calculated after the volume is complete. A recent survey of journals published in the UK suggests that the price per page of journals in the life sciences is relatively low; the high average subscription price is because the average number of pages published in a year is very high. The price per page is generally lowest for journals in the humanities and social sciences, and

	Humanities Soc Sci	Sci-Tech Professional
INCOME		
Subscriptions	85	74
Single-copy/back vol	6	2
Advertising/mailing list	5	2
Offprints/reprints	1	8
Permissions	1	0
Page charges/submission fees	0	12
Other	2	0
TOTAL	100	100
COSTS		
Production	58	56
Postage	6	7
Distribution	2	2
TOTAL	66	64
GROSS MARGIN	34	36

Figure 8.1 Typical breakdown of costs and income for journals.

highest for those on business and management. Part of the difference may lie in the perception of the market's ability to pay, and the usefulness of the information, but it probably also reflects the greater use of hired professionals for business and management publications. The size of the subscription list is also a factor.

Financial strategy

The financial strategy adopted by a publisher will depend upon circumstances and inclination. If survival is a prime consideration then the publisher is likely to want to generate cash and will be reluctant to invest in new projects; any development of existing journals will need to be self-financing. A publisher in a strong position may use the cash generated by existing journals to launch new titles and develop existing ones. The launch strategies may be high or low risk, again according to taste and circumstances (see chapter 10). Profits or surpluses may also be used to buy other publishing businesses, to set up overseas offices or to develop publishing services that can be offered to other organisations. Publishers also have to consider how much they should invest in the development of their own electronic publishing.

The publisher may be concerned with cash flow, the gross margin (either as a sum of money or as a percentage of sales), or with the final profit or loss. In practice a low-price, low circulation journal with a high gross margin may be less profitable than a high-price, high circulation journal with a lower percentage gross margin. Both commercial and not-for-profit publishers may be under pressure to produce profits (or surpluses) to support the investors, whether they are shareholders, a university, research institution or a learned society. Many organisations would have to curtail their activities considerably if their publications did not generate a surplus. There may be tension between those who want money now and those who are anxious to build up the business for the future.

Many publishers produce both books and journals and may want to keep a balance between them for various reasons, not just financial ones. Established journals have an advantage in the timing of payments. Most journal publishers demand money before they will supply a journal; they may be paid up to eighteen months before the settlement of the last production bill. The publisher has, in effect, an interest-free loan which can be used to make money in other ways. If no account is taken of timing, a book sold over two to three years, with an advance on royalties and the production bill paid around the time of publication, may appear more profitable than a journal. In reality, the journal may be the more profitable publication.

Budgets and cash flow forecasts

Financial control and planning requires information. Most serious businesses today have budgets and cash flow forecasts for several years ahead, regularly updated. A budget is a forecast of income and expenditure and hence of profit or loss (see figure 8.2). A cash flow forecast takes into account the timing of payments; it shows the cash deficit or surplus at a given time. If there is a deficit, as in the early years of the journal, it shows what the borrowing requirements are for the project; with an established journal it will often show a surplus available for investment elsewhere or to finance other projects within the organisation.

Since the income for a journal is received before the bills are paid, it is possible for a journal to have a cash surplus throughout the year, but to actually be making a loss. So journal publishers need both budgets and cash-flow forecasts (see figure 8.3). If the publisher has more than one journal, they will be produced for each title and cumulated for the business as a whole or for different sections of it.

Budgets for individual journals are first drawn up when a publisher considers launching a title and updated at regular intervals through the life of the journal. Very often they will be for three or five years ahead. The time span may be broken down into years, but some publishers will work on months or quarters. They are commonly revised each year when the publisher has final figures for the previous year, and again when costs and prices for the subsequent year are calculated. Cash flow forecasts are often month by month (or, possibly, for a very simple business, quarter by quarter). For a journal publisher they might be drawn up for about eighteen months ahead when the prices for the subsequent year are set.

Any forecasts which show a marked and unexpected change from the

```
Title......Serials Quarterly .........Volume(s)..17...........

Year  1997       parts/vol  6    pages/part 96   print number  950

Subscription prices
Current      Domestic.180...Foreign.190.. Special..80..(individual)
Proposed            .. 190        ..200....       ..90.....
Single parts         40        Advertising per page  300
Trade discount 5%
```

INCOME

Subscriptions	Net price	Number	Total income
Domestic (trade)	171.00	210	35910
Foreign (trade)	180.50	460	83030
Individual	90.00	30	2700
Retail (average)	182.00	85	15470
Special			
Free	-	45	-
Total subscription		830	137110

```
Other income
Advertising                                        5700
Offprints                                           500
Other e.g  permissions, CCC/PLS                     250

Back volumes                                       2200

         TOTAL INCOME                            145760
```

COST OF SALES

	per part	per volume/year
Production	8500.00	51000
Editorial fee		9000
Editorial expenses		10000 (secretary)
Promotion		6000
Distribution		5500
Postage		6800
Offprints		900
Other (specify)	(Ed board meeting)	2400
Total direct costs	15266.67	91600

```
GROSS PROFIT      (i.e. Income less direct costs)      54160
% of sales           37.16

OVERHEADS (Figure calculated separately: see text)     39355
% of sales           27.00
```

```
NET PROFIT(LOSS)  (i.e. gross profit less overheads)   14805
% of sales           10.16

Completed and approved by: Jane Bradshaw      18 May 1996
```

Figure 8.2 Specimen journal costing form.

| | | | | | | | | | | | | | | next year | |
	to Dec	Jan	Feb	Mar	Apr	May	June	July	Aug	Sept	Oct	Nov	Dec	Jan	Feb
INCOME															
Subscriptions	40000	25000	12000	8000	5000	5000	5000	2000	2000	1500	1200	1000	1000		
Other income															
Advertising					2000		2000		2000		2000		2000		2000
Offprints			500		500		500		500		500		500		
Other eg permissions & back volumes		100	100	200	100	300	100	200			300	100	200		
TOTAL INCOME	40000	25100	12600	8200	7600	5300	7600	2200	4500	1500	4000	1100	3700		2000
OUTGOINGS															
Direct costs															
Production (inc offprints)	500		8500		8500		8500		8700		8800		8800		
Postage		2400		2400		2400		2400		2400		2400			
Editorial		500	500	500	500	1000	500	500	500	500	500	1200	500		
Marketing		400				4000		450	250			900			
Total direct costs	500	3300	9000	2900	9000	7400	9000	3350	9450	2900	9300	4500	9300		
Operating expenses (overheads)	1500	2100	2100	2100	2000	2000	2000	2000	2100	2200	2000	2000	2200		
TOTAL COSTS	2000	5400	11100	5000	11000	9400	11000	5350	11550	5100	11300	6500	11500		
Cash flow in month	38000	19700	1500	3200	−3400	−4100	−3400	−3150	−7050	−3600	−7300	−5400	−7800		2000
Cash flow to date	38000	57700	59200	62400	59000	54900	51500	48350	41300	37700	30400	25000	17200	17200	19200

Figure 8.3 Cash flow month by month for a journal with six issues a year for a single subscription year.

previous year or that the journal is likely to make an enormous profit or enormous loss should be treated with suspicion. Has everything been taken into account? It is sometimes thought that there is more virtue in forecasts which understate income and overstate cost than the reverse. It is prudent to be cautious, and to assume that not all circumstances will be favourable, but the purpose of a costing is to give as accurate a forecast as possible. The consequences of an over-pessimistic forecast may be easier to live with in the short run but in the long it is likely to discourage further investment and may even provoke unnecessary and drastic action, which could undermine the business.

As well as providing information on what the financial future of a journal or the journals business might be, budgets and cash flow forecasts are useful tools for monitoring costs and performance; this is discussed below.

Costings

Costings are done to set the price (or prices) for a journal for the subsequent year; this is an exercise which should be completed by July at the latest (see chapter 5). Sometimes a Society will want to decide at an even earlier – for instance at an April AGM – and also to keep the price to members unchanged for a couple of years. Costings may be done on a number of different assumptions. For instance, what effect will an extra issue, a change of format or an increase in the editorial fee have on the price?

Budgets, cash flow forecasts and costings all look to the future; prices have to take into account changes in costs over an eighteen month period and budgets those for several years. The past can be a useful guide, but simply adding a percentage for overall inflation to earlier figures is too rough and ready. Grants (if any) may be fixed. Other items such as supplements and sales of advertising and offprints, or permission fees may vary greatly from year to year. Postage and editorial costs have risen faster than inflation and may well continue to do so (see below). Similarly, can the numbers of subscribers simply be extrapolated from past years? Are there factors which might affect different markets differently? What about fluctuations in exchange rates?

Before doing costings the publisher should also discuss with the editor and any sponsor possible changes for the next year. Has the time come to increase the number of pages – and perhaps the number of issues too? Are there any developments that will affect the editorial costs? Is any special promotion planned that should be built into the budget (perhaps a conference that the publisher should attend)? If there are special subscription rates for particular groups, should they change by more, or less, or the same percentage, as the ordinary subscription price. Will the number of copies needed for members or exchanges change significantly?

Spreadsheets have made it possible to draw up models which can be easily manipulated to provide costings, budgets and cash flow forecasts (see figure 8.3). That makes it possible to try out a large number of assumptions. The assumptions should be spelt out and every version should carry the date and the name of the person who produced it.

In earlier chapters we have discussed the different cost centres (editorial, production, marketing, subscription fulfilment and despatch) and also sources of income (subscriptions, back volumes, advertising, offprints, permissions, page charges and grants) in journal publishing. Here we look at them again in relation to journal costing and pricing.

Pricing policy

Policy is needed to translate figures from costings into prices to be charged. The publisher has to consider what costs to allocate to which subscribers. For an established journal not run in association with any society or library, and selling only to institutional subscribers, the answer will be fairly simple. Unless the price is higher than break-even after allowing for the timing of payments, discounts and commissions, the publisher will make a loss. How much above break-even will depend upon other income, the return the publisher and/or sponsoring society wishes to make, provision for future growth, and an estimate of what the market will bear. The publisher may want to keep the price down in the hope of attracting other journals to his list, persuading librarians that the publisher is not rapacious, or because he believes that he will sell more at a lower price. On the other hand, he may want to maximise his income, and so will pick the highest price which he feels will not provoke a rash of cancellations.

From a number of studies, and from publishers' direct observation, it appears that the price of a journal has only a very small effect on the sales of that journal. There are some caveats. Major subscription agents ask their customers to let them know of any cancellations months before the new subscription period begins. Librarians in turn are demanding that publishers announce prices before they have to make cancellation or renewal decisions. Until recently, librarians often made renewal decisions before they knew actual price increases for individual journals, so cancellations might not take effect for something like a year and a half after the increase is announced. More expensive journals are most at risk when libraries are trying to save money, for that is where the greatest savings can be made. And an increase in the price of one journal makes it more difficult to subscribe to another – perhaps another from the same publisher.

However, it is clear that libraries do not subscribe to journals they do not want because they are cheap, or refuse to subscribe to more expensive journals if they are heavily used in the library. Journals are considered on their merits, and not simply on the cover price. In any case, the cover price is not the only cost: the library should also take into account the costs of ordering, accessioning, and binding and storage. In addition, the subscription agent may add a surcharge to cover the difference between the publisher's discount and the margin he wants.

In fixing prices, allowance should be made for copies produced for sale (it is hoped) in later years. It will be appreciated that the back volume market is somewhat precarious (see chapter 6). Many publishers and their financial advisers therefore think it wisest to write off the unsold stock in the year of publication, if they can. It can be argued that that decision is hard on a new journal, but it should be remembered that, if the journal does not succeed, the back volume sales are likely to be very small. Back volumes and single parts cost the publisher more to handle than subscriptions, and do not have the same cash-flow benefits. A common formula for the single part price is to add something between 15 and 25 per cent to the subscription price and then divide by the number of issues.

Higher prices for subscriptions which go to other countries can be justified if the publisher bears the costs of currency conversion, uses faster and more expensive methods of despatch, or has a local office or agent providing additional services to the subscriber. Sometimes higher prices for export subscriptions are because of domestic price controls; then the lower price in the home market is an artificial one. If none of these obtains, or if the mark-up is very great, it will be resented by the overseas subscriber, who may try to find ways of circumventing it, by buying in the country of origin or using a consolidation service (see chapter 5). Publishers in the European Union are expected to treat all EU countries as their domestic market and price accordingly.

Discounts to subscription agents are discussed below.

New journals

A new journal starts with few subscribers, if any, so little income is received in advance. To start the journal and to get subscribers costs money. If the subscription price is based on the costs and the number of subscribers expected in the first year, the price is likely to be well above market rates and to deter anyone from starting a subscription. Consequently, a publisher setting up a journal needs to take the long view of it as an investment.

In the 1960s, publishers expected new journals to break even by the end of three years, and some journals managed to show a profit in their first year. Today, break-even often takes five years or more, and then the earlier investment still has to be recouped. In the meantime, the publisher carries the loss in the hope of future profits. Figure 1.1 shows the sort of sales pattern publishers have come to expect.

It can be argued that, as far as the overheads are concerned, the costs of adding a new journal to an existing list of journals are marginal ones, and so can easily be absorbed. If the publisher already has ten journals, and the existing staff and systems can cope with more, then adding another journal to the list will increase the overheads by much less than 10 per cent. But it should be remembered that the real overhead costs for a new journal are often considerably higher than those for an existing journal, for much time is spent on setting it up and on planning and executing its promotion. Marginal costing should be used with great caution; only a very small proportion of projects or subscribers can be treated as marginal at any time.

Special rates, members and exchanges

The decision to offer reduced prices to particular groups is often a marketing one (see chapter 4). If some individuals might subscribe to the journal, but not at the full price, then it may be desirable for the publisher to offer it to them at a lower price. The minimum economic price is the marginal cost of supplying these subscriptions, including the additional cost of having more than one subscription price. Any income above that will be a contribution to the gross margin (gross profit). If there are large numbers of individual subscribers paying more than the marginal cost, the institutional price could be lower than it would otherwise be. In practice, most journals, particularly in science and technology, attract few individual subscribers, other than members, at reduced rates. In recent years individual subscribers have become more significant, but, excluding society membership, are rarely more than 10 to 20 per cent of the total subscription list and often considerably less.

Librarians and others are often surprised by how low the marginal cost of a journal is. For instance, the production cost of the first 500 copies might be £8 each, but copies above that number might cost only £1. The variable overheads are also quite low. That makes it very profitable to sell additional copies at, say 50 per cent of the standard price to people who would not otherwise buy the journal.

Where a journal is associated with a society, then some, or all, of the members are likely to want the journal. Often it will be supplied automatically to all members, but some are available only on payment of an additional sum. As a general rule, unless the journal receives (or is credited with) a sum of at least the marginal cost of supplying these subscriptions, there will be a loss on these subscribers who may then be, in effect, subsidised by the non-member subscribers. A possible exception is where distribution to a large number of members makes it possible to increase the advertising revenue; even though they pay little or nothing for their copies the journal benefits financially from their existence.

Similar principles apply where a journal is run in association with a library and is exchanged for other publications that the library wants. The journal should be credited with some notional income for copies sent out on exchange. That might relate to the cost of the copies, or to the value of the publications received. Sometimes treasurers or librarians ignore the fact that, if the value of the publications received is less than the cost of those sent out, they are making a loss on the transaction. There may be reasons for continuing such exchanges, but they are not economic ones.

Special rates for subscribers who pay for more than one year at a time are more common for general and trade publications than for scholarly journals. Lower subscription prices and relatively large numbers of individual (rather than library) subscriptions for general publications mean that the cost of collecting payments is a relatively high proportion of subscription income. With a multiple-year subscription, the average transaction value is increased, and the costs can be spread over the whole period. Hence the publisher may be able to offer considerable discounts or incentives for multiple-year subscriptions; multiple-year subscriptions then become a marketing tool. If that produces additional subscribers, the publisher may be able to increase the rates charged for advertising. If there is an unexpected cost increase (for instance of paper), the periodical may be able to publish fewer editorial pages or fire a foreign correspondent.

Scholarly journals have much less flexibility. For many, subscriptions are virtually their only source of income, and they may be under pressure to increase the number of pages or their frequency to stay competitive. Publishers often lack confidence that the benefits from having sub-scription income earlier than they otherwise would, will outweigh possible increases in costs from inflation or from a greater extent. In any case, most of their customers do not have the funds available to take up such offers.

Costs and income

1 Bills paid to outside suppliers

Some items of expenditure change with general changes in costs, and suppliers may be able to give guidance about their future charges. But inflation affects different items differently: computing and software costs have fallen, but wage rates have increased in real terms in most countries. Changes in methods of production have enabled printers to keep price increases down; this applies particularly to typesetting, which is often a major item in the production costs. Another factor is the effect of changes in exchange rates on costs: if the local currency declines in value against those of other countries, imports will cost more. A journal printed locally may use imported paper.

Needless to say, changes to the journal will affect the costs. Changes in the number of pages, or in frequency of publication will change production and postage costs. Changes of printer, of production method, or changes in the content of the journal (more mathematics/chemistry/ illustrations/foreign language setting or other special sorts) will also affect production costs and may have an effect on editorial costs too. Editorial costs are discussed in chapter 2, but it should be noted here that they can vary greatly from one year to the next; for instance, if the editor is no longer able to call on voluntary help, or the institution in which he works is no longer willing to provide certain services free or at a very low charge.

2 Overheads/operating expenses

Some overhead costs may be attributable to a particular journal or group of journals: for instance, salaries paid to people in a section concerned entirely with journals. Others are part of the cost of running the organisation as a whole: rent, heating, lighting, auditors and so on. Unless the organisation produces only one product, there will be some arbitrariness in the allocation of overheads, even if it is done after the event, but it should be as fair as possible. Every section of every organisation is inclined to believe that they are expected to contribute more than their fair share of the operating expenses. If there is distortion, other publishers may be able to lure away journals on which overheads are being over-recovered, leaving those on which overheads have been under-recovered. Justice should be seen to be done, both between individual journals, and between journals and the other activities of the organisation.

If a publisher has a number of journals, all with about the same income and incurring the same amount of work, it is possible simply to divide the total overhead by the number of journals, and apply that figure to each of them, or to express the costs as a percentage of sales. This method has the merit of simplicity, but is inappropriate when there are great disparities between individual journals. There is an almost infinite number of other, more complex, ways of allocating overheads. One possibility is to consider that it costs a certain sum to publish any journal, however small. This figure might cover the general overheads of management, costing and the production of accounts, and some promotion. Beyond that, editorial and production overheads are likely to relate to the amount of material and its complexity. Distribution overheads will increase with the number of subscribers, and the frequency of the publication. Operating expenses on other sales (advertising, offprints, back volumes, permissions etc. – see chapter 6) might be reckoned as a percentage of the income, and not necessarily the same percentage for each item. One advantage of more complex overhead allocation is that the publisher may have more flexibility in tendering for journals. A disadvantage is that it makes the costing process more complicated.

Given the sort of scheme outlined above, the method of calculating overheads would be:

Basic charge
+ (number of issues [or pages] pa. × charge per issue [or page])
+ (number of paid subscribers × charge per subscriber)
+ (a percentage of non-subscription income)

A percentage of total revenue, or a charge per page, or a percentage of the production bill could be added in. There might be a lower charge per subscriber for those subscribers for which the cost of collecting money is small (for instance, subscriptions billed to the sponsor in bulk) or for which no charge is made.

Having decided how to allocate the overheads for the next year, the publisher should check that the total sum allowed for all journals is close to the expected total overhead on journals for the year. If there is a great difference, figures will have to be re-worked. Sometimes it is argued that the overheads should be 'fixed' (i.e. distorted) to make it possible to undertake some venture which could be very profitable in the long run, but which will be loss making in the immediate future. This is dangerous ground and should be avoided. The decision to publish something likely to be unprofitable should be made with one's eyes open. We discuss costings for new journals later in this chapter.

3 Income

The same sort of considerations apply to income as to costs. Forecasts should be as realistic as one can make them. For almost all scholarly journals, the most important source of income is subscriptions. To estimate the income, one needs a proposed subscription price, and an idea of the number of subscribers. Costings can be done to show the effect of several prices and, for instance, the number of pages (extent) that might be allowed at any given price, or the number of subscribers needed to achieve the financial targets at different prices or extents.

Many journal publishers quote prices only in the currency of their own country. This is obviously easier for the publisher (but may be more difficult for the subscriber). If prices are quoted in more than one currency, changes in the relative rates of exchange will complicate the costings. It may be necessary to do figures on optimistic and pessimistic assumptions, and strike a balance between them. If the publisher is sufficiently concerned, he can cover this risk, at a cost, by buying or selling currency forward. A publisher pricing in dollars should make it clear whose dollars he means; Canadian or Australian dollars are worth less than the US dollar. If the disparity between the prices in various currencies becomes too great, subscribers complain of being exploited, and try to buy from the country of origin rather than paying the higher price ('buying round').

Forecasts of non-subscription income can be done by extrapolating from previous years, inspired guess-work, or certain knowledge. A grant, for instance, will be fixed in advance; sponsored supplements may vary wildly from one year to the next. Sometimes it may be considered that the costs and the income for these items will approximately balance out. A journal may have a reasonable income from the sale of advertising, but also carry exchange advertisements for which no income is received, and supply authors with offprints from which there is no revenue.

Monitoring costs

Actual costs should be checked against forecasts. If there are discrepancies, where are they and how have they arisen? Incoming invoices should always be checked, both for arithmetic, and to make sure that the goods or services invoiced tally with both the estimate and with what was received. If they do not, suppliers should be informed as soon as possible. A quick check for production bills is the price per page; if this seems out of line with that for other journals, or other issues, then individual items should be looked at in detail, starting with the largest.

Wherever possible, firm estimates should be obtained for any goods or services that are being bought in. It is wise to discuss levels of costs with suppliers regularly and to get alternative quotations. Suppliers will sometimes suggest ways of saving money, but may need to be prodded into doing so. Changes in printing technology have produced economies, but savings can also be made by changing design, paper, method of despatch, invoicing procedures and so on. The exercise of looking at every aspect of a journal and asking 'why do we do this?' and 'what do others do?' is likely to suggest a number of improvements, and can produce substantial savings. (See also chapter 3.)

One classic mistake is to print more copies than will be needed. Accurate forecasting of print numbers is difficult, especially in the early years of a journal. It is tempting to think that it does not matter, for extra copies cost relatively little. They take up space and need looking after; the surplus is not just of one issue, but of many.

Monitoring performance

Budgets and cash flow forecasts are also tools for monitoring performance. Comparisons should be made between the forecast and the actual figures to date at the end of each period in the projection. This is not simply an academic exercise. It allows the publisher to see how the journal is doing in relation to forecasts, and to take action if need be. Some items may be higher or lower than forecast because the forecast figures were wrong or because the timing of payments is different from expectation.

If the subscription income to date is lower than forecast it could be that cancellations are higher than expected, renewals are coming in slowly (perhaps because of a delay in sending out reminders), something has gone wrong with the processing of orders, changes in exchange rates have upset the forecasts, or that there are payment problems from a particular market or agent. The publisher can try to identify the problem and see what can be done to remedy it. Perhaps the planned promotion has not been done or was less effective than hoped. Similar considerations apply to income from other sources: advertising, offprints, back volumes, etc.

Higher than expected income may be due to increased sales, changes in exchange rates, untypical sales of back volumes, or perhaps a growth in the sales of colour advertising – which will also mean an increase in costs. If the costs are higher than expected, that could be because they were underestimated, or there are more subscribers, or payments are being made earlier to suppliers. If business is slack, printers may deliver copies – and their invoices – earlier than scheduled.

If monitoring the cash flow suggests the journal is on a disaster course, then it may be necessary to reduce the number of pages planned for the rest of the year (possibly in a combined issue covering more than one part); change the method of production; or note that the price for next year needs to be increased to make up for previous losses. If, on the other hand, the journal is doing unexpectedly well, perhaps because of a 'windfall' from changes in exchange rates, or because it has been possible to keep costs down, the publisher might, for example, decide to increase the number of pages (thereby cutting the queue of articles awaiting publication – and encouraging submission of more articles).

Accounting for journals

Budgets and cash flow forecasts are concerned with the future. Accounts report what has happened in the past and how profitable, or unprofitable, it was. Most businesses in most countries are expected to produce some sort of accounts for tax purposes. Most publishers will produce accounts for individual journals for their own information or because they are needed for the sponsors of journals not wholly owned by the publisher.

If the performance has been properly monitored throughout the year there should be no surprises in the accounts. But they have a useful role in fixing attention on what actually happened and in showing trends in costs and sources of income both for each journal and in comparison with other journals (if any) from the same publisher. Some activities may be shown to be unprofitable and the appropriate steps can be taken; for instance, the cost of selling advertising space and printing advertisements may be more than the advertising revenue.

All costs and sources of income should be included and itemised as far as is reasonable. Any special factors that affect the accounts for that year only should be noted so they are not taken to be encouraging (or discouraging) trends. Care must be taken to ensure that sums received for issues not yet published are not included as income. Back volumes will normally be written down to a very low figure.

Accounts to sponsors should be as clear and simple as possible, and should be consistent with previous figures and with forecasts. If practice changes, it is helpful to rework the figures for previous years so the sponsor is comparing like with like. Otherwise there may be enquiries as to why one figure has gone up by 20 per cent, but congratulations on reducing another by 50 per cent when the only real change is in the presentation of the accounts. Needless to say, accounts should be with the sponsor not later than the due date. The agreement may permit the sponsor to appoint an accountant to check the publisher's records for the journal if they suspect the books have not been properly kept.

Credit control

Most subscriptions are sold on a cash-with-order basis, so credit control is not a problem. Purchasers of back volumes or single issues often ask for a *pro forma* invoice so the goods are not supplied until payment is received. Few authors default on offprints; most publishers expect payment with the order, or at least an official order from the author's institution. Advertisers may well be known to the publisher. If an advertiser has not paid for recent advertisements, then the publisher will threaten not to publish further advertising.

There can be problems for publishers if their suppliers' businesses fail. It is not always easy to get either copy or typesetting out of a printer which is in receivership. If another firm is used for subscription fulfilment the publisher should make sure that they have sufficient information to reconstruct subscription records should that be necessary. Payments should be made in the name of the publisher or the journal and not the distributor.

Care should be taken when appointing any exclusive agent (see chapter 4). If customers have paid money to such an agent and the agent then defaults, the publisher will still be expected to provide the goods.

Acceptable forms of payment

It is up to the publisher to decide what forms of payment are acceptable. Most restrict the currencies they will accept; for low priced journals, currency conversion can absorb a significant proportion of the income. US banks may charge $15 to $30 per check; in the UK, the charge is more usually £6 to £12 for a batch of cheques in the same currency drawn on the same country's banks. When the charge is made per batch of cheques, it can be more economic to pay in cheques in batches rather than daily.

If the publisher requires payment in his own currency, then the subscriber bears most of the bank charges. This is not negligible; for instance, Japanese banks charge something like 2000 to 2500 yen (about £15 or $25) for foreign currency transactions; that deters individuals from purchasing subscriptions direct from the publisher. If the value of the publisher's currency is expected to fall, some overseas customers will delay paying bills for as long as possible in the hope of a more favourable exchange rate.

Publishers are generally happiest with cheques or money orders for journals sold to institutions or through subscription agents. Letters of credit are more cumbersome. The international giro system can be convenient, particularly for individuals: it works better in some countries than others.

Getting payments from individuals is more difficult. Most subscription agents will not handle subscriptions from individuals. Many publishers accept payment by credit cards for journals, both for subscriptions and for offprints. This can encourage individuals to order without delay; it makes selling at conferences and exhibitions easier, and it helps with problems of currency conversion. Allowance must be made for the commission deducted by the credit card company in fixing prices. UNESCO coupons are subject to commission from both subscriber and publisher and payment may be slow. However, it is certain, and some subscribers find it difficult to pay in any other way.

Traditionally, many societies asked members to pay by a standing order to their banks. Frequent changes of journal prices have made this less attractive; members often either forget to instruct their banks to change the amount when the price is raised, or issue a new standing order without cancelling the old one. For that reason, direct debit may be preferred: subscribers who authorise their banks to pay by direct debit are given advance warning of the new price. Unless they stop the payment, the sum is automatically transferred on the due date. (See also chapter 5.)

Financing journals

For established journals, with cash received in advance, there is generally no problem of raising the money to finance them. Indeed, the question can be how to use the money to best advantage until the bills have to be paid. For new journals, the position is very different. Subscriptions can be slow to come in, and disappointing to start with. The publisher not only has to pay the cost of producing copies and his overheads, but also the very considerable cost of promoting the new journal. Cash flow forecasts will show the total outlay in the first few years.

If a publisher already has an extensive list of journals, new journals can be financed by existing ones. New publishers can seek finance from wherever it may be found. But a learned society may be restricted in what it can do. That is one reason why learned societies enter into agreements with publishers to publish journals for them. Other reasons include publishers' expertise, economies of scale and the problems of employing more staff. For a society, publishing is a means to an end, but it is rarely the society's main objective. Time spent on publications might be better spent on doing things which only the society can undertake. The next section looks at the sort of financial arrangements that are made between publishers and sponsors of journals. For comments on the other elements in the agreement, see chapter 7.

Publishing arrangements

Some journals are owned outright by their publishers. The publisher takes responsibility for the journal, and need not consult any outsider on business decisions, though it is often wise to ensure that the editor and editorial board are apprised in advance. All profit, and all loss, accrues to the publisher; he alone benefits from his sagacity or suffers for his folly. Learned societies that undertake the publication of their own journals are in the same position. But there are many journals whose sponsors, be they a society, an association, a research institution, or a university department, cannot or do not want to undertake the publication or the financing of the journal themselves. Provided the conditions are right, a publisher can usually be found who is prepared to undertake the publishing.

What is done by the publisher, and what by the sponsoring body will be a matter for discussion. Some will be happy to leave almost everything except the selection of material for publication to the publisher, including collection of money from members. Others want to be involved in every decision, using the publisher only for distribution and promotion; seeking, but not necessarily following, the publisher's advice on production, pricing and promotion.

Naturally, the charges made by the publisher will depend upon the amount of work involved. Where charges relate to a percentage of sales, or of production costs, then the percentage is likely to be lower for highly priced journals with larger sales than for low-priced journals with low print-runs. The possible financial arrangements run from the sponsoring body receiving a contribution to editorial expenses, to their paying the publisher a commission for services and carrying the financial risk themselves. Somewhere between these two extremes is a half-profit arrangement. Any of them can work out satisfactorily for both parties provided that there is trust and understanding between them. The half-profit arrangement is much favoured by some societies, but can be the most liable to dispute, since overhead costs can be difficult to define, and the costs often surprise those not in business. Some sponsors may recognise the cash flow for an established journal and expect to receive some payments on account.

Whatever arrangement is agreed upon, it should be covered by an agreement (see chapter 7) which should be clearly understood by both parties. If a sponsoring body has any doubts about what a proposal, an agreement, or an account actually covers, they should not hesitate to ask. The agreement should specify the dates by which payments should be made to the other party. If a variety of charges are mentioned, it should be clear whether these are to be added together, or whether perhaps one is a minimum, or an advance, and the other a maximum figure.

Subscription agents and trade terms

The role of subscription agents is discussed in chapter 5 but the discount that a publisher decides to offer has financial implications. Some publishers regard agents as acting solely for their own clients; others see them also saving time and money for the publisher. The latter, of course, are more likely to give discounts than the former, or to give larger discounts. At one time, almost all publishers gave a discount to subscription agents; the sum might be a fixed amount per subscription, or percentage, which might range from 5 to 20 per cent of the subscription price. Many publishers settled for 10 per cent. In recent years, some publishers have stopped giving trade discounts, or reduced them to 5 per cent, or a dollar a line, or some other figure. Sometimes the discount varies with the time the payment is received: those paying before then end of the year before the subscription begins might get an additional 2 per cent or 5 per cent. Some publishers argue that a subscription costs much the same to handle whether it costs US $10 or US $1000, and so offer a lower percentage discount on their more expensive titles.

Practice is changing. In recent years some major publishers have cut their discounts sharply. Some offer higher discounts if they receive orders electronically (see chapter 5), but not all publishers believe that a tape saves them time and money. In any case, it generally results in payments being received later than with paper-based renewals. Meanwhile, the agents compete to get library business and a key area of competition is the service charges to their customers. How the service charges are calculated is for negotiation between the agent and the library. A library with relatively few subscriptions, mainly to low-priced journals from obscure publishers in distant countries, is likely to be asked for a higher percentage of the invoice value than one which buys only the larger and more expensive scientific journals. In the hope of maintaining their margins, agents are placing more emphasis on relations with publishers and exploring how they can work together more effectively – and earn a discount.

There are arguments in defence of any rate of discount, or of none. Points in favour of a discount include the lower costs of handling subscriptions that come through agents (fewer renewal invoices; fewer financial transactions; less correspondence with subscribers); that agents circulate information on new journals to their customers and may advise on title changes, delayed issues etc.; the catalogues that agents put out; useful feedback from agents on the state of the market and the incentive that the discounts give agents to accept orders. It may be noted that in some countries (for instance, Japan), the agent is sometimes not fully paid, at least by government-funded institutions, until at least some issues have been received, while the publisher still demands cash with order. In the meantime, the agent is financing the subscriber.

Arguments against a discount, or for a very low one, include the view that the agent serves the library, not the publisher. With no discount, the publisher can put a lower cover price on the journal, though that may be in effect negated by the agent's charges. Some publishers have systems geared to handling single line orders; they claim that massive orders from agents disrupts the even flow of their work.

Any publisher uncertain what discount to give will find it helpful to get the trade lists of publishers with similar journals, to see what others are doing. The Allen Press catalogue is a helpful source of information. Whether or not a discount is given, the publisher should be willing to accept orders from subscription agents. Those who do not may lose sales; in some countries it is difficult, or even impossible, for libraries to get hold of foreign exchange or import licences. Exclusive agents, or those undertaking active promotion for a journal, naturally expect special consideration.

The financial year

For reasons which have been discussed in chapter 5, most academic journals run on a calendar year basis. Whatever the publisher's financial year, it makes sense to produce accounts for management purposes for such journals by calendar year. These accounts should show the position for that year's trading, so they include only income for the issues scheduled for the year, and for previously published issues. All costs incurred for that year's publication should be included, regardless of when they are paid.

If the publisher's financial year is not a calendar year, then the main accounts will have to allocate a proportion of the receipts to issues not yet published. In times of inflation that is not easy. If that allocation is too high, the profits will be understated; if it is too low, they will be over-stated.

Keeping records, paying bills, collecting money

Larger firms have accounts departments making sure invoices are checked, records are kept and bills are paid. But many journals are published by very small organisations, sometimes with no full-time staff. Without proper records, it is easy for financial matters to get in a mess. All receipts must be properly recorded and analysed: is the income for a subscription (if so, for which year or volumes?), a back volume, a permission fee? Sometimes a portion of the sum may have to be passed on to some other body, either on receipt or at some agreed date; this can apply to permission fees and royalties on reprints of back issues for instance.

Bills should be rendered promptly and statements raised when necessary. All invoices should be checked against the order and the goods or services supplied. Payments to editors are commonly made at fixed times without an invoice. Accounts to outside proprietors or sponsors may have to be presented by a certain date. A diary may be needed to record when such transactions take place so that they are not overlooked. Often the details are recorded in the agreement; those responsible for accounting and making payments therefore need to have easy access to all agreements relating to journals.

Insurance

Some publishers of academic journals insure against libel, obscenity or breach of copyright (see also chapter 7). This can be arranged through a Lloyd's broker. Others feel the expense is unnecessary. If there is substantial and saleable back volume stock it should be insured at an appropriate value; this need not be the same as the value of the stock in the accounts for the journal. Replacement cost would be a very high value, particularly for a few copies of each issue in a long run of volumes. An alternative approach is to consider the loss to the business if the back volumes were destroyed by flood or fire.

Valuation of a journal

Ownership of a journal may include ownership of the title, the subscription list, the physical stock, the copyright (at least in the typography and arrangement of articles) and the right to continue to publish it. If the ownership changes, what can the proprietor expect to receive? To become profitable, journals may need substantial investment on the editorial side and to build up the subscription list and this investment should add to the journal's value to the existing publisher and to any purchaser.

What another publisher will pay for a journal usually relates to anticipated profits, rather than past performance: a journal might lose large sums of money in its first five years, and show a healthy profit in the next five. Gross profit may be a better measure than net profit, because of difference in accounting methods between different firms. Journals in law and medicine and in scientific subjects with strong research funding may be expected to be more profitable than those in social anthropology or literary criticism for instance and so obtain higher prices.

In addition, there may be a separate consideration for the existing stock. With long established journals in most fields, back volume sales are small and the stock is worth little to the next publisher. The main exception is law, where back volumes continue to sell for fifty years or more. With a journal founded fairly recently, it may be hoped that as the subscription list grows, some new subscribers will want to have the journal from the first volume.

Increases in journal prices

Purchasers of journals complain that subscription prices are increased each year, usually by more than inflation. Earlier in this chapter we saw that overall, on average, journal prices have been increasing by more than twice the rate of inflation. Why have journal prices increased so much faster than the average prices for other goods? There are a number of reasons.

Firstly, we are not always comparing like with like. Other goods are sold by a fixed quantity (pound, litre, metre, tonne etc.); the unit of a journal is the annual subscription. Almost all successful journals increase the number of pages that they publish; in some cases, they may double in a few years. That reflects the need for academics and scientists to publish their work and the ability of the journal to attract publishable material.

Not only do journals increase in size, but to keep costs down, publishers have been getting more words on the page, using larger pages, smaller typesizes, with narrower margins and perhaps double column setting. At the same time, the content has become more complex. On average, journals probably contain more mathematics and statistics, more chemical formulae and linguistic symbols than they did in, say, 1976. Complex typesetting costs more than setting straightforward text. So even a page of a journal in 1976 is not the same commodity as in 1996.

Some journals still receive some benefit from voluntary work done by editors, editorial board members and referees, and from the support that editors often get from their employers, but this has diminished. Payments to editors have almost certainly increased by considerably more than inflation. That is partly because of the increase in material being published but also because the institutions in which editors work are often reluctant, or unable, to carry the costs of running the editorial office as they once did. Moreover the office that once needed a filing cabinet and a typewriter now needs a personal computer and printer with appropriate software, an answering machine, a fax and an e-mail link. Similarly, smaller societies have grown to the point where they can no longer rely on voluntary help. Additional costs will be reflected in a higher subscription price.

Another item in the journal budget that has risen steeply is postage.

Postal services are labour intensive. Apart from that, the postal authorities in countries that import a lot of printed material from overseas through the mail but export little themselves receive 'imbalance charges' to compensate them for the costs they incur for deliveries into their country. Postal charges have risen by much more for printed matter than for letters in almost every country. Further, many journals are now sent by air-speeded delivery to overseas subscribers. The service is better, but costs are higher.

While costs have been going up, the number of subscribers to most established journals has been falling. Fixed costs (see above) and unit production costs per subscriber are therefore higher. The weakness of the market has meant that publishers have had to work harder and spend more on publicity than they once did. New journals take longer to reach break-even point, and the cumulative loss has to be recouped sooner or later.

Further, many learned journals in the past were published at a loss. Some still are: of the fifty-five respondents to one survey of US journals in the humanities forty-five reported they were making a loss. Support for loss-makers is now less easily obtained. Many journals needed to increase their prices simply to cover their costs. The combination of inflation and a fall in the number of subscribers scared many publishers, especially learned society ones. Prices that might once have been subsidised may now include an element to build up reserves in case of future disasters.

This is not all. In the 1960s the finances of many established journals were helped by the sale of back volumes or royalties from reprinted editions or collections of papers. That income is now very small. Authors generally buy fewer offprints than they once did, and it is harder than it was to sell advertising space. Income from copyright licensing and document delivery is still very low although growing. Subscription prices have been increased to make good the loss from other sources.

All these factors have contributed to the increase in subscription prices. Fortunately, there are some things that have helped to prevent journal prices rising more steeply than they have done. Automation has kept down the cost of typesetting and of subscription fulfilment. Printers and publishers have sought cheaper methods of production and have redesigned journals so as to get more words on to the page, to make the best use of standard paper sizes, and to use production facilities most economically (see chapter 3).

Will journal prices continue to increase in the same way? Everyone hopes that inflation rates throughout the world will stay low. In spite of the economies that have been made, many journals could reduce their costs further, though in some cases the saving will be small. But there is little sign that the other factors which have led to the increase in journal prices will be reversed. Publishers are taking a harder line and are closing down or shedding those that seem unlikely to pay their way. Some journals have been stopped only a few months after their launch. While the average price of journals may well continue to increase by more than inflation, the increase in the number of journals published has been slowed, which may be some comfort to librarians.

Conclusion

Sound financial management cannot make a good journal out of a bad one, but weak financial control can lead to the demise of a good one. Every aspect of journal publishing has financial implications. The better this is understood by everyone involved, the easier it is for the journal to prosper.

9   Bibliographic aspects

Introduction

The object of good bibliographical practice is to make it easy for readers to use journals and to keep the cost of handling them to a minimum. Divergence from common custom confuses and irritates librarians, subscription agents and bibliographers; it may deter or confuse potential purchasers and delay the appearance of the journal on the library shelves. Many libraries have automated systems which refuse to function if not fed the appropriate data: for instance, every serial record may require an International Standard Serial Number (ISSN). One indication of the scale of the problem is that ISI (The Institute of Scientific Information) has a full-time member of staff recording and checking title changes, splits and mergers. This chapter discusses the basic bibliographic decisions which have to be made in journal publishing and makes recommendations where appropriate.

Mostly this is logical and straightforward, though not necessarily self-evident: few publishers get it right every time. It is foolish to invent a new way of doing things, if the customary method is satisfactory. In case of doubt, it is useful to check the practice of the leading journals in the same subject area. Two general principles can help to avoid some of the most common pitfalls. One is that journals are handled by clerical staff in publishing houses, subscription agents and libraries: they may be expert in handling subscriptions, but are unlikely to know anything of the subject matter of the journals they handle. Secondly, at least in principle, the final form for most learned journals is still a bound volume. It is helpful to think how that will be composed and to work back from that to the individual parts, indexes, contents lists and so on.

Readers are also referred to *Serial Publications: Guidelines for Good Practice in Publishing Printed Journals and other Serial Publications* which was partly based on a draft of this chapter. Though primarily addressed to UK publishers, many of the recommendations could be usefully adopted by publishers elsewhere.

Journal titles

Every journal should have a unique title. Useful sources of information on existing titles include *Ulrich's Periodicals Directory* (Bowker, New York), *The Serials Directory* (EBSCO) and catalogues put out by other major subscription agents. These should be available in any library with a reasonable holding of serial titles. The title should be brief while properly reflecting the content of the journal. Once, most journal titles began 'Journal' or 'Annals' or 'Archives'. That makes it harder to locate a title in a bibliographical listing and is no longer considered necessary. Terms such as 'quarterly' should be avoided, unless it is certain that the frequency will never change: the *Quarterly Journal of Medicine*, established in 1907, is now published monthly.

Inclusion of the country of origin in the title can discourage sales in other countries; it suggests that the content is parochial and of primarily local interest. It is assumed that a journal with 'International' in its title may be no more international than one without, but it can provide a useful variant if it is difficult otherwise to find a title that reflects the subject matter and does not duplicate that of an existing journal.

Journal titles are listed in catalogues and bibliographies in alphabetical order, often all in upper-case type. Many of these are now in machine-readable form. Consequently, non-alphabetic characters in titles should be avoided, as should titles which depend upon capitalisation of some characters only. Thus 'Tin and Zinc' and not 'Sn/Zn' for instance.

Journals are often known to their contributors and readers by the initials of their title. That is convenient within the 'club', but it should be remembered that many copies will go through librarians and subscription agents who may not be familiar with these abbreviated titles. In any case, they can be ambiguous: microbiologists refer to the *Journal of General Microbiology* as the 'JGM'; but that also stands for the *Journal of General Management*. A large academic library, or a company involved in biotechnology might subscribe to both journals. The full title should be the official title printed on the cover and the title page.

The words used in the title should be as far as possible ones which are currently internationally understood. 'Natural philosophy' is no longer commonly used for 'natural science', and the term 'moral sciences' is not generally recognised as meaning 'philosophy'. The proposed title for a journal of parliamentary history, *Parliaments, Estates & Representation*, had 'Estates' as the first word; that was rejected because it could be confused with journals dealing with property or real estate.

The title on the title page is definitive and should be identical with the title printed on the cover, with the contents list and in any promotional material. Even minor differences can cause confusion, for there are many journals with similar titles. Subtitles or translations of titles into other languages are permissible, and they need not appear on the cover.

Unnecessary changes of title cause great annoyance to librarians and bibliographers. Each title change requires the creation of new records and all existing catalogue entries and records must be amended with cross-references to the new title. Trivial changes such as that from 'International Accounting and Financial Report' to 'International Finance and Accounting Report' should be avoided. Even worse is where the change reduces the amount of information, e.g. from 'Instruments and Control Systems' to 'I&CS'.

Sometimes a change of title is necessary to reflect a change in the scope of the journal or because words have changed their meanings. In these cases subscribers should be given a warning and an explanation – which can also help to promote sales. The former title should be carried prominently on the cover of the journal for some years so that the continuity is recognised. The new title should begin a new series so that the first volume carrying that title should be volume 1; unfortunately, this is not always observed. A new ISSN is needed if the title changes (see below).

Numbering of volumes and issues

Journals are usually issued in volumes with several numbered parts to a volume. Subscriptions (see chapter 5) are commonly to whole volumes. It is most convenient if publication of a single volume, or a number of volumes, coincides with a calendar year. A volume provides both a means of charging and a reasonable number of pages to bind together with a title page, contents and index. Very large volumes are difficult to handle; very small volumes make it harder to trace items through indexes and increase the cost of library rebinding.

Numbering systems should be simple and clear; complex numbering systems (as with *Journal of Chromatography*) are disliked and cannot be handled easily by current automated systems. They should be consistent; changes may delay the checking in of issues or lead to claims for missing parts. Arabic rather than roman numbers should be used; outside Europe few people understand roman numbers and they are not usually clerks in libraries or subscription agents. Individual issues may be referred to as issues, numbers or parts. They should be numbered consecutively within a volume, so each volume will have a part 1, part 2, etc. If it is for some reason impossible to publish as many issues in a volume as originally hoped, then one or more can be a double issue with two numbers (e.g. parts 3 & 4).

Both volumes and individual issues should be dated. The dates on the individual issues are for readers (who talk about the 'May issue' or 'the issue of 17 April') rather than librarians who normally work from part numbers. Since a volume typically spans a period of time the relevant date is the year, or years, of publication. Individual issues should be dated by month not by season: 'Fall' is 'autumn' in Europe and 'spring' in Australia. Is the winter issue the last for the previous year or the first of the new year?

Sometimes the precise date of publication is required, as in taxonomy where the first published name for an organism is the preferred one. It may not always be possible to forecast the day of publication when an issue goes to press. In that case, issues may give the month of publication with the day and month printed in the subsequent issue. If the information is printed on covers which may be discarded when journals are rebound, the dates of publication of each issue should be listed on the verso of the volume title page.

Splits and mergers

Journals which split or which merge pose bibliographical problems. Ideally following a split, one journal should continue with the original title and numbering system, and the other start with volume 1 of the new title. Otherwise, the title is discontinued, and each has a new title, ISSN and numbering system. With mergers it may be possible to keep the title of one and its ISSN. If the title changes, then it will need a new ISSN and a new numbering system.

Supplements and special issues

An ordinary issue with a particular theme presents no bibliographical problems to libraries, provided the pagination is consistent with the rest of the volume. It can be helpful to readers to indicate the theme on the front cover. Supplements or special issues that are additional to the usual pattern of publication need care. They can confuse the numbering scheme and automated check-in systems. Within any volume there should be only one page one; repagination may be needed if the issue is to be sold as an independent publication. (See also section on pagination below.) Regularly published supplements that are independent of the main title should have their own ISSN (see below). See also chapters 2, 5 and 6.

Covers

Librarians and readers look to the cover for basic information about the journal and the particular issue. Table 9.1 sets out the information which it is helpful to give and indicates where it should be placed. If the inside front cover presents the basic information well, it can simply be photo-copied to make inexpensive leaflets with the contents list from the cover and an order form on the other side. Spines should be lettered downwards so that the title can be read when the journal lies flat. Covers are often removed when a volume is rebound. Information on the cover which is of lasting value (for instance, contents lists) should be duplicated some-where inside the complete volume.

Libraries often need to put a stamp or a sticker on the front cover for internal housekeeping purposes. They therefore dislike cluttered covers which do not allow any space; shiny ones, or very dark ones on which the stamp will not show up. Another argument against dark colours is that bar codes are easier to read if printed on a light background (see

Table 9.1. *Checklist of information which should be included on journal covers (assume outside front or outside back cover, unless inside is stated)*

Information	Position	Comments
Title	Front cover	At the top, because of the way some libraries display journals.
	Spine	Letter downwards, so it can be read when journal lying face-up
	Heading of contents list (q.v.)	
	Inside front cover	Useful; not essential
ISSN	Front cover, ideally top right-hand corner	
	Heading of contents list	
Volume & part number	Front cover	Information changes each issue; avoid reverse type and two-colour printing
	Spine	
	Heading of contents list	
Date of issue	Front cover	Give month and year, not season. US Fall is New Zealand's spring.
	Heading of contents list	
SISAC Bar Code issue identifier	Outside back or front cover	
Pagination	On spine	Helpful in finding an article
Date of publication of previous issue	Inside front cover, or at foot of contents	For journals publishing taxonomic work and unable to give the day of publication on the issue itself.
Publisher's imprint	Front cover	
Printer's imprint	Back cover, usually at the bottom	Required in UK publications.
Publisher's address	Inside front cover	Also useful at foot of contents list.

Information	Position	Comments
Sponsoring society	Front cover	If applicable.
Editor's name	Front cover, inside or out	
Editorial board	Front cover, inside or out	
Editorial address	With notes for contributors (q.v.)	
Frequency & months of publication	Inside front cover	
Prices	Inside front cover	Include subscriptions, single issues, back volumes, domestic & overseas, and postage.
Back volume availability	Inside front cover	
Notice about claims for missing issues	Inside front cover	
Copyright notice	Inside front cover	
Contents list	Back cover	Easy to find, and to copy
	Front cover	Only if very short; otherwise on an early page of the journal e.g. facing inside front cover.
Permissions statement	Inside front cover	Information about copying and re-use of material published in journal. Include CCC data if pertinent.
Notes for contributors	Inside cover	If cover very crowded print in journal. A brief statement might be included on inside covers.
Recommended abbreviation	With contents list.	

Table 9.1. (*cont.*)

Information	Position	Comments
Details of sponsor	If any, include on inside covers	
Advertising details	Inside covers	If relevant
US mailing notice	Inside cover	If required by US Post Office

issue identifiers below). For further notes on cover design, see below and chapter 3.

Imprints

Every issue should have a publisher's imprint giving the publisher's name and the address of their main office or offices. Some countries (e.g. the UK) also require a printer's imprint by law. Even where the name of the printer is not necessary, the country of origin should be given; some countries demand this on imports. The publisher's imprint also goes on the title page, and the printer's imprint on the verso (see below).

Contents lists

Every issue needs a list of contents set out in order of appearance. Retrieving unlisted items is difficult so book reviews, errata, editorials, notices of meetings, etc., should be listed. Some journals published in languages other than English also give a contents list in English as well as in the language of the journal. This is helpful for abstracting and indexing services and should increase international recognition.

For articles, authors' names are conventionally given first followed by the title of the article, and then the page number. Some journals give the numbers of the first and the last pages; this is useful in preparing references and for abstracting and indexing services. Authors are often given in upper case, with the title in upper and lower case. The different type-styles are particularly helpful if the entries might otherwise be confused by, say, a bibliographer unfamiliar with the subject (Mill 'On Liberty', ditto 'On The Floss'). Listings of book reviews should distinguish clearly between author, reviewer and title; they usually start with the author of the book, then its title, and then the name of the reviewer, followed by the page number. In other systems the page number is the first item, or goes between the author and the title. Some studies of the typography of contents lists are listed in the further reading section.

The contents list should be headed by the title of the journal, the volume and part number, the ISSN (see below) and the date of publication. It is also helpful to include the names of the publisher and the sponsor, if any. This is because copies of contents lists are reprinted by some organisations and circulated to library users: they are also the basis of *Current Contents* and similar publications. Contents lists like these provide complete bibliographical references and information needed for document delivery.

Contents lists are usually printed on the outside cover or on the first page of the journal. Professional, trade and technical journals, particularly large format ones, may list the contents on the front cover. Most scholarly journals, especially those in the natural sciences, use the back cover, unless the number of items is very small or the journal is able to sell that space for advertising. That leads to a cleaner design for the front cover; the space can be used for an illustration from that issue or to highlight any messages to readers. Longer contents lists may continue on the inside covers. If the contents list does not appear on the cover, then ideally it should face the inside front cover, so that readers can find it quickly. Since the contents list may be discarded when the volume is rebound, whatever follows the contents should begin on a right-hand page. Sometimes an indication of the main contents is given on the front cover, with the full list inside.

Volume contents, indexes and title pages

A volume should properly have a title page and contents at the beginning and an index at the end, though not all journals provide these. The title page should give the title of the journal, the volume number and year of publication, the name of the editor(s), and possibly the editorial board, and the name of the publisher, and of any other sponsor. The title page is always on a right hand page. The verso (back of the title page) should give the name and address of the publisher, the copyright notice (see chapter 7), the ISSN (see below) and the printer's imprint.

The volume contents list sets out the contents lists of the individual parts of the volume in order of appearance. If the journal is rebound as a volume, this contents list will follow the title page, while the annual index goes at the end of the journal. Therefore, both contents list and index need to start on a right-hand page. There are usually separate author and title or subject indexes; a subject index is the more helpful. The more items a journal publishes the more desirable this is (see also chapter 3). A few journals publish indexes in each issue which are cumulated throughout the volume; this is useful if there are a large number of short items – reports of legal cases for instance.

It is theoretically possible to print the title page as the first page of a volume, but the contents lists and indexes cannot be completed until the page numbers of the last issue have been finalised. It greatly simplifies administration for both publishers and for libraries if indexes and title pages are included in the subscription price and bound in at the end of the last part of the volume (not in a centrefold where they may be over-looked). If they are sent out with the first part of the next volume they should not be bound in (which means they may fall out and be lost); if the journal does not grace non-renewed subscribers, provision should be made for copies to be sent to subscribers who have not renewed for the next year. Title pages, contents lists and indexes should be allowed for both in costings and in the production schedule for the final issue of the volume.

Ideally, librarians would like a notice on the front cover of the final issue of a volume pointing out that it is the last part of that volume and that it contains the title page and index.

Cumulative indexes

A cumulative index to a number of years or volumes is sometimes an attractive idea. With computer-aided typesetting and automatic alphabetical sorting they can be more easily prepared today than was possible in the past. None the less, sales of indexes are usually quite small, with less than a quarter or a fifth of the subscribers taking them up. They can be included in the subscription price, but the question remains of whether subscribers find them really useful, particularly as abstracting and indexing services provide continuously updated subject-based bibliographical information.

Advertisements

Advertising in primary research journals is usually placed at the front or the back of the journal; advertisements for books and other journals may go into the book review section. This allows for easy production of off-prints without advertising matter and helps those libraries who wish to remove the advertisements before rebinding.

International Standard Serial Numbers (ISSNs) and CODEN

An International Standard Serial Number is an eight-digit code (two blocks of four numbers) unique to a serial title. Libraries and subscription agents use them for ordering and in their records. ISSNs eliminate confusion between journals which have the same or similar titles. ISSNs are issued by national agencies in different countries (e.g. Library of Congress in the USA; British Library at Boston Spa or their agents in the UK) and co-ordinated internationally by the International Serials Data System in Paris (ISDS International Centre, CIEPS, 20 rue Bachaumont, 75002 Paris, France). Publishers are strongly recommended to print ISSNs on the front cover of journals (in the top right-hand corner); with the contents list; on the versos of title pages; and also in price lists and any publicity material.

ISSNs are given for all journals listed in *Ulrich's*. A publisher wanting an ISSN for an existing title should send copies of it to their local ISSN agency. The ISDS International Centre can provide the address. ISSNs can be issued for new titles on the basis of advance information, but the publisher should send the agency a copy of the first issue to confirm that the serial exists. There is no charge for an ISSN.

Coden are five or six-letter codes for journals; they are assigned by the International Coden Service of Chemical Abstracts Service. They have generally been superseded by ISSN. Their disadvantages are that they do not have a fixed field or a check digit and that, since they are mnemonic, users may rely on faulty memories.

Issue identifiers

The issue identifier extends the ISSN to identify an individual issue within a series. It can be printed as a bar code so that it can be read with a light wand. This allows automatic check-in of journals by libraries with a considerable saving in staff time and is now being adopted as standard practice by major journal publishers. Most print the bar code on the outside back cover; librarians would prefer to have it on the front cover, but aesthetic considerations are against that. Standards for bar codes for journal issues have been laid down by SISAC: the Serials Industry Systems Advisory Committee (c/o Book Industry Study Group Inc., 160 Fifth Avenue, New York, NY 10010, USA).

Article identifiers

The ISSN identifies a journal by a standard number but for some purposes, including document delivery and payments for copying, it is convenient to have a standard means of identifying an individual article without having to give the author, title, journal, year of publication, volume, pagination etc. The results of a survey carried out by the stm Association on the use of document identifiers are shown in figure 9.1. The stm Association is also looking at information identification below the level of article which will be important to copyright holders as electronic publishing becomes more sophisticated (Armati, 1995).

In 1991 the American National Standards Institute approved a standard (ANSI/NISO Z39.56) for the Serials Item and Contribution Identifier (SICI); this expands the ISSN to include: date of publication; volume and issue numbers; number of first page; a title code if more than one article starts on the same page; and a check digit. One disadvantage is its length, which is a variable with a minimum of twenty digits and a maximum of thirty-

Use of document identifiers

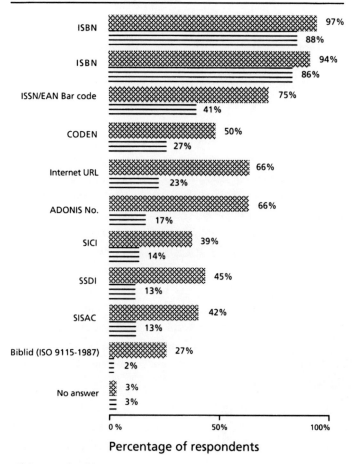

Percentage of respondents

This standard is...

known   used

Figure 9.1 The results of a question in a 1995 survey of members of the stm Association asking whether they knew and used a range of document identifiers.

eight. Another is that it requires the use of an unmodified roman alphabet which makes it less than international.

At the same time ISO (The International Standards Organisation) has been working on an alternative standard, Biblid. This differs from SISAC in giving the year of publication, rather than the full date; and the full pagination of the article; it omits the title code and the check digit.

There is also the ADONIS number, developed for use with the ADONIS system (see section on document delivery in chapter 6). A disadvantage is that it is page-independent, and so it is not possible to generate the ADONIS number from a copy of the article, nor, given the ADONIS number, to find the appropriate article within the journal without recourse to another reference source. However, since they are page independent, they can be used for manuscript control during production. Excerpta Medica includes the ADONIS number, where there is one, with its abstracts.

From 1 January 1996 a number of publishers, including the American Chemical Society, the American Institute of Physics, the American Physical Society, Elsevier Science and the IEEE adopted a Publisher Item Identifier or PII to provide a unique identification of documents they publish. They hope other publishers will follow suit. The code has seventeen digits and consists of:

1 A prefix, **S** for Serial and **B** for Book.
2 The ISSN (eight digits), plus last two digits of the year in which the number was assigned (which may well be the year before publication) for serials or the ISBN (International Standard Book Number – ten digits) for books. It seems open to the publisher to decide whether to treat books published in open-ended series as books or serials.
3 Item number. Five digits allocated by the publisher.
4 A check digit.

The only characters used for items 2 and 3 for serials are the numbers 0 to 9. X stands for 10 when that is the check digit for the ISBN or the final check digit. The PII is a number for life: an item retains the original PII even if it is reprinted in a different publication.

Besides these requirements for individual issues and volumes there are certain items of information to be given with each article. These are discussed below.

Titles of articles

The title heads the article. It should be unambiguous, informative, and as brief as possible. Titles such as 'Further studies on some organic compounds of tin' tell the reader little; 'The History of the Primates' might refer to monkeys or archbishops. A shorter version may be required for the running heads (see below). The better the title, the more likely it is that the item will be recovered by bibliographical searches. Misleading titles run the risk of being indexed inappropriately by the secondary services. Shorter titles may be needed for running heads (see below).

Authors

Authors' names are usually printed immediately below the title, though in some journals, or for brief contributions, they may appear at the end of the piece. Convention once was that men simply used initials and their surname, while women included one given name but this is no longer general practice. Today many science journals just give initials, while social science journals are more likely to use a given name. If there is more than one author, the order of names is usually decided by the authors; it may be determined by their relative contribution to the project, their seniority or the alphabet. If there are more than three or four authors the editor may ask that the number is reduced. Only those who have made a substantive contribution should be listed; the assistance of others should be recognised in the acknowledgements.

Authors' qualifications may be printed after their names. This adds little and is rare in scholarly journals. More common, and more useful, is the author's affiliation. Scientific, technical and medical journals, and some journals in the humanities and social sciences, customarily provide the full postal address, so that communications and requests for offprints can be directed to the authors (or to one author in particular). Addresses are best given at the foot of the first page of the article: it is helpful to readers and to abstracting and indexing services. If an article has a number of authors from different institutions the authors from a particular institution can be marked with a symbol (e.g. an asterisk or a dagger) and a common address given for each institution in a footnote.

Date of receipt

Scientific journals commonly give a date of receipt of the paper (or the revised version) and/or the date of acceptance of the contribution. Some like to include both, whereas others feel that doing so may reflect badly either on some authors or on the refereeing system of the journal. The information gives authors an opportunity to choose those journals which offer the fastest publication – provided that the journal is appearing on schedule. The original intention was to help determine claims to priority, but today they are usually decided by date of publication.

Abstracts and summaries

An abstract is a self-contained account of a paper; a summary may refer to items (e.g. figures and tables) in the text. The abstract should tell a reader whether this is a paper which he wants to look at in more detail. Informative abstracts, which set out the purpose of the work, the methods used, the results and the conclusions are usually preferable to descriptive (or indicative) ones. The latter simply state what the parent document is about.

Structured abstracts are required by many medical journals. They are helpful to both authors and to readers, for they set out the points that should be covered by the paper. The individual elements will vary from subject to subject. For instance, the headings used by the *European Journal of Surgery* are objective, design, setting, subjects or materials, interventions, main outcome measures, results and conclusions (Evans, 1995). Hartley and Sykes (1995) suggest that structured abstracts for papers in the social sciences may well be easier to read, to search and recall than unstructured ones. They suggest that the subheadings should be background, aims, method, results, conclusions and comment.

Abstracts have a number of uses. Readers may look at them first to determine whether it is worth reading the article itself. There are abstract journals for most subjects. They range from *Chemical Abstracts* which covers the whole field of chemistry and related areas, to very specialist ones, such as *Abstracts of Folklore Studies*. Abstract journals print abstracts of recently published papers in journals and sometimes symposia volumes. They may reproduce the author's original abstract, or they may prepare their own. A few abstracting journals allow critical comment, for instance *Abstracts on Hygiene and Communicable Diseases* and *Tropical Diseases Bulletin*. Many abstract journals are published in hard-copy and online versions; some are also available on CD-ROM. They provide a key to the literature for many researchers and information officers.

Authors do not always give abstracts the attention they deserve. The ideal author-prepared abstract is one that can be used by the major abstracting services without amendment; the better the abstract, the faster the paper will get into the system. (For guidelines on writing abstracts, see O'Connor, 1991.) Most scientific journals require authors to submit abstracts with their papers; they are less common in the humanities and social sciences but increasing there.

The abstract may be the most read part of the paper and so should be printed in a clear type of reasonable size. Paradoxically, most older journal designs had the abstract in a smaller type and with a line too long for easy reading. Some journals print abstracts in more than one language; most commonly, papers in other languages will carry an English-language abstract.

Keywords

Some journals, particularly scientific and medical ones, select and list 'key-words' – terms which indicate the principal topics of the paper. This may be of assistance for information retrieval, though there is little evidence that they are much used. Some journals use a controlled vocabulary, but since the introduction of new terms takes time, many allow free vocabularies. Alas, the latter are probably even less helpful for bibliographical control or retrieval than the former.

Pagination

Every page of editorial content within a volume should have a unique number, with even numbers on the left hand page of a two-page spread and odd numbers on the right. The first page of each issue follows from the last page of the previous one. This is sometimes forgotten when publishers produce special issues within the volume, and start them, too, on page one. If it is desirable for some reason that they should begin with page one (e.g. if they are also to be sold separately in book form), then the number should have a letter prefix or suffix e.g. 1S or S1 etc. (Avoid the letter 'p' sometimes used to indicate proceedings – it can be read as an abbreviation of 'page'.) Prelims (title pages, volume contents lists, etc.) and indexes may be given roman numbers; material which will not form part of the final bound volume should not be numbered.

Advertising is often in a separate section and removed when the journal is rebound. In such journals, advertisement pages should not be numbered in the main sequence; otherwise, when the volume is bound, it will appear that some pages are missing. If numbering is desirable, then they can be given a prefix or suffix letter, for instance, A17. If a society issues the proceedings of its meetings in a journal together with other material, but wishes to make the proceedings available separately to members, then again prefixes or suffixes should be used (e.g. 23X).

Right-hand pages are always odd-numbered and left-hand pages even-numbered. If there are blank pages (if, for instance, all articles start on a right-hand page, see chapter 4) then the number is not printed on the otherwise blank page, but the page is included in the total page count – which should always be an even number.

Catch lines

A catch line should be printed (often in very small type) at the top of the first page of each article of a journal – rather than, say, below the abstract. It gives the title of the journal, the year of publication, the volume number, the pagination of the article, and a copyright notice. Journals published in the UK also commonly add the statement 'Printed in (name of country)'. The catch line will provide the correct reference to the paper, and confirm copyright ownership. It also identifies the paper and its source from the first page of an offprint or a photocopy.

Copyright Clearance Center information may be printed at the bottom of the first page of each article (see chapter 7).

Running heads

Running heads are the headings which appear at the top of each page. Customarily authors' names are given on the left-hand page and the title (abbreviated if need be so as to fit on to one line) on the right. Book reviews might have 'book reviews' on both left- and right-hand pages, or the journal title on the left and 'book reviews' on the right. Other sections are treated similarly.

Binding

Libraries have traditionally had the individual parts rebound in hard-bound volumes at some convenient time after the index and title page have arrived; once many individuals did the same. The object is to keep the issues together, making it less likely that one will be stolen, and to stop them from falling apart. (That suggests that journals get considerably more use than some critics believe.) Rebinding is less common than it was, because of pressure on costs, but many libraries bind at least some titles.

When journals are rebound ephemeral non-editorial matter is often jettisoned. Thus advertising sections, society newsletters, and contents lists and indexes from individual issues may be thrown out. It is therefore important that there should not be anything of permanent value on the other side of the page.

Some publishers offer subscribers to certain periodicals (particularly legal ones) a bound volume at the end of the year for a small extra charge.

Formats

Chapter 3 on production considers the factors to be taken into account when determining the format of a journal. It should be mentioned here that librarians do not like large floppy journals which cannot stand up on a shelf without support. It is much easier for all users if the journal has a spine wide enough to print on; that usually means that each issue should run to at least sixty-four pages. At the same time, very thick volumes are difficult to open flat.

A change of format of a journal should not be lightly undertaken, particularly an increase in the height of the page. Library shelving is planned to fit the journals they hold and to avoid wasting space. A taller page may mean reshelving the journal in another location and recording the move in the catalogue. Of course, sometimes a change is inevitable; sizes may be uneconomic, or inappropriate for the material to be published. Should that be the case, explanations of the reasons for change can help to soften the blow. In no circumstances should a change be made part-way through a volume, for that will make it impossible for libraries to bind the volume properly.

Announcements of changes

Librarians are trained not to open up the journals they receive. A publisher who wishes to signal a major change, for instance of title or of publisher, a split or a merger, or that a particular issue is the last to be published should affix a note to the front cover of an issue, known as a sticker. This can be glued down one side only to allow it to be removed and passed on to the right people.

Summary

It is not difficult to adopt good bibliographical practices, but it does require clear and careful thinking. Publishers can make it easier (and consequently cheaper) for all parties in the communication chain to acquire journals and to retrieve the information contained in them.

10 Managing a list of journals

Introduction

Journal publishing is a business; like any other business it needs management to determine policies and objectives and to make sure that the necessary resources are available and used to their best advantage. Existing journals need regular review to ensure that they are fulfilling their potential; proposals for new journals should be appraised in the light of the publisher's overall strategy. Decisions have to be made about investment in people and systems, in existing journals and the launching of new ones as well as the setting up of overseas offices either for individual journals or the business as a whole. Policies on pricing, marketing, design and production, copyright and copyright licensing, document delivery, electronic publishing and bibliographical standards have to be developed. Management and staff need to be aware of what is happening in their markets and what their competitors are doing. This chapter looks at the overall management of journals and journal publishing strategies, including how journals are acquired, managed and developed and conversely how they can be sold to another publisher or terminated if necessary.

Some background

Most academic journals make their living from publishing the results of original research; unpublished research is worth very little, except as an experience for those who did the work. Not all research is worth publishing; even when it is, many submitted papers need substantial work before they are ready for publication. Throughout the world the amount of research being done has been increasing steadily. Journals play a major role in the assessment of research and hence of researchers; many people are under great pressure to publish in order to justify a research grant, gain promotion, tenure or the next job. Consequently the amount of material seeking publication has grown rapidly in recent years. Plagiarism, piracy, duplicate publication and the minimum publishable unit (publishing a piece of research in a number of papers where one would suffice) are tempting. Some assessors have moved from quantity to quality of research publication and it is hoped that this trend will continue.

The system is paid for by those who buy the journals, particularly libraries. For most, acquisition budgets have not increased nearly as fast as the rate of increases in journal prices plus new titles and so subscriptions have been cancelled (see chapter 4, marketing). Improvements in the range and speed of service of document delivery has made cancellation easier. Unfortunately, journal publishing has high fixed costs, so a reduction in the number of subscribers has the effect of further increasing prices.

Most businesses aim to grow and to increase their market share. There are two possible growth strategies for a journal publisher. One is to increase the size of existing journals. The other is to publish more titles. Publishers may launch new journals on their own account, split off new titles from existing ones (see chapter 2, editing), acquire titles from other publishers or enter into agreements to publish journals on behalf of other bodies. It may also be possible to merge a title with another from a different publisher. The next section looks at these possibilities in more detail. We also look at the other side: the publisher who wishes to dispose of a journal or journals unsuited to their list. If the worst comes to the worst, the publisher may decide to close down a title, so we look at that too.

But it is not enough to have titles. A journal is a dynamic entity; in today's competitive market when journals can easily lose status or market share, they should not be taken for granted or left to run from year to year with only a brief discussion when the subscription prices for the subsequent year are fixed. Over the life of a journal it is common for the circulation to rise in the early years, plateau and then decline slowly, even when the amount of material it publishes is growing. So this chapter also discusses methods of auditing the performance of journals and some questions to ask if a journal is failing to meet its targets.

Publishing policy

Two major policy decisions are the subject areas that the publisher will cover and the type of journal to be published. These may go hand in hand; it is difficult to imagine a wide-circulation journal of Indo-Scythian studies, or a journal on community nursing intended solely for the academic library market. When looking at any proposal, the editor has to consider whether the journal will fit in with the publisher's other journals without adding staff, establishing new routines or learning new techniques. If it cannot, then the implications of the new journal for the organisation as a whole have to be considered. Will this journal take the business in the direction in which it should be going? Is it likely to be profitable on its own account? Might it lead to other publications that will also be profitable? Could the expertise acquired from publishing the new journal improve the performance of the publisher's other journals?

For learned society publishers, decisions about the subject matter are usually determined by the interests of their members. The primary object of a learned society is to serve the subject and the interests of its members, though publishing ventures are commonly expected to support the society's other activities. New journals require heavy investment of time and money and carry no guarantee of success, so societies publishing on their own account usually concentrate on journals in their own field.

Similarly other publishers, whether commercial or university press, may devote themselves to a narrow range of subjects. Some publish only journals, but most journal publishers also publish books. The journals list may complement the list of books or a journal or group of journals may be seen as a way of breaking into new subject areas. Experience gained from publishing journals in one subject can usefully be applied to journals in other subjects, and there are economies of scale in journal publishing. Because of the methods of selling (see chapter 4) it is easier to handle a list of journals on diverse topics than of books.

In general, scientific, technical and medical (STM) journals incur higher costs, particularly of production, than journals in the humanities and social sciences, but their purchasers are accustomed (sometimes resentfully) to paying higher prices. That makes it easier to increase the number of pages and issues in STM journals if the editor is receiving enough good material to fill them. The increase – and the consequent price increase – will not be welcomed by subscribers, but the cost per page may be lower.

On the other hand, the lower prices of journals in the humanities and social sciences help to encourage greater sales to individuals. It also makes them less liable to cancellation: librarians needing to reduce expenditure on serials will usually review the most expensive titles first. Journals concerned with business studies and law often lie somewhere between STM and humanities and social science journals. The more academic will sell principally to academic libraries worldwide. Journals concerned more with practice should sell to practitioners, but the market may be limited by geography. For instance, few practising lawyers are concerned with the law in other countries.

The second major policy area is the type of journal to be published. A weekly journal has a different rhythm and very different editorial requirements from a quarterly, with usually a much stricter attitude to deadlines and publication dates and often a greater reliance on advertising sales. An international publisher may be inappropriate for a journal of mainly local interest. Selling to individuals (particularly if they are not members of a sponsoring society) or to businesses is different from selling to libraries; it may need a different editorial policy. A journal that gets a substantial proportion of its income from advertising has different concerns from one largely dependent upon library subscriptions. Primary journals (i.e. those publishing reports of original research) are very different from secondary (e.g. abstract or review) journals. Letters, trends, or preliminary communications journals are different again, often requiring very rapid publication, a quick response from referees and sometimes rather informal methods of production. Cover-to-cover translations depend upon finding a journal that merits translation and good translators who can cope with both the language and the subject matter.

Increasing the size of a journal

Since some of the costs in publishing a journal are fixed, increases in extent (the number of pages) can make economic sense. As we have noted above, the amount of material seeking publication in journals is growing. If pressure of space causes an editor to reject good papers that provides opportunities for rival journals to establish themselves or strengthen their position. Most good journals are under pressure to increase the number of pages published, however much librarians may regret that. Faster than average growth requires a subject in which research is growing and an editor and a publishing strategy that attract papers in competition with other journals. Pressure on editors to accept marginal papers to fill the pages is unlikely to be a good policy in the long run. Editors of integrity will resist it, and the reputation of the journal will suffer; that in turn can reduce the quality of submissions and lead to cancellation of subscriptions. The caveat is that higher priced journals are more likely to come up for cancellation review than cheaper ones, regardless of the amount of material that they publish.

There may also be a problem for societies who supply all their members with the journal; some may be getting a lot of printed paper of no interest to them (though there may be an electronic solution to that). Splitting the journal (see below) may be a solution. On the other hand, the editors or the council of a sponsoring society may feel a split would destroy the overall balance of the parent journal to the detriment of the subject. If that is the case, the editor may need to increase the rejection rate, but that could encourage other publishers to start their own journals in the field.

Splits, or twigging

A publisher may feel that a journal is growing too large, either for the editorial team to cope with it, or because the total price is a deterrent to subscribers, even if the price per page is relatively low. Sometimes the rapid development of a particular aspect of the subject throws out the balance of the journal. It may be sensible to split the journal into two or to twig off a new journal.

The overall economics of splitting are not clear-cut, particularly if a large number of members were getting the original journal. If with the new arrangements a member who wants both journals must pay a supplement, then either less paper will be sent to the members, or the income will increase. However, the costs of editing and publishing two smaller journals are higher than for a single larger journal and so are library handling costs. That may be a short-term problem. If the decision to split or twig off a journal was correct, then both journals are likely to grow to a point where both are substantial and the loss of economy of scale is outweighed by the convenience to the reader of having two distinct journals. In addition, one or other of the journals may appeal to subscribers who did not buy the original journal.

Launching new journals

Traditionally publishers have grown their lists by launching new titles. In the sixties, especially in STM fields, this was done with relatively little risk. With the right subject and a strong editorial team initial promotion would attract enough subscriptions to fund the first issue, further subscriptions would cover the second issue and so on; it was sometimes possible to launch a new title without going seriously into deficit.

With current market conditions the launching of a new journal may involve an investment of tens of thousands of dollars or pounds over several years and the risk of failure is high. It may be five years before the journal begins to break even and take longer than that to pay back the initial investment. Journal publishing is not a short term business. Consequently, publishers are starting fewer titles although in the humanities there has been a recent spate of new titles (Oakeshott, 1995); in the sciences the birth- and death-rates of journals are probably nearly equal (figure 1.3).

Chapter 2 on editing and chapter 4 on marketing look at the sort of enquiries that publishers make before launching new titles. Some useful insights can be found in the list of references and further reading. For instance, Janet Bailey (1989) discusses the steps by which a publisher decides whether to publish a new journal with interesting examples. She points out that just as most papers rejected by one journal are eventually published by another so most proposals for new journals from sponsors get taken up in the end. Charles Fischer (1990) describes how he launched a new business school periodical with no previous experience as a journal editor. He started by writing to the editors of approximately 150 business school journals for their advice and nearly one-third responded with 'a wealth of materials and suggestions'.

Publishers may have specialist subject publishers/editors seeking out ideas for journals (and books too). They should keep in close touch with the editors of their journals who will be conscious of which areas of their subject are growing fastest. They attend major meetings worldwide and watch the emergence of new sub-disciplines and meet the leaders in these and the officers of pertinent societies.

New journals often come from a partnership between a sponsor, for instance a society or some other organised group of researchers, which would like to have a journal to give it identity and a publisher with strong editorial presence in the field. The publisher provides the capital and publishing expertise and services. The sponsor provides the support of the research community which is invaluable in getting material to publish in the early issues. Another possible bonus is the existence of a body of members, provided they will pay more than the marginal costs (see chapter 8, financial aspects) to receive the journal.

A publisher who develops the idea and puts it to the sponsor is likely to become the publisher of the journal, although there may be some tough negotiating over editorial control and fees, royalties or a share of profits and charges for copies going to members. Occasionally the setting up of a journal will stimulate the formation of a society; the publisher can help with the administration of the new society by running the membership list if all members automatically take the journal. Sometimes a publisher will hope to gain the support of more than one sponsor; for example both a North American and a European society.

If the idea for a journal originates from the sponsor then the sponsor should not accept the first offer from a publisher. In some cases they will send out a proposal to several publishers, interview the strongest contenders and select the most appropriate.

In the early years a new journal may build up a considerable deficit (see figure 1.1) particularly if there is no sponsor to cushion it. The costs of publicity, sample copies and setting up the editorial office may far exceed the revenue from subscribers. A publisher can try to limit the losses by going for a low-cost strategy; on the other hand, if the publisher has adequate resources, faith in the journal, its editor and their own ability to sell it, a high-cost strategy may be adopted.

With a low-cost strategy the publisher may be able to persuade the editor to accept a low fee and budget for expenses. Publicity can be kept to a simple leaflet mailed to carefully selected lists backed up by letters from the editor to colleagues. The first volume may be only two issues of sixty-four pages each in a smallish format; CRT and DTP (see chapter 3, production) may be used to keep down the origination costs. As subscriptions come in and the supply of copy builds up the journal may be allowed to grow slowly, moving to slightly larger issues then three issues in an annual volume and so on, with perhaps a switch to a larger format.

Such a journal may not make a hefty loss in the early years, but it may never do much more than cover its costs (including overheads) and it may not promote the publisher's reputation. If there is competition from other journals, it may be difficult to attract good papers. But it may be the only strategy open in some subject areas, particularly in the humanities and social sciences publishing. And of course it is sometimes successful, especially when the journal is in a new and rapidly growing subject.

Publishers adopting a high-cost strategy do so in the hope that the journal will turn into a major title delivering a healthy profit in later years and paying back the early deficit. The deficit may reach something of the order of US $150,000 by the end of the third year of publication. A high-cost strategy is commonly used for STM and professional publications when it may be considered necessary to attract good papers and good editors with high status. The budget for publicity in the first eighteen months (covering the six months before publication and the first annual volume) will be at least US $30,000 with four-colour brochures, widely distributed sample copies and special displays at major meetings. Editorial expenses could include one or two meetings of an international editorial board, travel by the editor to attend key conferences and the setting up of an editorial office with an assistant and equipment with editorial software to cope with the hoped-for number of submissions.

Sometimes there will be editorial offices in several countries; for example, the United States, Britain, Germany and Japan.

Lavish production may be thought necessary to make people notice the journal. For instance, it might have a four-colour cover with a different picture for each issue, a large double column format, and high quality paper, typesetting, printing and binding. Rapid publication can be helpful; the publisher may aim for not more than ten weeks from acceptance of copy, but that requires frequent publication.

It is possible to switch from one strategy to another. Moving from a low-cost to a high-cost strategy may effectively be a relaunch. The journal already has editorial momentum and subscriptions but the publicity required to establish a new image will need to be well conceived and will probably be expensive. Moving from a high-cost strategy to a low-cost one will contain future costs but may not do much to recoup past losses.

Ideally journals are published on a calendar-year basis, but that timing may not suit the publishers' plans or the flow of copy for the first issues. Some publishers have launched a new title half-way through the year as a half volume, so that, for instance, three issues of a bimonthly are published in the first year. The advantages include being ahead of any rival publisher who may be looking at the same idea (waiting to publish the first issue in January gives the rival time to organise a competing title or even publish first); lower production costs for the first volume which will inevitably lose heavily as subscription revenue will be small. The editor may find it easier to fill the smaller number of pages. Another advantage is that it starts generating citation data earlier: some libraries only subscribe if the citation status can be seen and such data are only published after a minimum of two volumes have appeared. An alternative approach is to launch a new title with one issue in the first year followed by three (or more) in the second year to make up the first volume. That does not help with getting citation status quickly but it may get the journal onto the market sooner than otherwise or ease copy-flow problems.

The early years

Many publishers produce a five-year budget/business plan for the launch of a new journal; sometimes with best, worst and expected cases. The early years are an anxious time, with the editor concerned about getting submissions and the publisher watching the post for subscriptions and specimen copy requests and charting the circulation growth. Figure 1.1 shows how expectations have decreased as the market has become more difficult.

Many journals have fewer than 100 institutional subscriptions in the first year. Since many libraries take three years or more to allocate funds to acquire a new journal this may not be as hopeless as the outsider might assume. An increase in the second year to around 150 to 180 is encouraging. If the number is less than that, or there are immediate cancellations, that suggests that the journal should be radically altered, relaunched or even terminated at the end of the third year.

The third year is often critical. A journal which has done well in its second year may add only twenty in the third, putting it on the danger list, another may gain as many as in the second year and look more likely to survive. By late in year three the performance versus plan should be clear and a revised strategy might be considered. The audit checklist in the next section can be used. Another factor brought into the equation includes the flow of copy: if that is strong, the publisher may postpone the planned break-even point by increasing the number of pages. In the short term, the additional costs will increase the deficit, but it may be necessary if it is to develop into a journal indispensable to researchers in the field. On the other hand, if copy is not coming in as hoped, it is another signal that the journal has not found a niche.

Sometimes it will be clear in year three that the market or subject is not ripe for another major journal, but the journal can survive by cutting back to a tight economical design and employing the savings listed later in this chapter. It might be possible to break even by raising the price sharply. That could restrain further growth in circulation and perhaps should only be done if the journal is thought to be near to its maximum circulation.

When a journal is five or six years old it should still have some potential for circulation growth if a reasonable editorial standard has been achieved and there is sufficient interest in the subject. Figure 10.1 shows a histogram of subscription renewals over the year for an established journal (top) and a young journal (bottom). This type of analysis

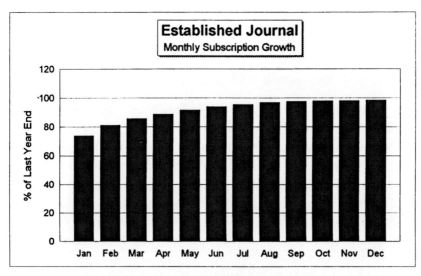

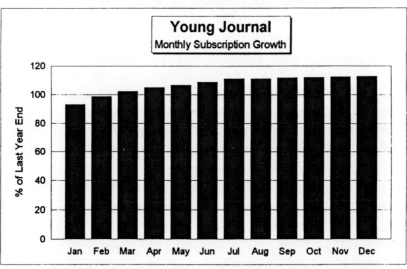

Figure 10.1 Histograms showing the build up of subscriptions over the year (1994) for an established journal (top) and a journal launched three years previously (bottom).

should demonstrate early in the year whether a journal is still gaining circulation.

Acquiring journals from other publishers

Another way of increasing market share is to acquire journals – or the rights to publish them – from other publishers. The publisher acquiring the journal may be able to offer a more suitable home, a fresh eye on the journal or economies of scale that would make it possible to continue the journal either on its own or as part of a merged journal (see below). A publisher may be interested in selling a list or part of it; sponsors are generally advised to maintain their ownership of a title when they take it to another publisher (see section on tendering for society journals below).

Chapter 8 discusses the valuation of journals. Prices paid have increased as publishers concentrate more on journals and less on books. Journals published in English from North America may fetch higher prices as they are often thought to have potential for growth, while journals published in, say, German or French usually sell for lower multiples because of the limited number of potential subscribers.

As much information as possible should be gathered before offering a bid. Who are the subscribers and how many are there? What are the subscription trends? Are there any special subscription deals which might not be renewed or which affect the income? The existing publisher may not be prepared to make subscriber details available to a competitor but might allow an independent adviser access to the lists in confidence to extract certain information. Information is also needed on advertisers and advertising revenue and any agreements with other bodies that affect the journal (e.g. copyright licensing, micro-form or electronic versions and so on). If the purchaser wants the current editorial team to continue they will need assurance of their commitment and full details of any contractual arrangements with them. The purchase agreement may include a warranty of some of these items.

One problem to be resolved is unearned subscription revenue. The acquirer may construct a three or five year budget to estimate the income stream under their ownership. If the seller has already collected some of these subscriptions under two or three year deals, the price paid should take account of that. If the transfer is made part-way through a year, there is the question of unearned revenue for the current year. If, say, the sale of a quarterly journal takes place on the first of July, the acquiring publisher will take responsibility for producing and despatching the last two issues and might pay for any work in progress on these two issues, but the subscription revenue still to be earned by these last two issues may be deducted from the acquisition price. It is simpler if the transfer is at the end of the subscription period when the respective responsibilities to subscribers are more clear cut.

If a journal offers an any-time start for subscriptions, the calculations are more complex. The usual method is to construct a table showing the number of unearned subscriptions for each forthcoming issue. This will require details of when each subscription was paid and for what issues. One cannot assume that the average subscription has six months to run: there may be a seasonal pattern with peaks in new or renewed subscriptions in the Autumn (Fall) and Spring or when there have been major publicity campaigns.

Subscription lists for journals taken over from other publishers may require a lot of work to convert them to the format and standards of the purchasing publisher. This should not be underestimated, and is part of the acquisition cost. The two publishers may differ in what they expect outside editors to do and what is done in-house; the editor and the new publisher will have to discuss and agree the procedures to be adopted.

There have also been cases of a sponsor buying a journal from a publisher. This can happen, for example, when each party owns a share and the sponsor has built up sufficient funds to acquire full ownership. The valuation of the journal is difficult and a compromise may be reached whereby the sponsor pays less than another publisher would pay, but in return, signs a long-term agreement with the publisher.

Tendering for society journals

Learned societies and other sponsors may put the publication of their journals out to tender. From the publisher's point of view, tendering is time-consuming; if every sponsor approaches six publishers, then only one-in-six tenders is successful. However, tenders can bring in journals that may not require a great deal of editorial development or initiative.

Tenders often ask for a quick response; none the less they require careful reading and research. Publishers who respond to a detailed tender document with no more than an invitation to lunch or a suggestion that they would be happy to undertake the publication but would want to double the price should not be surprised if they do not get the journal.

While the sponsor will set out the points that they consider important, the publisher may want to introduce other factors that seem pertinent. That is often welcome, but a publisher who attempts to talk a sponsor out of something they have firmly decided may get short shrift. Otherwise the response should be as for any other inquiry about publishing a journal. It may be circulated to a committee with no professional publishing background or advice, so it is worth taking time to make sure that details are spelt out clearly. (One firm lost an attractive journal because the society assumed that two sums to cover the publisher's overheads should be added together; in fact one was a minimum and the other a maximum.) It is helpful to provide some background about the publishing firm, its ownership, principal offices and main activities.

Extras, such as sketches of new cover designs, are helpful and can add a lighter touch. But they are no substitute for hard information on what the publisher would do; a costed publicity plan will carry more weight.

Appendix 1 sets out some of the factors a sponsor might include in their tender documents. Chapter 8 on finance outlines some possible arrangements and chapter 7 on legal aspects discusses agreements between publishers and sponsors.

Mergers

Sometimes a journal has little hope of standing on its own feet either in the present publisher's hands or in another list. In that case, the publisher might think of merging it with an existing journal on their list or with a title from another publisher. In either case, the merger will be subject to negotiation with the editors of the two journals. The scale can run from fifty-fifty participation in the new journal to one journal subsuming the other. In the first case, there might be a change of title and a new combined editorial board leading to a stronger and more broadly based publication, retaining, it is hoped, the subscribers from both journals. In the second, the subscribers from the journal being incorporated will be encouraged to continue their subscriptions.

Whatever the terms of the merger a key factor is the number of subscribers unique to each journal. Since neither publisher is likely to be willing to reveal their current subscription list to the other, an independent body may be needed to compare the two subscription lists and identify the number of duplicate subscriptions and the number of fresh subscribers that each journal can offer the other. It may be necessary to distinguish clear duplicates (identical addresses for the ultimate subscriber) from probable ones (very similar addresses) and from unknowns; each journal might have, for instance, the same number of subscribers in China, but the final destination of copies may not be known.

If two publishers are involved in the merger, the publisher may ask the vendor to guarantee not to set up a similar journal in the same subject area for a certain number of years.

Selling journals or closing them down

Not all journals flourish. Some ideas for dealing with troubled ones can be found in the sections later in this chapter on auditing journals and dealing with an ailing journal. If none of these seem likely to make the journal viable or appropriate to its publisher's list, then the options are to sell the journal to another publisher, to merge it with another journal (see above) or to stop it entirely.

Selling a journal or a list of journals

Earlier in this chapter we discuss the buying of journals from other publishers. But for every buyer there is also a seller. A publisher may find that some titles no longer fit the sort of publishing they wish to do and, rather than close them down, they may seek a buyer for them.

The process of getting bids for the purchase of journals is very like the process of getting tenders (see appendix 1). The publisher will need to decide what information to give to prospective purchasers and which publishers to approach. The journals may be sold simply to the highest bidder, or to the highest bidder whom it is thought will treat the editors and sponsors of the journals fairly and decently; they are not necessarily the same. To start with, the seller may wish to be anonymous and use an independent intermediary to explore the level of interest of different publishers before coming into the open.

Purchasers may look for guarantees from the publisher including, for instance, that there is a reasonable flow of copy; that the editors are prepared to work with them; that there is no reason to expect a drop in advertising revenue (because, for instance, a particular contract is coming to an end and is unlikely to be renewed); that the subscription list will be passed on in good order and that the number of subscribers is as stated. Provision has to be made for dealing with back volumes, claims for previously published issues, payments received by the present publisher for issues not despatched, royalties from micro-form, CD-ROM, online use, photocopying and electrocopying etc.

Closing a journal

Sometimes after examining all the possibilities the publisher may conclude that they have no alternative to closing a journal. To make this process as painless as possible (enquiries about a no longer published journal waste everyone's time) there are a number of steps that should be taken including those listed below.

1. Determine which will be the final issue of the journal. If there is a common subscription expiry date then, if possible, the final issue should be the one with which all current subscriptions expire.

2. Estimate how much material will be needed to fill the remaining issues. If too much has already been accepted for publication and the finances will not allow extra pages, some material will have to be returned to contributors. Other things being equal, the principle should be that the most recently accepted material is returned with apologies to the author and an explanation of why it is no longer possible for the journal to publish it.

The editor may also have commissioned some contributions – book reviews for instance – which it will not be possible to publish. The authors should be informed as soon as possible so they do not waste time working on things that the journal cannot publish.

If there is too little material in hand, then the editor might attempt to raise some more. This may not be possible, particularly if the reason for closing the journal is that the editor can no longer edit it. The answer may be to publish the remaining material in one issue but to number it so that it completes the volume – for instance 'parts 3–6'.

3. Material that cannot be published or orders or claims for volumes that will not be published are unproductive both for the journal and for its clients. The closure should be signalled as early as possible. Subscribers and readers are best alerted by a large removable notice stuck on the front cover stating that the journal is closing and giving the volume and part number and date of the final issue. Subscription agents rarely see journals and so need separate notification, both for their records and so they can advise their clients.

4. Typesetters, printers and binders should be informed as soon as possible. Some contracts require long notice. Suppliers may buy materials in advance and so need to estimate the quantity required. They will want time to find other customers to take up capacity released by the closure of the journal.

5. The editor or the publisher, or both together, should prepare a note for publication in the journal to explain why it has been decided to close the journal and to thank contributors and subscribers, as well as those who have worked for the journal (editors, referees, copy-editors, publishers, printers, designers, distributors, advertisers) for their support in the past.

6. Journals are sometimes described as 'continuations'; a journal that has ceased publication still has life after the last issue. It is therefore wise to have a stock of a standard letter or postcard that can be sent to enquirers after the journal has ceased publication giving the title, ISSN, the date and volume and issue numbers of the final part, together with any other helpful information, such as addresses for back volume orders, permission requests etc.

7. Determine what should be done about:

(a) *Claims for missing issues*. For some months after the publication of the last issue, there may be claims for that and for previous issues. If possible these should be treated in the normal way (see chapter 5).

(b) *Orders for previously published issues.* Arrangements need to be made for the existing stock. Should it all be disposed of? Is it possible to arrange for another body (perhaps a specialist back-volume house) to hold a stock of issues that might be saleable, either on commission or as an outright purchase?

(c) *Copyright matters.* There may be existing licensing arrangements for reprinting or photocopying; licensees should be informed that the journal is ceasing publication and given instructions for the payment of royalties in future. There may also be requests for permission to re-issue material published in the journal. To whom should these be directed? How will they be dealt with? The journal will need a 'literary executor'.

(d) *Contributions.* Authors may continue to submit papers, reviews etc. long after the journal ceases publication. These should be returned to the sender with the standard notice (see 6 above) that the journal is no longer published.

(e) *Books for review.* Publishers who have regularly sent review copies or catalogues should be advised that the journal is ceasing publication. Books received too late to review should be returned to the publisher with a note of explanation.

(f) *Press releases.* For many academic journals these are often more of a nuisance than a source of useful information. They should be returned (including the address label) to the sender with the notice that the journal is ceasing publication.

(g) *Directory entries.* Publishers of directories in which the journal has been listed should be informed that it is ceasing publication. *Ulrich's* and the *Ebsco Directory* are the most important, but do not neglect the others.

(h) *Advertisers, including exchanges.* Let all regular advertisers know that the journal is ceasing publication.

Auditing journals

Many journals pay their way and present few problems to their publishers. But it does not follow that they are achieving their full potential. Some sponsors may resent any intrusion by the publisher into what they regard as their territory, but others are happy to work with the publisher to find ways of making the journal more successful and more attractive to authors and subscribers. In either case, the publisher should regularly monitor the journal's performance.

Ideally an audit will involve editors, editorial board members and sponsors as well as all pertinent members of the in-house staff. They can contribute firsthand knowledge of what is happening in the subject. Everyone concerned should be encouraged to look ahead. Is a change of editorial policy desirable or feasible? Perhaps the editorial board needs strengthening in some areas; changes of content may affect the format, design or production process used for the journal. A change in policy that increases the range of topics covered will have marketing implications.

An audit checklist might include:

1 Design.
2 Production standards.
3 Quality of typesetting.
4 Consistency of style, terms and symbols.
5 Editorial policy.
6 Citation ranking (see chapter 4)
7 Geographical distribution of contributors, current and in the recent past.
8 Geographical distribution of subscribers and whether numbers in each area are static, increasing or declining.
9 Subscription price and price per page in comparison with rival journals.
10 Use in libraries.
11 Document delivery requests (BLDSC and Uncover data for example) and receipts from RROs.
12 Efficiency of editorial process: (a) acknowledgement of receipt of paper; (b) refereeing, speed and thoroughness; and (c) average period between receipt and acceptance/rejection.
13 Publication time; acceptance to publication (if possible in comparison with rival journals).
14 Unique selling points: why should people/libraries subscribe and why should authors submit papers?

15 Promotion.

16 Circulation in comparison with rival journals (if possible over several years).

17 Regularity of publication and reliability of delivery.

18 Number of free offprints; price, quality and speed of despatch.

The ailing journal

Auditing is preventative medicine, but even audited journals may get into difficulties. Treatment of the sick depends upon proper diagnosis of the cause of the illness. If a journal is in trouble, there is often more than one cause. The most useful diagnostic tools are the figures for the journal, if possible over a number of years; as much information as possible on other journals in the same subject area; and a cool look at whether the journal is meeting a real need. If changes have to be made, it is usually better to make them all at once. Among the benefits is that the changes can provide the basis for further promotion, which is a tonic needed by most ailing journals. If the price has to be raised sharply, it is better to do that at the same time as changing the production method and increasing the number of pages to speed up the publication time.

Here is a checklist of some common problems and possible solutions. It does not claim to be exhaustive, but it should provide some initial ideas. As a first step, they can be followed up by reading the appropriate chapter of this book, and any suggested further reading. Other publishers, or other societies, may be willing to give advice: there are also consultants who can help.

Are there enough subscribers ? If not:

Were expectations too high? Compare the figures with those for other journals, and rethink the journal in the light of experience.

Is the subject area of the journal too restricted; can it be made broader?

Does the title give a false impression of the content, thereby deterring some potential readers?

Is the journal publishing enough good material to justify the price?

The answer may reflect poor editorial judgement; long delays in publishing papers; high-handed editorial treatment of authors; too close association with a particular school of thought; the production may be inadequate for the kind of material authors want to publish, or the presentation may be unattractive.

Are there features which could be added to make the journal more attractive to authors and subscribers?

Are there potential markets (of level, of subject interest, or geographical) which have not been properly tapped: does the subscription list reflect the scope of the journal?

If it does not, can promotion be put in hand to remedy this?

Has promotion been done properly? Has everything been sent out that should have been? Was it all clear? Were the right lists used?

Have subscription agents been told about it? Do they know where to send orders and how much the journal costs?

Is the journal included in the appropriate bibliographic listings, especially *Ulrich's*?

Should the journal offer special rates to particular groups to attract new subscribers?

Is the income too low ?

How does the price compare with that of similar journals? Can it be increased without being too much out of line with them? (Remember that they may have to increase their prices too.) Will increasing the price cause such a reduction in the number of subscribers that the finances of the journal are made worse by the price increase? It is very rare for this to happen with journals. (The number of subscribers who would have to cancel to nullify the effect of the increase can be calculated.)

Is the trade discount much higher than customary for that type of publication? If so, can it be reduced?

Are the actual net receipts from an overseas subscriber much lower than for domestic ones? If so, consider restricting the currencies you will accept, and fixing prices in these currencies.

Are you suffering from bad debts? Many journal publishers work on a strict cash-with-order basis.

Could you improve systems to bring in the money earlier?

Is the journal being credited with enough for copies going to members, or sent out on exchange?

Can you increase the income from items other than subscriptions (see chapter on non-subscription income), either by selling more, or by raising prices?

Should members be paying more for their copies? Should the journal be made an optional extra rather than being sent automatically to all of them? Some may not even want it.

Are the costs too high?

Are there some costs set against the journal that really should be carried somewhere else? (This is a common problem with society journals.)

Could the extent or frequency be reduced, without building up long delays in publication?

Do you need a tougher policy on acceptance and rejection of papers, etc.?

Are there sections of the journal which are of little value, which could be dropped?

Can the production costs be sensibly reduced, without making the journal less attractive to authors and subscribers? Can you make real savings by changing the printer, the method of production, or the materials used? When were estimates for printing last sought? (See the checklist in chapter 3.)

Is work being duplicated, for instance by the copy-editor and the printer; or by keeping unnecessary sets of records?

Can distribution and/or despatch costs be reduced?

Are you paying a publisher/distribution service more than it would cost you to do it yourself?

Would it be cheaper to get the work done by a publisher/distribution service than to do it yourself?

Are there too many free copies? When was the free list last checked?
Should exchange copies be charged to some other budget, e.g. the
library?

Can you simplify office work? (Forms, standard letters and postcards
instead of personal letters; simpler recording procedures; more – or
less – automation.)

Have you too much material to publish?

Is editorial selection rigorous enough?

Does the journal cover too wide a subject area?

Can you increase the size of the journal, with a proportionate increase in
price?

Can you split the journal into two smaller, more specialist ones? (That
increases the overhead costs, but can make subscriptions more
attractive to libraries. It has an especial advantage for society
journals, for members might then receive only one journal as of
right.)

Is the journal short of good material to publish?

Can you and the editors make it known that you are looking for papers to
publish? A call for papers could be sent out. Speakers at conferences
might be approached for papers.

Is the editorial board doing all it should to attract papers? Can its
members be pressured into contributing themselves?

Is your publication time too long? How does it compare with your
competitors'?

Is your offprint policy too mean? Are your page charges too high?

Where are the papers you would like to publish being published? Why do
authors submit their papers to these journals rather than to yours?

Can you make your journal more attractive to authors?

Should the scope of the journal be broadened? Are there other topics on
the borders of the subject which could be included in its coverage?

Could other features usefully be introduced, e.g. review articles, abstracts,
short reports, proceedings of meetings?

Is the editor up to the job?

Is he (or she) willing and able to co-operate to make the journal viable?
Is his approach too narrow, or outdated?
Does he have enough time to devote to the journal?
Can he keep to schedule?
Is he giving offence to authors or referees?
Does he reject too much – or too little?
Is he overloaded with work?
Does the journal need a new editor, or more editorial assistance?
Could an additional editor, an assistant editor, or a more active and/or authoritative editorial board help?

Will tackling the items above be enough? If not, can you consider:

A complete revamp of the journal, and particularly of its editorial coverage, backed up by a proper marketing campaign?
Merging with another journal? If so, under what terms and conditions?
Linking up with a society (or for a society-sponsored journal, with another society in another country) and making the journal also the official journal of that society. That could bring in additional papers, and enough additional subscriptions, albeit at reduced rates, to save the journal, particularly if the society can help with promotion.
Finding someone to relieve you of routine chores, so you can spend time on more important matters?
Finding a publisher with whom you can work (or another publisher)?
Finding a body that will sponsor the journal by, say, buying some subscriptions for distribution to customers or contributing to the editorial costs. (This is not often possible outside clinical medicine).

Co-ordination

As this book demonstrates different publishers will have different policies and practices for their journal publishing. They are also faced with a variety of possibilities for electronic publishing and document delivery.

Which a publisher chooses will depend upon their list, their resources, their location and their inclinations. Those managing lists of journals need to co-ordinate their activities and the staff (editorial, design and production, marketing, order fulfilment and distribution, finance, bibliographical aspects, copyright and so on) so that unnecessary variants are not introduced inadvertently and that guidelines are adhered to. When changes are introduced they can be used to increase the publisher's expertise; wherever possible there should be controls to indicate what would have happened if the change had not been made.

Training in journal publishing

Training may be formal or informal, in-house or out-of-house. Out-of-house training has the benefit of exposing people to other ideas on how to publish journals, providing contacts in other publishing houses and allowing people to demonstrate their ignorance (or fly kites) without incurring any opprobrium from their colleagues. stm (the international association of scientific, technical and medical publishers), Book House Training Centre (London) and the Professional and Scholarly Publishers division of the Association of American Publishers have all run courses in journal publishing. Many of the bodies listed in appendix 2 (Some associations of editors and publishers of learned journals) run conferences, meetings, seminars and workshops which can be helpful in developing staff.

11   Electronic publishing

Introduction

The term 'electronic publishing' has more than one connotation. On the one hand, it can describe a situation where the entire flow of information from author to reader (via whatever intermediaries are necessary) is in machine-readable form. On the other, it has been used to describe information transfer in machine-readable form up to the final stage, when the reader is supplied with hard-copy. (Indeed, it has also been applied to the conversion of printed material into machine-readable form.) In essence, the various usages tend to blur into each other. For example, many readers prefer to read lengthy pieces of text from print-out rather than on the screen, even when the latter option is available. Nowadays, it is the first, completely electronic scenario which is usually meant by 'electronic publishing'. However, the best definition for our present purpose may be 'any type of publishing where the economic base is the machine-readable form, rather than the printed hard-copy edition'.

Some types of information are obviously more suited to electronic handling than others. Large quantities of reference material that must be sorted quickly to extract a limited amount of data provide one obvious example. Abstracts and indexing publications fall into this category, and publishers of these already have years of experience of providing their information in machine-readable form. To some extent, intending publishers of electronic journals can learn from this experience, but the differing requirements of primary and secondary journals (for example, as regards how the input material is provided and edited) mean that such transferral may be limited in its scope. Publishers of abstracts journals moved into electronic publishing early on because they handle small chunks of text in large numbers, and this proved to be a suitable task for a computer. Handling long pieces of text proved more difficult, but, in recent years, full-text handling – essential for electronic journals – has become rapidly easier. By 1992, some 2,500 periodicals were available online, and the number has continued to climb rapidly (mainly electronic versions of existing magazines, newspapers and related publications). In terms of contents, these have naturally been biased towards topics such as finance and business, where there are customers who are prepared to pay for quicker and better access to information. Most recent articles and books on the Internet will contain some mention of electronic publications (Krol, 1993), but the material dates very rapidly. There have been some surveys of authors' and readers' opinions of electronic journals (RS/BL/ALPSP, 1993; Schauder, 1993).

The sort of factors involved in electronic publishing can best be seen by looking at an actual example of electronic communication – the bulletin board. The concept of an electronic bulletin board is based on the physical boards for pinning up notices that used to be common in village shops. Anybody could pin a note on the board – concerning anything from sales and wants to meetings – and would expect it to be seen, and possibly responded to, by the local community. The basic requirements for access to an electronic bulletin board are a computer terminal connected to a network. The bulletin board, itself, can be set up with appropriate software on one or more host computers. Users can read information (and input, if they wish) from the screen, tracking down items of interest via a series of menus.

The analogy with a physical notice-board can be pushed further. The shopkeeper usually kept an eye on the board to ensure that it did not become too full, and that out-of-date or unsuitable material was removed. In a similar way, academic bulletin boards – the ones of most concern here – usually have a co-ordinator who ensures the smooth running of the system. Bulletin boards for the academic community are normally aimed at specialist groups and typically concentrate on a specified range of items (e.g. work in progress, forthcoming meetings). They overlap with other types of computer-based communication, such as newsgroups (which, as the name implies, are concerned with the exchange of research news) and electronic newsletters. This overlap is worth stressing. Unlike printed sources, electronic sources of information can blur into each other: so a bulletin board can readily develop into something else.

There is a parallel between these electronic activities and the early days of printed journals. These latter originated in part from the letters exchanged between individual scientists about their work. To obtain better dissemination, some of these letters came to be channelled through one person, who brought together the information reaching him and then distributed it to others in the research community. It was not a large step from this to a printed form of the letters with the person who collected them as editor.

A similar development may take place with informal electronic communications, such as bulletin boards. For example, *Hi-T$_c$ Update* was launched in 1987 as a means of keeping researchers in the rapidly expanding area of high-temperature superconductivity abreast of progress in their subject. It lists relevant preprints as they appear. *HEPTH (High-Energy Physics Theory)*, started in 1991, takes this a stage further. It not only lists new preprints, but also makes the full text of each available online. It only requires peer review to be introduced for this to become a fully fledged electronic journal. The difference from a publisher's viewpoint is that subscribers are not charged. This is possible because the networks and computer terminals are subsidised, and the editorial labour is unpaid. There can be no doubt that these developments are affecting traditional channels, especially letters journals. The electronic lists in physics have, for example, forced the American Physical Society to consider providing the high-prestige *Physical Review Letters* in electronic form.

Dissemination

The dissemination of electronic data depends on developments in information technology, i.e. in networks and in the computers attached to them. Electronic networks have been around in the world of research for some time, but they have changed gradually in their nature. Initially, they linked together the mainframe computers at specified institutions. For example, NSF Net in the United States linked together institutions involved with the National Science Foundation, whilst JANET (the Joint

Academic Network) linked British universities. Such networks, which join together geographically dispersed centres, are labelled WANs (wide area networks). Subsequently, the proliferation of micro-computers has led to the need to join them together within an institution, leading to the creation of LANs (local area networks). The basic distinction between the two types therefore relates to their level of dispersion, but there have been other points of difference. The most important has been that the bandwidth and speed of handling information for LANs can be considerably higher than for WANs. The differences in this respect are diminishing as the quality of long-distance transmission is improved. Their importance relates to the information that can be transmitted. Existing networks can handle text readily, but experience more difficulty in transmitting graphics (especially colour graphics) with reasonable speed. The new networks should get over this problem. In the early days, network use was particularly strong amongst scientists and engineers, but in the 1990s social scientists and people in the humanities have taken up the new opportunities with enthusiasm. Networked access to information now spans all subjects.

Networks extend internationally, as well as nationally. For example, there is EARN (the European Academic Research Network) which not only links European networks, but also links them to networks in North America. What is happening is the establishment of a hierarchy of networks, with LANs linked by national WANs which are then connected by international WANs. The logical culmination of this development is the Internet, which is designed to join together academic networks worldwide. By 1994, this had over 20 million users worldwide, with an expansion rate of perhaps 10 to 15 per cent per month. Aids to help users of the Internet have been, and are being, devised. For example, WAIS (Wide Area Information Server) allows searches for information in terms of topic, whilst WWW (World-Wide Web) provides a hypertext interface to information. The latter development is particularly important, since it seems increasingly likely that future electronic journals will require some kind of hypermedia links.

The rapidly improving access to networks has encouraged the growth of online publications in the 1990s. Scores of electronic journals and newsletters have appeared in recent years. A good listing of them is provided in the *Directory of Electronic Newsletters, Serials and Discussion Lists*, which is updated at intervals (see bibliography). Most publications in the directory, at present, are free of charge to readers, but some require a subscription. It will be noted that discussion lists are mentioned: they are very similar to news groups. All these groups originally tended to use LISTSERV software (often referred to as the 'list server'), which can be readily obtained by network users who wish to start their own electronic publication. There is a strong move now towards Windows-based software, but, as always, acquisition of the new interface will be spread out in time both within countries and between countries.

Many research networks are open to academic users without charge (though some of the network services may be charged for). Nevertheless, financial factors can still affect use. An example is the question of connecting to a LAN. Onsite connection is usually free to the users, but a connection from home will be charged at the rate of local telephone calls. Depending on how much this is, reading electronic publications away from one's desk may be encouraged or discouraged. Local charges are an important reason why far fewer British than American academics communicate electronically from home.

Inevitably, the growth of internetworking means that many users who can now access the Internet do not come from the academic/research world. Correspondingly, the range and level of material is becoming increasingly wide. One query that is attracting particular attention in the USA is this: given that the Internet is becoming a part of the general information infrastructure, rather than purely academic, should a charge be imposed for access to it?

Several networks used by academics are not available to outside publishers for general communication (though the signs are that restrictions will soon ease – for a suitable fee). However, there is nothing to prevent a publisher putting up an electronic journal as a database accessible via academic networks. Common carrier networks also have their problems. Providers of information on these are typically seeking for ways of adding value to their activities, in order to bring in more revenue. On such VANs (Valued-Added Networks) publishers may find competition to some of their traditional interests. At the same time, network access offers new marketing opportunities to publishers. For example, publishers such as Springer-Verlag have started to offer potential readers online access to the tables of contents and abstracts of their titles before each new issue appears.

Alternatives to online

Not all the problems of interconnecting users of different electronic networks have yet been overcome, and this is part of the reason for the rapidly growing popularity of facsimile transmission (along with its greater ease of use internationally). For journals, fax also has the great virtue that it can handle diagrams easily. In consequence, it is increasingly being used to support journal operations. One publisher, for example, claims to have cut by half the time from the submission of an article to its publication by using fax at all stages (including communication with referees). The appearance of micro-computers that can also handle fax has enhanced its value, though, of course, text and diagrams cannot be altered directly by the recipient.

Problems of online provision can be circumvented by storing the journal electronically on some medium that can be physically distributed. The current favourite is CD-ROM (compact disk read-only memory), so called because users can only read the contents of the disk: they cannot change or add to them. Generally accepted standards already exist for such disks, and they have the additional advantage that they can store graphics. But compact disks are not an ideal storage medium. Their choice for text is based on the popularity of such disks for purveying music, which means that the costs both of the production of the disks and of the players have dropped to acceptable levels. Other optical disks have been developed which can store considerably more information than a CD-ROM, but they only have restricted applications at present. The number of CD-ROM titles available is currently increasing by well over 50 per cent each year, with some two-thirds produced in the USA, and most of the remainder in Europe.

Roughly speaking, a CD-ROM can hold 100,000 pages of text in ASCII, or 10,000 black and white photographs, or 1,000 colour photographs. Unless a journal is lavish in the use of colour photographs, it should therefore be possible to get several annual volumes on a disk. This highlights the problem of publishing a single title on CD-ROM: there is far too much storage space for a single issue. This is not true of secondary publications, such as abstracts journals, where the amount of material can soon justify a large amount of storage space. Alternatively, CD-ROM may be a good way of providing current issues if several different titles are put together on one disk. Typically, the journal contents are stored as digitised text (SGML plus Postscript) with a separate image file; a package such as Acrobat can be used to store more on the disk. Readers can use their own search terms, as well as searching via standard bibliographical input (author names, titles, etc.).

One such CD-ROM development is the ADONIS project. In this, the contents of 650 biomedical journals from 72 publishers are put on CD-ROM and distributed, usually shortly after the printed versions have appeared. ADONIS was the subject of a prolonged period of experimentation before it was established in its present form as a not-for-profit operation supported by some of the leading international journal publishers. The disks go to major libraries to support document delivery, though some work has been carried out on direct use by readers (see also the discussion in the non-subscription income chapter). Currently subscribers pay for usage (any copy made of an article is charged at a rate set by the original publisher), but, in future, subscribers will also be able to pay an upfront charge (in effect an electronic subscription) for each journal for unlimited access to that journal. Storing the journal articles in SGML Postscript files handled via Acrobat, rather than as digital bit-mapped page images, will enable ADONIS to include more material on a disk with quicker access.

For applications of this sort, CD-ROM is becoming an increasingly attractive option in terms of cost. Currently, a CD-ROM costs some $1000 to master, whilst additional copies (for runs of fifty to one hundred) cost some $3 each. CD-ROMs can, moreover, be handled in a similar way to journals so far as obtaining subscriptions and dispatching copies are concerned. Recipients are clearly finding CD-ROMs acceptable, at least for reference and archival purposes. Librarians like them because, unlike much online retrieval of information, the cost involved is known beforehand. Readers like them not least because they can be accessed directly, whereas online retrieval has traditionally been done by specialist intermediaries. With the widespread availability of laptop micro-computers with CD-ROM drives it is possible to carry round collections of journals; the machine-readable form has become more portable than the hard-copy.

Exploration of the uses of CD-ROM is leading publishers to a range of new business contacts. For example, the Japan Electronic Publishing Association was established in order to bring publishers together with computer manufacturers, information-processing companies, software development companies and marketing companies. Nor is CD-ROM the end of this particular road. Multi-media, combining text, sound, still and moving pictures is attracting considerable attention (and could have potential for journals in such subjects as ornithology or surgery). The most rapidly growing field is interactive multi-media (such as CD-I) which has even more complex publishing requirements. At the moment, interactive publications are mainly reference or educational works, but possible journal applications can readily be envisaged.

Authors

The evident differences between printed and electronic journals raises a fundamental problem. Can electronic journals be made as attractive to authors as printed journals are? After all, besides wishing to reach the widest audience, which is not necessarily possible electronically, authors have to consider their own prestige in the academic world. Electronic distribution will lead to a more limited (though perhaps better-targeted) audience in the immediate future than can be reached via printed journals. At the same time, electronic journals still have to become fully accepted as publishing outlets: it will be some time before they carry as much weight in the academic community as traditionally produced journals. Experiments with synopsis journals in the 1970s nicely illustrate this point. Many authors saw publication in synopsis form as second-best to full publication. So, though the synoptic idea made sense to publishers, librarians and even readers, it failed to take off significantly. Nevertheless, at least one publisher has begun to experiment with an electronic variant, where the printed synopses are backed by electronic access to the full papers.

Newsletters, which are expected to be ephemeral, have had no major problems in attracting contributors; so any technical difficulties for authors of electronic periodical publications can clearly be overcome. But an electronic journal, if it is to attract authors, must be considered to carry good quality material and to be available to readers on a long timescale. In terms of quality, the best way to kick-start any journal is to ensure that it contains contributions from respected authors in the field. These are typically senior people, who may not be entirely happy with computers (though in science and technology they may well have research staff who are much more computer-oriented). Society publishers may find it easier than their commercial peers to persuade such authors to contribute to new electronic journals. But the main determinant for the immediate future will be subject matter. As is evident from the titles of electronic newsletters and journals already in existence, topics relating to computers and information can attract authors to electronic journals, since the workings of these latter represent, in a sense, an extension of their existing research activities.

Equally, research that is based on large amounts of data may find electronic journals a good outlet. For example, the electronic version of the *Journal of Fluids Engineering*, published by the American Society of Mechanical Engineers, not only offers the same papers as the printed journal, but also provides the extensive data on which they are based. In a research topic such as molecular biology, data are input to a number of databases by a wide range of researchers. This is usually referred to as electronic data publishing. The contents really form one vast multi-author paper, and raise the same kind of questions, e.g. regarding quality control. Such databases obviously require a commitment to long-term storage. More generally, if any electronic journal is to avoid the charge of being ephemeral, it must have a large storage capability available long-term to potential readers. It is worth remarking that parallel publication allows the printed version to be used for archival deposit. This traditional approach to availability may well prove attractive to authors whilst electronic journals are still in the process of establishing themselves. One factor in favour of electronic journals is that authors in scientific fields are beginning to compose papers jointly online, so that expertise in handling papers online is growing.

The *Online Journal of Current Clinical Trials*, launched in mid-1992 by the American Association for the Advancement of Science (AAAS) and the Online Computer Library Center (OCLC), illustrates the basic problems of establishing an electronic journal. Access to the journal has been carefully planned: text and simple graphics can be downloaded by readers, or they can be sent typeset-quality copies by mail or fax. The journal is peer-reviewed and carefully edited, yet each paper goes online within forty-eight hours of acceptance. Prior to launching this journal, OCLC developed its own Windows-based graphical interface (alongside a standard command-driven ASCII interface). This interface has since been extended to other journals. However, it has suffered the fate of many pioneering systems: the main thrust of development is now elsewhere. The subject field was chosen because clinical trials currently produce a great deal of information that needs to be published rapidly, and because medical authors and readers were believed to use networked micro-computers in their work. The journal suffered from some technical problems at the start, especially for readers outside North America. However, the major problem proved to be lack of content. Few authors were prepared to submit their papers. To encourage them, an agreement was reached with the *Lancet*, shortly after the launch of *Current Clinical Trials*, to print shortened versions of the electronic journal papers. Even so, the flow of material has remained slow and the ownership of the journal has changed. Here we have a case where the problem of attracting authors has been a major concern (though there have also been complaints from librarians about changes in charging).

Another approach currently being tried is to use a partially electronic format. The printed journal provides extended summaries, whilst the full papers are stored electronically in Postscript files. Subscribers can retrieve the full papers via anonymous FTP. In effect, this is the electronic version of a synopsis journal.

One point worth noting is the willingness of authors to submit material in electronic form for publication in conventional journals. At present, journals ask for such input on disk (though some are also experimenting with online input from author to publisher). Surveys suggest that some 75 per cent of North American authors are happy to submit papers on disk, as compared with some 60 per cent of European authors. Both percentages are growing, but the existence of a resistant minority (together with the problems of access to word-processing in many non-Western countries) needs to be kept in mind by publishers. Again, the nature of the research community is crucial. The electronic preprint system run by the high-energy physics community is a good illustration. Virtually all authors and readers in this field use networked computers constantly, wherever they are situated geographically. The community is small, well organised and needs rapid access to new information. Hence electronic communication of papers makes excellent sense.

It is worth noting in conclusion, that electronic communication is particularly susceptible to viruses (to hackers as well, but they are less likely to be hyperactive in the electronic journal field). Publishers of material in electronic form will need to have good virus detection procedures in place from the start, since authors can quite unwittingly submit contaminated data (see the discussion in the earlier chapter on production).

Readers

The need for some kind of terminal in order to access an electronic journal is, of course, one of its major disadvantages. Much journal reading is done at home, or whilst travelling. For both, but particularly the latter, printed journals may remain cheaper and easier to use than electronic media for some time; though the improving quality of computer print-outs may change the balance. In these early days of electronic journals, readers may need assistance in tracking down and using the new journals; they may also be unable to afford access out of their own, or out of departmental funds. The amount of material provided by an electronic journal may flood the computer storage space available to an individual reader. For all these reasons, access to electronic journals by libraries, as well as by individuals, is likely to be an important factor in the growth of their use and acceptance. There is a growing interest in the provision of integrated electronic services to both individuals and libraries by bodies other than publishers. For example, the CARL Uncover service (CARL = the Colorado Alliance of Research Libraries) is widely accessible and provides a database which is planned ultimately to cover the table of contents of some 25,000 journal titles.

Articles can be identified and ordered over the network from anywhere in the USA. Copies are faxed within twenty-four hours. (For material already in electronic form, the response time can be less than an hour.) The fee charged includes any payment for copyright clearance and can be paid either by credit card, or by institutional subscription.

In general terms, subscriptions to electronic journals can be decided on the basis of three parameters – the intended audience (individual reader or institution) and the number of concurrent users; the type of access (online or CD-ROM); the type of information (synopsis or full-text). There is as yet no consensus on how to price parallel print and electronic versions of a journal. In some cases, the electronic version is priced quite separately from the print version (though maybe at the same figure). In others, subscribers to the print version receive a discount (up to 100 per cent) on the electronic version. Another issue under debate is ownership after the subscription has lapsed: with hard-copy, subscribers keep the issues they have bought, while with electronic subscriptions some publishers argue that all access to the journal should cease if the subscription is cancelled (i.e. in effect the subscriber is 'renting' access to the journal). One attraction of CD-ROM is that usually the customer keeps the disks subscribed to.

One question, as yet unsolved, is whether subscribers to electronic journals will represent the same mix as for printed journals. Since delivery direct to the reader is so easy with electronic communication, it might be supposed that the delivery of electronic journals will bypass libraries – as most current electronic journals are doing. But only a few existing electronic journals charge, and most of these do so at a low rate to attract individual subscribers. It seems likely that, if higher charges are imposed, central purchasing by the library will be the commonest approach – as has already happened with CD-ROMs. Projects are therefore underway to see how delivery of electronic journals to libraries might work best. For example, the TULIP (The University Licensing Program) project, which ran to the end of 1995, delivered over forty titles in materials science published by the Elsevier/North-Holland/Pergamon group to fifteen US university libraries. Each university specified the hardware and software to be used, and Engineering Information customised the journals to the form required by each specification.

Bit-mapped images were provided along with an ASCII file obtained by uncorrected OCR scanning of the journals. (The latter was used for searching.) Three types of licence were available – for single-site universities, for multi-site universities, and for universities with external readers. A British experiment, which was also completed at the end of 1995, looked in greater detail at how an individual title, again in the materials science field, might be handled electronically. The project involved an extended pre-delivery phase studying how research libraries might best handle the receipt and distribution of the electronic version of the journal (Rowland et al., 1995). Both the US and the UK studies were particularly interested in evaluating reader behaviour and economic factors.

Publishers may be well acquainted with the design requirements for printed journals, but the design of electronic journals is still a relatively uncharted territory. Guidelines on some basic aspects – such as the amount of information that should be put on a single screen, or how best to use colour for emphasising text – can already be drawn up. But the basic question of what style of electronic presentation will best satisfy readers remains open. It may be that there is no single answer. Most readers of printed journals seem to expect that electronic journals will be presented in much the same way, with a cover, contents page, etc. However, readers with extensive computer experience expect electronic journals to be different, so as to make best use of the opportunities that electronic communication offers. Can such differing reader expectations all be satisfied?

Here again, investigations are under way. One example is the 'Red Sage' project, which brought together Springer-Verlag New York, AT & T Bell Labs and the University of California at San Francisco. Several other publishers contributed journals bringing the total up to seventy. Sophisticated software (RightPages) was developed to help users feel they are dealing with the equivalent of a printed journal. Readers are presented initially with a screenful of journal covers, laid out as on the new journals rack in a library. Once the reader has selected an issue, its contents page can be scanned and papers selected for browsing page by page. At the same time, the system provides facilities not available with the printed journals. For example, it can alert readers to the arrival of new journal issues which contain papers that might interest them. Early data suggest that readers are using the system to browse journals just as if they were visiting the library; relatively few articles have been printed off, so charging solely on the basis of articles printed off is unlikely to be sufficient to support a publication. Electronic subscriptions appear to be the answer. It has already become apparent from this trial that no university has the facilities to store digitally a wide range of journals for local access with this software. Even though the University of California at San Francisco has a powerful computing centre, at seventy titles its capacity is near the limit. This suggests that the electronic versions of most journals will be on the servers of publishers or specialist inter-mediaries. 'New players' are already showing interest in this role.

Economics

For a publisher, the bottom line clearly relates to the economic viability of electronic journals. Consequently, it is essential to be clear beforehand why the move to electronic publishing is being made. For example, is it a part of long-term strategy, or for more immediate gain? It seems unlikely that there will be great financial savings on the editing side, since most of the activities will still require human input. For example, copy-editing will still need human assessment, though this may be aided by automatic spelling checkers, etc. Again, though the selection of referees and communication with them may be made easier by electronic means, appreciable editorial input will still be required. In any case, electronic communication could just as well be used for supporting traditional forms of publication. Negatively, there will be, especially in the early stages, new queries arising from authors, editors and referees about the working of the system. Consequently, editing an electronic journal has clear advantages in terms of turn-round speed, but not in terms of effort (and so of cost). However, publishers of major paper-based journals are not necessarily expecting electronic publications to produce extra profits although electronic access and delivery might give some savings in cost as well as time (Russon & Campbell, 1996). The hope is rather that they will help sustain the profit margins of the print-based journals, which have, in many cases, been falling steadily.

MIT Press decided to launch a new electronic journal – the *Chicago Journal of Theoretical Computer Science* – in 1994. They estimated that, starting with 300 institutional and 150 individual subscribers in the first year, rising to 350 and 250, respectively, in the third year, they could break even in the latter year, given an institutional subscription of $125 and an individual subscription of $30 p.a. It was assumed that there would be no income from such traditional sources as offprints or advertising, though this would be somewhat offset by lower marketing costs. Apparently the result has been sufficiently successful to encourage MIT Press to plan further electronic journals.

Online publications available at present may actually charge considerably higher subscriptions than their printed equivalents (though they may also offer additional services). When the connect charges are added, customers are usually paying several times the price of the printed publication for electronic access. At the same time, the ability of the reader to pick and choose can greatly affect the economics of journal publishing. One example concerns advertisements. How can a publisher ensure that readers look at the advertisements in an electronic journal, if they are free to retrieve what they wish? The only suggestion has been to offer a journal at two prices: if the subscriber pays the lower price (subsidised by the advertisers) then they have to work through the advertising pages on the screen before accessing the articles. More fundamentally, can electronic journals continue to be sold as packages? Subscribers to printed journals pay for the articles that are not read, as well as those that are. If access to an electronic journal is charged for on an article-by-article basis, some articles may cover their costs, while others do not. The balance is likely to be less advantageous to the publisher than the present bundling of printed articles together. Since it is often difficult to tell beforehand which articles will be most read, the pricing mechanism for an electronic journal will normally need to be at a constant rate per article consulted: it will be difficult to recoup costs by charging more highly for accessing the more popular articles.

An analysis of the use of journals in a British university library, carried out in the 1980s, found that the average cost to the library of each article consulted was some £2 (when converted to 1996 rates). Libraries would therefore expect that electronic journals should provide access to articles at about the same cost. In fact, the charges for access to full-text via DIALOG are currently running at double, or more, this amount. For comparison, acquiring a photocopied article from British Library Document Supply Centre (BLDSC) costs some 50 per cent more than consultation of one's own library copy. Addition of any royalty charge would bring this figure even closer to the current cost of online access. The gap between internal consultation and external provision is not huge, but may well take some closing, especially in view of the potential loss of income from spin-offs, such as offprints. Accessing individual articles also implies payment on demand, rather than the up-front subscription which is such a welcome feature (to publishers) of printed journals. Finally, a library that has not handled electronic journals before will usually need to expend several thousand pounds, directly and in staff time, in preparing for their reception and handling.

Two obvious models of charging for electronic journals can be drawn from (1) the acquisition of information via online secondary services, (2) the purchase of printed journals. Online services originally charged mainly on a connect-time basis. As search speeds improved a per-document charge became common; now mixed time-and-hits charges are frequently applied. Compared with the printed journal, this has disadvantages, e.g. in organising payment beforehand. An annual subscription avoids this problem, but raises the question of who has access.

Some kind of site licence must be the answer, but this may be difficult to monitor (Pearce, 1995). It is worth noting that experience suggests that demand for machine-readable information expands rapidly as soon as readers can access it for themselves from their own desks. Major trials of the site licence concept are now under way and experience from these should be valuable. For example, in Britain the higher education funding councils have negotiated national site licences with three publishers. In this ambitious trial, the 165 Higher Education Institutes (HEIs) can subscribe to the journals from the three publishers (Academic Press, Blackwell and Institute of Physics Publishing) at a subsidised rate, have electronic access to all their titles, and make copies of articles for teaching and research. Another trial (known as Infobike) sponsored by the Higher Education Funding Council for England (HEFCE) gives the universities in Manchester, Keele and Stafford University electronic access to the journals of Academic Press and Blackwell Science through the Bath Information and Database Services (BIDS). Close monitoring should reveal valuable usage data: it is already expected from other BIDS usage data that undergraduates make greater use of the primary literature than previously assumed. Such usage data may be used to determine licensing charges. In both trials, sophisticated software developed by BIDS and ICL Fujitsu is being employed to manage the user's access to the database of articles held in Postscript files and compressed with Acrobat for rapid transmission.

If the charge for a site licence is based on likely usage rather than the range of publications made available, much fairer pricing can be established. For example, with conventional publishing a large university might be able to subscribe to four times as many titles as a small university and thus their students will have the advantage of a much better library. With licensing based on usage, a publisher might make available all its titles to both universities but charge the larger university four times as much as it has four times as many students. Students at either university will have equally good access to the research literature. Electronic publishing, therefore, has the potential to help less well funded organisations which was not what was originally predicted (see, for example, the introduction to Chernaik, Davis & Deegan, 1993).

Some of the difficulties can be alleviated by parallel publishing of the printed and electronic versions of a journal. The determining factor here is the effect that electronic access has on subscriptions to the printed version. Much of the expenditure on a printed journal is independent of the number of copies produced, though up to 20 per cent of the costs may relate to distribution. If electronic access reduces the circulation of the printed version without bringing in sufficient revenue from electronic document delivery and electronic subscriptions, the printed version may cease to be financially viable. Yet the income from the electronic version may not cover the additional costs of providing this new form of access. Judging from the experience of abstracts journals, no major financial problem arises so long as electronic access forms a small proportion of the total access. The dilemma that both versions may become unviable arises when electronic access becomes a significant fraction of total use. The natural reaction of publishers to this dilemma is, of course, to try and encourage institutions to subscribe to both versions by appropriate pricing of each.

Parallel publishing is a specific example of what some publishers are calling 'augmented print'. In this, the machine-readable journal is regarded as the basic entity; as described in chapter 3 (figure 3.3). From this basis, any other form – bound copy, individual paper, CD-ROM, online – can be generated according to the marketing mix considered economically desirable. To some extent, this already exists in the electronically typeset files of a journal. Thus the American Chemical Society has provided electronic full texts of its own journals (and some others) for several years past. However, these fall short of the ideal in a number of ways, e.g. inability to handle graphics.

In one sense, the question of individual versus institutional access to electronic journals is no different from the same question for printed journals – publishers will try to encourage both. The question of cost to the individual remains crucial in both cases. However, additional factors are at work in terms of individual access to electronic journals. The most obvious is whether potential readers have an appropriate terminal on their desks at work and/or at home. It is quite clear that usage of electronic journals will fall dramatically if terminals are not immediately to hand. Equally obviously, the terminals must be linked to an appropriate network. Even in developed countries, not all potential readers (and authors) fulfil this requirement, and the position is, of course, worse elsewhere. Hence, publishers of electronic journals will need to consider carefully what fraction of their potential readership can actually be reached. (It is likely to be appreciably greater in the immediate future if access is focused on the library, rather than on the individual.)

An alternative economic model for highly specialised journals has been proposed by Stevan Harnad. He accepts that with electronic publication there will still be the cost of organising the reviewing of material but believes that the other costs involved in creating a publication can be drastically reduced. He thus argues that savings of 70 to 90 per cent are possible. He adds that in the WWW environment researchers expect free access and authors should be prepared to fund this by paying page charges on the understanding that publishers use this revenue to cover their costs (including refereeing) and make the article available over the

Internet without further charge (Harnad & Hey 1995). One problem here is that such a mode of publication may not impart status to the author's work. Various studies (e.g. Coles 1993) have demonstrated clearly that the main factor taken into account by an author in deciding to submit an article to a particular title is that title's perceived status.

The need for electronic journals

Given all these problems, why should publishers consider introducing electronic journals? The positive reasons are that the cost of electronic communication is still diminishing, its capabilities are increasing rapidly and so is the number of users. In any case, the publishing of traditional journals now involves publishers in handling text in machine-readable form, so they are already at the half-way stage. It can therefore be expected that the key question, as for traditional publishing, will be the quality of the information. A negative reason is that it is becoming increasingly difficult to introduce profit-making new titles in traditional format. Electronic journals may open up new niche markets and new sources of funding for the purchase of information. It is worth noting that ISI, which provides much of the 'alerting' information on the primary literature, only obtained 11 per cent of its revenue from electronic products in 1988. By 1993, this had increased to 50 per cent.

Obviously, not all material is equally suitable for provision via electronic journals. Journals requiring online access to large amounts of graphic material immediately come to mind as problematic. However, the position is far from clear cut. Institutions are increasingly installing high bandwidth local area networks. They are also beginning to network the information on CD-ROMs. Hence, a graphics-oriented electronic journal on CD-ROM might be distributed locally in a way that cannot yet be achieved nationally online. Alternatively, the situation can arise where the national distribution has adequate bandwidth, but the reader's local system (especially if operating from home) does not. In general, it helps to concentrate on text-based journals for online distribution whilst remembering that the situation is changing rapidly.

Three types of publisher seem to be best suited to exploit electronic journals at their present stage of development.

1 Large commercial publishers, especially those who have an established interest in media other than print-on-paper.

2 Society publishers who can count provision of an electronic journal as a service to members, to be supported, at least initially, by membership subscriptions.

3 Niche publishers whose material is best handled in machine-readable form and whose subscribers are prepared to pay for the value-added element of an electronic journal. (This group may include individual researchers or academics who decide to provide a service to a small and scattered scholarly community.)

The material contained in an electronic journal must still be available to readers long after its first publication. Publishers – and this particularly applies to group (3) above – must therefore look at the question of long-term storage. If the journal is published on CD-ROM, it can readily be stored in this form (though there is still some uncertainty about the eventual lifetime of the data on such disks). An online journal requires more consideration. In the first place, the publisher may store the material centrally, increasingly on an optical disk. Alternatively, the online information can be down-loaded to CD-ROMs, and made available to subscribers in this form. If the material so provided includes the back-run of the journal, a publisher is likely to require return of any previous disk, to prevent its unauthorised use. COM (Computer Output on Micro-form) continues to be competitive for some purposes, especially where files need to be distributed to a number of sites and rapid access to the information is not an important factor. It has the additional advantage that the long-term stability of micro-form is well established. Discussions are currently going on in a number of countries concerning the provision of central depositories for long-term storage of electronic material.

Requirements

A vast amount has been written about electronic publishing in recent years (some relevant material is included in the bibliography, though much more could be added). Although journal publishers can gain much useful information from this literature, its emphasis is more on electronic book publishing along with desk-top publishing (DTP), than on journals. The following brief round-up suggests some of the main points that journal publishers need to keep in mind.

Introducing electronic publishing

This depends on the level of in-house expertise. If it is only moderate, a typical initial approach is to scan magazines and trade literature and to talk to other publishers. The idea at this stage is to isolate possible systems of interest within the budget available. It is vital that publishers set their own benchmarks before making any decisions. The next step is either to contact sales representatives and arrange demonstrations, or to call in a consultant for advice. In either case, the publisher will need to know about maintenance and training, as well as the suitability of the system for the planned operations. Whichever system is proposed, it must be tried out before installation to judge how user-friendly staff find it to be in operation. Publishers must also remember how rapidly the situation is changing, and so must plan ahead. For example, more than one operating system is available. The research world has increasingly moved to UNIX-based systems. If the potential authors use such systems it may make sense for a publisher to follow their lead.

In-house usage

Most publishers are purchasing information technology for more than one reason. It now pervades all aspects of publishing – administration; accounts; editing; production; distribution; marketing and publicity. Much of the equipment involved will be connected via a local area network, which raises two questions. The first concerns compatibility. Computer hardware and software date rapidly: a write-off time of three to four years is common. Hence, new equipment is continually being purchased to take over, or run alongside, existing activities. It is important that such equipment can support the inter-working required: which may put limitations on what can be installed. The second point concerns security. With electronic systems, it is much more necessary to consider who has access to which information, who is allowed to alter a computer file, and so on. Since electronic publishing handles large quantities of electronic data from external sources, it is also essential to guard against accidental (or even deliberate) contamination of the data files.

Input

An important question in operating a system is how will authors be inputting their material? Traditional printed journals are already gearing up to accept machine-readable input, so this is no innovation. Most, however, are expecting disk input: online input has been relatively less explored. Graphics obviously need special attention. An uncompressed full-page image may require several megabytes of storage. Hence, it may be easier for a publisher to obtain the original image and scan it in-house, if it is required in machine-readable form. The type (and cost) of the appropriate scanner depends on the complexity of the graphics involved, but the storage requirements can quite quickly exceed the capacity of micro-computer systems.

Editing and production

Originally, word-processing and desktop publishing followed different routes, with the former emphasising editing and the latter layout. The two activities are becoming increasingly blurred. The two most popular DTP packages currently – Quark Xpress and Adobe Pagemaker – are appreciably more flexible than earlier packages. Similarly, good DTP work can be done on a standard office PC: it is no longer necessary to have a dedicated Apple Mac. The system chosen will naturally depend on the journal. A small publisher handling a limited circulation journal may decide to carry out almost all the production side in-house. A large publisher with higher circulation journals may decide to use a DTP system as a flexible front-end before sending the material to an external service (e.g. for CD-ROM production).

Another factor relates to the type of material handled by the journal. For example, extensive use of mathematics requires special software. A package such as TeX can handle a wide range of mathematics, but needs a fair amount of practice to use properly. Since an appreciable number of mathematicians use TeX in preparing their publications, a publisher of mathematics journals may consider the effort involved in getting to know the package well worthwhile. A major plus for electronic handling is the ease with which changes can be introduced. For example, any good software package will automatically renumber tables or figures, if a new one is inserted in the text.

One area of activity that is required whatever the form of output used is tagging the text to record its structure. Such generic coding is now in widespread use, the prime candidate for coding journal articles being SGML (Standard Generalised Mark-up Language). This is supported by national publishers' associations (who can point enquirers to detailed information), though it still requires further development. There is now a standard (ANSI/NISO 239.59–1988) for electronic manuscript preparation and mark-up. At present, inserting the code is typically an in-house activity, though future developments may make it possible to devolve it to authors. Use of such coding is essential if the idea of augmented print, described above, is to get anywhere.

Output

For printed output whether in-house or at a printers, the journal publisher should know something of page description languages such as Postscript. These ensure that the output always appears correctly, but have the disadvantage that royalties are charged, which can put up costs appreciably. If the material is to be output onto a screen, however, the whole question of layout needs to be reconsidered. The points at issue can be appreciated by scanning the large range of electronic bulletin boards, newsletters and journals now available. Online access (as distinct from CD-ROM) requires, at present, negotiation with a database host. In this case, the handling and presentation of the material will depend in part on the requirements of the host.

Distribution

The distribution of a journal on CD-ROM is relatively straightforward. Along with the disk there should be instructions on how to use it. If there are several journals carried on the disk with each title encrypted (such as EcoFile where club members receive disks carrying twenty-five ecology journals), then, in exchange for the appropriate subscription, the disk should also be supplied with a password and any other instructions on how to access the encrypted files.

The main concern over making a journal available on the Internet has been security. It is now relatively easy to set up the electronic version of a journal on a server for access, although at this stage access does not mean browsing the actual text held on the server. It means identifying an article from the article header database, then having it transmitted (probably in Acrobat) to one's own terminal. Developments in software, however, have produced several systems recently that control access to a password holder and pick up mis-use of the password, e.g. concurrent usage of a password issued to an individual subscriber or usage of the password from the wrong terminal. Such systems can be used to handle an electronic subscription or sell individual articles based on a credit card transaction.

The issues of copyright protection and security are addressed in an excellent report by Dietrich Goetze entitled 'Commercial Electronic STM Publishing' (Goetze, 1995), distributed by the stm Association. He points out that although the WWW was designed to be cheap and always available, it does give the publisher some safeguards. For example, it is often easier for the user to leave the file on the remote host; when the information is needed again, the host is accessed again. This design provides copyright protection and creates the opportunity to build an additional layer of safeguards. Saving the file can be made dependent on a parameter which travels with the file. A document can be segmented in many separate files making it a tedious and time-consuming task to piece together as a single file for sending on to others. Files can be encrypted as part of an overall metering system. Finally, WWW gives the option of permitting the user to download the information or not; permission to download can be subject to charge.

Several organisations, such as OCLC, are offering to run electronic subscriptions on behalf of publishers. The advantage of OCLC is that they already have terminals established in around 15,000 libraries. One problem for the publisher, however, is that, having worked the subscription agents' discount down to under 10 per cent, they could now be faced with much higher 'charges' from these new players. A schedule might include charges for preparing the database (especially if the publisher cannot supply in SGML), storing the files and handling the subscription; at least one scheme also includes a service charge to the subscriber. Sales of individual articles from the database might pick up a further charge. The new player, or a subscription agent making a logical developmental step, may also propose marketing a cross-indexed package of journals offering a bulk discount to subscribers; this discount will come out of the original publisher's revenue. This package might be delivered on CD-ROM, enabling the subscriber to set up the database on a LAN for local use including genuine browsing. It will be difficult for a publisher not to participate in such schemes with their obvious appeal to the market yet not only would they be losing margin, but they would also risk losing their identity and direct contact with the customer (normally a feature of electronic publishing).

The publisher's response is likely to be to set up their own electronic subscription systems and perhaps pay a commission to intermediaries who route orders for journals or individual articles. They should also be prepared to negotiate lower charges perhaps linked to sales incentive schedules; without their journals, the new players will have no business. This could well be a competitive field, which should bring down charges.

The future

In view of the current rate of change it would be foolhardy to try and predict how electronic publishing will develop over the next few years. However, several projects are planned, or underway, that should help publishers who are contemplating the introduction of electronic journals. For example, the EUROPUBLISHING project, funded by the EC, is supporting two pilot schemes which should allow publishers to evaluate advanced authoring, production and distribution methods in a European environment. But a major point still remains to be decided: should electronic journals organise themselves along the same lines as printed journals, or not?

This one query actually subdivides into a number of separate questions.

For example, should the processes of editing and refereeing follow traditional lines? There is no reason why the refereeing of an article in an electronic journal should be restricted to a couple of referees only. It is just as easy with an electronic system to open the activity to the entire readership of the journal. Again, will the presentation of information to readers be changed? Much work is currently being done on hypertext, which allows text to be read in a non-linear way. It can therefore be used to bring in background information as, and when, on-screen reading requires it (e.g. if another article is referred to in the text, it can be called up and scanned immediately). In a similar way, the growth of multi-media communication offers the opportunity to include audio and video material in articles.

Despite this potential for divergence from the traditional journal, it seems likely that electronic journals will tend, at least initially, to mimic the established pattern. This seems the safest way of establishing the acceptability of electronic journals as a respectable outlet for articles. It may also encourage the evolution of existing printed journals into electronic form. Printed journals have the great advantage of an existing list of subscribers and the status which attracts articles. However, this can also tend to make them more conservative. Thus we should expect such transmutation to occur via a period of parallel publishing. In the longer term, it will be surprising if the inherent flexibility of electronic publishing is not fully exploited. Before that can occur, however, the current problems of electronic journal publishing will have to be resolved. They can be summarised as: (1) personal problems (e.g. what will encourage individual readers and authors to use electronic journals?) (2) technical problems (e.g. how should graphics be handled?) (3) organisational problems (e.g. do subscription agents have a role to play in handling electronic journals?) (4) infrastructural problems (e.g. how many of the potential subscribers can actually access an electronic journal easily?).

Appendix 1

Getting tenders for journals

An editor, a society or some other body seeking a publisher for a journal may be well advised to ask a number of publishers to tender. The sponsor must define the publishing services that the journal needs; for an established journal that should be part of an overall revaluation of the journal and its place in the market. Before any publishers are approached, consideration should be given to any changes that might be desirable. Several publishers can be approached at the same time, and their responses may incorporate suggestions for other improvements in the journal or the way in which it is marketed. Knowledge that other publishers are being approached makes it likely that the bids will be competitive, though some publishers claim they are reluctant to tender in case their ideas are fed back to their rivals.

The sponsor should allow plenty of time for the tendering process and then for the eventual publication of the first issue under the new arrangements. Eighteen months to two years before the first issue is scheduled may not be too long. If the journal is a new one, then the longer period will be helpful since it takes time to gather papers for the first few issues. Often the sponsor is an academic body without full-time staff. It can be difficult to get people together for visits to publishers. If decisions are normally dependent upon council meetings held at fairly long intervals it may be desirable to set up a smaller group (a publications committee perhaps) which can act on its own initiative.

Once the decision to go with a particular publisher has been made, many details remain to be worked out. Subscription agents want information about journals, including price information, by June or July of the year before publication and many advertisers (including pharmaceutical firms) plan and budget for a year during the previous summer. Designing a new journal can take time, and established journals may need to change their style, format, design or paper. Most publishers like to allow slightly longer to produce the first issue in case anything goes wrong and so as to have promotional copies in advance of publication. Design and format have to be established before typesetting can begin. Publicity people need briefing and time to work out plans. If the journal already exists, arrangements must be made for the transfer of subscription lists and any outstanding payments for subscriptions.

The stages in tendering are:

1 Draw up a document setting out the basis for tenders.
2 Draw up a list of appropriate publishers.
3 Send the tender document out to the selected publishers.
4 Compare their tenders, asking questions on points that are not clear or which seem at variance from other tenders.
5 Select the two or three tenders that seem most attractive.
6 Arrange to visit the publishers concerned to meet the people who would work on this journal to discuss the proposals.
7 Decide which publisher is the one most suited to the journal.
8 Settle the terms on which they will publish the journal.
9 Have a meeting with the publishers to run through the things that need doing before the first issue comes out under the new arrangements.

The first stage in the tendering process is to draw up a clear specification for the journal. Publishers will be more interested in journals that sound attractive and that appear to be run by sensible and business-like people than in woolly or half-baked proposals. The more specific the information provided the easier it will be for the publisher to judge the potential for the journal and to put forward constructive proposals.

The specification should include a statement of ownership and the present publishing arrangements (if any). If there is an existing publishing agreement how long is it before it can be terminated and what notice must be given? Who owns the subscription lists? If the journal already exists, why is the sponsor seeking another publisher? Is the service unsatisfactory, or is it just a matter of looking around? If the existing publisher puts forward the best financial terms, is the sponsor bound to stay with them?

What sort of publishing arrangement is being sought (see section on publishing arrangements in chapter 8, financial aspects)? To what extent does the sponsor want to be involved in carrying the financial risk? In principle, the party that carries the risk should have the final say on the price, though that may be after due consultation. If the sponsor owns the journal do they want to pay for promotion separately or for it to be included in the publisher's charges?

What are the aims and scope of the journal and how does it differ from existing journals in the field? Why should an author submit a paper to it, or a library take out a subscription? Are there any special features that make the journal particularly attractive and interesting? If the journal already exists is there a good flow of papers? What is the rejection rate? A breakdown of contributors by country and by speciality is helpful. What about citation rates and impact factors (see chapter 4)? What abstracting and indexing services cover the journal?

What is its market? Who should be expected to read the journal? What libraries do they use? In which parts of the world are they to be found? If the journal already exists then as much history as possible should be given of prices and subscription figures, differentiating between those paying the regular price and those getting the journal free or at any special rates. Renewal rates are useful (i.e. what percentage of current subscribers renew each year) as is a geographical breakdown of the subscription list. What efforts have been made recently to increase the sales of the journal?

What factors affect the design and format? If the journal already exists are the sponsors happy about the production standards? There is a trend towards larger pages, often with double-column setting. What about illustrative material (graphs, figures and photographs) or formulae? How many pages a year should the journal publish? How is that expected to change with time? What is the relative importance of speed, quality and price in the production of the journal? High quality and speedy production may not be cheap.

What are the editorial arrangements? How long has the present editor been in post and for how long are editors appointed? What about assistant or associate editors or editors for special features? Is there a planned editorial succession? Who is on the editorial board, where are they based and how active are they? What is the editor expected to do? Who looks after refereeing procedures? Who handles the correspondence with authors? Who does the copy-editing? Where and when are the indexes, title pages and contents lists produced? Who is responsible for paying the editorial costs?

Who sees that the copy is sent to the typesetter at the right time? Who looks after the flow of proofs between typesetter, editor, copy-editor and authors and makes sure that corrected proofs are returned at the proper time? Are things running smoothly at the moment? What about instructions for offprints for authors?

How is the journal despatched to subscribers? Who holds the lists? Are there special arrangements for copies for members of a sponsoring society, or are copies sent to them in the same way as other subscribers? (Some societies distribute newsletters or abstracts of meetings with members copies of journals.) What packaging material is preferred? Is it important to get the journal out by a particular date?

Who owns the copyright? Do authors assign their copyright to the journal? Is it registered with any copyright licensing scheme? Are there any licensing arrangements for editions in other formats, for instance micro-form, online or CD-ROM versions?

What about previously published volumes if any? Who owns the stock, and where is it held? What have sales been like in recent years?

What else should the publisher be told? Can the journal reasonably expect income from the sale of advertising or the rental of subscription lists? Are there other sources of income that affect either the income from the journal or the work that the publisher has to do?

The tender should ask for a statement of the publisher's interest in, and suitability for, the journal; the sort of terms on which they would publish; financial forecasts for the journal for say five years; and an outline of the proposed agreement. The basis of the financial statement should be clear; comparing production costs for different years and different formats is almost impossible. The tender might be on the current basis but offer the publisher an opportunity to suggest changes.

The tender document or covering letter should make it clear that the inquiry is confidential, and that all tenders received will also be treated as confidential. In principle, a sponsor could ask the publisher to sign a form agreeing to keep the information received as confidential and barring them from publishing a competing journal for, say, three years; in practice that is unlikely to be workable. There should be a closing date – preferably at least five or six weeks after the receipt of the letter. The publisher may need further information so the name, address, telephone and fax numbers and e-mail address of someone who can deal with queries should be given.

If the journal already exists, then at least one specimen copy should be provided for each publisher (with a note to explain how it differs from a typical issue); if more can be spared, two or three copies would be appreciated.

The tendering publisher may ask to see the subscription list on the grounds that they have found in the past that the number of subscribers has been overstated. This should be resisted, for the publisher could use it for unauthorised purposes. If necessary an independent person can be asked to produce whatever information is required from a list certified by the present publisher as an accurate record of the current subscribers at an agreed time.

Appropriate publishers

The sponsor might approach between five and eight publishers. More tenders than that can become confusing (and suggests that the sponsor has not been critical enough in thinking about possible publishers); it is not fair to ask publishers to tender if they are unlikely to be thought suitable. If there genuinely are more publishers who should be approached, it may be worth enquiring first whether they are seriously interested in tendering.

If the journal exists, the current publisher will probably learn pretty quickly if the sponsor is seeking tenders. Sponsors should let the present publisher know what is happening and explain why. If the reasons are strictly financial, then the present publisher might be allowed to tender after all the others with an indication of what the tender would have to offer in order to be successful.

Friends and colleagues involved with other journals and serials librarians may have useful advice to give on the choice of publisher. Communication is easier if the publisher is not too far away and can operate in the language of the journal. Mail can be slow, and fax is not acceptable for proofs. Different time zones can make telephoning more difficult. If the journal goes to a large number of members all in one country, the costs of distribution will generally be lower if the journal is printed in the same country.

A publisher who already has several journals in a given subject area is likely to be better able to handle the journals on that subject than one who has none. In principle, there should be better access to mailing lists and to potential advertisers, more chance of attendance at appropriate conferences, and more understanding of the subject. Direct competitors should of course be avoided.

Much is said about the relative merits of commercial and non-commercial (or profit and not-for-profit) publishers, most of it by people from outside publishing. In practice, many not-for-profit publishers are expected to produce a large surplus and to behave in the market place as commercial publishers do. (Much of the perceived difference in prices per page of journals comes from the higher circulation – and sometimes page charges and tax breaks – that the not-for-profit sector may enjoy.) A commercial publisher may have more autonomy or flexibility than a non-commercial one, but on the other hand it is more likely to be involved in a merger or takeover. Because of their reliance on sales to members, some society publishers may be less active in selling to overseas markets than their commercial rivals; others are able to make use of the membership lists to promote other publications. It is more important that the publisher should feel right for the journal than that it should have a particular status.

Evaluating tenders

One advantage of preparing detailed specifications for tenders is that the replies from publishers should cover the same points (though they do not always do so in practice). It makes it easier to set out the responses in a table and to spot where one publisher's figures are out of line with those of their competitors; it is not unknown for estimates of production costs to leave out major items (offprints or colour advertising for instance), or to be based on the wrong number of pages or issues. Sometimes it is necessary to get clarification of statements or figures that are ambiguous or are out-of-line.

The responses will also indicate how keen different publishers are to get the contract for the journal. Publishers who try to talk the sponsor out of the publishing arrangements that they have asked for, who clearly have not read the documents properly, who produce replies that are internally inconsistent, or who do not make a good job of selling themselves may also not be very good at selling the journal. On the other hand, editors may be wary of publishers who are too thrusting or who offer too many bright but impracticable ideas.

For most sponsors, the financial terms are a key consideration, but they should not be the only one. In any case, the financial return on a journal will generally depend upon the sales, and most would prefer a publisher who gives realistic figures and who, with luck, does slightly better, than one who promises the earth but delivers much less. Good service and a responsive attitude on the part of the publisher can save the sponsor much hassle; that is particularly helpful where the journal is run by volunteers.

No reliance should be placed on vague promises of improved financial performance and even guarantees should be treated with caution. Publisher's editors are under pressure to get journals; some may make offers which look very attractive but which are unsustainable. If they are successful in getting the journal, that will help their cvs. When the problems emerge the editor will be working for another publishing house; it will be left to their successors to sort out the problems. The authors know of one journal where the new publisher provided a very optimistic guarantee which the sponsoring society was very happy to accept. To meet the target income, the price was increased sharply and production standards were lowered. These measures contributed to an above average decline in the number of subscribers. Not surprisingly the publisher wanted to negotiate an agreement less favourable to the sponsor at the end of the first term.

The sponsor should be satisfied that the promised results stand a reasonable chance of being achieved, and that requires proper costings. Sponsors should have a say in the pricing policy (if they are the owners of the journal they should have the final word); however a publisher cannot be expected to issue a guarantee of income if they have no say in the price on which the guarantee depends.

Ideally the sponsor should visit several publishers. Firstly, one learns much more about an organisation by visiting it than by seeing one or two representatives in one's own office. All publishers have some staff turnover, but in some it is very high. The sponsor will want to know how long people looking after journals have been working for the firm and how long they have been in their present jobs. If the firm plans to relocate in the future there is likely to be disruption to the work and the present staff may not move with them. Similarly a merger or take-over is likely to produce upheavals; some staff may find the new management not to their taste and others may be made redundant. There is no way of ensuring against this, but a sponsor who knows a good deal about the firm they are dealing with is less likely to meet with unpleasant surprises.

After acceptance

Once the sponsor has decided to accept the tender from a publisher, detailed negotiations are needed about all aspects of the journal, including: the flow of copy, editorial style, format and design, prices, promotion, handling of members' copies, methods of despatch, arrangements for offprints, sale of advertising space, copyright assignment and copyright licensing. If the journal already exists then arrangements have to be made for the transfer of subscription records, payments from subscribers and back volumes.

Conclusion

Getting the right publisher for their journal is a worrying time for any sponsor. Any new agreement will be for a minimum of three years, but ideally will last for much longer than that. There are costs associated with any change of publisher. So it is important to get it right. Clearly there are many pitfalls for the unwary. Some sponsors find it useful to have a consultant with an understanding of journal publishing to guide them through the process, while others may feel they have sufficient expertise themselves.

Publishers' and editors' associations

African Association of Science Editors (AASE)
  President Professor Negussie Tebedge
  Faculty of Technology
  Addis Ababa University
  P.O. Box 385
  Addis Ababa
  ETHIOPIA
  Tel +251 1 122573
  Fax +251 1 552688/550911

Associação Brasileira de Editores Cientificos (ABEC)
  Secretary Rosaly Favero Krzyzanowski
  ABEC Secretariat
  Rua Lauro Muller
  455 - Botafogo
  22290-160 Rio de Janeiro
  BRAZIL
  Tel +55 21 5412132 R: 116
  Fax +55 21 2958499

Association of Learned and Professional Society Publishers (ALPSP)
  Secretary Professor B. Donovan
  48 Kelsey Lane
  BECKENHAM
  Kent BR3 3NE
  UNITED KINGDOM
  Tel +44 181 658 0459
  Fax +44 181 663 3583

Association of Earth Science Editors (AESE)
 Secretary Karhyn Lessing
 781 Northwest Drive
 Morgantown
 West Virginia 26505
 U.S.A.
 Tel +1 304 291 4679
 Fax +1 304 291 4403

Center for Academic Publications Japan
 Contact Masataka Watanabe
 4-16 Yayoi
 2-chome
 Bunkyo-ku
 Tokyo 113
 JAPAN
 Tel +81 3 3817 5821
 Fax +81 3 3817 5830

China Editology Society of Science Periodicals (CESSP)
 President Dr Yon-qin Weng
 Room 716
 86 Xueyuannanlu
 Beijing 100 081
 CHINA
 Fax +86 01 202 9375

Commission of Editors of Journals Concerned with Clinical Chemistry
 Contact Mr P. M. G. Broughton
 Wolfson Research Laboratories
 Department of Clinical Chemistry
 University of Birmingham
 BIRMINGHAM B15 2TH
 UNITED KINGDOM

Committee of Editors of Biochemical Journals (CEBJ)

Chairman Professor K. Siddle
Department of Clinical Biochemistry
Addenbrookes Hospital
Hills Road
CAMBRIDGE CB2 2QR
UNITED KINGDOM

Conference of Editors of Learned Journals (CELJ)

Contact Professor R. A. Shoas
English Department
University of Florida
Gainesville
Florida 32611-2036
U.S.A.

Council of Biology Editors (CBE)

Executive Director Ms Cindy Clark
One Illinois Center
Suite 200
111 East Wacker Drive
Chicago
Il 60601-4298
U.S.A.

Editing and Publication Association of Bangladesh (EPAB)

Contact Hasan Ahmed Shareef
Associate Editor
International Centre for Diarrhoeal Disease Research
G.P.O. Box 128
Dhaka 1000
BANGLADESH
Tel +880 2 600 171-8
Fax +880 2 883 116

European Association of Science Editors (EASE)

Secretary-Treasurer Ms Maeve O'Connor
49 Rossendale Way
LONDON NW1 0XB
UNITED KINGDOM
Tel +44 171 388 9668
Fax +44 171 383 3092

Finnish Association of Science Editors and Journalists (FASEJ)

Contact Mrs Kerttu Tirronen
Technical Research Centre of Finland Information Service
Head of Publishing Division
P.O.B. 42
02151 Espoo
FINLAND
Tel +358 0 4561
Fax +358 0 456 4374

Indian Association of Medical Editors

Contact Dr Samiran Nundy
Editor
The National Medical Journal of India
All India Institute of Medical Sciences
Ansari Nagar
New Delhi 110 029
INDIA
Tel +91 11 661123 (ext. 335)/667540/6863002
Fax +91 11 6862663/6868516

International Association of Anthropology Editors (IAAE)

Contact Dr James Spuhler
University of Michigan
Department of Anthropology
Ann Arbor
MI 48109
U.S.A.

International Association of Scholarly Publishers (IASP)

> *Contact* Prospero M. Hernandez
> Rutgers University Press
> 109 Church Street
> New Brunswick
> NJ 08901
> U.S.A.
> *Fax* + 1 932 7039

International Council for Scientific and Technical Information (ICSTI)

> *General Secretary* Daniel Confland
> 51 Boulevard de Montmorency
> 75016 Paris
> FRANCE
> *Tel* +44 33 1 4525 6592
> *Fax* +44 33 1 4215 1262
> *e-mail* icsu@paris7.jussieu.fr

International Association of Scientific, Technical and Medical Publishers (stm)

> *Secretary* Mr Lex Lefebvre
> Muurhuizen 165
> NL-3811 EG Amersfoort
> THE NETHERLANDS
> *Tel* +44 31 33 656060
> *Fax* +44 31 33 656538

International Federation of Science Editors (IFSE)

> *Contact* Miriam Balaban
> School for Scientific Communication
> Mario Negri Sud
> 1-66030 S M Imbaro
> ITALY
> *Tel* +39 872 570316
> *Fax* +39 872 570317

Middle East Association of Science Editors (MEASE)

    Secretary Professor Dr Mohammed Refaat Shalash

    Journal of Veterinary Science

    National Research Center

    Al-Tahrir Street

    Dokki

    Cairo

    EGYPT

    Tel +20 2 701211/3921762/701849

    Fax +20 2 700931

Netherlands Association of Science Editors (WERK)

    Contact Ing. Bran ten Cate

    DLO-Staring Centrum

    Instituut voor Onderzoek van het Landelijk Gebied

    Postbus 125

    6700 AC Wageningen

    THE NETHERLANDS

    Tel +31 8370 74482

New Zealand Association of Science Communicators

    Contact Dr Jaap A. Jasperse

    Executive Secretary

    DSIR Publishing

    Cubewell House

    16 Kent Terrace

    P.O. Box 9741

    Wellington

    NEW ZEALAND

    Tel +64 4 858939

    Fax +64 4 850631

Nordic Publishing Board in Science

    Secretary Mr Ingvar Isfeldt

    Swedish Research Council for Science

    Stockholm

    SWEDEN

North American Serials Interest Group (NASIG)

    Contact Susan Davis

    7721 Levington Road

    Batavia

    NY 14020-9345

    U.S.A.

PEPET (Malaysian Editors)

    Mr Bin Haron Hasrom

    Chairman

    Penerbit University Kebangsaan

    43600 UKM Bangi

    Selangor DE

    MALAYSIA

    Tel +603 825 0001

    Fax +603 825 6484

Society for Biomedical Communicators (SBC)

    Contact Dr K. Satyanarayana

    Deputy Editor, Publications and Information Directorate

    CSIR

    Dr. KS Krishnan Marg.

    New Delhi 110012

    INDIA

    Tel +91 11 584846 / 5725990

    Fax +91 11 5731353

Society for Scholarly Publishing (SSP)

    10200 West 44th Avenue

    Suite 304

    Wheat Ridge

    Colorado 80033

    U.S.A.

    Tel +1 303 422 3914

    Fax +1 303 422 8894

Ukranian Association of Science Editors

Secretary-Treasurer Tatyana Pasechnik

Institute of the Problems of Mathematics, Machines and Systems

42 Glushkova Ave

Kiev

UKRAINE

Tel +007 044 2667005

Fax +007 044 2136184/2287272

UK Serials Group (UKSG)

Secretary Jill Tolson

114 Woodstock Road

Witney

OXFORD OX8 6DY

UNITED KINGDOM

Tel +44 1993 703466

Glossary

AAP	Association of American Publishers Inc.
AAUP	American Association of University Presses
Acrobat	Previously 'Carousel': Adobe Postscript PDF and display software
ADONIS	A document supply service on CD-ROM covering 650 biomedical journals from 70 publishers; subscribers receive disks weekly and print out articles for a usage charge fixed by each publisher
ALA	American Library Association
ALPSP(UK)	Association of Learned and Professional Society Publishers
ANSI	American National Standards Institute
ARL	Association of Research Libraries
Article Clearing House	UMI's article delivery service, all subjects
art paper	Paper coated with china clay and polished to be shiny or matt, suitable for half-tones
ASA	Association of Subscription Agents
ASCII	American standard code for information interchange. Each symbol in ASCII code consists of seven data bits and one parity bit for error checking
ATM	Asynchronous Transfer Mode: enables digital data to be transmitted more quickly
B. H. Blackwell (BHB)	Largest UK-based serials agent
BIBLID	Bibliographic identification of contribution in serials and books – ISO 9115
BIDS	Bath Information and Data Services
bit map	An array of pixels which together make up an image for screen display or printing out
BLDSC	British Library Document Supply Centre

bleed	to bleed is to extend an illustration beyond the trimmed edge of the page
blueprints	Contact dyeline proofs made on paper from film
BPIF	British Printing Industries Federation
BRAD	British Rate and Data – publication listing UK publications and their circulation and advertising specifications
Browser	Generic name for search/view software needed to work on WWW, e.g. 'Mosaic'
BSI	British Standards Institute
CARL	Colorado Alliance of Research Libraries
CAS	Current Alerting System
cartridge	Printing or drawing paper with good dimensional stability, bulk and opacity
CBE	Council of Biology Editors
CCC	Copyright Clearance Center (USA)
CD-I	Compact Disk – Interactive
CD-ROM	Compact Disk – Read Only Memory
CIS	Campus Information Service
CISTI	Canadian Institute for Scientific and Technical Information
citation studies	Pioneered by Eugene Garfield, founder of ISI: tracking, mapping, plotting, cross referencing which articles cite each other, in order to develop theory of 'impact factor' of a particular article and/or journal
CITED	Copyright In Transmitted Electronic Documents
CLA	Copyright Licensing Agency (UK)
CLARCS	The Copyright Licensing Agency's Rapid Clearance Service
CODEN	Unique and unambiguous permanent identifier for a specific serial title
CODATA	Committee for Data for Science and Technology (ICSU, qv)
colour separation	The separation of artwork into four process colours by means of filters or by electronic scanners. The resulting continuous-tone films are screened to make printing plates
CONTU	National Commission of New Technological Uses of Copyright Work (USA)
CRC	Camera-Ready Copy, originated material ready for photographing, usually for reproduction by litho printing

CRT	Camera-Ready Typescript
CWIS	Campus Wide Information System
DAT	Digital audiotape
Dawson's	Major serials agent based in UK and owner of Faxon
DIN	Deutsche Industrie Normalien (German Standards Bureau)
DOCUTECH	Xerox's all digital, scanning, printing, binding system with 600 dpi capability available in a 'network publisher' version
dpi	dots per inch
DTD	Document Type Definition – an SGML model of the structure or content of a document (or group of similar documents). This model identifies the tags that will be used in document, and the permissible relationships between the information elements identified by the tags
DTP	Desktop Publishing – the production of fully made-up pages on a microcomputer
EANA	European Article Numbering Association
EARN	European Academic Research Network
EASE	European Association of Science Editors
EBSCO	Serials agent in USA, probably the largest
EDI	Electronic Data Interchange
EPS	Encapsulated PostScript – a format used for storing graphics suitable for printing purposes
EUSIDIC	European Association of Information Services
even working	A total number of pages in a publication which can be produced entirely by printing sections of the same number of pages (e.g. sections of 16 or 32 making up an issue of 64 pages)
fair use	Copyright doctrine that individuals have the right to make a copy of an article for personal use without permission from copyright holder
Faxon	Major North American serials agent now owned by Dawson's
FID	Fédération Internationale de Documentation
FTP	File Transfer Protocol – enables a client-server system to transfer files
GII	Global Information Infrastructure

Genuine Article (The)	ISI's article delivery service linked to articles cited in ISI indexes
GUI	Graphical User Interface
Guidon	Graphical user interface developed by OCLC
half-tone	Illustration created by dots of varying size giving the impression of continuous tone
HCI	Human–Computer Interaction
Home Page	First document seen by user when connecting to a specific URL on the WWW
HTML	Hypertext Mark-Up Language – used to prepare a document for access over the WWW
HTTP	Hypertext Transfer Protocol
Hypertext Link	An embedded macro that identifies a document location that the user will jump to when the link is clicked with a mouse
IAS	Individual Article Supply
IEPRC	International Electronic Publishing Research Centre
IASP	International Association of Scholarly Publishers
ICEDIS	International Committee for Electronic Data Interchange in Serials
ICSTI	International Council for Scientific and Technical Information
ICSU	International Council of Scientific Unions
IFFRO	International Federation of Reproduction Rights Organisations
ILL	Inter-Library Loan
image document	Bit-mapped images of documents (as used in ADONIS) created by scanning; requires more space than ASCII; not searchable unless text manipulated further; advantages are graphics and layout
Impact Factor	A value given to a journal based on the number of citations to that journal divided by the number of articles published in the previous two years (see Citation Studies)
imposition	Arrangement of pages in a sequence which will read consecutively when the printed sheet is folded for binding
INIST	Institut de L'Information Scientifique et Technique (France)

IPA	International Publishers Association
ISBN	International Standard Book Number
ISDN	Integrated Services Digital Network
ISDS	International Serials Data System: the worldwide network that allots ISSNs
ISI	Institute of Scientific Information – publishers of *Current Contents* and *Journal Citation Reports*
ISO	International Standards Organisation
ISO 8879	ISO SGML standard (Official ISO name = 8879-1986[E], Information processing – Text and office systems – Standard Generalised Mark-Up Language [SGML])
ISSN	International Standard Serial Number
JANET	Joint Academic Network (UK)
JICST	Japan Information Centre for Science and Technology
keystroke	Pressing one key on a keyboard; an operator can achieve around 10,000 keystrokes per hour, i.e. about 10,000 words per day
Kinokuniya	Major Japanese serials agent
LA	Library Association (UK)
LAN	Local Area Network
LATeX	A text formatting system written in TeX
ListServ	Mailing list programs to facilitate group communications
LOC	Library of Congress
make-ready	Setting up printing equipment for a specific job
Maruzen	Major Japanese serials agent
NASIG	North American Serials Interest Group
NII	National Information Infrastructure
NISS	National Information Services and Systems (UK)
NREN	National Research and Education Network (US)
OCLC	Online Computer Library Center (US)
OCR	Optical Character Recognition
offset	Printing using an intermediate medium to transfer the image onto the paper
OPAC	On-line Public Access Catalogue
origination	The first phase of production, from the author's edited work (either on paper or disk) to a form from which published copies can be made

PA	Publishers Association (UK)
page description language (PDL)	Software that makes up pages of text and graphics (e.g. PostScript)
parser	See SGML parser
PDF	Portable Document Format (e.g. a file in Acrobat)
perfect binding	Pages are bound together by glue on the roughened back edges rather than sewn
permanent paper	acid-free paper made for archival purposes. The specifications for manufacture are laid out in America standard ANSI Z39 1984 and cover neutral pH, alkaline reserve, chemical finish, tear resistance and fold endurance.
PIRA	Printing Industries Research Association (UK)
pixel	PICture ELements – the smallest element of a displayed image
Postscript	Page description language from Adobe which is device independent and enables pages to be compressed, transmitted, and displayed on Acrobat
PLS	Publishers Licensing Society (UK)
PPA	Periodical Publishers Association
RRO	Reproduction Rights Organisation (e.g. CCC)
RTF	Rich Text Format – common format containing tagged typographical information which typesetters can use
SAIID	Serial Article and Issue Identifier
SDI	Selective Distribution of Information
SFEP	Society of Freelance Editors and Proofreaders
SGML	Standard General Mark-up Language – an international standard for the mark-up of text. A language for describing the structure of documents or information and describing a tagging scheme to delineate that structure within text.
SGML parser	SGML software product that verifies DTDs against the rules of SGML and also checks a tagged document against the rules of its DTD
SI	Système Internationale – the internationally agreed metric units
signature	Folded section of pages from one printed sheet
SISAC	Serials Industry Systems Advisory Committee

Site licence	Single upfront payment for use of copyright material as defined by contract
SSP	Society for Scholarly Publishers
STM	Scientific, Technical and Medical (publications)
stm Association	Association of STM publishers affiliated to the International Publishers Association with strong interests in journals and copyright
STN	Scientific and Technical Network
Super JANET	The upgrade of JANET that allows rapid transmission of graphics
Swets	Largest serials agent on Continent of Europe
SyQuest	Removable hard disks available in different storage capacities
tag	A special marker inserted in a document to identify the information contained in that part of the document
TeX	A text formatting system with particular capabilities for typesetting mathematics and equations
TIFF	Tagged Image File Format – graphic file format developed by Aldus and Microsoft that compresses bit-mapped information
ToC	Table of Contents
TPI	Title Page & Index
UKOLN	UK Office for Library and Information Networking
UKSG	UK Serials Group
Ulrich's	See bibliography
UnCover	Alerting and document delivery service from CARL now owned by Knight-Ridder
URL	Universal Resource Locator – code for an electronic address
WAIS	Wide Area Information Server/Service, where individuals can access a multiple of databases through intermediation of hypertext, AI-assisted searching etc.
WAN	Wide Area Network
web	Continuous roll of paper used on web-fed press, as opposed to sheet-fed
WIPO	World Intellectual Property Organization
WWW	World-Wide Web – gives rapid access for Web browsers

	to combined text and graphical information with links to related informatiom
WYSIWYG	What You See Is What You Get
z39.50	ISO standard for an information retrieval protocol for intersystem searching

Bibliography

Anderson, D. C. (1989). Journals for academic veterinary medical libraries. *Serials Librarian*, 16, 81–91.

Armati, D. (1995). *Information Identification*. A report to the stm Association of Scientific, Technical and Medical Publishers, Amersfoort, The Netherlands.

Aronson, L. (1994). *HTML: Manual of Style*. Ziff Davies Press, California.

Ashby, P. & R. Campbell (1979). *Microform Publishing*. Butterworths, London.

Association of Subscription Agents and the Publishers Association Serial Publishers Executive (1986). *Electronic Communication between Publishers and Subscription Agents*. The Publishers Association, London.

Bailey, J. D. (1989). New journal decision making. *College and Research Libraries*, 50, 354–9.

Ball, S. (1995). Viruses: from curiosity to Computer Armageddon, and back? *Learned Publishing*, 8, 233–43.

Bann, D. N. (1986). *The Print Production Handbook*. Macdonald and Co. (Publishers) Ltd, London.

Barnard, M. (1986). *Magazine and Journal Production*. Blueprint Publishing, London.

Baron, D. N. (1988). *Units, Symbols, and Abbreviations, Second Edition*, Royal Society of Medicine, London.

Bero, L. A., A. Galbraith & D. Rennie (1992). The publication of sponsored symposiums in medical journals, *New England Journal of Medicine*, 327, 1135–40.

Bishop, C. E. (1984). *How to Edit a Scientific Journal*. ISI Press, Philadelphia, PA.

Bodian, N. G. (1984). *Copywriter's Handbook*. ISI Press, Philadelphia, PA.

Bodinham, M. & R. Campbell (1992). The survival of the journal: a simple spreadsheet model for predicting the outcome. *Learned Publishing*, 5, 153–9.

Brown, D. (1993). Current awareness and document delivery: the changing market. *Serials*, 6, 29–39.

Bryan, M. (1988). *SGML, An Author's Guide to the Standard Generalized Markup Language*. Addison-Wesley Publishing Company, Reading, MA.

Butcher, J. (1992). *Copy-editing: The Cambridge Handbook*. Cambridge University Press, Cambridge.

Campbell, R. (1992a). The commercial role in journal publishing: past, present, and future. *Logos*, 31, 27–33.

(1992b). Document delivery and the journal publisher. *Scholarly Publishing*, 23, 213–21.

(1992c). *Journal Production: Principles and Practice*. Publishers Association and the British Printing Industries Federation, London.

Cavendish, J. M. & K. Pool (1993). *Handbook of Copyright in British Publishing Practice*. Cassell, London.

CBE Committee on Economics of Publication (1982). *Economics of Scientific Journals*. Council of Biology Editors, Bethesda, MD.

CBE Style Manual Committee (1994). *Scientific Style and Format: The CBE Manual for Authors, Editors, and Publishers*. Cambridge University Press, Cambridge.

Chernaik, W., C. Davis & M. Deegan (eds) (1993). *The Politics of the Electronic Text*. Office for Humanities Publications, no. 3, Oxford University Computing Services, Oxford.

Coles, B. (ed.) (1993). See the Royal Society *et al.* below.

Compier, H. & R. Campbell (1995). ADONIS gathers momentum and faces some new problems. *Interlending & Document Supply*, 23, 22–5.

Cooter, M. (1991). 'Countdown to the *BMJ*'. *British Medical Journal*, 303, 1615–19.

Council of Biology Editors (1988). *Illustrating Science: Standards for Publication*. Council of Biology Editors, Bethesda, MD.

Cox, J. (1991). Subscription agents: why librarians love them and publishers take them for granted. *Logos*, 2, 154–8.

Curwen, P. J. (1980). *The UK Publishing Industry*. Pergamon Press, Oxford.

Daniel, H.-D. (1993). An evaluation of the peer review process at *Angewandte Chemie*. *European Science Editing*, 50, 4–8.

Day, R. A. (1989). *How to Write and Publish a Scientific Paper*. Cambridge University Press, Cambridge.

Denley, P. (1989). *Word Processing and Publishing: Guidelines for Authors*. The Publishers Association and the Association of Learned and Professional Society Publishers, London.

Diehl, R. L. (1990). Electronic Manuscripts: A Low-Risk Approach. *Scholarly Publishing*, 22(1), 29–39.

Digital Libraries (1995). Special issue of *Communications of the ACM*, 38 (4).

Directory of Electronic Newsletters, Serials and Discussion Lists (1994). Association of Research Libraries, Washington, DC.

Drew, Barbara (ed.) (1989). *Financial Management of Scientific Journals*. Council of Biology Editors, Bethesda, MD.

Estes, R. (1985). *Dictionary of Accounting, Second Edition*. MIT Press, Cambridge, MA.

Evans, M. (1995). Structured abstracts: rationale and construction. *European Science Editing*, 56, 4–5.

Faigel, M. (1985). Methods and issues in collection evaluation today. *Library Acquisitions: Practice and Theory*, 9, 21–35.

Fischer, C. C. (1990). Launching a new academic journal. *Scholarly Publishing*, 22, 51–62.

Freitas, D. de (1983). *Copyright System: Practice and Problems in Developing Countries*. Commonwealth Secretariat, London.

Geiser, E. A. & A. Dolin with G. S. Topkis (eds) (1985). *The Business of Book Publishing: Papers of Practitioners*. Westview Press, Boulder, CO.

Goetze, D. (1995). *Commercial Electronic STM Publishing*. stm Association, Amersfoort, The Netherlands.

Goss, F. D. (1985). *Success in Newsletter Publishing: A Practical Guide*. Newsletter Association of America, Washington, DC.

Hamaker, C. (1988). Library serials budgets: publishers and the twenty percent effect. *Library Acquisitions: Practice and Theory*, 12, 211–19.

Harnad, S. & J. Hey (1995). The scholar and scholarly publishing on the Net. *Networking and the Future of Libraries* 2, edited by L. Dempsey, D. Law & I. Mowat. Library Association Publishing, London.

Hartley, J. & M. Sykes (1995). Structured abstracts in the social sciences; presentation, readability, search and recall. *European Science Editing*, 56, 6–7.

Hemingway, C. & R. Campbell (1995). An ordered migration? The publisher and the network, in *Networking and the Future of Libraries* 2, edited by L. Dempsey, D. Law & I. Mowat. Library Association Publishing, London.

Herwijnen, E. van (1990). *Practical SGML*. Kluwer Academic Publishers, Dordrecht.

Hunter, K. (1993). Document delivery: threat or opportunity. *Learned Publishing*, 6, 21–4.

Huth, E. J. (1982). *How to Write and Publish Papers in the Medical Sciences*. ISI Press, Philadelphia, PA.

(1989). 'The information explosion'. *Bulletin of the New York Academy of Medicine*, 65, 647–61.

International Committee of Medical Journal Editors (1994). Advertising in medical journals and the use of supplements. *British Medical Journal*, 308, 1692.

Kassirer, J. P. & M. Angell (1994). Violations of the embargo and the new policy on early publicity. *New England Journal of Medicine*, 330, 1608–9.

Katzen, M. (ed.) (1980). *Paper, Postage and Distribution of Journals and Books*. Association of Learned and Professional Society Publishers, London.

King, D. W. & J.-M. Griffiths (1995). Economic issues concerning electronic publishing and distribution of scholarly articles. *Library Trends*, 43, 713–40.

Krog, L. & C. Binder (1990). How can an independent journal survive its 40th Anniversary? *European Science Editing*, 40, 4–6.

Krol, E. (1993). *The whole Internet*. O'Reilly and Associates, Sebastopol, CA.

Lee, Marshall (1979). *Bookmaking: An Illustrated Guide to Design/Production/Editing*, R. R. Bowker, NY.

LISU (1995). *The L.I.S.T. (Library and Information Statistics Tables)*. LISU, Loughborough University, Loughborough.

Lowry, A. K. (1993). Copyright and licensing in the electronic environment. *Scholarly Publishing Today*, 2, 3–5.

Macdougall, A., H. M. Woodward & J. M. Wilson (1986). Modelling of journal versus article acquisition by libraries. Report to BLRRD, project SI/BRG/47.

McLellan, M. F., L. D. Case & M. C. Barnett (1992). Trust, but verify: the accuracy of references in four anaesthesia journals. *Anesthesiology*, 77, 185–8.

Maguire, M. (1994). Secure SGML: A proposal to the information community. *Scholarly Publishing*, 25, 146–56.

Martyn, J., P. Vickers & M. Feeney, (eds) (1990). *Information UK 2000*. Bowker-Saur, London.

Meadows, J. (1991). What makes a good journal. *Serials*, 7, 14–15.

Mills, J. L. (1993). Data torturing' *New England Journal of Medicine*, 329, 1196–9.
    (1994). The practicalities of journal design. *Learned Publishing*, 7, 239–43.

Moline, S. R. (1989). The influence of subject, publisher type and quantity published on journal prices. *Journal of Academic Librarianship*, 15, 12–18.

Oakeshott, P. (1995). *Trends in Journal Subscriptions 1994*. The Publishers Association, London.

O'Connor, M. (1978). *Editing Scientific Books and Journals*, Pitman Publishing, London.
    (1980). *Model Guidelines for the Preparation of Camera-Ready Typescripts by Authors and Typists*. Ciba Foundation, London.
    (1987). *How to Copy-Edit Scientific Books and Journals*. ISI Press, Philadelphia, PA.
    (1991). *Writing Successfully in Science*. London.

Olsen, J. (1994). *Electronic Journal Literature: Implications for Scholars*. Mecklermedia, Westport, CT.

PA and BPIF (1984). *Book Production Practice*. Publishers Association and British Printing Industries Federation, London.

(1985). *Customs of the Trade for the Manufacture of Books.* Publishers Association and British Printing Industries Federation, London.

Peacock, J. (1989). *Book Production.* Blueprint Publishing, London.

Pearce, A. (1995). 'From books to bytes: the user at the centre of the scientific information system. *Learned Publishing*, 8, 203–8.

Peterson, C. (1992). The economics of economics journals: a statistical analysis of pricing practices by publisher'. *College and Research Libraries*, 53, 176–81.

Publishers Association (1981). *Machine Readable Codes for the Book Trade.* The Publishers Association, London.

Rowland, F., C. McKnight & J. Meadows (eds) (1995). *Project ELVYN: An Experiment in Electronic Journal Delivery.* Bowker-Saur, London.

Royal Society, British Library and the Association of Learned and Professional Society Publishers (RS/BL/ALPSP) (1993). *The Scientific, Technical and Medical Information System in the UK.* British Library R & D Report No. 6123, London.

Russon, D. & R. Campbell (1996). Access to a journal. *Logos* 7(2).

St Aubyn, J. (1995). Copyright and learned journals: some questions answered. *Learned Publishing*, 8, 75–86.

St. Cyr, W. A., L. N. Domelsmith & K. V. Ratnakar (1980). Experimental approaches to the date of origin of Koopmans' theorem. *Journal of Irreproducible Results*, 26, 23–4.

Satyanarayana, K. & K. V. Ratnakar (1989). Accuracy and completeness of references cited in selected biomedical journals. *European Science Editing*, 36, 5–6.

Schauder, D. (1993). Electronic publishing of professional articles. *Journal of the American Society for Information Science*, 45, 73–100.

Shelock, E. (1985). *Learned Journals Pricing and Buying Round.* Epsilon Press, Letchworth.

Silverman, R. A. (1989). Desktop publishing: its impact on the academic community. *Scholarly Publishing*, 21(1), 57–63.

Singleton, A. (1980). *Societies and Publishers: Hints on Co-operation in Journal Publishing.* Taylor Graham, London.

(1994). Charging for information – pricing policies and practice. *Learned Publishing*, 7, 223–32.

Singleton, A. & A. Cooper (1981). *Role of Subscription Agents: With a Supplementary Report on UK Libraries' Trade with Agents.* Taylor Graham, London.

Stern, B. T. & R. Campbell. (1989). ADONIS – publishing journal articles on CD-ROM. *Advances in Serials Management*, 3, 1–60.

Strong, W. S. (1993). *The Copyright Book: A Practical Guide.* MIT Press, Cambridge, MA.

Tibbo, H. (1994). Specifications for camera-ready copy: helping authors be more productive. *Scholarly Publishing*, 25, 221–32.

Trevitt, J. (1990). Permanent paper – progress in the US and UK. *Logos*, 1(1).

UKSG (1994). *Serial Publications: Guidelines for Good Practice in Publishing Printed Journals and Other Serial Publications*. United Kingdom Serials Group, Witney, Oxon.

Ulrich's International Periodicals Directory. published annually by Bowker-Saur, London.

University of Chicago Press (1993). *The Chicago Manual of Style: The Essential Guide for Authors, Editors, and Publishers*. University of Chicago Press, Chicago.

White, H. S. (1979). Factors in the placement and cancellation of journal subscriptions. *Society for Scholarly Publishing Proceedings*. Washington, DC.

Williamson, H. (1983). *Methods of Book Design*. Yale University Press.

Woodward, H.& S. Pilling (1993). *The International Serials Industry*. Gower, Aldershot.

Woolf, P. K. (1993). Integrity and accountability in research and publication. *Scholarly Publishing*, 24, 204–13.

World of Learning. Published annually by Europa Publications, London

Xu, Zhao Ran & D. H. Nicolson (1992). Don't abbreviate Chinese names. *Taxon*, 41, 499–503.

The following serials also contain useful information:

CBE Views, *European Science Editing*, *Learned Publishing*, *Logos*, *Newsletter on Serials Pricing Issues* (online only), *Scholarly Publishing*, *Serials*, *STM Newsletter*.

Index

Printed in the United Kingdom
by Lightning Source UK Ltd.
124299UK00001B/169-171/A